RESCUED AT GUNPOINT

Heralyn Toling's Spiritual and High School Diaries

BY

HERALYN TOLING

AuthorHouse™
1663 Liberty Drive, Suite 200
Bloomington, IN 47403
www.authorhouse.com
Phone: 1-800-839-8640

First published by AuthorHouse 12/30/2008

ISBN: 978-1-4389-2505-9 (sc)

Printed in the United States of America
Bloomington, Indiana

This book is printed on acid-free paper.

WARNING:

30/69/95/98/125/136
150/177/207/214/328/14
[August 10, 2008, 7:41 PM]
HERALYN MORALES TOLING [H.M. TOLING]

WILL BE HARZARDOUS TO YOUR HEALTH!!!!! THIS HAS BEEN CAREFULLY THAWED OUT & PRINTED EXACTLY AS IT WAS WRITTEN. HA! HA! IRRITATING GRAMMAR FROM A FILIPINO-AMERICAN IMMIGRANT. (WRITING IN ENGLISH IN THE FOLLOWING STYLE):

1) RUN ON SENTENCES THAT KEEPS YOU GOING LIKE THE BATTERY YO' MAMA is USing FOR HER HEARING AID! [THANK U!!! I'LL BE HERE ALL WEEK. Plez write your first name herre:_________]
2) WORDS THAT iz SPELLED IN EBONICS, SLANG, IN DA HOOD & *"White Chicks"* or *"Malibu's Most WANTED"* Movie Stylezzy [Whatzitcalled__?__NOSTALMAGICAL!]. . . Forcheezzzzy bb___ _____! COMPLETELY MISPELLED WORDS COZ I HAVEN'T BOUGHT THE "HOOKED ON PHONEX (See!, I can't even spell it.) WORKS 4 ME." STILL, DON'T HAVE IT! That makes me ILLiTERATE ALREADY! You bought this book bcoz I know You-me spiritual.
3) I stick to da ORIGINAL WRITING girlfriend like PAM's original spray. I NEVER GONNA BE A COMEDIAN IF THAT'S ALL I CAN THINK OF COMIN' BACK FROM A LAS VEGAS VACATION. IT DOESN'T SEEM LIKE A JOKE.
[January 1, 2005, 11:05 PM, Saturday] April 8, 2008, 8:42 PM, Tuesday. RAGP:HTSHS&CD [THREE STEPS TO SPIRITUAL MOTIVATION]w/JM&MROCKTARS deadline due goal on February 2010.

☺ P.S. ALMOST 1/3 OF THE COST PRODUCTION OF THIS BOOK IS FROM THE U.S. GOVERNMENT-2008 REBATE CHECK. TO FIND OUT MORE! BUY THE DVD AND WATCH MY 2ndINDY MOVIE THAT I DIRECTED, PRODUCED, & WROTE. TITLED: **"MY VENTI FRAPINOA SKETCHDEZORTDRUNKENPHRENIA WEEKENDS"[HITS in theaters 2018-2019?]**

☺ **[DEDICATION PAGES]] [THANK U PAGES]**

THANKS TO:

WHO TO THANK? THANK YA' ALL FOR READING THIS CRAZZY NOVELLA /BOOK-DIARIES. I THANK 1ST & FOREMOST , MYSELF, THE ONE WHO MADE IT POSSIBLE TO WRITE INCREDIBLE WRITINGS 4 DA LAST 29 YEARS IN DA MAKING. **KIDS WANTED TO GROW UP TO BE FAMOUS ONCE.**

OH MY GOD!!! TO MY GODS & GODDESSES & STO.NIÑO & THE VIRGIN MARY [THE PATRON SAINT OF THE PHILIPPINES]. TO MY MOMMY , I CALL "ME" AS HER NICKNAME, [ARLISTINA MORALES MARR & DAD [HENRY TOLING] & MY 2 STEP DADS [ARTHUR MARR [R.I.P] & ONE NOW RON ODEING -THANKZ TO THEM 4 LETTIN' ME BE…AHHH!!! TO MY FUTURE RECORDING LABEL & RECORD MANAGERS & PRODUCERS & SINGERMATES & SONGWRITERS @ **TOLINGLIBEDO RECORDS{♥T.I.M.E}**. WAIT, I'M A WRITER, NOT YET A SINGER OR ANTI-SUPERFICIAL FAMOUS ROCK STAR. I'M JOKING AGAIN. DATS FOR ANOTHER DEDICATION PAGE. UMM YEAH !!! ESPECIALLY TO MY PUBLISHING COMPANY 4 MAKING DIZ POSSIBLE… IF I GET DIZ PUBLISH. THANKS **AUTHORHOUSE BOOKS** .

TO ALL MY FRIENDS IN HIGH SCHOOL, [CLASS OF '98] I CAN'T WAIT TO GO TO MY **10TH YEAR REUNION TO SELL THIS BOOK.** NOT REALLY! JUST KIDDING!!! TO THE WHOLE CLASS OF 1998 @ EL CAPITAN HIGH SCHOOL. THIS IS 2 FUNNY. TO THE HIGH SCHOOL CLUBS - I LEARNED TO GROW & MATURE AS A **YOUNG LEADER** IN THIS COUNTRY U.S.A. & CREATING/HAVING A POSITIVE IMPACT I COULD INFLUENCE/AFFECT IN DIS UNIVERSE; OUR WORLD TODAY & THE FUTURE. TO MY DREAMS, ASPIRATIONS [TO BE…] & INSPIRATIONS [PROBABLE VISION TO TAKE ACTION ON MY GOALS], TO HIP HAPPENING HOPING SOMEDAY IF I EVER WANT TO BECOME AN ARMY OFFICER, A POLITICIAN, DA FUTURE 3RD, 4TH, ,5TH OR 6TH POSSIBLE FEMALE/WOMAN PRESIDENT OF MY COUNTRY, MY HOMELAND, DA PHILIPPINES OR DIS WONDERFUL OHHLALA COUNTRY CALLED UNITED STATES OF AMERICA. GOOD LUCK TO DA GUY I PLAN ON MARRYING. MY HEART GOES OUT TO U, TO WHOEVER YOU ARE. OF COURSE, DA GREAT, CARING & DEDICATED TEACHERS, TO NAME A FEW, LIKE MRS. BENJAMIN, SRA. FONSECA, MS. DOUGLAS, MR. VAN & TO ALL MY TEACHERS I WORKED WITH IN EL CAPITAN HIGH SCHOOL 1994-1998. THANKS!!!! ***TO UNDERSTANDING THE TRUE MEANING OF FREEDOM OF SPEECH … STILL LEARNING TODAY.***

TO MAKE **EVERYTHING BETTER** ON ANY BUSY, HECTIC & CRAZZY SCHEDULE OVER DA LAST FUCKIN' 6 YEARS @ GROSSMONT COLLEGE… .[DUH! WILL SOMEONE GIVE ME ALL A'S TO GET OUT OF THERE, I GUESS NOT!] DA PEOPLE THAT CREATED A POSITIVE IMPACT ON MY LIFE ARE MY TENNIS TEAMATES LIKE CHRISTINA MOLINARO, BRIANNA

PINNICK, SAYAKA FUKUMOTO, YUKI HAGIWARA, MAYUMI, STEPHANIE IRWIN, SUNNY. TO MY TENNIS ASSISTANT COAHES DONNA & FERNANDO. OF COURSE, MY FAVORITE COACH IN THE WHOLE WIDE WORLD . . . THANKS COACH ___?___. [TO ALL MY MALE TEAM MATES/ TO ALL THE GUYS WHO TOOK THEIR SHIRT OFF @ DA TENNIS COURTS]. [TO ALL MY CURRENT TEAM MATES IN DA NEXT 2 YEARS@ DAT COLLEGE_(YEAR_ ______UNIV. OF SANTO T.,MANILA) ,ANY DAY NOW, ANY DAY NOW … BLAH. BLAH.]. OF COURSE, WHO NEVER GAVE UP & GOT ME TO LOOSE 30 PLUS POUNDS [JUST KIDDING!!!! I did it myself.] & COUNTING COZ I WORK HARD @ DA TENNIS COURTS & THE GREAT COACHING POINTS "AIM HIGH" "NO FEAR" "BE AGGRESSIVE" " FAST FEET, SLOW HANDS" "HAVE CONTROL, NOT POWER". MY COACH MEAGAN HABER [FORMALLY KNOWN AS COACH LOWREY], WHO HAS HELPED ME GET THROUGH MY TENNIS COLLEGE CAREER GOALS. TO HOPEFULLY SOMEDAY… MY HARD WORK WILL PAY OFF, TO GET A FULL RIDE SCHOLARSHIP TO **CAL STATE LOS ANGELES/CALIFORNIA STATE POMONA {WILL I FINISH MY U.S. ARMY ROTCDAYZ? YEAR 1-2-3-4-AND BEYOND?}**[IF THEY CAN AFFORD ME & OF IF I HAVE THE $ MONEY TO GO BACK TO COLLEGE…. TO TAKE TIME OFF FROM WRITING. I CAN'T IMAGINE NOT WRITING.]TO HAVE THE SAME MAJOR LIKE THAT MAIN CHARACTER IN *LEGALLY BLONDE* "ELLE WOODS" , WHO MAJORED FASHION MERCHANDISING/FASHION DESIGN. TO CHRIS RAY, [& TO THE WHOLE GANG OF ATHLETIC TRAINERS/DOCTORS @ GROSSMONT COLLEGE] WHO HELPED ME POP BACK MY [THRU NUMEROUS THERAPIES] 1ST SHOULDER DISLOCATION & HEARRING "DDDDDDIIIII IIRRRRRIIIITTTTTTTTYYYYY" FOR DAT IST TIME IN THE ATHLETIC TRAINING ROOM DURING MY 1ST SHOULDER [LEFT] DISLOCATION. [DA 5TH WORLD RECORD ON LEFT SHOULDER DISLOCATION] WHICH LEADS ME TO THANKING "XTINA" CHRISTINA AGUILERA, BRITNEY SPEARS, MARIAH CAREY, MISSY ELLIOTT, LIKE A VIRGIN GIRL["Material Girl"]-MADDONA "ESTHER", TO KELLY CLARKSON (YEAH! LIKE I'M REALLY LOOKING FORWARD TO WORK ON DAT MOVIE …I WROTE ABOUT "JAWING 'MR'. & MRS. ROCK STAR") & JANET JACKSON FOR THEIR GREAT ALBUMS DAT MAKE MY LIFE A LIVING REASON TO KEEP GOING & FOLLOW MY DREAMS [OOHHH!!! 4 THOSE GREAT DANCE MOVES I'VE SEEN AT THE NITE CLUBS LIKE THE MELSEVEN & THE PUSSYCAT DOLLS] A SHOUT OUT TO THE G-FORCE AND THE ASAP FAMILY. YEAH! Look I'm not getting lucky with any of them coz we're ******. Go S*** me if you *** ??? Picture in thiz book. OF COURSE, TO EVERYBODY IN ROCK & ROLL MUSIC & MOVIE BIZNESS WHO HAS MADE MY LIFE GREAT & FUN…TO DA DANCE BIZ & PPL. WHO

HAS PUT AN IMPRINT ON ME DAT I CAN DANCE HIP-HOP ON DA DANCE FLOOR LIKE MELISSA ADAO, MY DANCE TEACHER & HOPEFULLY TO WORK TOGETHER ON MY UPCOMING ALBUM 4 CHOREOGRAPHY[IF I EVER GET SIGN] & TO MOST TALK ABOUT CHOREOGRAPHER , TINA LANDON ABOUT HER LIFE & REPUTATION. MAYBE WE CAN WORK ON THOSE PROJECT TOGETHER [IF I EVER GET TO MEET MY CHOREOGRAPHER IDOL TINA LANDON]. DID I MISS OUT ANYBODY? _?-TO DA GIRL I COULDN'T SPANK BACK [REGARDLESS WHY SHE FELT LIKE SPANKING MY ASS] THANKZ 4 THE FREE DANCE MOVES/LESSONS & TO ANYONE WHO TRIED TO BUT DIDN'T… DON'T EVEN THINK ABOUT IT! DOUBLE STANDARDS WORK BEST, WHEN AGAIN? I SHOULD BE JUST KISSING UP TO U RITE NOW. LASTLY, THANK GOD! REWRITING SUCKS !!! BUT NOT THE LEAST, MY NEIGHBORHOOD HOMEY LAKESIDE BARBERSHOP WHO CUT MY MOHAWK HAIR LAST SUMMER 2004[6/25/04]. THANX U!!! JANELL & JANAN SHUNNARA "YOU'LL GO OUT A DIFFERENT PERSON." WHO CONVINCE ME EASY DOES IT ON MY 1ST HIGHLIGHTS DERE . TO MARY@ TRIM RITE BABERSHOP. {Still thanking the new owners @Trim Rite… I swear ? Why do I see JO***** @ L.A.? *I JUST NEED TIME TO LIVE DERE. YEAH bb!}* TO PHOTOMAKERS & 4 PICKING MY GUD SIDE IN PHOTOGRAPH FING ME. TO PHOTOGRAPHERS: DEBORAH KANG & BECKY PINNICK 4 DA COOL PHOTOS ON THE COVER & INSIDE IN THIS BOOKZINE… MY 2ND NOVEL. A SHOUT OUT [TO DA ONE I'M SLEEPING WITH. OK I DON'T REMEMBER SLEEPING W/ ANYONE COZ MAYBE THE PERSON COULD HELP ME PAY THE RENT HA!HA!] [MY JOKES ARE NOT DAT FUNNY HUH?] OF COURSE, THINKIN' ABOUT LAKESIDE, DA PLACE I SPEND HALF OF MY [ADULT] LIFE [ALMOST AS GOOD OF RESIDENCY TO BECOME A SENATOR] [OOH! TO ALL THE GREAT WORLD LEADERS & SENATORS, TO HILARY CLINTON, MR. OBAMA,& BARBARA BOXER 4 WRITING DAT BOOK ABOUT HER LIFE. MAYBE I'LL END MARRYING SOMEONE WHO IS U.S. PRESIDENT BOUND [THIS IS TOO FUNNY]. WELL, THEY ARE BOTH GREAT INSPIRATIONZ TO US ALL . OK! I NEVER READ NEITHER ONE OF DERE BOOK THOUGH.] TO OPRAH WINFREY, J.K. ROWLING & MTV. TO DA GREAT LEADERS THAT KEEP THIS NATION GREAT & THE WORLD SAFE. KEEP UP DA GREAT WORK!!! TO MY WORK @ KFC WHO HELP ME PASS BRAIN FART/GAS THINKIN' ABOUT WHATEVER …& MY STORE MANAGERS VIRGINIA, JUSTINE & MINDIE 4 GIVIN' ME DA 35-45-60 {$.50/YR.} CENTS RAISE… TO ALL MY KFC/A & W CO WORKERS… & DOSE 2 ILLEGAL MEXICANS [PLEZ DON'T CARPOOL GOIN' BACK TO MEXICO LIKE THE LAST 2 MEXICAN COOKS DID. TO DA JOKES WE TALKED ABOUT. WE DON'T CLONE OUR CHICKENS!!!!! BELIEVE ME! GO COLONEL SANDERS, WHO CREATED HOMEY CHICKEN THAT WILL HELP ME WIN THE U.S. & WORLD TITLES IN KARATE & TAEKWONDO [HEAVYWEIGHT] TO DA ROAD TO MY OLYMPIC DREAMS…[YEAHHH!!!]

November 23, 2005 (WEDS, 7:41 PM) revise 2/16/07 9:36 PM

A SPECIAL THANKS

4 BUYING AND READING THIS BOOK

A PERSONAL ESSAY

RESCUED AT GUN POINT:

WRITTEN BY :H.M. TOLINGLIBEDO

?

Font 48/ 4 DA LOVE OF MY COUNTRY [COUNTRIES]{WORLD}
WEEKEND # ?________________DATE__/___/__
*LIVEDO [✈]check when done, write it
after being rescued at GUNPOINT!!!

THE END*

…A SNEAK PEAK SAMPLE FROM THE "SEX & MUSIC LITERATURE 101" SEQUEL "DAMUARTE²MIL 107" COMING SOON & HIGHLIGHTS FROM ***R.A.G.:HERALYN TOLING'S [SPIRITUAL]HIGH SCHOOL & COLLEGE DIARIES[3S 2 SM] W/ "jawing 'mr.' & mrs. rockstars"***

Da Mu Ar Te² MiL♥ 107

171 DAM!!! GHETTO GIRLS TO LIVE THE MILLION DOLLAR MANSION DREAM HOUSE

2/26/04

"Where should I park my car?," Christina stops suddenly, a brake release from her energy.

Oh I get it! Retard writer cumming thrue...
I 4 got to explain . . . LARISSA Newly bought pimp mister mobile ..a FORD MUSTANG GT ~~was in front~~ was about to be monstrously crash to/into/ of Christina Mercedes BENZ…

"AAHHH!!!"..............(15) A loud voice. We laughed coz some of us where in the van on our way to SANTA BARBARA,CA.

"It's in the middle of? A ghetto in INGLEWOOD," said HEATHER with pigtails ...reddish brown hair.

{ITZ TIME FOR THAT BRITNEY SPEARS MOMENT... U KNOW... I SAW BRIT AT THE MALL... BLAH... BLAH... SHE HAD A LOT OF FANS WAITING FOR HER AUTOGRAPH/SIGNATURES. I WANTED TO BAIL TO & LEAVE THE FASHION SHOW. I REALIZED I WAS ONLY 16 OR 17. It was a hot summer... I recall her singing 3 songs that went #1. _the e!}

"Does anybody have a highlighter?," I said. *"I have in the underwear bag..."* Sayaka showing off her underwear pinkish latest fashion in 4 putting on the pencil & school writing utensils. A happy cheery person who smiles a lot.

"Alrightden.." [___?___]

"Oh you save me a spot." [C.P?... dere was a buckteeth girl? I didn't know dat! In my Tennis team.]

"HA! HA! I save you a seat. You should seat here so SUNNY would seat heRe. Coz Ashley sits here," B.H. *[Dat would be weird to hire/get an actress with this initials.]*

OH MY GOD! I CAN'T IMAGINE WORKING HERE...
AND SITTING HERE LAUGHING ABOUT THIS BUCK TEETH
GIRL IN DIZ VAN. I SHOULD MOVE IN MY OFFICE-
VIRTUALLY IN SINK REALITY TO MY FAVORITE #1 N.Y.
TIMES BEST SELLER.. "SO WAT ARE U DOING TODAY?" [H.T.]
"I CAN'T.. I'M OFF TODAY." [unknown #1 N.Y. bestseller]
"DOESN'T? ANYONE OR ANYBO DUUY WANNA SHARE MY JOKES..UR JOKES WITH ME?" [H.T.]

"Larissa your choices are large or extra small...
...if you feel better here's a medium." [Coach Meg]
"Nike doesn't make those black ones." [L.Lohan]
"That's a large." [Larissa]

["I don't even remember how I fit in mine last year.] I thought. Thank God I'm just a road manager. (I could only wonder why Director __? Is wearing a black tennis skirt. I'm over you... ALRIGHDEYDENTTTTT!!!!)

"Rise and shine HOT SHOT!" [Linday's road Maniger -? only H knows.]
What is her name? Covina, L.C.___ Jail cell. The next C.A. of POP MUSIC INDUSTRY.

"Good Job you guys... Everybodyz on time. Everybody bought their books." COACH HABER.

The tennis ball key chain . . . One of the stuff I got from Briana's Mom.

*"Oh! Hi Heralyn. …*** %%$#@^&&***!!!!"*

"Check out my CADILLAS XLT in that parking lot." Check him out. [8:13 PM Friday 2/6/04]
A day after my B-Day… or a couple days after my Birthday. FEB./ 04

☺ I LOVE MILKI ♥WAY TAKE ANOTHER GOOD NIGHT SLEEP TODAY DREAM ABOUT NOON AFTERNOON DANCING WITH ME. I LOVE Rock & Roll. I wana get back To the Eagles CD buying them see how many they made and check out the best thing ever happen to me… that's Easy 4 me right no getting sick faking it to last longer in the business of being lazy. Just when you think itz over… You remember Pilot pens where to get this type BP-5Fine.

10:35 PM 2/9/04

Remind me the many playful player mates.(I love it. I hate it.) BLONDES DO HAVE FUN!!! AND ******ES TO WATCH AFTER THEM. OKAY! The Quote is… that is it! "OKAY FIND THE ONE! ***I THINK I FOUND MYf7***ING SELF!"***

♥

☺ **PART ONE**: Heralyn Toling's 1ST DIARY

☺ THE SOPHOMORE YEAR:

☺ THE CLASS PRESIDENT &

☺ POPULARITY ROCKS ! ! !

Sept.3, '95 (12:45)

Finally got my own Diary. I showed it to my Dad and he said when you are 60 yrs. old, you are gonna look back and read it. I laughed. I know I'm going to look back anyhow but for now I'm just going to concentrate about my life. I hope everything will be great for me towards my goals in life. Days seem to go by so fast, the next thing you know its been months then years past. Goals during this summer may not all that work out but I must go on TO GET READY FOR THE FUTURE.

TONIGHT'S THE NIGHT. AFTERSCHOOL WAS TOO BUSY AND THE TIME WAS SO LONG. 2 weeks of work, people EL CAP, PARENTS ARE WATCHING US. I had butterfly in my stomach. It went by so fast. Every body was loud and I had lot of fun just being on the float. It was great. I got thirsty, my throat was dry and my feet are sore. I got to get inside to watch the game, fireworks etc. We deserve to win first place. The announcer said first place is (Oh my god Sophomores) Sophomores. I shout loud. I got off the bleachers to share the moments. I scream "WE WON!" too many times and hugs. I was so happy, the happiest one. What's embarrassing was…

My Dad asked me who's the happiest persom. Then I answered, "I AM." OF COURSE, THE STRESS, WORK & BEING A SOPHOMORE PRESIDENT I AM THE HAPPIEST PERSON ON EARTH TONIGHT. I DON'T WANT IT TO END. ALSO, THINKING HOW I DIDN'T CONCENTRATE MUCH TO POPULARITY COZ OF FLOAT. TONIGHT. I REALIZED IT'S NOT ALWAYS POPULARITY WILL GIVE A CHANCE OF BEING IN ASB. LIKE LARISSA GREGERSON, TONIGHT CROWNED HOMECOMING QUEEN. SHE DESERVE IT. She hangs out to everybody. Doesn't care about popularity …WE LIKE HER BECAUSE SHE HAS A GOOD PESONALITY. WE ALL LIKE HER. I CAN BE WHAT I WANT TO BECOME AND THINK I CAN BE IN ASB PRESIDENT or HOMECOMING QUEEN or BOTH. IF I WILL BECOME AN OWNER OF A COMPANY. THEN ANYTHING IS POSSIBLE IN THIS WORLD. IF THEY CAN DO IT, THEN I CAN. I BELIEVE I WILL BE COZ I KNOW I CAN.

WHY CAN'T I GET A BOYFRIEND? AFTERSCHOOL WAS FUN. In ASIAN CLUB ~~wasd~~ we went to the DOJO PLACE next to Blockbuster Video. I found out Celest Dad's is the owner of the DOJO. I was going to talk to him about registring for taking TAEKWONDO but didn't have enough time. Mrs. Martinez & I were boxing & she hit me right on my right eye. I guess I gonna tell everybody about it.

Okay, glimpse of ____.. . He is so cute. He's out of my leaugue. If he does likes me and he showed signs of that proving he like me then WHY WON THE ASK ME. That is the most annoying part. Then again, if he doesn't that's okay, that means he not my B-Day wish from last year. Hey, it could happen. … I thought about how I'm gonna be driving soon supposibly tomorrow but not until next year. OH WELL! -DYED MY HAIR..but…

April 18,1996

This week's frustration is over it; about running for TREASURER. I ran for TREASURER LAST YEAR and lost 2x in a row. ~~She~~ My Spanish club advisor told me, the 3rd time is for sure. I hope so. I'm counting on it. It's would be so IRONIC to me to run for TREASURER Next year. OR maybe run for PRESIDENT. It's a gamble I have to win my 3rd one no matter what it takes. It's hard. On Monday I slept till 3 in the morning and only got 2 ¾ hours of sleep. On Tues night I slept till 1:30 in the morning. I had to get up, and NOMINATING CONVENTION was a whole lot ~~of exper~~ better that last year. I broke 3 boards. Got 2 cuts and hit KELLIE [KELLY] LUNDEEN on ~~the~~ her face by the board fly at her face. I chicken out at the dares. I knew I would. I'm so afraid of it, it was the only part I didn't like and I wish I prepared my skit a would lot better and said something to the delegates.

"GOD, I'M SORRY. My life at age of 16th is been full too many disappoint on disappointment I remember but very little accomplishment I know I achieve of my goals. Some yet to want the goals/dreams I haven't achieve and I'm talking about bigger goals ahead for me in the future. I know myself well about my dreams in life and it has become my biggest fear in life if I don't succeed. I'm so much WRAP up into success that I want it so much my life wouldn't be a complete puzzle without it. I can't believe I said that my dreams are the missing puzzle. THANK YOU GOD BUT that's the problem. I'm a dreamer with big dreams. That's why Im afraid coz I sometimes think I'm not confident enough or I won't get accepted in the Air Force Academy or ROTC…

BUY THE MOVIE/DVD "SPEECHLESS" - A MODERN VERSION OF "GREASE"/"CLUELESS"- INSPIRED FROM DIZ BOOK

"HERALYN M. TOLING's SPIRITUAL HIGH SCHOOL/COLLEGE DIARIES"[3 STEPS TO SPIRITUAL MOTIVATION] WITH "JAWING MR. & MRS. ROCKSTAR"@ AMAZON/AUTHORHOUSE/BARNES&N?.COM-

☺WRITE DOWN YOUR CURRENT DREAMS/GOALS:______________________

____

☺WRITE DOWN HOW TO ACHIEVE THIS:_____________________________

I WILL ALWAYS FOLLOW MY DREAMS AND NEVER STOP DREAMING. I WON'T STOP RUNNING TILL I GET WHAT I WANT IN LIFE.

☺*December 31, 2004, 10:07 PM*

-From The Heralyn Toling's HIGHSCHOOL/ COLLEGE Scrapbook

☺ (given from a friend Elizabeth Decker at last period AP BIOLOGY class

☺ -unknown source/revise) **THE STORY OF JACK SCHITT**

☺ **"H Shit is the 'son' of L Shit and O Shit. L Shit, the fertilizer magnate, married O Shit, the owner of the HBG&LP Shit Innyho-hohotel. H Shit married N Shit and they produced 16 children. Holy *SpirituAL*-IT, their first passed on shortly after childbirth. Next came twin 'sons', D Shit and DD Shit, two daughters, Pola Shit and G Shit, and another 'son' Bull Shit. DD Shit married CLULEZ Shit, a high school dropout. D Shit married Love Shit and they have a son named Chickenflirtymeal Shit. Pola Shit and G Shit married the Happening brothers/sisters. HA!HA!HA! The Shit-Happening children are Down Shit, BullUP Shit and HipHophoray Shit. BullUP Shit just married a spicy little number named Pieceof Shit and they are waiting the arrival of Baby Shit."**

☺ **Now you can proudly proclaim, "I know the true story of H Shit."** ***whatever "shit happens" -F. Gump movie***

I feel like shit today. Maybe because I'm in a bad mood since Period 4. …My pissy mood will be gone after I do kickboxing. I plan to exercise after writing in my diary. I feel a little better after I listened to **[NO DOUBT RULEZ!!!]** Sublime, Sprung Monkey, and A. Morrissette. I still have a little T.V. to my surprise but nothing is on that is worth watching. I love MUSIC♥. It has cheered me up on so many bad d~~b~~ays and I can relate my life to it. T.V. is crap most of the time. As usual, writing this calms my nervous system down. Back to realization therapy. So what…my classmates just wrote what they wanted to say. No harm done there. ~~I~~ Like getting an F on Calculus or a C in Govt. or a C in Physics or a C in Bio or a C in English. At least I have one B in Spanish. Just one of the classes I worked hard for. I EITHER WORKED HARD for something OR I DON'T. I should have stayed at McDonalds and surf my 2nd semester. But I had a plan for 2nd semester, and it blew. Oh well! I did everything.

A RESORT AREA WILL BE PART OF YOUR HOLIDAY PLANS. [Fortune Cookie]
Dat soundz good @ ____

[February 12, 2005, 4:26 AM [SAT]] I was gonna try to find about OPRAH's SHOW…in my DIARIES but I couldn't find the one about PSALMS ..27... [But hey! I just wanna be on OPRAH'Z BOOK CLUB.] *remember the 6-7 months of p.celebrity vacation*

GRATITUDE LIST

Everydays Gratitude as of Nov. 30,1997 -"Life is great no matter what!"

Jan 13,1998-

"It's better to live and die ful~~l~~filling one thing you want to happen or desire and hope for than to live and die fulfilling nothing at all." [I get it now. I see it. Good quote.] "Fulfilling something that came from the heart is fulfilling A LIFE'S PURPOSE."
The overall "GRATITUDE LIST" 4 letter word L-I-F-E. I have the air to breathe, healthy lungs and heart, people around me, Life precious moments, a list just continues but it all continues but it all comes down to **me**, **my soul**, **my life**.

↑ ↑ ↑

Jan 20, 1996

….50th Inaugural Day for Clinton for another great 4 years…..

Jan 21, 1996...

I'm happy to get this far. I DON'T WANT TO BE POPULAR. JUST SO I COULD HELP THE SCHOOL -SOMETHING DIFFERENT OTHER THAN CLUB OFFICE. Heck, I've been helping the school since I feel in love getting involve and the rewards are…great leadership I have help me decide to study POLITICS. I think it's weird -HERALYN IN POLITICS. But I'm thankful and grateful; a

stepping stone in my life. ☺

HERALYN MORALES TOLING SENIOR quote:

WEST POINT and ?ARMY LIFE.

Girls KICK ASS!

RUNNING 140.
CHINESE PROVERB:

THE MORE YOU SWEAT IN PEACE.
THE LESS YOU BLEED IN WAR.

THANKS Heralyn 4 not dying.
I will live past my 27 b-day.

Christmas Tree ME Productions
founded on year of 2006/
M.V.F.S.W. deadline June30,2016?

[3 steps to *SPIRITUAL* MOTIVATION]

STEP 1

P L A N

PLAN on writing your short-term and long-term goals. Prioritize your GOALS. In simple terms, find or know what is important to you, about your life right now and family influence, cultural, political. PLAN the ideal formula for success.

STEP2

D R E A M

DREAM about your goals, recapture your ambitions, rethink everything!

STEP3

A C T I O N

ACTION [TAKE FULL RESPONSIBILITY, TAKE ACTIONS IN fulfilling your goals, dreams and ambitions. Never ever GIVE UP! Opportunity knocks when you start believing in yourself. Find inner peace.

♥

☺ PART ONE:
Heralyn Toling's 1ST DIARY
☺ THE SOPHOMORE YEAR:
THE CLASS PRESIDENT
& POPULARITY ROCKS!!!
♥ The BOMBMISH DAYZ OF OUR LIVES!

Sept.3, '95 (12:45)

Finally got my own Diary. I showed it to my Dad and he said when you are 60 yrs. old, you are gonna look back and read it. I laughed. I know I'm going to look back anyhow but for now I'm just going to concentrate about my life. I hope everything will be great for me towards my goals in life. Days seem to go by so fast, the next thing you know its been months then years past. Goals during this summer may not all that work out but I must go on TO GET READY FOR THE FUTURE.

Sept.8, '95(9:50)

TOO BAD THIS WEEK OF SUMMER THEN SCHOOL AGAIN. WHEN DOES IT END. SEPT 5, I bought a health ball & my Mom's birthday present. That night I scrape my left knee from falling off my butt playing roller blading on my Mom's birthday while playing tennis, actually while running trying to get the balls to serve. I twisted my right ankle & scrape my left knee. What have I done to deserve this maybe the health ball is bad luck. Chinese says; their good for your health they say. Maybe I didn't respect it. Also that day I got a headache, my colds got worse then yesterday almost got an accident after my Dad picked up KELLY ROSSI. It's weird, but this little voice inside me ~~keeps~~ told me what will happen. Today, my left ear feels weird & keeps bumping to torny plants or something. WHAT'S WORSE? I found out I couldn't get in ASB. Only good thing about today is I got to know more about KELLY LUNDEEN playing doubles with her. I'm really glad I didn't regret her instead of SARAH SHAFFER.

October 27, '95

How long has it been since the last time I didn't write on my diary. I've been so BUSY and STRESS out lately. First day of school I got it all figured out, join clubs, be popular etc. I wanted to say Hi! to people I know but sometimes I couldn't even if my conscience told me to. Everyday always thinking to say Hi! talk, meet new people then I wasn't into it because of the Homecoming float. Being the President, as a leader I'm serious on doing my duties. I always wanted to be class officer for a long time. We had 3 weeks to work and get organize. 1st week was so stress out thinking about the float. I never been stress out for a long time. Monday of the first week was our first meeting and over the weekend I called AMBER BARNES & KELLY MASSEY about it. Amber didn't have to run the whole meeting, I only asked her to talked about the float on her experiences. Oh well! On Weds. ¼ people came than on Monday. We watched the movie of 7 Brides and 7 Brothers. I was nervous when I talked to a big group of people. Friday we talked about Jessica's house float meeting. It was a waste not doing nothing for 1st week but called for Fri. night for Monday meeting only because we have to talk about what we need on materials but ended up changing the float ~~theme~~ topic to ***Peter Pan*** on Sunday night 6:00 right after I got pick up from school. That weekend was **LEADERSHIP CAMP**. It was fun but wanted to cry because ~~it didn't~~ sometimes I feel left out. That first speaker guy said have you ever had that feeling after camp is over you don't want to go home because you felt you belong. I don't think I felt that way coz I almost cried twice. On the bus, no seats left I felt I wanted to cry but nice AUTUMN NINTEMAN offered her seat to me. VANESSA JEFFRIES was mean to me. But I think I had fun all of the people in ASB know me. 3 guys in ASB I liked. #1 his named is James, I think whom I played Ping Pong. #2 John whom we did 2 people touch and #3 I forgot his name but his the tallest person in school. Almost forgot Nikki Huck's brother. Back to float….. Monday night meeting at Jessica's house and Mon. Lunch meeting changed to Peter Pan. We had meeting on every night working on the float. Sometimes I feel left out and sometimes not. Its over, looking back on working on the float & time, hard work and everything we've done. **TONIGHT'S THE NIGHT. AFTERSCHOOL WAS TOO BUSY AND THE TIME WAS SO LONG.2 weeks of work, people EL CAP, PARENTS ARE WATCHING US. I had butterfly in my stomach. It went by so fast. Every** body was loud and I had lot of fun just being on the float. It was great. I got thirsty, my throat was dry and my feet are sore. I got to get inside to watch the game, fireworks etc. **We deserve to win first place. The announcer said first place is** (Oh my god Sophomores) **Sophomores.** I shout loud. I got off the bleachers to share the moments. I scream ***"WE WON!"*** **too many times and hugs. I was so happy,** the happiest one. What's embarrassing was I said we won 1st place then the mascot peak of the hand thing. I just stood there and later on what I did. Before this happen I remember my visions of having Peter Pan Float. I pictured the ship. I said, "Wouldn't that be cool if we do Peter Pan then a week later we did. If we win first place the Juniors wish they never changed their Topic. I believed we will win 1st place & Judgement to our float was ours the Best. One guy question "Who float is this?" "the Sophomores its Peter Pan." Then he said "How sad." I was thinking he'll wish he never sad that. I am so happy, my mind is on about the FLOAT. IT REMINDED ME OF The TALENT SHOW. I COULDN'T GO TO SLEEP COZ thinking about the float. My Dad asked me who's the happiest persom. Then I answered, "I AM." OF COURSE, THE STRESS, WORK & BEING A SOPHOMORE PRESIDENT I AM THE HAPPIEST PERSON ON EARTH TONIGHT. I DON'T WANT IT TO END. ALSO, THINKING HOW I DIDN'T CONCENTRATE MUCH TO POPULARITY COZ OF FLOAT. TONIGHT. I REALIZED IT'S NOT ALWAYS POPULARITY WILL GIVE A CHANCE OF BEING IN ASB. LIKE LARISSA GREGERSON, TONIGHT CROWNED HOMECOMING QUEEN. SHE DESERVE IT. She hangs out to everybody. Doesn't care about popularity but to know them & meet people. WE LIKE HER BECAUSE SHE HAS A GOOD PESONALITY. WE ALL LIKE HER. I CAN BE WHAT I WANT TO BECOME AND THINK I CAN BE IN ASB PRESIDENT or HOMECOMING QUEEN or BOTH. IF I WILL BECOME AN OWNER OF A COMPANY. THEN ANYTHING IS POSSIBLE IN THIS WORLD. IF THEY CAN DO IT, THEN I CAN. I BELIEVE I WILL BE COZ I KNOW I CAN.

NOVEMBER 7, 1995 (10:28 P.M)

Its passed my curfew but I have to get up 5:30 in the morning or else I'm grounded for a month. NO WAY! I'm writing with a flashlight. Can you imagine going to 2 clubs at the same time at LUNCH. It's not easy. Today at Key Club I got appointed for CLUB TREASURER & my first meeting on CSF. WHY CAN'T I GET A BOYFRIEND? AFTERSCHOOL WAS FUN. In ASIAN CLUB ~~wasd~~ we went to the DOJO PLACE next to Blockbuster Video. I found out Celest Dad's is the owner of the DOJO. I was going to talk to him about registring for taking TAEKWONDO but didn't have enough time. Mrs. Martinez & I were boxing & she hit me right on my right eye. I guess I gonna tell everybody about it. BO, the president of the Asian club lead the class in teaching us one form of self-defense. BO is cute & a gentleman. Every time I saw him he was very COOL, he always act & look COOL. Too bad were about the same hieght. Meeting new people from clubs, new classmates or prevuos I MUST SAY HI!, talk with them in activity & find a way to get to known them. I would spend 7 hours on the public library last Saturday from 10:00-5:00 to work on our BIOLOGY PROJECT. IM GLAD. IM WITH NANI KAHANANUI & DANEILLE IDLEMAN IN THE GROUP. TODAY From 4:15 to 7:00 we stayed on the library to work on it. I DON'T EVEN WANT TO THINK ON WHAT DAY WERE GOING TO THE LIBRARY AGAIN.

(Sun) 12-10-95

I'm kind of sleepy and tired. I do really want to write to my diary coz I want to go to go to go to sleep. It's probably for good I have to write coz it's been a wonderful weekend for me. Yesterday I had a slumber party. SHELLY MCDANIEL, Kelly Rossi and LAURA HUNTLEY was here. Each has their own character , still Kelly a shy one, Laura a boy crazy girl and Shelly who I don't really know quiet well yet. Shelly I prefty and I love her clothes. Very excited for her first tournament and slept all night will we weR watching a movie and sleeping bag wrestling 2:45 in the morning. Day dad was great. He bought pizza, cooked cookies and breakfast. He is great.

At the tournament, I wasn't nervous as I saw on my 1st one. I didn't want to make the same mistake before about being upset to not winning. TOO BAD SHELLY FELT THAT WAY. LIFE* NOT FAIR.. Good I wasn't diapund being 2nd place again. Afterall there was only 4 girls. Maybe next time but best part was the kata. I was suppose to do my basic form I made up but I change to Kung Fu in the middle of my ~~m~~ form. I was thinking, " What am I doin?" I was daze and confuse all the was to the tournament.

Jan.18,96(Thurs.)

Yesterday was SARA NEPHEW's birthday. I gave her a card; drawed a picture of her holding the estinguisher and she wretch the car. She laughed. The day before her birthday I said " I bet you $10 box It's going to rain tomorrow." I wanted it to rained because I didn't like her at that time. It only rained later on that day but not on her birthday. She said, "Somebody must hate me because it's going to rain today." I could have said "I hate you, that's why!." But I didn't. What can I say I'm jealous of her and that's why I hate her. She has the characters that I want but I can't have and tried, like excellent grades & friends. I remember I broke my pencil at Math because she made my day a bad day. It's just she always get the credit, Sara this, *"she's the queen bee" "smart"* I WISHED I WAS HER. SHE HAS ONE OF THE MOST IMPORTANT THING I WANT RIGHT NOW. I never would taoght today would change my feeling about her. I always feel every time I see her I have a bed day which is like everyday. Tonight I felt different about her. I didn't expect this. We went to El Cajon Library and ended up looking for it for 30 minutes. On our way we went to Yogurt Mill, and she started taking about if ~~how~~ She look down on people because the girl (classmate) told me she does. She explain to me what happen and how ~~she~~ I asked her of her driver's test and how she laugh but the girl got the wrong idea and the girl cried and said guess who: the trouble maker is in this class. She talkative. Sara said "Sorry." I had to tell her the truth. TRUE she looks down on people. I shouldn't have said names about SARAH WHYTE, CHERYL BILLSTORM, ARIANNA FAHEY but I did. I hope she doesn't get mad at them or hate them for what they said about her. Also explained on how she said to ~~Jan~~ Joe. " Youre jealous of me." When she said that my mind said "I'm jealous of you if you only knew." I taught she was serous but she said she was joking. I can't believe I spread rumors on what she said to people, at that time I hated her and that's why? I will never forget about the Yogurt Factory and we sat talking about it. At that moment I felt different about her. Stuff I taught I was wrong and judge her character badly because of jist JELOUSY. I DIDN'T GET ABOUT POPULAR PEOPLE & UN POPOLUR and in HUMANITIES CLASS. She said she will fix this trait of her. I hope so. I'll be booking forward to it. Other quality is she pride of how she is the best and It can also be a good thing. One on one with Sara made me realized something special about her. HOPE TO SEE FRIENDS WITH HER AND

KNOW ABOUT ME. I wonder what she will talk tommorrow. What will she do, something different of what happen today. Will she treat me better? How will she thinks -if I write her a letter about how I felt before? MAYBE TOMMORROW WILL BE A GOODDAY. I happy of what happen today. I just hope I don't think negative as before GOOD NIGHT TILL THE NEXT STORY OF MY LIFE.

Feb. 6, '96

The day before my birthday. It was mostly a happy day. 3D-aRt- I was sleepy. Algebra II- felt out of place (surprise I ~~lov~~ taught I did it-over but sane feelings as the past 3 years. I have to improve somehow. But I got a chance of junior friends. Let's see how I handle them. I will make them adore me. WILL SEE! Spanish-got an OLEE. What's wrong here; be more friendly to your partner and everybody around to know you. WAKE UP HERALYN! 4th period BIOLOGY- Okay, glimpse of SCOTT MCLAUGHLIN. I think he mentioned to his friend his birthday on Feb. 26-or 27. He is so cute. He's out of my leaugue. If he does likes me and he showed signs of that proving he like me then WHY WON THE ASK ME. That is the most annoying part. Then again, if he doesn't that's okay, that means he not my B-Day wish from last year. Hey, it could happen. HUMANITIES -very upbeat. Kati talked why she cried because she is afraid she might get cancer. I was shocked; Speechless.
I don't know what I would say to her because it's hard for me to explain my emotions words but only deep inside me. What she did was brave to talk in front of the class. I learned not to misjudge someone especially if you don't know what's going on/about. Like Cati & me both have similar problems people might not like her who sees almost everyday but at least she talks to them. What about me. I'll be lucky if SHAWN WOODY talked to me.

Afterschool hasn't change much for me because I always think about popularity, more friends and more friends and popularity. I just can't get over it. Somehow it has gotten so important that affected my schoolwork and everytime I think about just ~~sho~~ slowed down my self-esteem lower because it only improve by a short amount. I could write on and on about this but not tonight… Maybe some other night. I could talked for hours about popularity from my head. Went to El Cajon library to drop book from **Renaissance**. Stop at Saturn Dealer for lookout of used car for $5,000 for Mom. I ~~taught~~ thought about how I'm going to be driving ~~soon~~ supposibly tomorrow but not until next year. OH WELL!- DYED MY HAIR-WARM BROWN But didn't come out like nothing still same hair color- Well, maybe next time. I can still ~~colo~~ curled my hair. Red Lobster-Ate shrimp, lobster and crab was good and cake- a piece of cake with a candle. That was GREAT and DELICOUS. Wore my new outfit dress. I looked liked sort of fat. I don't know if I should wear it tomorrow or not. Tonight a while ago I was thinking about my past birthday parties of my childhood. I had 9 or 8 consecutive birthday cakes that are huge and lechon. Big relative/family party. Those were the days I could imagine how little and my cute smile with my unpretty teeth showing. My 6th B-day party always haunted me and reminded me of APRIL MASCARIÑIAS- my first best friend. Tomorrow I will be 16. Which I am now if Philippine time. I wonder how many ballons I will get. Ther is more important than just ballons tomorrow. I don't know what to expect. I start the day waking up early. Only feared of BAD DAY. I just want to have a GREAT DAY TOMORROW. FEEL GREAT AND WORRY FREE.

FEBRUARY 7TH -SWEET 16TH

Today was a very special day for me because it's my 16th Birthday. It started out when I woke up 5 A.M in the morning doing my Spanish homework. I did my every morning before I go to school except I blowdried my hair, wore makeup & high heeled shoes to look good. I was suppose to wear it on my dress today but didn't, and planned it wearing on V-Day. Sorry! I didn't want to be late; not making up my bed and messy coz didn't have enough time. I bothered Kelly R. saying why she didn't bring ballon for me. I think I was being rude. I just wanted more ballon or at that point just a ballon so people would notice me and say "Happy Birthday." Somehow being notice has been so important to me. I love attention from people. Always has and will on popularity, talents, compliments, class, compliments from teachers. You know me. When I saw ELIZABETH DECKER who bought a balloon. It made my day GREAT because of one ballon. I felt important and will be noticed. Arianna didn't bother to greet "Happy Birthday!" She I heard later on from JUNI UNDEN that Arianna talked about my shoes and didn't bother to say happy birthday and something about my personality but I'm not sure. That time I wanted to talk bad stuff of her to but later on it was her opinion and learn she is just the same Ariana before and she is entitled to her opinion. 1st period went fast. TANDY MASTELLER's B-Day today, also had a (1) ballon. We greeted with great smile. A saw about 3 people who had birthday ballons carrying them around at school. KRISTI JENKINS, A.S.B, Com. of Athletics who doesn't know me. I wanted to talked to her but didn't get a chance to. 2nd period-all day in between periods people would greet me which is "COOL" KARINA BUETTGENBACH didn't bothered to say/greet "Happy Birthday." I wonder why?- I don't know what she thinks of me. Karina, the person who I liked to be my friend didn't greet to me. Sara N. said "Happy Birthday" 2nd period. Of all the person I believed she said it to be so sweet from her sweet voice at 6th period personally in the library. That meant a lot to me. How she said it, behind it all that smiling face tells how she thinks of me as a friend. That was special. Having a sub for Spanish was great. Taking to April as my partner. Adam and COLLEEN WOOLRICH said it with exclamation expression especially Colleen. ~~The~~ A group of ~~us~~ them in class smiled like Naomi. 4th- I wanted Scott to say " Happy Birthday" to me but he didn't. KELLY BRADY sang it all the way till we got to BIO classroom. NAOMI HERNANDEZ was one of my favorite of the day. Bothered Mr. White "let's say we did & not ." LUNCH A to J club Regina greeted me 1st. JESSICA S. came along. Asked Larissa if she ~~come~~ could come to my Birthday Party. replied "I don't know yet." I was touched by Olivia Barner's speech while doing my poem for Humanities. I pictured myself every time whenever I'm at A to J club ~~askingif~~ I would be taking and one of the future guest speaker. ~~is the~~ Telling them how I felt I will be a speaker. Talked about God, me, experiences in school, my goals and drems- what I found about it ups & down. Picturing that in future and come true is something to feel happy. Humanities still Kelly Brady sang it in Spanish. The whole class sang " Happy Birthday" to me. I was surprised it was a big tone of voices and no ~~way~~ it be like Spanish but at least Ill get olless. I hope CLINT MARSH give me flower. WHY DID ELIZABETH HAD TO LEAVE? NOT FAIR FOR ME OR ESPECIALLY HER. Karina still didn't say anything. That's okey: Karate tonight. Spend 20 dollars on gifts for Friends on V-DAY cards is tonight and last night I reflect on the past birthday parties. Those were the memorizes. I remember when April visited on my 6th B-DAY. Tomorrow I start track and Football. Goodnight.

3-5-96

UPDATE IN FEB. I WENT TO DISNEYLAND ON CSF NIGHT. I'm glad finally I got in a group and didn't feel neglected but I wish I was talking to the big crowd. My Slumber Party was a blast and I didn't want it to end. I HAD 10x much fun than last year. I got the people I like at my party. JESSICA STOKES, one of the best and nicest freénd of mine. Kelly Rossi, 2nd thoughts of not letting her to my party coz I thought she wasn't good enough. How dumb of me but she is my shigiest friend and she was on my party. I had to ditch Shelly McDaniel but felt less for others and wished I had more of my friends to the party. NIKKI HUCK.-thinks she will become an actress. WOW! She is pretty, nice, cheerful and of course she drives. JESSICA STAMPER too drives and she is wery understanding, always happy & considerate person. Larissa Gregerson was one of my best guest coz she is a Senior, goodly popular, everybody loves her, smart, caring, nice etc. She is one of the people of El Cap I looked up to. It was so much fun! I did hypmatize them, watched movies till 4 in the morning and talked.

This month wasn't always have been great at all. My Dad got mad at me for not having umbrella and a poncho on a showering afternoon. The day of my very first football game. I just don't want to talk about this.

NOW. Present day-night of 3-5-96 I'm grounded till April. Hey! At least I can say now I been grounded. Low grades. I have to wake up #:30 tommorow morning.

TODAY on my horoscope said I was suppose to have a lucky day. Afterschool 5th 6th period class Scott was letting our classmates read the letter I gave him. Worst enough, SHAWNI FLINT connented to Kelly Brady "WHO IS YOUR LITTLE PHYSCHO FRIEND." That made me feel like I want to crush him or Shawni. I can't believe he let his friends read that letter in front of me. I felt I wanted to melt and k+ll him. His friends were just astonisly laughing. GO AHEAD LAUGH. After school I felt, so bad and rotten and not still over it. BAD DAY! But I went to a Hawaiian restaurant called the Island. It was superbly delicious.

Back to Scott. Cheryl and Danielle complemented me for I have the guts and courage. YEAH RIGHT! Now I wish I didn't write him a letter and stop now. I don't know I wish he'll give me a letter. I wished he liked me but that is impossible coz his friends will be laughing at me coz… you know why? Everything is opposite now so for my feeling of him coz of what he did.

Let see what will happened tommorow. Good Night!

3-7-96

I am so deeply in trouble at school. I haven't been actually been doing my homework and studying. I fake in 2nd period I lost my graph paper so I couldn't do my presentation. I did a good job. Sara Nephew said, " I hope you'll find your graph paper." when I passed by her to 3rd period class. She care so much____? me. COOL! I like her. I wan't her be my future ~~e~~capaign manager. She could give me a lot of vote I just hope she is not a student senate. I'll talk to her tomanorow.

I personally gave Scott a letter from me to him. I told my friend wanted me to give this to you. After that I felt so low again. I had to hear them talking about me not knowing who I am. "She give me all these clues and it's scaring me."

" Maybe it's a guy" "Do you know who it is?" I felt so horrible but at lunch I laughed about what he said. I got mad because " he is so dumb he couldn't go figure the clues I give him." It turns out we are both mad at each other. Later after 6th period, Kelly told me what Scott said, "He will not write you a letter. He wants to know you but I told him she will tell you when the time is wright."

I had second thoughts of not telling him my name. I think I should but not now. I won't write any letters and tell him 2 weeks or 1 from now. I hope everything will be fine.

I must wake up tommorow. When will I get a boyfriend. I want one.

3-13-96 (Weds) 4:46 PM

I haven't done my homework yet since I got home 3 oclock. I wanted ~~ah~~ time for me to think about myself as always. I'm looking for my identity. Am I okay looking? How do people see me? Will I ever get a boyfriend? I want my 15th B-Day wish. None of my wishes come true yet.

Tomorrow I will tell him I want to met you next week. I hope Monday. I'm going to ask him some questions. Will see? I don't know, It doesn't matter if I told him ~~orI not~~ like him and if he doesn't like me. **That's okay** too. He doesn't have to like me as long as I told him I liked him personally in front **of his face** and get this off my chest. I don't know if I will feel better, probably not if I worry about that 3rd letter then I think I would not want to be around him when he knows. If he has a girlfriend at school. I should look around and watch him more often: Should I talk to the love doctor tonight. I'm only attracted or Il think he's cute but I °liked CORY THOMPSON coz he is so sweet especially when he flirts I just turns me on. I know he's not really cute but his a keeper for me. I'm going to ask ádvice from him about what to do about this guy I liked. I'll ask advice from my clique of classmates. BACK TO REALITY NOW.

✈☠♒●✸⬆♥☺Do Homework!!✝🌍♥↘❷⓿❶⓿☆

3-14-96

Today has been the worst day of my Sophomore year. Perhaps my high school ~~year~~ days! It turn out to be a great and fun filled day. At start of the day I was cramping for **Biology** test and worked on worksheet packet. I always do this since from the start of the school. I keep saying I will study but never. Period 1-3D **ART** was okay. Shannon asked me to help her on her project. JILON BLACK got caught in my so called "candy temptation." She asked about the dance, a Cindy Hopkins Dance. But I didn't answered. I must have this dance. Will see. I want it bad enough to taste it. Yeah Right. Per.2.- Hang in there. ~~at~~ for Homework quiz in ALGEBRA II. I want an A in that class. Everyone in the group got there attention on me when I talked about Martial Arts. Per.3- Spanish. Mrs. Benjamin is weird. She is so nice in her personally but her evil side of strictness makes me hate her. I just don't get her. Per.4-Biology. Goosh! I didn't study and wasn't ready for the big test again I can't flunk that class. I want an **"A"** in that class. The test was hard and I didn't know the answers at all. Scott M. still don't get/know I like him. I wonder if he likes Abigail or Valerie or Nani or what about **"ME."** OH WELL! He is just cute. He's too out of my league. Lunch went weird coz I had Science Club meeting today. Only15 people ~~shouell~~ showed up. CHRIS MCLAUGHLIN did something that they were talking about which he was suppose to do but didn't. The New Officers, Chris' girlfriend argue who's idea was it for the field trip this next friday…I envy them. I went to Spanish club meeting but not one was there except a guy who took a test & the new Spanish teacher in R7. I think she'll do good as an Advisor. I was the 3rd one to sign up for the meeting. I'm willing to help that club a popular club. Hey, you get scholarship. Why not join. After a little chat and she bought a $ candy bar from me. I went to a new group in front of the pool where the grass is. Jessica Stokes, KIO LANCE, Kelly and Yakes are few people who do swim hang outs there. ~~Its's fun~~ I did a little homework but didn't finish it. I went to R7 again to ask if there is a treasurer of the club. NONE! NADA I got the job. Start of a COOL DAY. Jessica came up to me when I was walking up to my Period 5 & 6 Humanities class and asked if I want to play tennis. I said, "Will see." Which I did. My Humanities class I had a sub. It was fun since we pretty much didn't do anything big. No check of homework. Read the **"Paradise Lost."** Last period was just about talking to counselor for your schedule next year. That's ~~mu~~ pretty much it. Then socialized. Afterschool with Jessica Stamper was fun. We went to "BURGER KING" and had a nice chat about stuff. I was so surprised I started talking and discuss about my situation. I felt confortable and knew her for years. She is the most understanding friend that I know of. Did I mentioned she is funny and always happy. We played tennis afterwards at court 6. Right next to where in court 5 DANIEL HUCK and JASON GREGERSON was playing doubles with their tennis team going. Little did I know afterwards. Jessica are I were stopping and talking them play and talk till we end up talking them play and talk till we end talking about guys. I told her I wrote a letter to this guy and so on. Also, I told her that I like 2 guys on the tenins team. He ended up liking J. Gregerson. I laughed and so unbelievable. It's so funny I can't believe it. We started taking about him. Now I know why she was talking how guys are dumb when we chat when playing tenis. I just can't believe it. I know why she is MAD at him coz she wants him to let him know she likes him and hope he'll like her. That's how exactly how I felt about Scott now. Good Night!

April 18,1996

This week's frustration is over it; about running for TREASURER. I ran for TREASURER LAST YEAR and lost 2x in a row. ~~She~~ My Spanish club advisor told me, the 3rd time is for sure. I hope so. I'm counting on it. It's would be so IRONIC to me to run for TREASURER Next year. OR maybe run for PRESIDENT. It's a gamble I have to win my 3rd one no matter what it takes. It's hard. On Monday I slept till 3 in the morning and only got 2 ¾ hours of sleep. On Tues night I slept till 1:30 in the morning. I had to get up, and NOMINATING CONVENTION was a whole lot ~~of exper~~ better that last year. I broke 3 boards. Got 2 cuts and hit KELLIE [KELLY] LUNDEEN on ~~the~~ her face by the board fly at her face. I chicken out at the dares. I knew I would. I'm so afraid of it, it was the only part I didn't like and I wish I prepared my skit a would lot better and said something to the delegates. I asked a delegate to nominate for me for Elections but someone else who a cute guy in CO-ED cheer named Jeremy got nominated instead of me coz he's more cute & popular. Either way I had no chance against ~~him~~ him or Lacey if I made the ballot. I told Jorge ~~to vote~~ GOOD LUCK! I hope you'll win. But its said to say he will lost but I'm just supporting him. Mostly, senior bound gets to win for office who are Juniors now coz there more populaR. Today I woke up quarter to 6 very tired and so sleepy. I wasn't awake till I ate 100 grand chocolate at 3rd period. It gave a big effect on me somehow. I have 3 of them. People asked me if I made the ballot but I didn't but I'm not upset about it coz Mr. Saffers gurantees of me in ASB. Cool ha! Then I can go out with thez guys I like in ASB. OH YEAH! Jessica Stamper is gonna be so jealous. I bet you there are few guys that likes me on ~~ny~~ EL CAP but I don't like any of them. I ~~g~~ was at the McLab till 7 I called ~~till~~ at 7 to pick me up and called 7: 10 and noone answered so I just went honne to walk. The lights was on and my parents were gone. It turns out they been looking for me for 1 hour. I felt so bad, it almost gave them a heart attack. I will never do that again. I so exiced for Jessica's STOKES PARTY.

4-20-96

On Fri, Yesterday was Jessica's Stokes B-Day. Her 16th B-DAY. Today was her party from 12 P.M.-10P.M. I got there at 12:20 P.M. We, all 7 of our friends went to the rodeo, box seat baby! It was cool! Too bad Sara N. and Crystal had to leave. People from Cross Country & track showed up about 15 of them. There was a group of guys and one of them I liked but I think he's a freshman but he's still cute. We went swiming and in the spa. At the end, these guys were talking something. I could have sworn he likes me or APRIL CARTER. I'll ask April on Monday.

April 23 1996, Tues

I'm still hanging from the edge of the rock. Somehow I have to find a way and do everything I can to climb back to the top. Yesterday, when I came back from school I remember about Jessica's B-Day Party. About JOSH FREESE if he thinks I like him or if he likes me. You know if he thinks he's all that cool, he must rate me, doesn't he does that to other girls? I would have like him a lot better if he's nice and have the personality like the guys I would want to go out with. If he asks me out, I'll say "I will never go out with you, maybe in another lifetime." Ha! Ha! He's a Jerk(.) Period. Just as I suspected the guy I liked at the party is a freshman, who ever he is. But, there's others guys in the world. I wish I know what they are talking about when I left. Jon Boland, I remember back in Leadership Camp I liked him ever since till I found out he's a senior and has a girlfriend. Well, don't worry Heralyn, there's other guys. ← this is the 2nd time I mentioned this sentence. Scott is cute! OH Yeah! I think that's the only one I liked about him. He will know it's me this week. Only thing I want to know if did he like me and then he's actions months ago about me & him. I just want to know what will happen if he finds out. I don't expect him to like me coz its his choice plus he's going to go out with Nani anyway. I have to mention this 3rd x in a row. Don't worry Heralyn- there's plenty of guys out there. Cory broke up with his girlfriend. Good news for me but bad news for him. Let's see if he falls for my charm. I would love to go out with him because he has an awesome personality. Very rarely I find his personality in other guys now a days. Next year, I have to go out with Jacob G. and Matt F., I must be in A.S.B. next year. I want Jacob first and I'll use my charm and I have to tell Matt I like him because he is so shy and I think he'll go out with me. WHO KNOWS! WISH MYSELF GOOD LUCK.

April 24 '96

I didn't even do my homework yet. I feel weird today. When I looked at myself in the mirror I felt like I'm confident, smart, pretty, nice, feeling good. I never felt this way before. Last year I can't look at myself in the mirror for 10 secs. But now its okay. I feel better. I feel I can do anything. I'm confident about my goals but fear time is running out and I will never achieve it. I have to, it contains everything about my future. I CAN DO ANYTHING! About Scott, let's just say not today but tomorrow. Im gonna be pretty busy tom. But I feel okay! O YEAH it's AMANDA BAUDERS17th B-Day tomorrow. I gotta go do homework. What else is there to do?

April 25, 1996

It started out to be a bad day because of homework/School crisis. And I'm also upset about the class officers not doing their work. Hello! I cryin out for help. Lunch I had to go to Key Club meeting. TREASURER AGAIN. Ariana's B-DAY is today and I gave Amanda her present and gave DYLAN CONFORTH a caramel chocolate. It was the thought that counts. After-school ~~of~~ Oh! Almost forgot Jessica Stamper volunteered to give a letter to Scott finally signed my name on it. I felt like I wanted to die. I had to stay at Mr. Van's Bio. Room coz I didn't want him to get the clue first. I played tennis with Jesicca. WHo else did we talk about? JACOB GREGERSON. OF COURSE! The heat was on. Dan yelled out my name, **" Heralyn, did you win for TREASURER?" "NO! ~~But~~ "There's always next year." "Yeah!"** Jacob was on the next court but I didn't know if he said something. I won't remember. But I did remember that rewine It so happen I accidentally, this time, the ball whent over the fence to Boy's court. It so happen Jacob was playing there. But he didn't pick it up, some other guy did. But he was looking at me. I went back to my court. I was full because we went to BurgerKing. Me & Jessica went to see CHRISTINA PRINCIPE race 100 relay. There was a track meet going on. I was talking with clinque friends I just went with Jessica then Josh come up to me and said, "Are you gonna be at Jessica's pool party tonight?" "There is a pool party, I 'll try to go then." I have to find a way to get to Jessica's Party by convincing my Dad to drive me there. I had to sell tickets at the Freshman Orientation Dance and only sold 4 tickets. I talked with SUMMER HUDSON[HODSON], MICHELLE DAY and AUTUMN MOODY, just hangin with them. Jacob came along talking with Summer and saying " How come there is no Boy's Tennis here." He crossed out and fillout sheet and changed it to ~~g~~ boys and put his name on the list. 4 other boys got on the list. I told my Dad this boy asked me out to go to Jessica's party with me. That was the only ticket way to get in. I did it. I got picked up and went directly to the party. Darn! I don't have a bathing suit. I felt so totally miss out coz I don't have my swimsuit. I had to talk to people. I talked with particular people like Matt Freeman. He's easy to talk to Jacob. That was the hard part. First gig! I listen to his conversation with his friend. "FRIENDS SUCK,… I like Summer Hudson. I came and talk to her at the Freshman Orientation today and still no clue." I felt like I wish Jessica Stamper was here. ~~n~~ I'll invite her next time.

Oh! she gonna be jealous. The party made me feel lonely but in the end it turn out good. I watched him play Jenga with his friends. He boomed it. He asked Jessica "Is this game right here. I like connect four." It was close to it but look different. We played and I lost against him again. He always wins. He won playing ping pong with me at Leadership Camp. He is fine! I talked with a group of people and I pretended laughing and didn't know what this guy was talking about. My Mom called so I told her to tell Dad to pick me up. I thought that was it. But when a few people were still there so I just chat with them. When Jacob came back and couldn't find his keys. I asked where he is. Jessica said " He at the back door." I went there. "Couldn't find your keys. I grab it where I found it and saw it in the middle of the party was going on. I glance at it but din't know who it was. I feel like something between the 2 of us is unique and ended up playing and I help him. Jessica asked "You found it. How did you find it." "Oh! I just saw it and gave it to him." JACOB REPLIED " She must have the eye like a hawk." I think I said Bye to him. That's What I call a perfect touch endeing of the party. Rewind: Almost forgot, SHAWN WOODY said "goodbye girls" he reached for my hand but I think I slapp it but sort of like a shake. FIRST TIME I GOT TO HOLD HIS HAND. That's the closest I'll ever get to. It's so funny. I don't know but he was flirty with Kristi Jenkins. He holdstive her hands. I looked at them. They looked like the perfect couple. He hugged her from behid. "Wait come back," holding back, "I love you," like a whisper but not lovel. It was just a 30 sec. Romance. K.J. didn't seem to care. Somehow she didn't want to talk to Shawn after that. I got to sit next to her. We both said "Hello!" I wished I said something interesting. Next party with a group of people. I need to know them and be able to talk and get on with the guys I like at the party. I will promose a party again at my best friend's house will be 10x better. I PROMISE . It's Destiny we are talking about! I told my Dad, I didn't like him, "So he turn out to be a bum HA! I hope you'll find the right guy." I hope so, soon enough like next week. I don't know what Scott is thinking right now coz I have to go back to school on Monday. I don't know what he will do or what to react to him. I HAD A VERY INTERESTING AND FUN DAY! HIGHLIGHTS OF THE WEEK. I'm telling Larissa that I like Jacob. She'll laugh. Just for the heck of it. I'm numbering my guys.

May 4th, 1996

I'm so tired of so tired of so many things to worry. I did a lot of activities. I hate being stress out. I don't know if everything will turn out alright or not. DECIDE FAITH IS LIKE TOSSING A COIN. My grades suck and I need to bring them up fast. I'll talk to another topic. On Friday, I played tennis after school with Jessica and her new friend who is 20+ yr. old guy. He's pretty good in tennis. I didn't get home till 10:35. I watched the SWIM TEAM and Softball girls. After that, 5:30 I changed at the gym bathroom and decorated. Vanessa Jeffries still makes kind of four fun of me. JULIE MENNE is nice and a good officer. Surprise! 10 people showed up, a few were freshmen. but its okay as long as you help. Jessica left me. the only reason she might have stayed if for sure Jacob was there. I really didn't think I would have fun but I did. I ~~saw~~ met Carol. Who lives in my apt. complex. She looked at me and said, "Hi! Heralyn! You guys this is Heralyn," with eagerness. I said "Hi!" I felt akward dancing at first but when HIP HOP MUSIC play. I was on the groove. "Go! Heralyn!" All night dancing I was right on the money. Finally, watching the GRIND works and paid off. I didn't really have trouble fitting in but well a little bit. I get better from experience. I think when I see new people that I already know I should smile always and say "Hi! With cheerfulness. Like Jessica Stokes & Larissa G. methods of "Hi!" I just hope Summer and her friends said nice things about me. I hope I didn't smell. I was tired after the dance and we had to clean up. I had a pizza and a soda. I was so hungry. Summer Hudson drove. I just didn't believe it. She got through by directions. ~~I was~~ Her Mom walk me towards the door to make sure I was fine. I didn't went to bed till 11:20 I was thirsty so I drank water. I had to wake up early because of the Jr. Olympics. Jamie is in it, and baby sitting her while working for KIWANIS. Her team won 3rd place for 400m relay. Rachelle's step dad drove us home. I came back home and told my Dad I'm going to get TACO BELL'S application. I did that to get to do Carwash. Mrs. Martinez has been bugging me. But I went over with what she said. I got there and started washing cars. MAGGIE ESCUDERO was there. Amber asked me if where are the class officers. I told them about it but there are not showing up. Maggie asked who is in ASB. Amber said she is. Amber said, "Heralyn the Class Pres." Maggie shocked my hand," Congratulations, I didn't know." I left at 2:15 P.M. and ate at TACO BELL and got an application. Still

I was hungry. Thinkin back: REWIND Jessica & me talks about Jacob all the time and we have a few things in common. It's weird but we get along well. She is still crazy about Jacob Gregerson even still she says, "I hate him." Only because she not gatting attention. I like him too. I know how she feels ~~but still~~ coz I still liked SCOTT and when I think I hate him only because he ignores me, and still I wish he knows. I can't believe he's going out with NANI K. I ~~hen~~ hinted he ~~thinkll~~ likes NANI or Valerie. I just didn't expect they would go out. I'M STILL CURIOS, DOES HE STILL LIKES ME? OR DID HE EVER LIKED ME? I wished hed tell me. Maybe he'll broke up with Nani on the 25th. And he'll interest in me. It could ~~say~~ mean from my horoscope at **Seveenteen**. sTart liking him made me feel I could go out with him. It boost up my self-ESTEEM BIG TIME coz of LIKING HIM. I told Danielle I'm going with a guy named DANNY who is a senior at EL CAP. Also, he is the guy I broke his nose and we a getting ready for Canadian Tournament this summer. I'm so good, only because to tell him I got over with him. BUT I DO ADMIT I'M JEALOUS AND UPSET He's going out with NANI. LiFe's not fair. Of course, there's other code guys #2 & #3 but #4 will wait next year hopefully. I think I'm starting to like the real Danny, he's #5. I can't believe it, My first impression of him was a geek and fat but he is actually nice, good sense of humor and funny. He thinks I'm ~~so~~ cool. He told Jessica Stokes at the Spring Assembly. I wonder if he ~~think~~ likes me. I wonder if what he said to me at the library was on way for me to notice him and start talking to him. CAN'T I JUST GO OUT WITH SOMEONE. I NEED SOMEBODY TO LOVE & ADMIRE MY INNER PERSONALITY. I went to the mall with Marylin and Jamie. I bought a new sunglasses. I met Dylan whos in my humanities class. I can't believe this happen! Miranda came up to me saying, "Youre Dylan's friend. He told me about you. He thinks youre smart. He's obsessed about you. I interupt, "Please don't tell me he said about me being a martial artist." "He did and how youre so talented and in KARATE." I smiled

"Oh! I'm MIRANDA by the way, Dylan's girlfriend!" "Oh you're the famous MIRANDA. He wrote your name on the bulletin bord. Mrs. Coffin-Prince is upset ~~to~~ Dylan and the whole class is laughing at him. He doesn't do that anymore because he doesn't want to get in trouble? She laughed. Somehow we separated. I saw Dylan but I didn't feel like talking to him. He had some cute friends so I was embarrassed. I can't believe I got to meet Dylan's girlfriend and word **OBSESION** came to her mouth about me.

***TO STOP* AND THINK ABOUT IT.** Who would be one who sees me about my inner personality aside from Dylan. I hope he's around somewhere, BUT WHO? He understands me. He's perfect for me. Still waiting! I'll get that wish.

May 22, '1996

Normal day like always. I'm a fourth so far writing this diary and you know my writing is bad and I need work on my grammar. It's 10:23 P.M and my radio is on star station. I was going to write something on May 15 (Weds.)= The worst day of my entire Sophomore Year. Did you ever believe in a saying "Whatever you do in the past will reflect your future? It did on that day. One #1 = Everything I worked for becoming and wanting to be a successful artist hasn't ~~become~~ come true. I was suppose to turn in my poster ~~co~~ coz it's due today but I didn't turn it in till after school when the judging was done. I wanted to win so bad. I walked in Mrs. Benjamin's Spanish room and turn in my Poster and she said "Too late now, we just got done with the judging." I replied "After all I've been through working on this poster."/ "Yes, after all that." I left immediately and tears coming out of my eyes and stand at a corner so no one could see me. I tried avoiding the people after that. You might think its silly to cry but the Poster Contest (Language month) was important to me because it reflects part of me. When I was a little kid I've always wanted to be the best in art. As I grew up, people appreciated my work but someone always get picked to win. I never won an art contest in my life except one of my drawing got in art exhibit when I was in 6th grade. It was a portrait of Paul Lawrence Du~~d~~nbar and won only one art contest in Lakeside Middle School for designing a brochure of a PTSA. I got picked out of other 8th grades art students. I didn't like art as much as I like Martial Arts because I didn't think I was good at it no matter how much I tried. Someone better always gets the credit. I always Hate that: 2nd reason was I wanted to run for a junior class office but couldn't because my G.P.A. is low by .5. My grades right now is not even me. As the school got empty and everyone started leaving I observed people and compared them to me. Like example, Sara Nephew was walking by ~~to go home~~ to leave school and I was sitting by the Quad area were the benches were. As I saw her I compared myself to her. What's the difference between her and me. One of my goals was to be #1 in my humanities class and she will be #2 but its not happening. What's the difference? What does she got that I don't have? We are both PERFECTIONIST. I compared myself to other girls who wore nice clothes and they got the looks and body to wear it. Why can't I be her. This is the #1 thing wrong with me. Whatever I do I am and never had been satisfied ^ about myself for the last 15 and 5 moths. Go figure!

LET's talk about other stuff like GUYS. Okay, I don't like Scott but I still want to be friends with him. I will force myself to talk to him. I don't care if he looks at me funny. Hey! At least I'm getting his attention. Now he knows its me, so what's the big deal. #1 I liked him is because his cuteness and style and later his sweetness. I think I only like him coz he's cute. I do like other guys. Por ejemplo #1 right now is Cory Thompson. You should have seen me when I gave him a birthday card after the day of his birth day. The conversation when lik this: "IS it someone's B-Day today?", he asked. "It's for you. It has your name on it." "Thank you Heralyn" "I always give my friends something on their B-Days. Really! Ask them." I was blushing at this time. Then he hugged me not face to face but side to side while we were walking towards to our Bio. Class. I gave him a funny card. A clown in the bathroom. I wrote that he deserves this card because he's nice and sweet person. I want to go out with him so bad. Whenever I see guys I like or talk and stand next to him I asked myself ,"Does he knows I want to go out with him. I wished." Cory is still flirting with girls and very sweet. He flirts with me too. I think I'm beginning to like Vesna. I didn't expect it but it just happened. "Does he have feeling fo me?" "Why does he talks to me in the 1st place?" I think I'm begen. ing to like him. Let's talk about something else.

I have Spring practice For Tennis. A 4 day weekend and Talent Show coming up. Bye!

date-5/27/96

I'm hoping this one will be a lot shorter that the other ones. I had a 4 day weekend and didn't have much fun as I wanted to but I got invited by Jamie's Mom to come to her party, which requires age of 21. I know it won't be fun for me as much as they will have fun. The adults I mean. Liquior and dancing! She didn't ask me to babysit Jamie but I ended up when we got bored and she slept over at my house. Since the 10 year old Jamie is the only certified best friend I have in this apartment even though she is acts like a brat sometimes and immature just to annoy me. I told few of my friends were cousins like I told ~~Celine were cousins~~ the Tennis team were cousins. FRIENDSHIP Seems LIKE A LUST TO ME. Okay, back to reality! I wished I would have gone to parties and to the beach or a sleepover during the 4 day weekend. Last week I beat Kelly Lundeen in a game 6-0. Today at practice I beat her winners up and ~~lows~~ losers down in a 2 to 3 game. Coach will give me a prize. I'm honored without Summer Hudson for the past l~~ast~~ 5 days of practice. Summer #1 in tennis team in singles. I think I'll tell everyone I'm playing singles to get away with Alecia question. I don't want to play doubles with her. I don't think of her bad but I'll rather have Kelly L. to be my partner again. We have the ingre dents to be #1 if we want to but she getting a little rusty. No, not that, ~~she~~ It's first time I beat her before. I'm glad I played Tennis with Jessica Stamper earlier this year for practice. Yap…remember those practice syping on Jacob G.

I'm glad at ASB room today because I don't want to get stuck in the middle where I have to be there to my friends who ~~wouldn't~~ didn't win. It's hard, take it from my own experience for the past 2 years of high school elections. I glad SARAH CELESTE won for Soph. Secretary, CRYSTAL WOZENCRAFT for Junior Pres. & SUMMER HUDSON for Junior V-Pres. I'm upset JESSICA STOKES lost for Junior Treasurer. I can't believe VEASNA won against her. I kind predicted it because the crowd voters ~~wante~~ knew him more than JESSICA plus VEASNA is smart & ran for school office this year. YOU WIN SOME, YOU LOSE SOME!

May 29, 1996

3 more weeks before school ends and I have to find a way to bring my grades up. WHAT'S BEEN HAPPENING? Talent Show is cancelled tomorrow and will resume next week coz of Baseball CIF finals at Jack Murphy Stadium tomorrow. I wished I could go but there's next year which I doubt. Friday, Walk on Water Contest after school. I volunteered to help coz Science Club is organizing it. Still waiting for ASB for interview. This will be the biggest thing ever which will reflect next year and my Senior year. I just have to be in ASB next in order for me to get paRt of my DESTINY to be a president and more

likely to be V- Pres. It's not easy. I have no idea what I will do if I don't get to be an ASB to many things I've hope and wanted so long and its time I get this chance to be an ASB rep.

I heard on the #39 international news ~~that~~ about Baganga . It was about the spread of Cholera. My Mom was upset and depressed. I'm to kind of person who doesn't know how exactly to react on circumstances. HARD to EXPRESS my FEELINGS. Suddenly I felt for my Aunt's Jojo's 2 kids in Baganga and my Mom's family who are my relatives. I feel awful about this It's not like I don't hear the cry of the ~~Philippine~~ Pilipinos when I hear stuff on the news. I lived there for 12 years. I used to feel lonely & homesick during my 1st year in U.S. but I'm not coz I've adopted this life. I know I will not be able to visit there till 4 years or so from now. I could go on telling about Philippines but works cannot express my feelings for me and everything else in this world.

I realized I needed Help and guidance for so long and didn't get it. Didn't get what I want last year, some came true and mostly didn't. I've gain confidence and self-esteem. I have a lot to learn in life. What happen to my dream? I need to get back on ~~the~~ track to hope on what's ahead.

6-10-96 Mon.

Today seem to be a perfect day. A+ on Sci. Met. Project. and everything else went fine even if struggle in Humanities for oral project presentation was today. STILL, I had a bad day. I asked Jeff Gladstone to sign my yearbook. I said, "I gotta have the Junior Class President to sign my yearbook." I signed his yearbook not knowing well what to write but he wrote something meant more than anything else in the world matters when you are feeling low. He told me he didn't ~~cant~~ make ASB Rep. And he didn't see my name in it but I didn't believe him. I went to ASB room and saw nothing "NADA" my name wasn't out there. From outside ~~the5~~ leaning to wards the glass I see the ASB room. So empty. I wanted to be in this class more than anything else since the VERY FIRST YEAR of MY HIGHSCHOOL CARRER. Noone could stop me from my leadership dreams. I tried all my best , tried, tried , tried. Lost treasurer 2x, didn't run for class office coz I know I wouldn't win with any way and low grades and sad but true AFTERALL I BEEN THROUGH, experienced leader in school, surprise, surprise, one thing I've been wanting most aside from a boyfriend, I didn't get. ASB was suppose to be my ticket to popularity but I don't care about popularity, I got myselF and my friends who cares about me. ASB is my ticket for me to run for PRESIDENT, V-PRES or TREAS. One day a week after I lost school Treasurer ballot I told my friends "Your looking at the future School PRESIDENT Right here." I'm not the future anyMore but **someday I will be the future OWNER & PRES. Of a billion dollar company.** I felt exactly the same when I lost the ballot for last today. It's their lost. Jeff wrote "Never give up and I didn't look at me I'm the Junior Class President and if you keep on trying **VICTORY** is near." He's right. For some victory is there . . . JULIE GODFREY. Soph. Class Pres & School Pres. KANDACE ETCHINGS. Soph. Class President ~~and~~ Com. Of Publicity and Com. Of Activities. I thought I had bright future ahead of me like them but I guess not. Julie likes me, voted for me and maybe wanted me to be in A.S.B.- I wouldn't mind being in her shoe. Kandace is popular one of most popular, =) leadership, full of character and says "HI!" to me in my Freshman year. I have so many good ideas about this school and how to improve and I have talents that only special people have. **I don't really want to be in Journalism but I guess I have to and I don't think talking Art will help me to Air Force Academy. I sacrifice for my best belieF. One day, I'll remember the day** of the interview for ASB Rep. And think I may not have made it but I have my on GOVT. now. To be my own school Pres and to use my talents and leadership skills in a big building of my own. WHO KNOWS Jacob Gregerson might WORK For me one day. I'LL BE MY OWN BOSS. ANYONE CAN TAKE MY OPPURTUNITY of MY DREAMS and HOPES BUT **I ALONE CONTROL MY DESTINY.** I don't care whatever happens in high school as long as if I made AIR FORCE, you can take my freedom for this and 2nd thing is my AMBITION to be a billionaire.

Elizabeth is an awesome friend. I have to apologize to her one day coz I never did listen to her problems used to be everyday but today was a problem day For me and she was there For me to cheer me up. You gotta reaad the poem and story she wrote for me. I have to be me To understand how I Felt ~~ah~~ or one of my closest friend who sees the inner soul of Heralyn. Thank's for everything Elizabeth. It help me made feel better. I couldn't have done it would out her and Jeff. INEVER GIVE UP TILL THE LAST BREATH I take. I WILL HAVE MY DREAM one day come [TRUE] because I never give up. VICTORY WILL BE MINE! A LAST!

June 13, '96

Can't wait till school is out. I hope I got in to driver's ed this summer. I can't wait to drive in which I don't know when. Never. Need money for it. I think I will have a better year this year than last year. It's been a tougher year than my freshman year. I did so many things in my Soph. Year, it's hard. I don't know about my Junior year.

Today still It's natural for me to go to the library everyday in the morning coz I arrive here at 6:35am and need to do homework or study. 3-D art class my dragon is coming along pretty good and can't wait to finish it. I get the best attention while working on this project. A guy in photo class came up to me twice talking about how great my project is. I think he's a football player, could be a senior or a junur. He looks kind of scary but tough type bouf guy. He mets my type my macho boyfriend type. I wish he told me his name. Who knows maybe I get to talk to him again and I'll talk about photo class. Algebra II had a test-getting along well with the group. I have MARK GUREERO, Varsity football player in my group and others LISA BROWN who work at Rally and my friend AMANDA BAUDER. Spanish -Surprise! I can't believe I'm getting along with 3 guys who sits around me, one is JEREMY RUNYEN, a football player my partner and, Erin, a Science Club President whos a junior and Miles who I have no idea about him. Biology- YEEPE! No more Project Sci. Met. Rushing to McLab the day before, today was oral presentation and that was it. Lunch in A to J club I wanted so bad to be an officer but didn't expect to win a club office because no one knows me very few, but I lacked showmanship of leadership. I can't wait for the party, June 27. I do better next time. Humanities was a whole 2 periods class report on CATI'S BALLET. She has an awesome talent like me in martial arts. She's lucky coz she gets to do one thing she loves most to perform her talent. WOW! She's talented. I could look into her soul that she seem to have hard times last year and interference with we she lies to her DESTINY. It's been tough for her but I'm sure she looks evry minute of Valley preforming. I wish I get to be top women martial artist in tournaments in the future. If I had the chance to be an Olympian I would love every minute of it. I could give up my college degree for Martial Arts.

All the guys I like, every single one of them, good ones, I hate. Why are they more successful than me. Veasna, got chosen in ASB and not me. Wow, I have no hope for MATT FREEMAN, small chrush since freshman year, he's the V-President of school next ∧ school year and Jacob Gregerson, Comm. Of Academics, love at first sight at Leadership Camp. Too bad I don't think ~~th~~ I would end up with a nice boyfriend next school year. Cory is still my #1 crush. Guys I like may be more succesful than me but no man in this world will interfere with AirForce Academy and big American dreams of owning a company. I won't let them. Competitive guys, butt out! I WILL HAVE A BIG FUTURE.

💣 LIFE MAY BE A LIVING HELL BUT I CAN JUMP OVER THE FIREBALLS AND NOT GET FRIED.

☺❷⓿❶❷✝❷⓿❶❼✈❽♥❾✪❿☼

6-17-96

YAP! It's just a normal day for me. Today is the last day of a regular full day of my Sophomore year. AT LAST. I hope I do great on my tests. A while ago, tonight after all I've done, I asked myself if my grades and accomplishments in my Soph. Year will help me go to AIRFORCE ACADEMY. Idon't know if it is destiny. I rather live in Colorado than here. Theres something about it on the first day I visited it. I was fascinated about this place. I feel Colorado is my destiny, maybe that's where I have my company. LET IT BE! IF AIR FORCE is destiny. Then I'll follow it the best I can but best is not good enough, Let it be, find another chain to put back and continue searching foR my dreams. Personally, I'll rather go to out of state college, a great college.

So Cory T. signed my yearbook last week. Today, he firtled with me ~~than~~ and Danielle. I can't believe he was all over her. If he likes ~~Cory better th~~ Danielle, I want to die. Wait till next year, I'll use my charm techinque level two. **HA! HA! I want to change big when I came bavk to school. AUsual, I'll be worried about my financial Junur Carrer. I don't know what to expect. Thers things, more things I did to improve than what I did my FRESHMAN YEAR. I had so many responsibilities and I did my best to stay in track COULD I ASK FOR MORE? I learn not just me but the SCHOOL.**

BACK to CORY. I just have to write this. Danielle and I talked about guys and we said to CORY "Not many guys are like you. Most guys are jerks and your sweet and nice." He replied, " I know I'm a stud, Thank you." I want to go out with him. BYE, I need some sleep.

6-19-96

AHHh!! Tomorrow is the last day of my Sophomore year. I want to have a sleep over. Today, I found out I got a D in Biology and had a C on Test final. It will show on my report card. I hope I get lucky if I get a B- in Spanish and B in ~~Biology~~ Humanities. Mrs. Coffin-Prince adores me, a teacher's pet who's not getting an A in her class. Dylan Conford ask me why I got a bad grade in this class when he ~~gave~~ handed out my test essay on the Book "THings fall apart" in which I got a C. I didn't answered him. I felt bad. I'm worried about my future, worried about my G.P.A, worried about…. My Junior year, College, Air Force Academy; if I get in, basically the future. I wonder what my Dad will say? Will he say the same thing to me as he did the day when I got my 1st semester report card. I don't care if he says, "Whre's the A's? Have you been working hard?" I'll tell him "You were the one who told me whatever my grade was as long as I gave my best you would be happy for me. There's far more than grades I received in my Soph. Year. I learned about myself, my capabilities, I have self-esteem, improve my character, learn to be prompt on the project/ jobs assign,.. About school, about people, ben responsible person and etc…I'm only a Sophomore and the **ROTC** recruiter wants to meet me because of my overall performance this year. I had a toughest times and suffered a lot. It's not easy…" I'll confront him with no tears and emotions but only facts.

Today I learned more about my best friend Kelly Rossi about her opinions and the future. We talked about ROTC and college. We are like Ying & Yang. She's smarter than me but very little leadership. I also have outstanding leadership and smart but needs work on grades. We both have good future. I'll help her, I've been supportive to her to doing activities and help. I still haven't seen her change. It's hard to know about her characteristics coz of her bashful side. I called information about ROTC, ***I felt better when the guy I called wants to see me personally and get ready to talk about the program benefits. ISNT THAT GREAT. He said, "I'm the kind of person there looking for."***

Sometimes I wished I was a kid again. A little kid who loves to play and be happy/ worry free. It's hard to think about my future at an age ~~and~~ stage and know what to ~~do abo~~ become.

☺I'll make it happen. I control my Destiny.

6-20-96

Today is the last day of school. Unfortunately for me I didn't seem too happy about it. Some people worried if I will ever maintain a good grades with at least a GPA of 3.0 in my report card. My step Dad probably won't say anything and he will say something if he cares now. AS the infamous saying goes, "Destiny is destiny: let it be." I'm not upseting my ~~de~~ life because of disappointments from the past but only to improve.

It's been a crazy night. I got home and talked to Kelly what's happening. We planned to ~~g~~ do something today but she couldn't because she has to get ready for BAND GROUP Preparations at GRADUATION. LISTEN COZ it's going to be a long story.

I felt sad but when I called Jessica and she invited me to go to Graduation. Perfect, This is going to be great. YOU KNOW WHAT? The REST OF THE STORY in which I didn't really expect tonight and unprepared for the circumstances of leaving behind the people I know for only one year will be leaving Highschool. The memories I have with them will live forever. Those memories are precious and I wouldn't trade it for anything. There will always be a place for them in my hearts.

So..... , I got dressed with platform shoes. It made me feel uncomfortable but It's ~~is~~ okay. Jessica I is a great person to be with. We always talk about different things we come up with in our minds. "People come and go." It's hard to let go, to say goodbye. Sure I hugged and congratulated them but still El Cap next year for me will look empty or not the same without them, not seing their faces with a smile when I talk to them or just to say Hi! There will be noone ever I met in this world ~~un~~like Larissa. The world would be a perfect place to live in if everyone has the personality like her<-6-21-96-> Jessica and I were looking for Seniors we know to Congratulate them. We saw Nikkie with her brother but I didn't ~~see~~ got ~~him~~ a chance to congratulate him. Goosh! A lot of people were around Larrisa. Everyone knew her, adores her. What she got I haven't got. I'm very fortunate to know her this year. For Jessica, she wished she knew Larrisa not just this year. She regret she didn't participate in track. I wished I knew Larissa better. I congratulated and hugged Larissa. She will be a great teacher. I see her future of a teacher loved and respected by her students and everyone. I can't have her personality. I'm nice but my personality characteristic is the shows the quality of a person who is ambitious, virsatile, willingly to be successful etc. I'm a unique person unlike Larissa or Jessica. Jessica cried but I didn't quiet understand who she felt. It's her ~~experience~~ feelings but I was there to listen for her and try to understand. It's hard to understand coz I didn't knew how she felt. It's hard to relate something on how one person can screw you up and how one can change you. Like Jennifer, why would she want to pissed Jessica? Why does she have to act mean to Jessica? Jennifer used people like a con artist. I just thought of something. My Soph. Year, I wanted to be popular coz fitting in was #1 hard thing for me. I didn't know a lot of people my freshman year. In fact only 8 people I knew well. It took me one day to figure my mirror of reflection of me in my Junior Year. I thank the Lord for this, for helping me realizing tonight of what I might be if I become too greedy to be popular. Sure, I made lots of friends at El Cap this year. Learned about how popularity works and how why my conclusion of the end of my Soph. Year I would rather be who I ~~am~~ want to be, just me, just want to feel great about me. Now I don't want to follow the rules to popularity coz I would lose myself who I was and what I'll become. The rules like start wearing popular trendy clothes, I did half and half my baggy original old me look, to know different kinds of people by hangin out with groups of people and some who I still hold on to are the ones I call my friends. There's a 2nd level to popularity oR I think the last used people. Use~~d~~ people who look good for image by just be friends with them, go out with a guy for image by just be friends with them, go out with a guy for image or just be fake to people if you think youre to good for them just so they would think youre cool but truly think you're a BITCH. This is the tricky situation why they really become popular coz people talk about her of how much her ego is the size of Jack's beanstalk and her BIYACH PERSONALITY. Now I know why really popularity isn't what I want to make me succeed to be a school officer, to please everyone etc. Larissa is popular and when people talk about her, they think she's smart, nice, sweet etc. All good comments, overall just who she is: *identity*.

I would never be like Jennifer. I'll rather be me and hope everyone will say good stuff about me. Some will say something bad because maybe their envy of me or just plain like Jennifer. I hope Jessica will not worry about being mean to her but think how dumb Jenifer is and should complement her acting personality of being a fake and snob person. Jessica, don't let anyone make you feel bad for whatever reason. Like me, some people, especially guys give me bad reputation coz I know martial arts. I always keep in mind I have an awesome talent and I think their ego is the size of their brain and joke around to ask for a fight with me because their jealous and I'm a girl and they think they can over power me. No way José! Another example like Sara Nephew, some people hate her part personality coz of how higly her mind thinks greatly and even though she is smart they think she's weird coz of her optimistic opinions from her point of view. Like Jessica, she's worried why everyone comments; she's always happy. She doesn't think of it as a compliment. Maybe because she wanted people to say something about her. I think coz she sees herself not happy, she only wants people to respect her. She's nice and not everyone take her seriously. I hope she doesn't feel to be opposite of herself. Like me, my 9th grade, as a shy person only thing my classmates know about me was my high intelligence of getting A's. That's the only ~~o~~ attention I gotten but I turn opposite and not wanting to get A's. I wished my classmates knew about me more that just my intelligence and talent. It was hard to show them because you can't please people and expect them to like you.

Yesterday will always be rendered as a turning point (I learned values) of my life. I greatly helped me reflect about me and others. The 1996 Graduation was memorable for me as it was to more valued to the Graduates. I have 2 more years then it will be my spotlight. A lot of unexpected things will happen. God was always there for me and helped me tonight not to go to the limit of greediness. I thank him for everything.

To wrap up my story. I told Larissa I liked herr brother. She said, "You too!" I told her to tell him in the near future. I won't have a shot with him anyway nor with Dan Huck. Too bad Dad is leaving but I'm not worried. I can't believe I just shoke his hands and I was about to hug him and I split. At his family party we got invited in which I got to ~~his~~ know his family circle. There was a time I glance at him and looked deeply into his soul, I felt great success for him and sense his not my guy or I'm just afraid if I met a guy like him or him would just swift my hopes towards life. At AMBER TROMBLY's house was a fun party. Like mostly other party I was shy and don't know well to talk around people. Amber's house is awesome. I loved it! Jacob wasn't there which was an upset for Jessica. Jessica is still crazy about him. I hope both get to be couple before they graduate. Next year's graduation will be emotional for me since most of my friends will be Seniors. I had lots of fun too bad we had to leave at 2:00 A.M. I was tried and only write ~~not X~~ 3 pages from my Diary.

As for me, I never put so much thought tonight writing this journal but It's worth it. My dreams are the reason/ purpose me here.

6-26-96 (Weds.)

My Summer? Not much is happening. I'm taking Dr. Ed for Summer School with exemption it only on Tues, Weds, Thurs. morning/2hrs. a day. Tonight, I will be talking about my goals/dreams as if this is the turning point in my life. I've been thinking about College. My Parents can't afford $60,000 for 4 years college fees. It's wise for one to get scholarship ROTC because it will help my future greatfully with blessings. **4 years of ROTC to go to the best university in the country and have 4 years job to travel around the world. What more could I ask for?** What about the ULTIMATE GOAL OF MINE TO GO TO AIR FORCE ACADEMY. If I get accepted it will be my golden ticket to Paradise but I have to go through hell. It won't be easy. My Dad told me about AIR FORCE ACADEMY and I'm glad he told me about it and about the opportunities in life for me. He helped me a lot. He didn't make me want to plan to go to AIR FORCE but It was my choice. It would be one of the greatest achievement of my life. I feel it's my Destiny to go there. Believe it or not! When I got the opportunity to travel across U.S. from OHIO to California, Colorado was breathtaking. I feel in love with the place I got to see Denver & Colorado Springs(city). It was spectacular. This was the best part I enjoy about my trip and Colorado was the only state I visited I remembered vividly. DESTINY AWAITS.

Whenever I feel low coz I did accomplish my goals at school. LET IT BE BUT I TRIED and I WILL TRY TILL I WIN, AND IF I DON'T I'M STILL A WINNER. Maybe making ASB next year wasn't meant to be or I was too good for them. I ~~ka~~ know well enough I was qualified to be in ASB. I will do my very best to prove them next year with all my night. THAT HAS TO BE DESTINY COZ I BELIEVE IN ME. Maybe to be in Journalism afterall is DESTINY. Don't ask me why I Think of that. I hate to write, especially essay or topic. I'm not interested. Maybe God wanted me be in Journalism.to put use of my ability and my weakness will no longer be ~~but~~ and it will improve. But I have great ideas and will be useful. Plus, research about the school will help me use my expertise and know more about the school and express it in writing.

AIR FORCE MOTTO on the catalog says "AIM HIGH" I always aim high. Im a very ambitious person always have been always will be. My Dad says "Why settle for satisfactory when you know you can achieve with all you might the glory of success." I'm that type of person who always aim high. I ran for Treasurer (ASB) coz that was highly classified of what I think I will do best and no commisioner of something, no low ranks. In fact, I think I want to run for V.President. I could, that's another story. It's too ironic for the 3rd time and lose. But hey that's life.

I WILL ALWAYS FOLLOW MY DREAMS AND NEVER STOP DREAMING. I WON'T STOP RUNNING TILL I GET WHAT I WANT IN LIFE.

(Thurs.) 6-27-96 10 P.M.

I can't believe I've gotten more than halfway writing all about my life (less than a year). All the sleepless hour writing my journal. Today I learned important lessons that I may sometimes don't think reflecting upon me and just let it slip by. Whenever I'm sad, I always let it slip by.

I was excited about thius A2J party. 6 hrs. at The Honeycutt's house and It's over. I had lots of fun. I always remember after every party big or small I feel the emptyness of being wanted because I feel like my mouth is sealed. I want to speak up but I don't know how exactly I wish I'm like Jessica Stamper who is a wacko and show emotions and it made like caring people like her.(Andy F. & Larissa G.) or Jessica Stokes who is so funny and have always something to say about topics. Or be like Andy or Larissa who has a lot of wonderful traits. I could be like them in my own way to prove people, so people could admire me and be inspirations to others. IWANT TO KNOW HOW TO TALK TO PEOPLE aproachably and with Friendliness to show my characterer. I WISH TO SAY TO EVERYONE: **"LOOK I don't talk much but TRULY I'M A GREAT PERSON INSIDE."** I don't know how exactly to show it to people. Volleyball was fun. A lesson of this was learning something I don't want coz of embarrasment and not good playing and it took me this party to like volleyball. I got bruises. ANDY FELDSCHER always slip an JINX when she made the volleyball net ball with her. Like ~~volleyball~~ basketball, I like the sport and I think having fun and just try it will make me more confident of the sports.

I especially like the part when the guy talked about his experiences. How he's been working to people who wants/ looking for hope in their lives. Brent is an incredible guy with a big heart and he's into his work to help people (to make an example). He found I mean he heard God/ God lead him to what he is now and he ~~do kn~~ heard ~~feel~~ God's voice. WoW! HE's happy with his life and glad of who he is. He help kids who is in gang, the kids were hungry for Christ. It's hard to explain. Taggers or kids who do graffiti some he helped and some are still out there. His point about how gangs are potrayed as who we see them but he sees gang ers differently that only people would not understand. It's like you have to look into the person's soul to understand an individual of their own uniqueness. It's even hard for me to look into my soul than others because of my reasonable ~~be~~ doubt of me, not sure or not content etc. I can look at myself in the mirror and say to myself I look good, I feel good unlike before I didn't like the reflection on the mirror I say. I have confidence and self-esteem & improve better but still doubt/ looking for something and can't find it. I'm not stopping till I find it whatever it is I'm looking for. I think everyone goes through this stage in this life. To succeed of wanting something and need to find it to complete the puzzle. ANNA ACOSTA found it found the puzzle tonight, heard God's voice. God's said "~~You~~ Anna, you've been inspiration to all and you can make a difference to all. To Touch other people's lives." "God? When is the day I hear your voice? What's my Destiny? How will I touch other people's lives? How will I help the society? The world? You probably know more about me more that I know about myself.

"GOD, I'M SORRY. My life at age of 16th is been full too many disappoint on disappointment I remember but very little accomplishment I know I achieve of my goals. Some yet to want the goals/dreams I haven't achieve and I'm talking about bigger goals ahead for me in the future. I know myself well about my dreams in life and it has become my biggest fear in life if I don't succeed. I'm so much WRAP up into success that I want it so much my life wouldn't be a complete puzzle without it. I can't believe I said that my dreams are the missing puzzle. THANK YOU GOD BUT that's the problem. I'm a dreamer with big dreams. That's why Im afraid coz I sometimes think I'm not confident enough or I won't get accepted in the Air Force Academy or ROTC or my biggest dream to have my own company. Sometimes I lack the strength and determination because I look into my soul too harsh. I have that characteristic in me because those characteristic made me succeed. Tonight you made me help to look into my soul and touched my life.

You've always been there for me when I needed strength and courage. I've help me through life when I feel low. But the past years I've been running away from you like how I was running away from myself over the years. Running away of what I've become from my fears, afraid people ~~wh~~
Would comment or me negatively (true or not) sarcasm and other things. You know how it feels to feel low and not knowing how to talk to people. Since I moved here from Phlippines and not knowing my expectations in U.S.A. Remember, for the first years living here and feeling sad and lonely, wishing new kids would come and talk to you and invite you to their group, hard to fit in and feeling everyday at school I'm invisible. Sometimes people only think I'm smart, the straight A student HUH ! Today I'm not anymore. The only main reason why I regreted my studies and not getting good grades my Sophomore year. It seems I turn opposite of one of my biggest assest so people don't say "You always get good grades. Can you help me with this problem?" I wished they really knew me more than that not my brains. I don't know how my parents will react with my grades and I'm very unprepared on what to say. I'm afraid my bad grades will affect my future. I have many things I worry about everyday of my life.

Please I ask- help me succeed. Lead me to the LIGHT OF DESTINY OF MINE. GUIDE ME. I'M CONFUSE. SO MANY QUESTIONS AND FOUND LITTLE ANSWERS. HELP ME ENLIGHTEN TO BE ABLE TO EXPRESS MYSELF AND SO PEOPLE WILL SEE ME. THANK YOU FOR EVERYTHING LEADING ME TO THE ROAD OF DESTINY.

June 29, '96 Saturday 12:15 P.M.

My eyes isn't very tired, still widely awake. "Seize the day." Avery famous quote by a guy I don't know but I remembered it said from one of the valedictorian address speech. I did. Woke up late this morning and was 30 mins. Late for Key Club meeting. It was so hot today. I had to walk to the library and back home. I came back 3:15 P.M. After the funny laughs and future Key Club planning meeting, the fun just started. **AS IF!**

Well, I ate my Taco Bell lunch and 4 of Key clubbers strolled around the park picking up trash for 35 minutes. I was about ready to give up but I volunteered at the library for one hour stacking up children's book. Then I searched for poems to Xerox copy for AP English Summer assignment. A last! I walked to home and stop at Dairy Queen to get a soda for quince thirst. THE HARDEST PART TO DEAL WITH was when my Dad looked through my report card. I wasn't there when he look at it and I didn't ask or come to him about my grades. I FACED MY FEAR. Hoping He would just accept my grades and I know he will always be proud of me no matter ~~how~~ what grades I get as long as I did my best. I'm not upset of my grades even though I could have done better but It was my best. I went scan through the Air Force Catalog to make myself happy. IF AIR FORCE WONT ACCEPT ME, It's ThEIR LOST. EVERY STEP OR STUFF I DO IN MY HIGHSCHOOL CAREEER WILL HELP ME GET THERE. I'VE DONE SO MANY THINGS, JUST ALL FOR THE DREAM OF GOING TO THE ACADEMY. I WILL ALWAYS THINK or AIM HIGH TO RISE. I'm SO Dedicated, if I put all my effort into what I want, motivated, a leader, etc. WHY WOULDN'T THEY WANT A PERSON WHO GOT THE CHARACTER OF A WINNER.

TODAY I GOT TO TALK TO 2 OF my most favorite cousins in the world. It's been 4 years past. Like what I said before, Tani & Lali were my puzzles pieces of my past. Remembering those childhood fun memories. They were like my sister considering I was the only child. Even though as a young kid whose hope was gold but low class, still they made me feel I belong to a family. Sometimes when I think of them I wished I could see them and be that little kid again but I doesn't work that way. Yeah! I'll come back as a mature adult and seeing them so differently. True, one is nicer that the other but people mature and change. Lali is my favorite one because she always made me feel equal all the time unlike Tani. I treat them equal coz its just me. I just hope they won't be fake to me. I felt the warmth cheering personality first time I talked to Lali. We were always getting a long. She was my buddy. Tani I don't know. I wonder how much they change. I wonder how they think of me, now I'm in U.S.

My Mom said my biological Dad stills looks for gold. Same old guy. Lucky me, I have his ambition, only I wont be like him wishing for gold but I will only look hard for my gold. My Mom said " WILL SEE." I'm not gonna be "BOT BOT" like him. I'M LIVING HERE. THE LAND OF OPPURTUNITY. I CAN DREAM ALL I WANT.

July 1 11:01 P.M.

What's the difference between a dreamer throughout his/her life and a dreamer achieved a dream without knowing this is how his/her life will ~~thu~~ turn out to be. I was reading through different type of people who aRe rich in "FORTUNE" magazine. All of these people have same thing; *software*. Their business made big bucks because of *software*. I went to the new Wal-Mart at Lakeside today with my parents. As I was looking around I saw a paperback book at the book department. It was all about COLLEN POWELL's life, who is today a military chief general. As I was scheming through the pages I looked if he went to ROTC or Academy. I found he went to ROTC at CC New York University/College. I thought at that moment he, "he must be an outstanding student." But actually in fine print ~~at a yo~~ in high school he barely got a C grade. There must be something about him why he got the ROTC scholarship. He's a great leader. He led an army to Gulf War and the 1st African American to be military general chief leader. WHAT MY POINT IS, DID THEY EVER DREAM ABOUT HOW THEY WANT THEIR LIFE TO BE. DID THOSE PEOPLE EVER SET GOALS TO BE RICH WHEN THEY WERE KIDS. DID POWELL ~~KNEW~~ DREAM AS A KID TO BE GENERAL. I'M SURE NO MATTER HOW TOUGH AS SOME POINT IN THEIR LIFE, DID THEY EVER SET GOALS 20 YEARS AGO THAT THIS IS HOW THEIR LIFE WILL BE, which is today. Maybe some people think I'm crazy because I tell them I dream to become a billionaire and have my own successful big company business one day. Becoming rich was my childhood dream, always like my Dad except I'm not like him. I'm going after it. It's not gonna be a *software* kind but something with better technology. What about me…what if I wanted HONOR than POWER? HONOR-serving this country or POWER-I don't ~~like~~ think money is power. I don't know. But I will aid thousands of people for jobs if ~~people~~ people have to work. Sometimes I fear technology will end this world. How people will lose their jobs and they won't be able to feed their family. Maybe my mission is to make technology a good way but I don't have those answers yet. I'm a woman and I want to make example to women out their that business world is not ruled by man all the time but men will come to me under my command. They will for me. I think I will make a great example as one of future leaders as a woman in future world. NOW THAT POWER. Power in business industry.

I always set goals, achieve it or not and not achieving it will only want me to improve and never give up till I get it. I gota job at McDonalds with my Dad's help the flyer. I can't wait. I LOVE MONEY. MONEY AND ME ARE CHEMISTRY.

(Thurs) July 4th-Independence Day

Yesterday was Wednesday-like any ordinary day I had certain task to do. I spend all my afternoon sittin at McDonald's restaurant waiting For the store maneger to talk to us about the orientation to all 3 of us got hired. Fortunately there was one girl out of the 3 of us. Fortunate, It's me. During the waiting of two hours I got to know the 2 other people who got hired. They are working for their car insurance. One perspective of me knowing what will happen if I won't go to ~~g~~ college is working at a minimum wage like McDonald's. One of ~~th them~~ the 2 is 19 years old who graduated El Cap ~~fo~~ 1995. I qualities I first notice about him are his cuteness and social personality showed. Between the 2 hours of waiting a homeless guy showed up and went up to talk~~in~~ to us ~~but~~ and knew Mike(19 year old guy). He Started talking to him. The homeless guy seem dirty but not so dirty and his breath sinks from drinking. The most important thing I will never forget is when he said "Mike are you gonna make maneger in 3 months?" I said, "I… What do you mean? How will he become a maneger , what's the secret?" " It's no secret. 1st of all he smiles and you don't….(rest of the words It was all a blurr to me but I think he said something about his personality)" Then he came back to us later, his last sentence "Are you ready to work maneger, (pointed to the other guy) crew member, (then his eyes went to me) dish washer cleaner." IF HE ONLY KNEW ME WELL BUT WHY SHOULD I LISTEN TO THE PERSON WHO CAUSED THE EL MONTE BRUSHFIRE (which I found out from Mike) AND TO A DRUNK PERSON AND I DIDN'T SEE ANY QUALITIES OF HIM THAT MADE HIS LIFE A LOT BETTER. "DON'T JUDGE A PERSON BY THEIR APPEREANCE." I DIDN'T JUDGE HIM BY HIS OUTSIDE APPEARANCE BUT SHOWED RESPECT TO HIM. HE'S DIRECT PERSON OFF THE TOP HES THE KIND OF PERSON WHO WILL TELL YOU WHAT HE THINKS. I remembered he said, "Shy people don't say anything because they think their learning by listening to the people who talk who ~~doe~~ has something Ho Say about the topic" Phy way to WHOEVER TREADS THIS ASIDE FROM ME AND ASKS WHY I WROTE SOMETHING ABOUT THE GUY WHO APPEALS TO SOCIETY LOW. I DON'T THINK OF HIM LOW. MY POINT WHY IS THIS 3 PAGES OF MY DIARY IN THE FUTURE WILL REMIND ME OF HOW THOSE DAYS OF MY LIFE WHEN PEOPLE THINK OF ME I'M NO GOOD: NO YOURE NOT DOING A GOOD JOB ~~LIKE~~ AS A PRESIDENT, THOSE TIMES WHEN I FEEL LOW COZ PEOPLE JUDGE ME ~~MY~~ -THOSE PEOPLE ESPECIALLY DON'T KNOW ME WHICH IS TRAGIC. THOSE TIMES WHEN I WANTED TO ACCOMPLISH SOMETHING BUT FAILED. NO I DIDN'T FALIED I TRIED WITH ALL MY MIGHT AND EVERYTHING IN MY WILL BUT I'M NO LOSER COZ I DIDN'T QUIT.

NOBODY TELLS ME WHAT I CAN'T AND CANNOT DO. I MEAN NOBODY. I'VE GOT A LONG WAY TO GO: TO BE… A BETTER LEADER, BETTER PERSON ETC. THE WORLD IS OUT THERE FOR ME TO SEE, AWAITS MY LIFE MY FUTURE. THE AMERICAN DREAM!

TODAY WAS A VERY SPECIAL DAY. TODAY THE U.S. celebrated America.. Whenever ~~the~~ I hear someone singing the song of the national anthem I felt what it is like to be an American.. To be proud, lucky to be here in U.S., point of my life awaits me to seRve ~~my f~~ the U.S., this country, I can't wait to be an American citizen to call this my country. I WILL BE PROUD TO SERVE AND HONORED TO SERVE U.S.A. ~~WH~~ PROUD TO SERVE THIS COUNTRY WHO AIDS MY COUNTRY AND SERVE WITH PRIDE.

TODAY MY PARENTS AND I ATE AT Chinese Village instead of Black Angus but didn't go to see fireworks in which I'm glad coz ROBIN SEIBER called me that JENIFER BURBANK is leaving and going up L.A. Why of all people who I just got to know ~~this~~ in 10th grade have to leave. She is nice, caring and funny. I miss those times when I see her on the hallway saying " HI!" and I just got to know her. Another thing I like about her loving and caring personality to ~~people~~ others, to her friends & to God. We need people like her in A to J and that's why she's one of the leader in A to J in which the respondsibity I'm ~~was~~ willing to accept in my junior year if I got choosen. Of course, not noone knows anything what I contributed to the club but Jenifer was there cooperating to help the club. I LEARN THAT FROM HER. Remember the saying "PEOPLE COME AND GO." I WISH GOOD PEOPLE COME AND NEVER GO AWAY. I WAS READY TO ACCEPT THE SENIORS WHO'S GONE BUT JENNIFER I'M NOT READY AND CAN'T ACCEPT KNOWING Jennifer will never be there when you needed support, good laughs and he uplifting personality. MOST OF ALL I CAN'T BELIEVE IT WAS JUST A ONE YEAR WARRANTY FRIENDSHIP. FRIENDSHIP IS SO PRICELESS. IT'S A LOT HARDER FOR HER LEAVING, LEAVING EVERYTHING BEHIND. I'VE BEEN THERE ONCE. IVE BEEN HERE LONG AND BEING ACCEPTED BY OTHERS MADE ME STOP FEELING OF MY OLD TIMES.

I got this fortune cookie which met a lot to me because over most of my life I've been comparing myself to others and think of myself to others and think of myself feeling low and no self-esteem. I REMEMBERED WHEN I WAS A FRESHMAN SAYING TO JUNI UNDEN " I WISH I'M SOMEBODY…." SHE REPLIED "YOU ARE SOMEBODY, YOURE HERALYN TOLING." IT'S hard to find a friend who listens to you and understand how you feel. I'VE BEEN LEARNING ABOUT OTHERS AND ESPECIALLY ME. IT HAS HELPED ME TO GROW AND UNDERSTAND ABOUT Part the meaning of life. A person's individuality, improvements of myself and learning to accept the world and myself and others.

JULY 15, 1996 (Mon 8:45 P.M.)

TODAY I GOT A CHANCE TO TALK TO ONE OF THE **ROTC** Recruiting officer, Lt. Gilbert. We talked about AIR FORCE ROTC. Did I mention it took my Dad and me 1 ½ hrs. to get to ROTC building. I feel great knowing I want to have a great future and think ahead of life. There was one girl got to scholarship this year's graduating class of EL CAP (MONICA HESS) There wasn't one day I didn't think about me at Air Force Academy 2 yrs. from now. What fears me MOST: IS IF I WON'T GET ACCEPTED TO AIR FORCE ACADEMY; my react[ion] would be my faults at Soph. Year basicilly failing of grades at that time. If I won't make it to the Academy. I will apply again under ROTC category which is harder: only top 20 gets in by the time I'm in college. I can't just give up coz I didn't get accepted… like always, Heralyn never gives up…. I gotta try again. My Dad is a GREAT INSPIRATION TO ME. I VERY LUCKY than just to have a Dad. I HAVE A DAD who taught me how his life experience for the last 60+ years of all his life. My Dad was a orphan and was born & grew up at Oklahoma. He didn't have parents like I have now. I'm happy to have a Dad now. Best gift I got when I was 12. He told me served in the army for 7 yrs. & served to Korean War. He told me about his experienced in the war but told me I myself or others unless a soldier who served in the war would not understand what he went through during the War. I think he's right. He told me how he had to make 5 yrs. Sacrifice of only 4 hrs. sleepy at night & working 2 jobs to get ~~the job~~ his college degree(mechanical engineer) It wasn't easy because in oRder for me to suceed: he never worked so hard in his life. For the next 6 yrs. Of my life: I will work so hard and pay the ultimate sacrifice to get my ultimate goals in life. Wish me all the luck in the world.

WORDS DON'T MEAN ANYTHING BUT ACTION MEANS THE WILL TO PROVE NOT JUST WORDS BUT THE WILL TO DO WHAT IT TAKES TO GET THERE. MY MOM SAID NO ONE CAN TAKE AWAY YOUR KNOWLEDGE or TALENTS: IT'S YOURS FOREVER TO GUIDE *YOU IN LIFE.*

July 19, 1996

Tonight is a very special night the world celebrates its 100 years of Summer Olimpic. The dreams of thousands of athletes come all together in Atlanta to take a part in their lives of living a dream. "Billy" Payne, one of the people who worked to make this Olymipic to remember, said in his last few words, "We are here to have a peaceful Olympics and yet it will ~~be a~~ unite to all of us for hope for peace- to a peaceful world." Sports is friendship, education and teaches us the value of a dream. Edward Alan Poe once said, "To dare dreams alive is what few mortals dream." A civil rights leader, Martin Luther King was born in Atlanta. Martin Luther King is a respected leader who live and hope for a dream a dream that's stand alive for all of us. Theres a lot of pride in each 197 nations. Each athlete with honor and pride ~~to be~~ to reach is ultimate dream. I wonder what it feels like to be one of the athlete just to live and make the dream come true. Muhamad Ali did it.

July 23

Today I started my very first ever job at McDonalds. It's a lot harder I thought it was going to be but I expected that. It was a very heartwarming as I watched T.V. in my bedroom, watching the women's gymnastics. The U.S.A won the gold. It was inspiring to see KERI STRUGG of her will to give it her best despite of her pain on her left ankle. This is an example to be proud to be human. The will to succeed. I wonder how I would feel if I participate in the Olympics.

Every person in this world has the power like every others have done has the power to succeed. A power to make their life a success by their own will from small to big dreams to make it happen. Success is the way you want to live it. A fellow's will and courage to succeed and the ironic truimph that echoes in their dreams will someday come true if the person's will is strong enough to make it happen. It not an easy task. Every person leads a different life and have they ask themselves this: Have I accomplished my ultimate dream in life? Have I done the ultimate sacrifice to hope I will get my goal come true? Has my life's work worthy of success & all that stands about me?

I asked myself and think as a young youth of 16 and so many dreams in life, sometimes I think it's impossible but my character is strong, the character that I always had regretting it for the past years because it was easy to regret when I feel so low about myself and I needed to be strong to regain the power of will. **Anything is possible, it's all in the heart, mind, spirited soul & character of believing in yourself.**

IF ONLY EVERYONE WHO IS YOUNG Like me realize the importance of a goal in life then the young will mature to flowers of the world. It's sad to look at some of my friends, to wish maybe it's to young to think about the future just have a goal & the will to succeed. For those who have tried & failed, I hope they will never give up and follow their dreams and learned from the past to make them stronger & better for a better world. When I feel sad, lonely, depressed or low I say chin up my child like my Mom said it to me and I will climb the highest ladder and if I fail I will climb back again.

July 28, 1996 (8:42 PM)

Im watching a taekwondo match on T.V. Sometimes I don't feel like watching A movie or game of something to do with martial Arts. WHY? When I feel how much impact of who I am, a part of me, a part of my goals ever since a young kid, a goal still I'm looking for answers for the last 16 years, perhaps the oldest goals of mine and wanting answers. The answers of hope and faith that someday I become a black belt & compete to be a competetor and world class competitor. What I'm I talking about anyway. As a little kid, it was fun at my Uncle's backyard practicing karate even though I wasn't a full participant coz my Mom thinks its only for boys and I'm too young and a little girl is no place for a guys sport. I don't think how my parents or my Mom when I was a young little kid or even today understand how much martial arts and impact in my life mean so much to me. How much? = if I picked my life in another parallel dimension earth I would pick it to become the worlds best in competitive world sport of taekwondo or karate or kickboxing and I hope I'm a female and still have my personality and character. Even now I wished I have the full support and the training I get, but nope, nada, nothing. I would give up just about my dreams to be in the military career and successful job making big bucks & owning a company and making the american dream. **OKAY! SO AM I THAT SERIOUS. Surely it won't make me a millionaire, maybe if land a job as an action star, and have the right looks and know how to act then it's a possibility. Then AGAIN LIKE ANY OTHER LIFE, it won't be easy. Hey, I could retire and open a ~~mart~~ Taekwondo studio , train kids and be a coach. Someday, I hope to be in the Olympics. HA! HA! HA! I**t's like saying I said before, I want to be a billionaire. It's like a joke, dreaming big is a joke but you'll never know. MY LIFE TIME DEFINION OF MY GOALS IS THE MIRROR OF MY FUTURE. IF I SUCEED, I WILL BECOME A PERSON OF WHAT I BECOME. I WANT TO LIVE NOT JUST SERVING THIS COUNTRY & BECOME A SUCESSFUL COMPUTER ~~ANALYST~~ PROGAMMER WORKING IN A BIG COMPANY. NO! I WANT SOMETHING MORE, I CAN DO MORE, DO BETTER, I CAN BE MY OWN BOSS MY OWN BUSINESS EMPIRE, MY OWN BUCIM HAM CASTLE, AND NOT JUST SUCCESS BUT TO AID OTHERS. THE MOST SPECIAL THING ABOUT ME IS I CAN DO MORE THAN WHAT I CAN DO:I WANT TO SHARE MY TALENTS TO PEOPLE, HELP THE KIDS OF THE FUTURE GENERATION AROUND THE WORLD. THAT'S EVEN GREATER.

JULY 29, 1996

My consience tells me I should open my eyes & not go to sleep just to write something dramatic about my life at 11:15 P.M. Yap as if . . . , someone will dig up my diaries and make a movie out of it or write a book. Like who would want to know about what I did in my life. Back to business here . . . , okay I had trouble sleeping tonight so I pretented I would be in this gymnasuim 10 years from now to be one of the competitors fighting for National Championship in taekwondo I pictured in my mind having a one on one match determines who will win first place. So I thought it would be ironic if my opponent knows me off and I get up feeling sore and possibly bleeding in my nose or mouth. I get up and still wanting to continue, took a deep breath 3x, closed my eyes for 3 seconds and open it and looked my opponent with fired eyes & determined person by just looking at my eyes. I kept thinking in my mind I came this far, win or lose, I'll give it all my best. Then I pictured myself in a hospital and injured minorly and this guy came in my room and talked to me he recruites for taekwondo USA Olympics and he wanted me. I didn't pictured myself winning 1st place at that National tournament because I want it to be special someday if it ever happens. It didn't matter coz I gave it all 1st, 2nd, 3rd , 4th or last. Then I cried not in my dreams but in reality on my bed because I said to the guy, " I've been wating for a guy like you to make me feel and wanted to be the person that I am now and it took me 27 years. Sometimes I wished my life was like the Karate Kid movie who found a great friend and made him more of what he had & made him a champion. I guess it will never happen to me because ~~my life~~ that movie is fictional and it doesn't happen to normal people. Ive been waiting and waited like when I was 16; I tought I'll find and old sensei and aid me to quench For my thirst to fill my talent and sharper it better and better and then I can call myself a black belt & a champion."

I'm so emotional , I once cried to my parents to go back to Karate and begged them. They just don't understand what I can do with the talent I have. Martial Art mean a lot to me in the world for more than all the millions of money. Since I all ready envented my own FungFu not knowing how I got it, I might as well teach myself karate & taekwondo
To get ahead than just not continue because that someone is not here yet, not getting me there, I need that teacher sensei to prepare me for one of the battles in my life but

for now I can stand own my own. As I'm writing this diary, I looked in their eyes and I could looked thrugh their souls and feel I'm like them at that tournament in my dream perhaps I'm already one and been at the 2 tournaments I participated.

Aug 1, 1996 (4P.M.)-(10:00)

No one understands me and I think I don't even understand myself. Perhaps I'm only human, making mistakes as my life goes on. Sometimes it will take a person if he/ she is willing knows it will take 3 or more than one making same mistakes not unless he/she realized what he/she has done and from realizing and reflecting only from the past mistakes he/she has made and from that he'll/she'll learn more about themselves and others too. I've made mistakes in life because I went and turn the wrong direction *unsafe* on the road. So What! I keep changing lanes which is good sometimes and sometimes bad depending the reason why I want to change lanes. Last year I made the wrong change of lane because I felt low of myself, I wanted more than just getting outstanding grades, I wanted straight A's, I wanted people to know I'm not shy and it annoys me I'm so shy & quiet and and if I don't consider myself shy and change to be someone who will be notice by making more friends, buy new clothes, mostly socialize more, exceedingly better than average I pushed myself too far to popularity only because I felt unsatisfied of myself in which it affected my grade but changed my perspective of desire to want to achieve in setting goals. I learned the biggest ingredient I have to know before the desire to achieve my goals… That is respect myself, accept myself, feel confident about myself, have high-self-esteem, feel great, don't compare myself to others thinking they are better because of the qualities inside and outside especially and keeping in mind to always do my best & the best is as far to think is the absolute perFectionism coz no one perfect. MY PARENT ARE WRONG, IT WASN'T JUST TO BE POPULAR.

MISUNDERSTANDING, mishalf with Dad, it happens once every 2 months minimum,. I don't hate him coz he's helped me a lot realizing to how to shape my goals in accomplishing it. I don't have to feel sorry for myself. I'm sure deep down my Dad still cares. My Mom told me tonight while ironing **that Sto. Niño had a tear on his eyes & that it looked like a warning sign coz, Mom said something in the house will happen**

every time She told me also "just to maintain high grades & go to college & get a job and not have to do what my Dad said of a carreer in the Air Force." My Mom ~~didn't like~~ seem upset to him. I'm glad my Dad said about career in military air force because it will help me to succeed more chances than others who just graduated without experience or lack of experience. I don't want to work 2 jobs to pay for college when I can get $60,000 scholarships. I want to get ahead & air force will help me that. Also, I plan to continue to have a carreer in taekwondo and by luck and Faith I might win national title and maybe the Olympics if possible. OF COURSE, ITS POSSIBLE I HAVE THIS FEELING OF DESIRE TO PARTICIPATE & JUST Participating will make me feel I accomplished a lot & made my dream come true & a happy kid with smile I will keep in mind achieving it for so long. I plan to invest in stocks at age 16 and continue for so many years. I plan to work for a computer company business coorporation. Quest to FIND ~~GREAT~~ THE ULTIMATE DREAM OF THE BEGINNING IS TO HATE MY OWN COMPANY BUSINESS. OF ALL THE RICHES IN THE WORLD I WILL ACCOMPLISH, I WANT TO HELP MANKIND IN WHATEVER I CAN I HAVE GREAT IDEAS. THE POWER OF THE MIND. I WANT TO BE POSITIVE ROLE MODEL TO KIDS WHO WERE ONCE LIKE ME COULD LEARN A LOT IN MARTIAL ARTS, YOUNG ATHLETES OF THE FUTURE AND THIS WOULD MEAN A LOT TO ME. A SPECIAL THING ACCOMPLISHMENT HELPING KIDS OF THE WORLD TO ACCOMPLISH THEIR GOALS IN LIFE. I HOPE TO HELP MY COUNTRY IN WHATEVER I CAN. I WANT TO BE REMEMBERED… AS A PERSON ON A MISSION TO LIVE AN EXTRAORDINARY LIFE.

Aug 4th, 1996 (9:41PM)

Okay! I'll tell you a secret. Finally! I'm always serous about writing my diary, it's always focused deeply emotionally about me. I went to LeAnna's Sweet 16 B-Day party and spend the night with my friends Kelly Rossi & my old classmate (8th grade) Linly. This is not my party. I had milk and guys were dumb and hopeless. I was a tag-along in the group of the party coz I didn't know only 4 out of 15. I never meet anyone like LeAnna we has a phone bill of $450.00+ in one month. Last night, she talked on the phone for at least 5 hours. I woke up and looked at her ~~seeing~~ and shoked by amazement she feel asleep with a phone right next to her ear holding it. Then laughed and went asleep again. I got home knowing my parent are at Barona and no keys with me. I broke into the screen window of my parent's bedroom and got in. I didn't want to spend 5 hours sitting on the porch starving & already have a stomachache. I DONT FEEL GUILTY.

I watched on T.V, about the top few Olympian Athletes. It was very touching knowing how they accomplished their dreams and what they had to do to get there.

Today I thought about simple and complex things in my life and this earth. I watched about interviews about the chief officers general in pentagon. It gave me more idea about the military forces. The Army Air Force chief of staff told his story on how he got in the army. Get this: He got called out by their town district attorney coz of his Halloween prank he took part in. But the district attorney had hope for him & he told him he could sign up for the Academy since there hasn't been one for a long time. After he graduated 33 years later he's a chief of staff. WOW! After I threw the garbage and I saw this little boy cryin for his Mom, yelling Mom and for a while no one was there and I think he hurt his leg. As walking towards him, he looked at me and I smiled & thought "I wonder if he's a bad or good boy. I bet his Dad is in the Navy or something. If he grows up to serve his country & he could be the next one." It's funny how you look at little kids playing, some are worst than others and hope they'll become someone they are proud to be & even greater. No one really knows right? Walking and just telling myself I'm young, great & feelin good person. Enjoying simple things in life like the flowers, trees, surroundings & material possessions etc. A person who is rich can't say that's just glory in their life. I would say the glory in every accomplishment is how it happen, history of life & what's behind it all purpose.

Muhammad Ali had dreams he will become heavyweight champoin of the world & become the greatest boxer ever lived. Imagine he meant it and age like me. Remember I asked: What's the difference between some one who has goals & dreams he/ she will chase after & having the desire to want to make it happen and someone who never expected it will ever come true and uncertain not planning it could happen coz you didn't think of it.

I'm like Muhammad Ali when he's young like me who plans to do great things in their lives; to conquer the world.

I learned Wilma Radloph won 3 Olympic consecutive gold medals. Her coach had a dream she would win 3 gold medals and shared it but didn't believe it. She who wore braces on her legs at age 10 and 10 years later at age 20 would one day become the fastest woman in the world. She died 2 years ago. Jace Jones-Kace, Marie Lou Retun, Kerri Strugg and the devoted dedicated woman athletes if not for them, there would be nothing like the centennial games with more women athletes. A salute to them all. I hope someday, if this will come true and destiny is the vision. I see in San Diego Olympics . It's true yet it will be San Diego 2008 or 2012. My parents don't really care about my Martial Arts talent but I do and I will give the ultimate sacrifice. Maybe I will win anything at the Nationals, but I tried. I've been touched deeply in this Olympics and plan to be there more likely as a spectator but very less likely to be one.

I HAVE FULL OF HOPE AND STILL I'M YOUNG TO think much about my future. One of those things I'm happy about me is I always want to stay ahead
In anything I do. I always strive to the top will my overall best in everything I do. * Anyone can have a dream but not everyone feels & hopes their vision in life. Anyone can wake up in a dream but a vision means youre chins are up, I could see it in my head, in my eyes & In my work.

Aug. 13, 1996 (10:22P.M.)

Like any ordinary boring summer day of mine, I had to go to work. Considering I had enough trouble at work such as giving the wrong food to customer, like how hard is frieng french fries by now when still manegers are still giving me advice on how to fry it, and not to mention I got in trouble for showing up 19 minutes late on a 10 minute break and a write up the next day for bad food procedure. I bet cha! Ramon, one of the maneger, can't wait to fire me someday. I'm counting on it. **RESTAURANT JOB IS NOT FOR ME.**

I was suppose to work ~~for~~ from 5 to 9 but got off 7:30 I think. On my way to go home, as I got off the restaurant. I meet this this old guy again. I chat with him and asked I'm interested in reading his book. I wanted to believe him for curiosity sake & to see if the story is good enough to publish. While waiting outside for him and his old friend to come back I knew it's trouble from then on. An old saying "CURIOSITY IS TROUBLE". I know because I've been into lots of them. Not to mention I got in trouble taking to him on my break already.

His first page would make you want to read more, as I thought he would have a lot of bad experience but to my surprise he didn't. He said, " When you don't have anything but hope and way someone will be there for you to help when you ask for help and you been helping people; no one will help you." I think I read ¼ of it tonight. I remember he told me if you believe in God and pray, he will be there For you. I believe in God, in him because he has done many miracoulous thing for me and others. He have done a lot for me & made me realized about myself. I'm about to ask him for guidance tonight. My opinion about all this is the old man should finish this story with a reflection and conclusion and hope someone will help him to type it so he could get it publish someday because for what he had done to himself and wish from his friend back in Georgia to ride cross country ~~across U.S~~. and write a book about it. It took him a year. IF it's going to be me, Lord, if I help him, from your guidance, I hope I will not get into too much trouble if not me. I hope someone will help him. Knowing I thought I'll get away ~~him~~ from all this and go home not hoping my parents will know I've been talking to strangers tonight. Surprise, It was my Mom saying they called "MickeyD's" and saying I got off work early from big trouble. I should have known better. My Dad showed up and I stayed at the phone booth till he came and ignoring the 2 old new friends I made tonight not saying" Good Bye" when I left. I had to just to be on the safe side. My Dad called the cops and we came home my Mom worriedly waiting for me. I told them I chat with my friends at "McDo" and stayed in & pretending not knowing the time at all. I said sorry sorry to made Dad knowing how worried my parents were. My Dad cried. I feel guilty for what I did and lie. MAY GOD FORGIVE ME. Like any other teenager I had to lie coz I'm already in trouble. I have a terrible headache & want to throw up. I'm going to bed.

August 19, 1996

[TURN THIZ INTO A L.B.$ SOMEDAY19.1996]

Tonight, I was suppose to be at Kelly Rossi's house spending the night. Of course ~~If~~ I ~~had~~ asked my Mom and should have known better I should have ask my Dad earlier. I'm expert in lying now to my friends & parents. To told Kelly my parents are going out for a dinner which is a lie. So here I am stuck in my room. It seems like summer is endless. I can't believe Im saying.."I can't wait till school starts." THIS IS SUMMER SUCKS BIG TIME… WORST THAN LAST YEAR! THIS SUMMER ~~IS A BAD SUMMER~~ IS A FUCKIN BORING SUMMER ! OKAY!

EXCUSE MY FRENCH! I Feel expressing yourself and say what you want is okay. THIS IS AMERICA …YOU CAN SAY ANYTHING. SOMEONE OTHER THAN ME WILL READ THIS WILL UNDERSTAND. I JUST DON'T LIKE THE IDEA OF BEING BOSS AROUND..TELLING ME WHAT NOT AND WHAT OKAY TO DO. I RESPECT MY PARENTS & CARE DEEPLY. I JUST WANT TO BE FREE TO DO WHAT I FEEL I WANT TO DO. I CANT WAIT TO BE 18 and graduate. I HOPE I GO TO AN OUTSTANDING COLLEGE. THIS HOUSE IS LIKE A JAIL TO ME.

I KEEP TELLING MYSELF TO THINK OF BETTER FUTURE SUMMER TO COME. I HAVEN'T EVEN DONE BUNGI JUMPING, SKY DIVING, SNOWBOARDING, SCUBA DIVING , SKIING, BCT (BASIC CADET TRAINING) ARMY STYLE FOR 1+ MONTH PLUS ETC. & I HAVEN'T TRAVELED AROUND THE WORLD & I HAVEN'T HAVE MY OWN STOCKBROKER.

I WATCH THIS SHOW FOR THE 2ND TIME ABOUT THIS GIRL WHO IS A SOPHOMORE IN HIGHSCHOOL. A SWEET GIRL, SMART, TALENTED IN WRITING, IN YEARBOOK STAFF BUT LIKE ME BEFORE, SHE FELT UNACCEPTED. ANGELA WANTED TO BE POPULAR LIKE THIS GIRL. SHE'S OBSESSED OF THE FACT SHE'S NOT LIKE HER & WISHES TO BE SOMEBODY ELSE. I'M VERY MUCH LIKE ANGELA BUT I DIDN'T KILL ANYONE WHO I WAS JEALOUS OF. I THINK ANGELA WAS A VICTIM PARTLY OF SOCIETY AND OF HERSELF & HER INNER EMMOTIONS. I'M SO MUCH ALIKE LIKE HER AND I KNEW HOW SHE FELT. ONE YEAR AGO I'VE SEEN THIS MOVIE BUT IT SEEMS I UNDERSTAND BETTER OF THE MESSAGE IT WAS TRYING TO TELL ME. YES! COZ I WENT THROUGH SAME THING SHE DID BUT NOW I REALIZED WHATS GOOD FOR ME THAN POPULARITY. I PAID THE PRICE LESS THAN ANGELA, MY GRADES BUT LEARN GREATLY ONLY I UNDERSTAND FROM EXPERIENCES & LESSONS OF A LIFETIME.

Aug 20, 1996

Do you have any idea what time it is? Its 12:41 AM 20 minutes ago, I had the best idea I would sacrifice working on it. Npoe it's not for me. It's a tribute to women around the world. It's awesome! I can't sleep as always, so I think. I step on lala land world. I asked myself how do I want to be remembered as… I want to go down on the history books. I want to do something; great things for mankind. I want to see happy faces little kids, to me they possess the future. I want to be just an ordinary individual who deeply cares for others in need. I want to do something for this world; great joyous things. But I only imagine it in my visions of hope right now but I will do everythting in my will power to make it happen.

Ambitious girl I am, I asked myself, **"What can I do? My mind possess it." I've always love history**, maybe someday I will go down on the history book, In what? Doing what? After all history book have chapters. "I love history, I've gotten and learned how history gave me inspirations. An Encyclopedia of the human kind=history=and maturity of Planet Earth as it evolves for millions of years."

"Lying on my bed asking myself in my thoughts, how much I know about history. I thought about the Egyptian pyramids and the pharaohs, Olympics, Wars & battles, to the greatest poets, leaders, writers, artists, ~~musi~~ composer (musicians), inventors, anonymous entertainers ~~of the past~~, soldiers, or athletes of the past etc.

Big question pops up when I thought about books, poetry, story or an author. William Shakespeare is known back then & now & other great writers or poets we are taught at schools have contributed greatly to mankind in their talents. Although, writing isn't my specialty, isn't my specialty, it's my weakness, I have thius dream maybe I'll be a writer & write books someday. THE BIG QUESTION I ASKED MYSELF WAS: IF I WRITE A BOOK ~~RIGHT NOW~~, WHAT WILL IT BE ABOUT?" My mind completely went blank for a minute or so. I thought I can always do something risky, like roller blade or skate across United States or talk about the places I will travel around the world someday but then anyone can do that. THEN A 6 Letter word SPORTS and a 5 letter word WOMEN just a snap in my finger. To me they were visions from GOD. I could do a tribute to all the WOMEN Athletes way back, the present & the future of women athletes they hold. HOW ABOUT TO ALL THE WOMEN IN THE WORLD - A TRIBUTE TO THEM BY WRITING A BOOK. I THOUGHT ABOUT THE TITLE: PAST, PRESENT & FUTURE. WE'VE COME A LONG WAY. IT'S ALL ABOUT WOMEN FROM THE PAST (WHAT THEY DID), PRESENT (TODAY'S WORLD DIFFERENCES FROM THE PAST) AND THE FUTURE FOR WOMEN. WOMEN from homemakers, Engineers, artist, entertainers, leader to athletes of today. WE HAVE COME A LONG WAY. I CAN DO IT IN 2 YEARS LESS. I WILL FACE PROBLEMS LIKE: BASICLLY THE FORMAT OF THE BOOK (INSIDE & OUT) BIG RESEARCH, PUBLISHING, WILL IT FIT AND OKAY FOR EVERYONE WHO READS IT(MEN, WOMEN, KIDS) & BIG PROBLEMS I WILL FACE, which is right & wise to do and which is not. THIS MIGHT NOT COME OUT NOT PUBLISH or I might not do this till my 20's. BUT I LIKE THE IDEA OF A 16+ year old writing a BIOGRAPHY FOR WOMEN. I HOPE ADULTS WILL TO. HELP ME LORD. I'M NOT DOING

THIS FOR THE MONEY. I DON'T KNOW HOW FAR IT WILL GO. WHAT I'M I GONNA DO. THIS MIGHT NOT BE A GOOD IDEA. I NEED AN ADIVISOR. IT WILL BE A PAPERBACK HISTORY BOOK ABOUT WOMEN WHO DID GREAT THINGS IN THIS SOCIETY & THE WORLD.

Aug 21, 1996 10:49 PM

I'm at my bedroom watching Miss Teen USA Pageant. It's down to Texas, Pennslyvenia & California. What's weird was when Miss Texas was introduced at the beginning of the show, my inner voice told me she's the lucky woman tonight. Could it be?

YE! I'M RIGHT. I feel like I won too. I predicted events come true before and thought it was a lucky choice prediction. Such one like this I felt Miss Texaz will win from the first part she was introduced. IF I COULD PREDICT MY FUTURE; could I think like NOSTRADAMUS. MY INNER VIOCE HAS BEEN GIVING ME ADVICES, TELLS ME HOW MY FUTURE WILL LOOK LIKE, WHAT'S MY DESTINY. COULD IT BE TRUE WRITING THIS BOOK HAS HOPE. I'M NOT SURE ABOUT THIS UNIQUE TALENT. DO I HAVE THIS TALENT- A VISION TO SEE THE FUTURE.

Aug 29, 1996

I waited this day for so long this month because it's the only fun day I will ever have this summer 1996. Looking forward to spend it at Family Fun Center with my best friend KELLY ROSSI. BUT I DIDN'T EXPECT TODAY REFLECTS THE BRIDGE OF A SUCCESSFUL SCHOOL YEAR & TENNIS SEASON. This is the 1st week of tennis. I'm feeling very depressed & confused knowing I won't have a great tennis season this year. I didn't want to waste my time playing a game with each one who waits to play singles knowing I may never make singles Varsity but I want to make Varsity and I needed someone to make Varsity Doubles with me. TO BE PLAYING DOUBLES WITH ME AS TEAM, SHE HAS TO WANT THE DESIRE TO WIN, TO PLAY TOUGH, TO ENJOY AND HAVE FUN, TO HAVE THE SAME ABILITY LEVEL AS ME, DEDICATED TO THE SPORT, I HAVE TO FEEL COMFORTABLE PLAYING TENNIS AND OFF COURT AS NOT JUST A DOUBLES PARTNER BUT A **FRIEND** TO BE TRUSTED. Alicia has been very nice & friendly person and I want to stay as good friends with her. Alicia is a good tennis player and I have a lot of respect for her. When she ask me to play doubles with her but I'm positive I don't think I said "YES." I ALREADY DEFINE THE PROFILE OF WHAT I WANT MY

DOUBLES PARTNER SHOULD HAVE THOSE CHARACTER. Alicia doesn't fit the profile, if we become doubles partner I may never be in Varsity & her character doesn't show she's a hard worker. As I look back last year tennis season, I didn't know it was going to be like that. I FINALLY KNOCK SOME SENSE IN ME UNTIL I REALLY LOOK BACK AS A FRESHMAN RANKED DEAD LAST AND WORK MY BUTT OFF TO THE TOP & I WOULDN'T BET THIS GOOD THIS GOOD OF A TENNIS PLAYER RIGHT NOW IF I HAVEN'T WORKED HARD and PLAY MY BEST EFFORT. MY DAD SAID 2 years ago I PLAYED 110% during practice PLAYING WITH KELLIE [KELLY] LUNDEEN AS DOUBLES PARTNER WAS A SHOCK TO ME. MY FIRST EMPRESSION OF HER WAS; she was too good for me. She's pretty, blond & one of the so called popular student and I don't hang with people like her at school and always thought she was mean & QUEEN SNOB. I THINK AT THAT TIME WE WERE THE BEST J.V. DOUBLES even if we rank # 3 because we keep winning all our games. We build as a team on court, we communicate as a team on court, we played tough, our best effort. YET WHAT'S WRONG? We only know each other ON COURT AND I Tried trying to be her friend, to hang out off court just be friendly talking BUT THERE'S ALWAYS A GAP, A BIG GAP THAT SEPARATES US TO BE FRIENDS. FRIENDSHIP WAS MISSING BUT YET SHE BRINGS OUT THE BEST IN ME. SHE WAS A COACH BY MY SIDE TELLING ME MY MISTAKES AND HOW TO IMPROVE MY SKILLS AND AS A TEAM AND HAVE MY SUPPORT SO WE COULD WIN AS A TEAM. I JUST REALIZED NOW AND MAYBE I ALREADY HAD BUT NEVER BROUGHT IT UP. I DIDN'T GAVE HER THE SUPPORT SHE NEEDED WHEN SHE FACED TOUGH PROBLEMS WITH HER DAD. BUT THEN HOW COULD I GIVE HER THE SUPPORT AND EVERYTHING SHE HAS DONE FOR ME WHEN WERE NOT EVEN FRIENDS NOT KNOWING HOW TO REACT AND I DIDN'T HAVE THE POWER LIKE HER CHARACTER TO HELP HER. IT WAS JUST A BEST SEASON EVER & I DIDN'T THINK NOTHING WOULD SPOIL IT. BUT I WAS WRONG! OH! WELL! I CAN ONLY LOOK BACK FROM MY PAST AND LEARN SOMETHING FROM IT AND USE IT TO BUILD [A]BETTER FUTURE.

TODAY AT PRACTICE I FELT LIKE A BOUNCING PINGPONG BALL AND WISHES SOMEONE WOULD SLAM THE BALL SO I WON'T FEEL CONFUSED ANYMORE. A BIRD SHIT LANDED ON MY RIGHT HAND, it looked small like a dot, I didn't know where it exactly came from but I thought of it as an omend from GOD a good sign of a good day. Brent, our coach, made me play doubles with Regina. Regina is good. If she only knows how good she is. I never seen anyone in the team like her, she can slam that ball with her backhand like a Pro traveling 90 miles per hour. If she had my desire to win, to succeed, to be the best then she would have been my best choice of doubles partner but she doesn't have those character like me. She she beat it, she can beat anyone the team if she had the desire to but she has to work for it. Did I mention she's the only one on the tennis team who wears makeup and makes sure her hair's perfect. THEN AGAIN, I WAS WRONG ABOUT THE GOOD SIGN FROM GOD and still confused. After the match playing doubles with Regina hoping I may never end up as her doubles partner this year. I ANALIZED ALL THE TEAMATES, WHO'S DOING SINGLES, WHO'S DOING DOUBLES, What's my chances making Varsity. Finally I had the urge to go up and talk to Brent during my break discussing about the candy sales. Brent questioning me about what I plan to do about playing singles or doubles. I asked him who's playing singles, a lot of names he mention but singles it's not for me right now although it would help me to become the most dedicated player recognized on the team but trophies don't matter because I already had that from my heart. I was born to be dedicated, to be dedicated is natural way of competitiveness to help me make the best in what I do. Brent mention there might be a spot for me in Varsity doubles #3 but I needed a partner, a partner who want to be in Varsity too. Brent ask me who I want to play with. I had a big questioned mark on my head. He said to come up to GALE and introduced myself & asking her if she wanted to play doubles with me. TOUGH CALL. I HAD TO DO IT. I walked up and introduce myself with full name. Asking her name & told her I wanted to play doubles Varsity & looking for a doubles partner. Telling her that Brent told me you wanted to be in Varsity. I went on and told her I wanted to play with someone who has the same ability level as me and told her I prefer to play doubles because you play with someone as a team, someone is there for you to help you out and singles is too competitive and I'm afraid singles will take a fun out of tennis if I play for singles. She said "SO DO I," she went on, "ALICIA ASK ME TO PLAY DOUBLES WITH HER BUT SHES NOT MY TYPE OF A DOUBLES PARTNER." "SHE ASKED YOU TO PLAY WITH HER, SHE DID THAT TO ME TOO BUT I WANTED TO PLAY WITH SOMEONE WITH THE SAME LEVEL & WANT TO MAKE VARSITY."

THANK YOU LORD FOR TODAY, THIS IS PROBABLE MY MOST MEMORABLE SUMM DAY, only one this summer. I DON'T KNOW what bad flaw to expect this year because it will be the BEST YEAR EVER. I just hope Alicia will understand and not make me Autumn II (backbiting me).

GALE [GAIL LEDERMAN] is like someone I hope I can relate to someone I see my reflection. I think this is a miracle for her to go to EL CAP her senior year when she's from CHRISTIAN HIGH. SEE HOW SPECIAL I AM. When we were talking, Jessica came up to us listening to our conversation interrupting telling us we were the same height. Expect I could have said I weigh more. I don't know her skills well but I see myself when I look at her because she has level skills with me, the desire to win & have fun, play it hard & want to kick butts.

I spend my afternoon with my best friend Kelly Rossi, Family Fun Center was fun but I will never go to the Pirate boat ride again. NEVER! I rode the Ferris wheel ride for the 1st time. I FEEL SO GREAT TODAY THAT I STILL FEEL THAT TINGLING FEELING INSIDE MY STOMACH, EXCITED OF TOMORROW AND HAPPY OF TODAY. Her parents are nice and I actually went swimming on the pool. We talked about Air Force and how we want to get out so we could get a job of our choice but I told her I wanted my own business. **She brought up BILL GATES, Microsoft owner of a company and richest person in the worlds. I WOULD LOVE TO** BE IN HIS PLACE. I hope to meet him someday, maybe I should marry him or take owe the company by being a CEO. Anyway. Kelly will be my lifelong friend.

Sept.2 (9:53)

I just got lectured from my Mom telling me I have to get good, better grades and I have to think about tennis, quiting if I don't have a ride home. NOW I SEE WHY HE'S MAD AT ME, MY DAD HAD BEEN MAD JUST ABOUT EVERY SINGLE FLAW I GOT, if it's not my unskinny body, bad character something had to be a new Flaw. The biggest one yet..., my flawless defeat of bad grades still haunts me by my Dad as the ghost. He's still pushing me by mot giving me ride aFter tennis so he wants me to concentrate only on my studies. He's right, he's always right. He wants me to do my Best. I WAS BORN TO LIVE THE RULE OF ALWAYS DOING YOUR BEST AND BE HARD WORKING PERSON.

I cry at my faults because I'm not stRong enough and I'm too sensitive and I hates to see my flaws showing I HAVE TO BE STRONG!!!

I want ~~to to stay go~~ to school soon this summer telling myself. But Im not ready at least I think I don't feel ready because knowing myself I never keep my promises, that's promoses, that's why probably why I think of myself good profile of a politician. Ive been telling myself, "Sure Heralyn, you're a junior this time, 2 years of flaws and your telling yourself you'll get better grades." Ooops! I don't think my sophomore year was bad experience all the way but thought of it at the end of school year as one step OF MY SELF-ESTEEM HIGHER & A BIG LEAD OF A BETTER PERSON.

CONCLUSION: LAST YEAR I SAID my accomplishments didn't work out during summer but this summer I think I accomplished 80% of my goals.

Right now I'm ~~listening~~ watching on T.V. about WOMEN FIGURE: THE WAY WE WANT TO HAVE PERFECT BODY. Right now I don't feel fat but I'm not skinny. I'm just 15 lbs. Overweight and need desperate toning oF my body. THEN AFTER THAT I CAN SAY I'M SKINNY. TOO BAD, WOMEN ARE PORTRAYED in society to have a skinny perfect body. I tHINK WOMEN LEADS A tougher harder life than men. → TOMMORROW is 1st Day of school and I'm really not ready but I just want to have straight A's real bad, concentrate on my studies, feel great about myself as one of the outstanding student in school, hoping my SELF-ESTEEM WILL GET HIGHER, MY CHARACTER HOPING WILL BE BETTER, STOP COMPARING MYSELF AS A LOW LIFE PERSON, WANT TO HAVE MY PROMISES NOT JUST PROMISES BUT TAKE ACTIONS, MANAGEMENT IN TIME ETC.

SEPT 13 (Friday the 13th)

1st Day of school, Sept. 3, wasn't that scary as I thought it was. I was worried about my AP English summer assignments the night before the school starts. I like all my subjects and my teachers. JOURNALISM will be a new experience for me, alternative to ASB, and entend to do what it takes to make THE HORIZON gain ∧ more popularity in school and play a big role, enough to be appointed as an EDITOR but like: THAT'S GOING TO HAPPEN.

CHEMISTRY Honors I have a humorous teacher, Mrs. Rosenburger. AP English class is a challenging class and having Mr. Landry as my teacher who is GREAT teacher. Mrs. Trochta, my Pre-Cal teacher was in the nay and I liked the way she teaches expect I don't understand what she's saying. My 3rd year Spanish teacher, Mrs. Fonseca gaved advice to us on how we can use beyond with the Spanish skills we got. THEN THERE's Mr. Yocom, a humurous knowledgable teacher in AP American History. Only in a week, he gave me partial answers of WHAT I WAS LOOKING FOR. FOR A SECOND JUST ABOUT ALL MY SCHOOL-FAME PROBLEMS WAS ANSWERED BY MR. YOCOM. HOW MAN ARE SELFISH AND ONLY CARE FOR THEMSELVES AND WE ALL WANT TO BE FAMOUS. HE ASKED THIS CHEERLEADER IN MY CLASS, " WHY DO YOU

HAVE A NAME PRINTED ON YOUR CHEERLEADING UNIFORM? DON'T YOU WANNA BE POPULAR?"

I HAVE MY OWN ANSWER TO THAT. OF COURSE, TO BE FAMOUS. HE MADE A POINT THAT ALL MEN ARE GREEDY, SELFISH; ONLY CARE FOR THEIR OWN PERSONAL BEING. HE ASKED THE CLASS "WHY DO WE WANT TO PUT OTHERS DOWN WHO ARE BETTER (students, smarter etc.) THAN US. WHY DO YOU WANT TO PULL THEM DOWN?" One girl answered, "To get our own Fame, to be more competitive."

I wanted to answer my point of view but didn't. When the bell rang, I told him directly that we want to be better than others so we want to pull them down to get our FAME only because we are JEALOUS OF THEM.

9/26 (9:51 P.M)

To continue from where I didn't finish because I've been so busy lately. It seems like ~~the longer~~ the longer the school days passed the longer breaks/time-out I get.

I'm talking about right now on how a Marine pamphet ~~chan~~ greatly affected me. It talked about the voices inside me, telling me on making the right decision. The tough brave person inside me, showing no FEAR, CHALLENGED EVERYDAY OBSTACLE, the one who gives me pure great power For better person. The one who never gives up and always give her best. Sometimes I ask her, "How do I live to people's demands? Is my confidence higher/better? OR AM I JUST PLAIN LOW?" I have what it takes but some puzzles are missing and I don't know how I will handle and unexpected delima of becoming a MARINE or AIR FORCE. I'm building to b~~r~~ea better person and there is no last stage to accomplish to be better because no man is perfect. I can only improve for better for the rest of my life. There are things in my life I need to work on. I worry about what people thinks about me more than what I think of myself sometimes. My Mom thinks, I have a very high PRIDE" I still don't get her. I just have things for me to make my life balance as possible because what's school memories without FUN memories. My step Dad is still not talking to me. I asked him if I could talk to him but he said theres nothing to talk about. He gave up on me. I don't know how much he expects of me and what he sees in me. I have the biggest gratitude "OTANG KABUBUT ON" to my Step Dad. If not for him I would have never be in U.S.right now. And I would not have the opportunity of bright future. Where would my Mom & I be then if not for him, where do we stand. Of

Course not spending the rezt of my life living in another relative's house. Yap! When I was 9 my Mom lost her job and we couldn't afford to rent the house after that. The next thing I know was I spent the next 3 years living in a house wher e you just glad you are living in to have been sleeping on the streets. I don't know how she did maintain to keep me in a private school somehow. Lord was always beside her and blessing of hope was near and it is now. My Mom is strong and I'm not going to cry over problems but be strong and find solutions if no solutions learn to deal with it in a positive way.

There are things I would have added but right now, its all I've got to say.

I'M GONNA TAKE ONE DAY AT A TIME and do make each day with big great happy smiles, joy feelings, seize the day(CARPIE DIEM), appreciate myself, others & things I see etc.

☯ **I NEED BALANCE & need to solve the missing puzzles.**

9/28

Yesterday I had my 1st yearlong break to go to the movie with a friend . It's like thw 1st time going out to watch a movie in year 1996. Really ! I watched THE FIRST WIVES CLUB with Robin Seiber. She's easy to be friends with and I'm glad she's keeping in touch with her higschool's friends who are still in El Cap. She's the type of person who cares for others and help you if you need it. GOING OUT TO HAVE FUN ON FRIDAY non school even if I had to finished up 2 articles at school. Fun was a kick-off For me.

Today ~~Yes I~~ was a very special day. My Mom took an oath becoming a new U.S. citizen. I'm happy for the both of us. FINALLY ! I had a bad mood I took on my friends . Then she started blaming me in which I was expecting and ~~it~~ I was just being moody coz I wanted to eat eaRly then she took it on me. SHE BLAME I CAUSED PROBLEMS IN TIS HOUSE & I DON'T LISTEN TO HER. I Remembered WHEN I WAS YOUNG whenever she gets mad or someone said something that made me cry, All I HAD TO DO WAS NOT LISTEN TO THOSE WORDS. MAKE THE WORDS PASSED TO YOUR EARS. UNTIL NOW I STILL DO THAT. IF IT INVOLVES MY MOM [STEPMOM], MY STEPDAD AND ME, it's my fault. OOH WEELL ! _ . . . LETS GET ON WITH THE REST. Where else but in EL CAJON FREINDSHIP FESTIVAL you get to see 2 monks, Miss Universe

'96, entertainment and learn a lot about a culture from Food to Tradition. I came close to Miss Universe 3 feet waiting for my Mom. Miss Universe is about 5' 9" , didn't really wore an elite clothes, just blue long sleeve shirt & black pants. I wanted her autograph but I couldn't . She could walk to McDo. to order something and I wouldn't know who she is really. Maybe I will think she looks like a model. My point is, she's just normal people except she's Miss Universe. She is only 19 from Venezuela but her speech I could have done better but I still liked it. She's still is learning speaking English & translated it to Spanish.

→ 10/2/96

IT WAS SAME OLD SCHEDULED SCHOOL DAY TODAY. THE WORST EVER YET. HUSSLING THROUGH DOING HOMEWORK IN THE LIBRARY, CLUBS AT LUNCH & sometimes I pretend not to let things happen or are now bother me but I can't help it. Spanidh is a drag, I have a witch teacher, no worst than a witch, but she can teach well. I space out a lot in that class. I did my homework but turn in late. Not a good impression about me if I ask a letter ~~resume~~ of recomendation from her in the future. Gail & I played a match with Heidi & BobI who made Varsity D.[Doubles] #3. I wanted that spot. I wasn't what I expected to be from Gail but there is no perfect, last year wasn't good and needed something lacking like this year but I think I chose the Varsity # 3 Doubles are better than us they get the spot. It made me feel in between the match we played when Heidi or BobI served to me I wanted to be on Varisty for a long time. I think "THERE ARE THINGS IN LIFE YOU GET AND DON'T GET NO MATTER WHAT?" It's a better motto sometimes than "TRY, TRY, & TRY until you succeed." When playing I asked never felt I got what I wanted in life. WHY? WHY? WHY?

☺**All my life I wanted to be President of something in school.** I wobn President of Soph. Class because nobody ran against me. GOD HEARD my CRY. Now I've gain more leadership ever and big leadership responsibilities. Tennis! WOW? I've come a long way from my freh man yar. Long, Long way. Not a clue about tennis, I'm glad I joined tennis for I got more than I expected for, greater than wanting to be on Varsity. I got other things too…. .. But I'm selfish. I've spent my life questioning my abilities, my limitations, skills, leadership, how people think about me, my talents, my I.Q., etc. etc.

etc. Basiclly, I'm doubting myself still. Brent said it today when we ask him if we could call him Coach Ford. He said it doesn't matter because at our age (teenagers) we experiment and he went through that. **It still haunted me when I was on the bus. When I was a kid I wanted to be an architect not knowing about it at all. I thought architect means an artist but It still fits me today.** I thought that was my father's occuation and I wanted to be like him. I don't really know much of 16 yrs. living the blood that runs through my vain feeling not a FATHER'S WORD to live by only a Dad 'at wants a perfect daughter who never had a child and didn't grew up living with his parents. What more do I want, I could be homeless living on the street in the Phils. With my Mom right now. What my Dad has done is far much as what my Mother gave me. **America is my opportunity to do whatever I desire in life.** My stepfather/Dad has given me a lot already. I didn't want him to neglect with my irresponsibility. I always remember more about my FAULTS than what I accomplish: But I think I lost a lot of battles and won little but sruggling to get what I want. I want TO WIN THE WAR. I'M STRESSED OUT ALREADY. **I HAVE TO BE STRONG. BECAUSE I WANT MY GOALS TO COME ALIVE.** I'm so Full of bullshit, I say it but never take **actions**. I want to get to AIRFORCE ACADEMY REAL BAD RIGHT NOW, **I WANT TO GO TO THAT scholarship for Washington D.C. trip more than Sara means it, I want to get straight A's knowing I have F's in class *right now,*** I want a real Dad, not just when I do accomplish great things in school & not make me a robot, (I like said before, nothings perfect), I want a car so I could no longer worry about rides or unsafe ness in the bus at night, I want money to buy clothes for…., I want a boyfreind to go to the Prom, I want to be on Varsity next year, I want to loose weight; to be able to run 1½ in 10 minutes, I want my personalities and character to be better, stronger than ever. I want to be in ASB as school TREASURER, I want to be an honor student, I want to gain leadership & office clubs/school. I DON'T CARE ABOUT THESE WANTS REALLY AS MUCH AS I WANT THE MOST FOR A LONG TIME. I don't care if I don't win to be school treasurer and be defeated by a popular student or not make Varsity next year. I MUST MAKE IT TO AIR FORCE AND GET GOOD GRADES, BE ABLE TO BE A WELL ROUNDED STUDENT. TO BE ABLE TO ACCOMPLISH MY FUTURE GOALS.

I worst part is when thinking about it is right now, I'm a dead tree like my leaves are dying & falling. **I need water , sun & nessecities etc. to GET MY GOALS. I'M FIGHTING TO SURVIVE, TO LIVE UP MORE THAN WHAT I EXPECT WHEN I CAN DO MORE OR BETTER THAT ANYONE IN THIS WORLD WHO WALKED on the FACE OF THE EARTH.** I'M SELFISH, I WANT TO SUCCEED AND I WILL DO ANYTHING IF I HAD TO EAT WORM I WILL. NOT JUST TO ACCOMPLISH MY DREAMS, TO SHOW OFF TO OTHERS, TO HAVE IT ON MY RESUME BUT EVERYTHING ABOUT IT STANDS ABOUT ME.

↙ I'm not

a **dead tree ∧ anymore my roots are new and young and my leaves are sprouting and even more....BUT There's more to learn.** ☆✈●🚑🏝☺❺❹♥**SDIB**☼

NOTE FOR PEOPLE WHO HAS READ OR WILL READ THIS DIARY. PLEASE READ THE 2nd diary (green (flower design)) on date Jan 18, 1998 which is today for me.

NOTE: MARCH 2,'97

I read the 3-4 last pages and I also wrote journal in my diary today. I'm afraid now and before when I wrote the last pages if THE
ONLY· TAING MATTERS TO ME IS MAKING ONE OF THE ACADEMY.
I'm afraid if I don't make it to one of them (West Point), everything that I stand for, worked for, sacrific, acomplish and especially my (weaknesses (now and before) (ie. Academics, limitation personality, some of my characteri have I've been trying to make it a positive outlook that for the worst etc.) IS NOT WORTH ANTHING ANYMORE. BUT I KNOW IT IS, I'VE EXPERIENCED and SUFFERED GREATLY & SUCCEED and failed. I know HOW MUCH IT'S WORTH = ACADEMY. **THE HARD PART IS WILL I EVER HAVE THE COURAGE TO SUCCEED and DESIRE IT THROUGH COLLEGE TO TRY and TRY and TRY without any REGRET of my making it the FIRST TRY? ✉ ☺**

♥

☺ **PART TWO:** Heralyn Morales Toling's 2ND DIARY

☺ **THE UPPERCLASS YEARZ:**

☺ **(MY MATURITY LEVEL Grade "A" Popularity)… in other words/…**

☺ ... THE PUBERTY OVERFUNRIDEZ TO CRASH & BURN ON MY AMERICAN TEENAGE YEARRSSZZZZ !!!

OCT. 6, 1996 (8:24 P.M.)

This week was tough as usual but I'm still breathing to survive. I'm so stressed out, know I know how much damage STRESS last year did to me 100x worst than it was compare to right now. I try to do as much fun as I can if possible to FORGET ABOUT STRESS; school, family, future etc (all the problems I release my worries out when I have fun with my friends, to get away from my parents, to forget about my failures, unhappiness & STRESS. SURE, IT DOESN'T LAST LONG, its like eating a food to make me happy & feel good but after the last bite I go back to face REALITY AGAIN.

My friday night, on Oct. 4 I took the ________ to go to school to ~~get~~ watch with my friends the football game. It was fun after ~~th~~ getting home and stared at my dark room lying in bed and ~~lelu~~ realizing just then I can say I HAD FUN and GLAD T.C. ask me to go with her group of friends. Only drawback was, me not a socializer hanging out with people who are ~~fr~~ her friends, to them I don't exist because I didn't have something cool to say and not forgetting feeling ~~me~~ desperate having to have a boyfriend to cuddle up with especially when you are surrounded by couples hugging and kissing in the group of friends of T.C. T.C.'s boyfriend is cute (so…so..so..) and sweet coz T.C. brainwashed him. I'm so jealous. I need a ride home which T.C. offered me. Football was Boring even though we won. It's no fun anymore, football is old to me being a junior and that was my **1st** game I saw this season.

MY FAVORITE PART was TOILET PAPERING Sara's house. But I have to tell you this. We (the group) didn't end up going to the pizza place but instead to RALLY' S. THEY WERE SHARING Jokes and we laughed. Cory Thompson and his girlfriend showed up. I ignored him but when we left to Sara's house he tried to get run over by Tiffany's car as a joke and I saw him when we left so I waved gooBye. ~~And no response.~~ We had to pull over to the side of a curve road so Tiffany, Laura and this guy I don't know had to Piss. So they did along the Bush. We ~~did~~ the group dicided to toilet paper Sara's house part of it was the group seem to not appreciate her attitude (she thinks she's better than us or acts like it) I still thinks she does but I have a lot of respect even all that I want to have ~~like~~ her ~~mind~~ brain. We did pretty good on her gate considering it was open and they did her car and trees. Unfortunately, all those ~~loudness~~ whispering and squeky noises, I saw her or a woman looking out at the window door but only a glance and didn't seem to bother at all. I hate for the fact she get to go to Leadership Camp.

7:55 PM NOVEMBER 20,1996

WOW ! I must have been really busy past these months because I haven't had time to share & write about my life in my diary. This time, I'll make sure I can read my writing, it's bad enough my sentences stinks- that some can't understand what the hell I'm talking about. NOT TO WORRY, I CAN STILL REMEMBER OCTOBER and this past days of NOVEMBER LIKE YESTERDAYS EXCEPT NO WORDS CAN EXPRESS THOSE FUN STUFF in every OPPORTUNITY to have fUN WITH MY FRIENDS. I SUPPOSE YOU ALREADY KNOW WHY? OF COURSE ! TO FORGET ABOUT MY WORRIES IN LIFE & JUST HAVE AN AWESOME TIME SO AT LEAST I CAN LOOK BACK AT MY HIGHSCHOOL YEARS WASN'T SO BAD AFTERALL. I'll make it the best years of my life, jusr a BIG Leap before the real world. It's bad enough school is a prison but just leaving it the way it is, school is a prison. I plan on making choices that deals with my school activities to dealing with homework and not to mention social life with friends. I don't know if I made the wrong chioces like-
(1) become a social partyer to go out with cool friends to kill time filled with fun & laughter (2) join school clubs and sports to test my leadership skills, courage, strength, know my weaknesses, better me, help the school, show students I care but no one cares about what I've done for this school or maybe I haven't done anything great.
(3) choices of feeling sorry for trying in running school office ASB (4) I ~~slip~~ went from a loner loser in high school as a freshman to what? I don't know? NOTHING! NOBODY! (5)

if I choosed 1 year ago I stick being a loner loser who gets radical grades because doesn't have a life, what would my I ve become right now. Probably a nerd jock jock, meaning a person who gets good grades who plays sports but in the lowest status of all.

THOSE ARE THE 5 biggest choices I have to change for my own beneficiary. I think it was a flawless defeat for me because I still feel SOMETHING LACKING IN MY LIFE, PROBABLY THE LACK OF ACCOMPLISHMENTS I'VE GOTTEN gotten the same old me running away TO DO BETTER THINGS.

I HAVE SO MANY CAPABILITIES AND PERSONALITIES/CHARACTER THAN VERY FEW GOT. FROM LEADERSHIP SKILLS TO SPORTS/ATHELETIC SKILLS TO MONEY MAKING ETC. WHAT ELSE I'M NOT CAPABLE OF?

LAST MONTH, WHICH WAS OCTOBER went by fast. I got a new friend who graduated last year but we weren't close Friends as we are now. I got to see THE FIRST WIVES CLUB with Robin Seiber. She's nice. It's great to see her support our Tennis team watching our game after school. I'm glad she's going to the banquet but a problem when she needed ~~the~~ a ride to get there. I felt bad after what she has done for me. I had lied to my ____ just to get away with stuff. Like on Halloween Night. Friendship is back to where I can relate to my old group of friends. Hilary hasn't change that much and Arianna is still the same. AFter that DCM (Key Club) at the Boardwalk was fun. El Cap Key Club looked bad overall but I got to bowl and eat with my friends. I got home 10 PM at that night.

I had to cancell a bowling night on Oct 26 because I wanted to go to the A2J club party. I got my way of getting rides- I got a ride From Jessica Stamper because I invited her and Nikkie Huck and told her Jacob Gregerson (the guy she worship) will be at the party. It turned out to be a sucky 1st annual Halloween A to J Party and last party (Halloween). Only because Katie Camp thought I was doing some kind of HOCUS POCUS. AS IF! everyone wanted to see me hypnotized a person to see if it's possible. On the contrary, I was the highlight of the party but I feel sorry for what happen that Jessica Stokes and her Mom got the blame for it. I can't believe Katie misjudge it without even seeing the group and me doing the hypnotizim.

On Halloween weekend, not forgetting Kelly Brady's sweet 16th party. Goosh! It's been a long time since I've been to my last slumber party. That party rulez! They had a spa, a billiard pool, big T.V. and we dance. Also, we did light as a feather stiff as a board but I felt low because my hypnosis didn't work. But that's okay I had loads of fun! After that you had to go back to reality again.

I went to Elizabeth's house for the 2nd time. It was nice to have a company friend who you can talk too. Her Mom was kind enough to give me rides not to mention I owe her big time for getting rides home. I wish Elizabeth would go to the movies with me with Hilary, Ariana and Kelly even if the movie suck. I don't go to watch movies but I best thing is the time spending with your friends and staying out of the house not to mention worry-free. Elizabeth has so much potential in her future but she doesn't care. OH WELL! I can't wait for Christmas and cool gifts.

Magic Mountain was the BOOM! I spent $ 40 bucks and only ½ discount ticket price. I got loads of memories, all great stuff-Viper-rode 2x, Revolution 2x, Flashback 2x, Colossal, Batman-dangling feeet, etc. All the good expensive food. I was in heaven but all good things must come to an end. I wish Elizabeth was there, she would have enjoy evry minute of it, just like me, Hilary and Kelly did.

Homecoming game was the BOOM! Sina Barnes and Jacob Gregerson won Homecoming Queen & King. As if I didn't know who would win. I got to take pictures so I got the radest spot ever. I had to pretend I was a real journalist photographer; not feeling stupid. Against Santana -63-0. El Cap is in CIF playoff now. I wonder what it would be like Homecoming Queen? You gotta be pretty darn popular. It's not like it will matter 20 years from now. My group of friends left early 15 minutes before the end of the game to go to **"Lytherbee's."** Sara, Tiffanny, T.C., Tammy, Robin and me were there having fun & talking about nonsense (nothing too important). That place is expensive. Nice that Tiffany came out when she saw me at the phone booth outside. I'm not sure if she was going to call or just waiting for me. Friday night's are awesome ! ! !

Today, Period 1-4 we took a test to help us what carrer choice we might fit in. I will never trust the result of that test in choosing a carrer choice. NO WAY!

November 28, 1996
(Thanksgiving Day 8 PM)

As always, my lazyness, my unwillingness to succeed has stop me to get things done.

Let's start by where I left off. **TENNIS THIS YEAR IS BETTER THAN EVER & IT ONLY GETS BETTER THAN EVER -ONE MORE TOUGH YEAR. Being a junior at El Cap, I wanted to be in Varsity tennis. I had no way of ride home after school tennis practice/ tennis games so I had to take the bus. Not to mention sacrifice, my 1 way of part of success. Tennis has always been different to me. I never *taught* in my life I will end up liking a sport….**

Jan 31, 1997

Well, gee, are we having fun yet? I'm gosh darn lazy but I must go on from where I left off. Where should I start. The sentence where I left off way back Nov. '96 Let's just pretend it Nov. '96 and I'm finishing a sentence and telling the story as it unfolds. I'll will do my very best to write every detail from that point of my life to now, so help me God to reflect on my deepest thoughts about my life like it was just yesterday.

Tennis has always been different to me. I never taught in my life, I will end up liking a sport…. By having the courage to join and keeping my dedication 120%+, PROVING MYSELF THE MOST AND OTHERS WHAT I'M MADE OF KNOWING THE FACT I WAS NEVER AN ATHLETE AND BECOME ONE. TELL ME HOW MANY PEOPLE IN THIS WORLD HAVE MY CHARACTER. I'VE PROVEN IT IN MARTIAL ARTS, BUT MARTIAL ARTS IS DIFFERENT COZ I LEARN HOW TO SET IT ASIDE THEN START AGAIN, VICE VERSA, & I HAVE MY UNIQUE WAY OF TALENT. IT'S HARD TO EXPLAIN. AFTER ALL THOSE YEARS AND ONE MORE TO COME WAS SO UNCERTAIN. I KNOW HOW MY TEAMATES SEES ME AND (MY COACHES) Playing tennis with pure dedication, talent developing, positive, achiever, competitive etc. that's how I see myself and discover my about myself in all the different things I do in life. NO REGRETS ONLY SUCCESS ! ! ! & MORE. NO PLAQUE OR TROPHY AWARDS prove it. It's the whole me shows it, nothing else. Need more to say. Let's talk about intensity here! Doubles partner with Gail It was awesome. I wish most blond people are like here. She's not snobby as I thought, She is so nice. Wishing we could have been friends. So did she know the bait or she she just being nice. I will just remember her sweet friendlike personality and I appreciate that in my memory 10+ years from now. She not like them, also I found out from my erotological approach thinking them are all snob coz I blame them but who cares realy, some are nice, REALLY! I will never

forget her envious big white F250 Ford Truck. I will never forget how we are short but she's even taller now. I will never forget the banquet; My Mom stole the flower, Robin being there, Gail, Nicole, Jessica, Nikki, Kelly, Mindy etc. ★ I BELIEVE YOU PAY A PRICE → Say What? WITH EVERYTHING YOUR DESTINY LEADS YOU. I made J.V. but wanted Varsity but J.V. expressed the idealistic of having the best times and Varsity just gives you PAIN but you get P.E. credit and a bigger letter. It's like balance and like them and I want them to show the real me, others should be able to feet
[fit] in the group, J.V. girls look up to me and I don't mean wanting attention. It's just gets better, huh! The adrenalin gushing trugh your face pumping blood thrugh your body, facing your ultimate challenge of the day with games. I gave it all I got- like a pure dedicated player. Shelly was the radest giving me all those secret Pal gifts. Tennis is fun! Nicole is my futeure doubles partner. She's just like any student around; average like mosr of us. I think she REFLECTS ME, SOMETIMES I THINK SHE'S BETTER, Like me. She goes afer evry single ball, dedicated, positive lift up spirit and have the DESIRE to be #1 like me. I expect simple GREAT THINGS ~~since~~ over the past 3 years for next year coz I know I will do 150%

I'm tired just to let you know it's 11:40 PM I need sleep. See ya tomorrow More Like see you tonight. A week later not tomorrow. Tonight is my B-Day 17th. Well, I better write down my feelings Being 17. It's my 1st sign I have to be mature. It's like I don't want to grow up. As Freshman, I see this seniors act matuRe, as if HOW? Even the way they walk, act, talk especially the smart people, they are so mature as if they know everything like adults. Part of me want to be young but I am but still a sign of maturity-responsibility wanting and waiting to be 18 to have that responsibility,feeling I have to control my life my way always, but its different now I have to be mature because I realized for all the past 1 year ½ making my own decisions- right or wrong- it was a sign of maturity and it made me STRONG and Better. Even wiser, so I'm fired up for another level of a new experience in liFe and this time I'm watching my back. No school on my B-Day. My Mom gave me money and a nice letter but I had to tear it up, so told me to. Ate my lunch and took a shower and clean up my room. My Mom called me and Hilary was thoughtful to call me B-Day. Isn't she great! She's the only friend that called me today except toHelar and gave her $ and greeted me Happy B-Day. Mi madre and yo went to Hometown Buffet, people (watreses) say Happy B-Day and got belly full of food. BongW [Bought] me a $20 Airwalk, black one except I hated the laces holes I wanted it like my Vans shoelaces so I cut all the fringes and bought a $20 sale brown boots-both shoes made in China. I say, you can tell a lot about people in their shoes; their style, moves, color etc. Only one difference buying a shoe in Ross ~~fron~~ and the mall, in Ross you set dirt cheap but at the mall you ~~pay~~ set the same thing except you pay 5x more and the shoes is heavier coz youre carrieying the weight price of the shoe. I prefer it lighter if you know what I mean. Mr. Hoss explain a thought for the weekend last week, one of my favorite saying, you have to let go of the past to live for the future and enjoy everyday with no regret. A kid when I remember that, I could not comprehend but when you experienced it, you know it. Today was great and I'll let go of it with hope like the ballons I let go of today from the restaurant. So I'm moving on and my summary ~~from~~ since the Beginning of the school year is short yet simple.

I wish I could remember my feelings because that meant more than anything because that meant more than anything else but just priceless memories. Putting it in my journal is priceless and all the money $ $ $ I spend or wasted for from is recorded in my journal turn nothing but memories. Christmas was just great. Yukie spending in us for 2 weeks. She made us sick but I learned a lot, meet new people; spent $100 for fun in Sea World, Zoo, etc. but I saved entrance fee. I got $100 from my Mom and bought a CD Boom Boox. **I miss Philippines way of celebrating and New Year** was just another night here but half way around the world its celebrated better. The only thing you can relate to for me is my Mom. She reminded me of Christmas all the time, wher she chaze me with a stick coz she got mad at me. Days go by fast, Friday nights was just staying up late watching TGIF. December was a dead month except it was the best dam Winter U.S.A. Break vacation. Elizabeth, my dearly friend still proves a better friend; she gives me ride home and make me feel especial as a friend. Remind me not to exchange gifts with Kelly this year. It was funny when I showed up at the conversation meeting with 17th magazines.

They loved it, one girl mentioned to me wishing they had big boobs. I laughed hard. They went crazy over their favorite movie stars. I went shopping gazillion times except they were rude and wanted to separate so I brought my friends. Right Now, I'm not in a mood to write so I cant get a good feed back. It was the past. Basketball was fun with Kelly, and Helen. It was nice how she drove us not to mention we got KFC for free except the drink. The look on Kelly's face as if she had to pay it. I spent $25 on fast food lately. I heard it was the best game they saw. I agree. We were seating at the edge close to the gym entrance dooo so it was easy for Gail to spot me. She surprised me with an attention greeting HI. I felt like I had to shake her hands. I told her,a dum move , "I saw your friends up there, "where", up there." … as if why so. I saw Jacob; I melted ~~by~~ but I can't believe I went to academic League at lunch insted of A to J when he greeted me across the way over, "Hi Heralyn hows it going." I didn't even have feeling for the guy. It was a dub move. Last club meeting we as a group hold hands to pray. I took the chance of sitting next to him. So this is how it feel like holding hands with one of your crush… All I know is I can't have any distractions right now and it never turns it like the way I want it to be even B-Day wishes . . . can't come true. No Fairytale I'm sick of it. Get REAL !

I went to the Mall with my Mom. I wanted an Airwalk shoe ($80)but I wanted more. Then she argues about thethey way I wear. I feel low when someone especialy her tells me whats wrong about myself coz I dont need someone to tell me about my flawless defeat. I should have took the shoe huh? I was thinking of that this morning but I'm glad I didn't coz I got something better.

To top the morning its 1:49 AM. Yesterday, after work I went with Helen to Boardwalk, crusin around to the Family Fun Center, Go Kart ride. I have to write it coz I ~~it was~~ had a great time. It was nice of her to treat me and to top it off her brother race us home and I got worried if we were pulled over or any accident. But it was FUNNN ! I spent $25 that night. It was a wise decision instead of tonight coz I would have to cancel it anyway and hopefully I will have a chance to go to one concert in my Junior Year. I'm planning on having a Bowling Party next week. I'm not spending $25 for my friends some don't exist in the next years of my life. YOU CAN ONLY HAVE A FEW GOOD FRIENDS I LEARN THAT HARD WAY and REALIZING ALL THESE FRIENDS AKA CLASSMATES/SCHOOLMATES DON'T LAST-NO LIFETIME WARRANTY.

NEED I NEED MORE TO SAY-GOOD Night! ALAS PORYORICH! WHATEVER! IT'S 2:05. I'M seventeen, full of confidence, hope, hapiness, faith, leadership, knowledgeable, etc. I CAN BE ANYBODY I WANT TO BECOME. NO ONE CAN STOP ME.I'M READY TO MOVE ON. Thanks Mr. Hoss.

Feb. 19, 1997

Today was a really weird day for me. It always seems like I'm there, then here but I'm really not prepared inspirationaly (it's gone-almost vanishing into tin air) academically, motivated but I am well aware of the facts. Weekends are so short now, not like before.

I'm so lucky to go the Unity Community Breakfast Forum. Considering I had to beg for it. It would mean a lot in my future goals and benefit from it. I loved the speakers, it's nice to see them as leaders being positive role models for us- future generations coz we are the leaders of the world. How we went for ice cream in Thrifty to kill time it made my tummy happy with what I had in Hilton Hotel for that 'awful' breakfast except the muffins. Aside from that I met new friends. I went to Human Relation Task Force meeting at 3PM -5PM today with Mrs. Villegas and Mrs. Martinez. It was crazy how they fight. Showing up first in time in the meeting I investigate and hopefully I'll bring up questions next time. I predict ANYTOWN will be here I hope so. As you can see I had a purpose of being a student and I took it as a serious responsibility. The looks on Mr.Matz. Face today and Mrs. Villegas all they want is a program. They care coz they know there making a difference and the people I saw today and a Few encounterment with them to talk are making a great ideal "diversity" as community members. That's what I learned and develop to pursue with the club success, activity supporting it, my student responsibility I want to…, and with this experience today I CAN USE IT AS A BUILDING BLOCK FOR TOMMORROW. MY GOAL TO BECOME a politician. I'll never forget U.S. attorney of Cal. Face when I ask a ??? from him. He told me "good luck" I want my academic stressed to the strongest strength as a big block to a path of success as well as like in my community → That's my Destiny-then GLOBALLY

[I scream RACISM STILL EXIST TODAY !!!]

* Does diz mean diz book gets to be #1 on AMAZON. COM ... probably not...... why ? my money & trying?

Feb. 23, 1997

Pretty darn crazy short weekend. I started out on Fri after school to RECOLLECT THE PUZZLES I STARTED LONG TIME AGO and the puzzles I lost, I need TO FIND. I NEVER REALIZED HOW MUCH WORK I needed to fished. If I didn't started this week then WhEN? It will be just another weekend. I started out on Fri after school to RECOLLECT THE PUZZLES I STARTED LONG TIME AGO and the puzzles I lost, I need TO FIND. I NEVER REALIZED HOW MUCH WORK I needed to finished. If I didn't stated this week then WheN? It will be just another weekend. But I accomplished something GOOD for myself & my future. I hope I get some scholarships recognitions, more conferences,, trips for me. I BELIEVE IN WHAT IM DOING IS A GREAT RESPONSIBILITY and HONOR TO BE A LEADER, SOMEBODY WHO IS ME CARES ABOUT MY SCHOOL, COMMUNITY, the people and ALL COZ OF A FUTURE I DRED FOR SO LONG, A DREAM, A GOAL I WANT TO ACHIEVE (AIR FORCE ACADEMY) TO KEEP IT ALIVE NO MATTER WHAT. I SUFFERED CONSEQUENCES ENOUGH AND STUMBLED and FALLEN UPON MY WEAKNESSES. WHAT AM I SUPPOSE TO DO. GIVE UP ! NO WAY ! I gotten this far in life. I don't care about the people who think I'm no good for this and I must move on from my mistakes and weaknesses coz it's the only best way. THIS MEANS A LOT TO ME. TO GIVE UP EVERYTHING I STARTED SO I COULD BE THE BEST APPLICANT EVER IS A MISTAKE; ITS JUST THROWING YOUR LIFE AND EVERYTHING YOU REPRESENT. WHATEVER IT TAKES ! COUNT ME FOR IT ! I'M STRONG, A LEADER, HARD-WORKER, KIND, HONEST and DETERMINED AND MANY MORE. I SUFFERED, GOT BEAT UP, STAND UP, BEAT UP, STAND UP and FALLEN etc. OKAY, THIS TIME IM STAYING STANDING PROUD AND NO ONE WILL STAND IN MY WAY, ONLY ME KNOWS THE WAY COZ it's my DESTINY. I FEEL IT IN MY-MY HEART ITS FOR ME. LORD JESUS THANK YOU FOR GIVING ME A VISION OF ME, anything is possible. THANK YOU FOR GIVING ME THE GUIDANCE I NEEDED. I HAVE DESTINY I'M WILLING TO TAKE A RISK AND A MISSION YOU SELECTED ME FOR THIS WORLD. I'M VERY OPEN TO VISIONS AND IDEAS AND I HOPE TO HAVE MORE SO PLEASE HELP ME. THANK YOU.

Feb.28, '97

Today is the last day of Febuary then it will be March. Days go by so fast. I would never thought I would make the toughest decision as early like this moth towards my life. I knew, I wanted to be in the military but I don't know what branch I will be on depending on how good I do and which scholarships I get or the academy's. O I choosed the Air Force thinking that was better than others next to Marines and Navy but isn't that how my mind is program from other sources. Asking Mr. Hoss yesterday; that day but still had a doubt of it. I told him today and he said, "Youre decision you ~~will~~ should not regret it or doubt, if you don't then have all the power in the universe." I'll remember that always. I was happy of how my Mom supported me but I hope she understand of oth week BCT this summer and one weekend a month. That's the hard part.

THIS LAST 2 weeks had been the longest and it took me that long to decide. I will HAVE NO REGRETS AT ALL JOINING THE ARMY NATIONAL GUARD. You know what's ironic the Lord has showed me is that I ranked Air Force Academy (most likely to get into) ROTC scholarship (and least likely to get- weird). But West Point I consider it toughest one and I wanted to apply just For the heck of it, that was a Dumb thought. That's one of my weakness; limiting myself to the highest. MAKING WP is the ultimate goal-it means everything I worked for that would make me the top applicant with all my might and when I stumbled and fallen then got up so I could keep up not limiting myself into anything. It would mean the hardest times of my high school for preparation could give me a relief/satisfaction WHEN I GET ACCEPTED IN THE WESTPOINT. I hope I get the Army ROTC scholarship coz I need it desperately for back up if I don't make it to West Point but applying for WP in college will be harder because only about top 5 year get selected from ROTC ARMY. I hope the Army National Guard will me an advantage towards that goal & beyond and hope ~~my~~ till make a big impact in my senior year.

TONIGHT I WAS GLAD I WENT TO THE KEY CLUB CONCLAVE. KEY CLUB- HA! HA! Key Club- I get it. IT WAS AN OPPORTUNITY TO SEE HOW GREATLY IMPACT I HAVE TOWARDS MY EL CAP KEY CLUB as a Leader, a pres. And service to the community in which I possess greatly. EL CAP REPRESENTED the last rank I want to boost EL CAP and Pump up for next year. HOW? WHAT? I need a vision I don't want to pride ~~my~~ our club of who has the ~~best~~

rank #1 or close but I want a vast improvements not by points but by growth … I was suppose to do that speech but ~~I~~ didn't happen.

FULL POWER NEXT MONTH and many more great days. HERALYN, changing from (1) I am now ARE YOU FIRED UP FOR IT? Just Don't forget to keep your heads up. (2) to change in future.

MARCH 2, 1997 4:37 P.M.

I hate how fast Sat. & Sun. goes by so fast especially when you work and have to do other stuff at the same time. IT'S GREAT HOW I TRIED MY BEST TO PREPARE FOR MY FUTURE. Iglued 3 of my latest fortune cookie message. TO ME IT REPRESENT HOPE. I'm playing this game like this: I clean my room, to eliminate trash I don't need, I throw away schedule paper to do list in my past in which I tried to do so hard, I create an organized and flexible atmosphere for myself by doing this. It's great how I'm going on a 8th week boot camp. I'm excited but I must not waste my unfinished business in my Junior years which will reflect my achievements and success in the summer, senior year and the future for me and the well-being of my school. I cannot tell what lies ahead for me and what challenges I take in this whole responsibility the path I chose. I'm not afraid- My courage will grow !

March 12, 1997 (8:35 PM)

Today was the big event I waited for so long. I was very glad I did this and once again this was one of my genious idea to write an article about it. I did procrastinated a little with preparing for this event but I made it according to my well- thought plan. I wanted this, and I ~~would~~ did my potential best to make this happen. What A crazy day IT WAS. Spending 7 ½ hours in a Clasy Hotel for a typical student on a school day to cover up a very important event and more important than I thought it ever was. I'm really tired right now and my bottom up the spinal cord hurts. Probably coz I was sitting most of the time.

I was really glad of getting a ride from **KARI JENSON**; just to drive us there early morning just made my moring. This was the only way to get there coz it's impossible to get there in time for the luncheon, the only way was getting there early morning. Plus, we would get free breakfast if we chow up at the Leadership Forum sponsored by the National Conference. I told them later we weren't suppose to be there: A valuable indeed, It's not what you know, it's who you know. Though this violates the rule of code ethic of society of Pro Journalist still it help me understand more about the NATIONAL CONFERENCE. I trly appreciate how hospitable, wonderful & great people they represent. The topic→***Diversity*** was very delecate/ sensitive coz it's very terriotorial for every person and a big problem. Other than my 2 colleagues are not interseted about it. I hated waiting for 3 hours in the lobby. I'm happy that they invited us to do this and free food that is not worth $30 plate each. I'm glad I didn't pay for Hilary coz I would have felt bad. I didn't realized how much impact, me as a young amatuer journalist towards the conference, this day and everything it stands for in general. It was an unforgettable experience and to be a part of it means something valuable: something I will carry and lead on in the future. I can't believe we were surrounded by journalists, community leaders, bussiness people, etc. who got invited.

I can't believe I talked to one of the Lady in KNSD, 7-39 Susan, she is so nice and sweet. I felt uncomfe and supid just coz she was there interviewing her. It was a highlight for me. She ~~mention~~ responded why she became a journalist because she was curious about the world about the TRUTH and us journalist have the responsibility to represent the TRUTH. I like that no wonder why I fit the profile of a journalist, CURIOUS RUNS in me always I wonder if I ever thought of becoming a Pro journalist. If I did in which are: T.V., paper etc. If I did I guarantee you, it will be an ambitious one and I must work hard to achieve and also I had to be one of the best. But I really have no regret coz I choosen something really important portraying a role as a leader. I aked myself many times already if I know I will be portrayed as a loyal political leader, someone with great leadership and ETC. IN WHAT WAYS WILL I BE ABLE TO DO THAT. WHAT IS MY ULTIMATE TASK FOR THIS NATION, OTHER NATIOIN, MY NATION THE WORLD in contributions? That vision will come true and right now I will ~~pre~~ prepare myself for my future. I hope this article will be the best one yet and I hope I will realized how much this will impact my life and journalism.

FOR THE PAST DAYS NOW I REALIZED how much I need to do to achieve my goal and the GREAT RIVER I WILL CROSS. TODAY at the Chinese Food I got this fortune cookie, IT said just that.

☺ I HOPE I DON'T DROWN AND IF I START TO, LORD I HOPE I CAN GRAD INTO SOMETHING TO BREATHE as early as possible and I NEED TO GET MY STRENGTH to get it more importance: REMIND ME RIGHT NOW.

April 4, 1997 (9:31 P.M.)

I wished I could record/ write every minute of my life in my journal so you would understand my feelings, my lifestyle, my sorrows, my desires, my rapture ness, in generaL MY LIFE.

It's weird ! → what I did today or spring break may not be remembered vividly in my heads always. Since time goes by so fast, one week is just one day. So just for the record let me tell you my Spring Break '97.

March 28th (Fr.) we had a half day. Afterschool would be going to the beach with Elizabeth and Danielle but just as I predicted it would not happen. Danielle couldn't use the car so I was out. Well, I didn't want to go to volunteer at the Library coz I needed to prepare for Hilary's 16th B-Day party. When I got home from taking the bus, I decided I would give Hilary another gift anyway. I spend $12 of ballons and a candle mushroom. The party was fun. I enjoyed the pizza and the cheese cake. I loved the movie. FOXFIRE. Boys /GIRLs and Hate movie was okay. I went home 11PM & I had to go to work the next day morning at 8AM-4PM. The Saturday was just work day then when I got home from work I just kickback and relax in my room and watched T.V. The next day was Easter Sunday. Jamie and I was supposed to go to the mall so I got up early to get dressed. Well almost early about 9 A.M. but I waited 12 PM for them to show up. Jamie didn't wanted to go because she doesn't have money. I still planned on going by myself to take the bus. It was one of those DAYS DECIDING WHAT THE REST OF THE DAY WOULD BE LIKE A FLICK OF A FINGER. I went to MCDo to buy the famous #5 meal I think it was a waste of money then waited for the bus. The bus got there alright except I walked away and went back to Marlyn's apartment to see what Jamie was up to. They watched MATILDA. I gave the kids the gummy bears and TWIX I bought from my Mom's $10 money she gave me partly coz she want caramel apple but I inted to ~~give~~ buy her one this Sun Day or Tomorrow. Jamie's Mom invited me to have dinner there. It was free. After watching Matilda we went to Stizler Park (past my school 3 miles from Barona). Jamie and her Mom had argument about Jamie's Dad (Nicole's father is Jamie's Stepdad) Lucky Jamie got a Dad her age but I didn't have one. Her Dad sounds okay to me coz he's caring about her even thouh Jamie's not his real daughter. Marlyn pointed out to me as an example I to Jamie I had no father and I turned out okay. We ate Dinner and watched Jack movie Rented. I rented 2 other action movie in which we didn't really watched when Jamie and I get to my house. Jamie spend the night over my house. We ~~do~~ planned to go to Riverview school to have a pinic. I turned to be an all day of fun unexpected things. Hanging out with 2 ten yrs. Old. Did I have a life ? Siayra was too much for her age. Hiking up hills and going under a fence that below to you is a dam. How supid I was. I had fun and not to mention the stinky Hallway of Hell next to Lucky's. I had to work on Monday that day at 5P.M. Kelly and I ran in the morning. Well at 10-11:30 A.M. We went to a Kiwanis Breakfast before we ran. It was a fundraising event for Key Club. ($50) On Weds. I saw LIAR, LIAR movie with Kelly and Kelly's brother. I went to Wal-Mart with Marlyn and her 2 daughers and she even gave me free dinner at Apple-bees. It was the best hot wings I've tasted.

I wondered why she's so nice to me and invites me to places with her and kids. Maybe she wanted Jaime and me to have fun and be friends. I asked Jaime to spend the night again. We watched Beverly Hills 90210 show. The next day I went to Ross with my Mom & Judy (My Mom's new friend) I was so hungry I went to eat buy food at Arby's spend the day with Jaime. On Thurs. Me and Kelly took the bus to Ross and tried to see if there's any good movie to watch but turned down because we weren't old enough. (NO ID). Sat. morning I had to work and stayed home lazy that day. The best kick-off of the Spring break was going to the ARMY NATIONAL GUARD with Sgt. MCGraw. Hilary's Dad. That day I realized this would be a carrer I will truly like. NO DOUBT ABOUT IT. The tip of the ICEBERG. I loved those bigton U.S. Army trucks. Sitting inthose hammers were quite a trill. Watching how they put an engine in the truck and how they work as a team. I met everybody there. The supply room; I wished I had those uniform with me now. The library is actually a trailor full with important manual in serial code #'s. Keeping track of them. This would be my job. I'm not so sure what else my duty really is yet. Meeting the 1st Sergeant and the Captain was awesome. These were the highest ranking people I've met so far in the military. Next to the recruiting office's If I had to choose to take place of one of the job there. I have to be the CAPTAIN< The UNIT COMMANDER. IT'S WHO I AM and WHAT I STAND AND WANT FOR. I have to be the leader. I love being a leader and love to lead. I have to be on top of all the Rest. That shows you as a 17 yrs. old tells you how high my ambition is. I could see it now Capt. Heralyn, unit commander # baltallion, B company or something bigger. I wondered what it would be like to be a Colnel or a General, 5'2" (if I don't shrink) a big shot. I never met one. ~~People~~ I mean soldiers were nice to me; I asked questions & they gave me advice. I wished I remember this Sgt. Name but he told me about Officer's Candidate School and said

"Character is everything." He spoke softly and clearly so I had to listen carefully. I told Sgt. McGraw I saw the new lady recruiter who replaced Sgt. Wynnhammer look mean but truthfully I was uncertain and nervous to meet her. But I'm glad she's a female, shes like a role model to me now. She helps me motivated since the day I met her. She was nice to me. She's from Virginia and has a Virginian accent. She's only live in California for 4 years. I can't believe shes 34 yrs. old but she looks around 25-27. She said if you exercise and eat right you'll look young. Yeah! That's something to look forward to. She got an opportunity to goto OCS but didn't 2 ½ years of college only. IF she did she could become a Capt. but I guess it varies with different people in their ambition in life. Every opportunity counts to me but this one is just beginning. I'll make it to West Point and I should be able to go to the Prep School because that's a chance for me to review high school academic and prepare for the rigorous & demanding experience in WP it will give me an opportunity to what I learn 4 years in WP will give me leadership skills, high standards of academic, challenge etc. I want to PLAN SO I COULD STAY AHEAD OF EVRYBODY ELSE. I WANT TO ACHIEVE THE IMPOSSIBLE to be possible. I will be tested. I might not get it, (Rhodes Scholar) but if not I hold I will get the TRUMAN in my Junior Year and a scholarship of graduate degree-masters degree. I WONDERED WHAT IT WOULD BE LIKE TO ACHIEVE THE HIGHEST RANK in Cadet Corps Capt. This cadet must be one heck of a great leader along with spectacular grades and impressive military performance. I HOPE it will be me. That day I felt like a soldier. Like the lady in the ARMY commercial, "Fell the Ribbon beneath your chest, you will be the soldiers ~~there~~… that gone before you. You will be a soldier." Something like that. I felt a sense of pride and honor during the formation saluting the flag. The flag- I wanted to feel freedom. That day It really click why I want to join the ARMY. I was glad I came. . .

On April 8, Tues, I scheduled an appointment. They picked me up from my ~~house~~ apartment at 3 P.M. I remember that place so vividly. This is where I will believe it happens so fast too soon. This school year is ARMY style ~~was~~ fashion. I wanted to have my own pair of boots & ARMY pants. What I got WAS MORE THAN I ASK FOR. This coming end of school year: I will be a soldier. All have all those uniform. I guess, be careful for what you wish for……. It's weird how life is. THIS PAST MONTHS HAS BEEN A TURNING POINT IN MY LIFE. I think it's un expected and ironic. I WAS AFRAID TO CHANGE MY GOALS, especially my ultimate guide to DESTINY. I wanted to be in the AIR FORCE, then suddenly thse 2 RecRuiters came to my school and I had the urge to walk into Mrs. Coffin-Prince to meet them. Why Not? I've been talking to them when they come to my school from different branches. It would help increase my knowledge . There's nothing to loose as long as I stick to the (AIR FORCE ACADEMY(plan. I shook their hands & I introduced myself to them. They said they were from te ARMY NATIONAL GUARD. I never heard of them They have this thing for Juniors can go to boot camp and serve reserve (1 weekend a month) I DOUBT THEM BUT I NEEDED THE MONEY BUT WHAT ABOUT AIR FORCE. I WAS AFRAID TO CHANGE MY GOALS COZ IT MEANT a lot to me. This turning point was a big question WHY? I gotten advice from my teacher, Mr. Hoss to help me make my decision. He didn't tell me what I should do BUT HE SHOWED ME TO WHERE I WOULD GET MY ANSWER. THAT IS ME (the answer) I can't believe how great things has happended to me. The challenge was to would have to put my ambitions higher and every standards to be higher. I have to go to WP. Stupid me, I limit my standard of not going to WP coz it was the best academy, a lot of people apply etc. I didn't want to go to WP because I didn't think I was good enough especially in academics. FROM THEN ON EVERYTHING I STAND FOR IS HIGHER THAN I THOUGH to Be AND I KNEW I WILL GRADUATE in WP. Being in National Guard will increase my chances of ~~the~~ getting there and spot to Prep school or an ARMY ROTC scholarship to go to VMI= (I would be the next 5th, 6th, …. Female) I DON'T CARE WHAT OTHER PEOPLE WHO IS IN OTHER BRANCHES OR NOT ABOUT ME joining the ARMY might not be the way to go. I ∧ Believe I SERVE A PURPOSE IN THIS WORLD TO Become one of the best leaders ever and I will be a soldier of what I DREAM TO BECOME. I know so. I went to the Chinese restaurant with Hilary and her Mom. I bought a fortune cookie It said: **YOU WILL BE SUCCESSFUL IN YOUR CARRER. Need I say More. I responded- I sould write a book- Heralyn's Fortune Cookies.**

APRIL 18th (FRI) 1997

What an awesome day. First time my name is on the newspaper as one of the assistant editors. Took the Chemistry test and didn't catch the bus. I ~~watched~~ walked with disappoinment to the library so I could call Sgt. J. Maynered thinking she's probably on her way to get me. Trying to catch my breath and sweating using the phone to call, I thought my day is done. But I was halfway through it. I sold a candy from the Librarian. It so happen. I had to miss the bus so I could get my reward from volunteering. I got a pateful of cookies & hershy kisses with a red ribbon. Covered with foil and a certifcate for volunteering. It made my day. I walked halfway home, took the bus at the Dairy Queen so I could be there home in time. I was in a hurry so I was kind of rude to Stanley when he wanted to buy a candy from me. He said it was a rip-off. OH WELL ! He finally showed up. Her truck TOYOTA RANGER, IS AWESOME. ~~I~~ This is what I would get as my

2nd car when I turned 30. I lost 2 pounds and 1.5% body fat in 10 days. WOW ! I got a coffe mug printed **"ARMY NATIONAL GUARD**." I was happy. I got my paycheck from McDo. My friends and I went to a Mexican restaurant and off to The rodeo. I felt blame by Hilary coz I said 9PM would be over. Knowing Kellys parents had to pick us up. But it was a bummer taking pictures even though I got in for free. The next thing I know, the night was over. I thought they would call me to go to bondfire with them. I spend my weekend writing letters, going to the church and to National City(suburb of San Diego… I think!. It's school time again. I have a bad headache and I'm sick, I got the colds. Jaime's 10th B-Day party was fun. It was a chance for me to be young again. What a slumber party would mean to me if I was 10 like her. Although (me & Jaime) we had the same thing in common= (our father's didn't give a dam about us, I don't think she went to the same thing or understand what it feels like. I'm jeaulous because she has a Dad and has Grandaparents. Only thing I had really at her age was my MOM. Yes, My Mom means everything to me. Jaime's Grandma reminded me of Mama Maria. I remember at the hospital, like I knew she was saying Farewell to me and my Mom at age 11. ♥She knew my life will be great. I miss her and her food. It was nice to know that someone cared about my ambitions. Jaime's Grandma told me; she admired how I have great ~~admission~~ ambition in life . I wish my Mom could tell me that but she will. My Mom is great. My relatives were great. I miss Lali & Tani and I miss my →homeland [PHILIPPINES]. Thanks GrandMa Maria & Thank you Lord…It feels like my headache is goone It felt like you /we me or you were next to me but you didn't want me to be scared. It's nice to know and remember you again. I hope I can talk to you mindly without being scared. Good Night!

I hope I get to visit Jaime's grandma when I go to WP and Prep school. Oh by the way Mama Maria. Thank you for being there for me and my Mom. There's always a special place For you always in my heart. You filled my childhood memories with great things and a full stomach. I miss your adobo. No one makes the best adobo like you.

May 24th (Sat) 9:20 P.M.

I finally got my lazy butt to write my journal. It's been so long. TIME GOES BY FAST LIKE ALWAYS. There is a lot of things I would want to include stuff in my diary. How can I put 5 weeks into writing, just read along. I would advise myself maybe next time I write a journal day by day because I know my feelings ultimately and in the mood to write it.

Like always I have weekdays of school, work and weekends. I LEARNED TO ENJOY EVRY MOMNET OF IT, EVRY SECOND AND EVRY MINUTE ABD EVRYTHING CUNTS FOR ME NOW… EVERY OPPURTIONITY KNOKS. WHAT A LIFE I HAVE. I FEEL LUCKY… 3 years ago I went the wrong way to look for me, but I didn't know what I wanted. IT WAS VERY IMPORTANT GROWTH OF MATURITY ~~OF~~ FOR ME. I learned a lot, creid, I got knocked down, truimph, shove, push, stood up etc. and I FOUND ME. It was the ANSWER to my questions and my character depends upon the paths or Doors/ Roads I took or walk in. It turned out great. I never feel low no more and no one can knock me down . . . Did you hear me (as if I'm yelling to you) I MEAN NOBODY. I am tough, smart, kind, ambitious and much more. No criticizm of me or about me can bring me down not even my Mom keep reminding me I'm FAT. PROGRESS IS MADE IN VIRTUE. I WILL PROBABLY TALK MORE ABOUT A REVIEW ABOUT THESE PAST YEARS, specificilly in HIGHSCHOOL as a year in review this summer.

Well, anyway I lost a few pounds and I can run just about 2 miles with Kelly. We ran almost every day. It helped me more energetic and it feels great because I'm working towards a goal= and is a very important one. I never want to exchange anything about myself anymore. . . I'm Heralyn ! It feels great to be here and alive. I love my life. I have no regrets. . . I did all I could and I know I could have done better, and I did, I did a whole lot better than I thought I would… that's me- Heralyn. I'm unpredicatable! I really did try to balance things. . . And I did this towards the end of this school year. ITS NOT EASY. BUT I got more than I bargain for. I didn't have to bargain. . . I will get the BEST and ONLY THE BEST I DERSERVE IT and I WILL GO TO WEST POINT… WHATEVER IT TAKES. I KNOW I WILL. Ha! Ha!

I went with Kelly on THURS on Apr. 24 or 17 or something but I knewIt was on a Thurday coz I called in sick. Kelly invited me to go to a WESTPOINT PRESENTATION where they invited the outstanding top students in San Diego Area to get to know WP along with their parents are invited to come. Kelly got an invitation coz she got a 1450 on SAT and her

grades are awesome. I just went coz I want to go to WP and it will help me more info. I went with my letter Man's jacket and was the only one wearing it. It lasted for about 2 ½/-3 hours presentation. I meet 3 West Pointers. One was a major, who is a head rep. For this region of the country. He is.. . I don't know what's the word but if he was an action figure, he would glow in the dark and I felt his character glooming, by the way he act, talk, walk and his uniform made him twice the person he was. He was very re[S]pectable and highly person. It took him 13 yrs. To be a Major. I saw a vision of me, like ~~him~~ his glowness soul's is like me. Comprende. I would I will become a WEST POINTER. One of the rules I learn is never doubt epecially about yourself and your goals. The Major talked about WP and I pretty much knew about what he was talking about. "West Point… blah, blah… Duty, Honor, Country. This is what you.. And will be.. These 3 hollowed words… and I knew what he was talking ~~about~~ about as if I could ~~repeat~~ read his lips. It didn't matter if I was not invited, I got info, and It didn't matter ~~if~~ I was surrounded by very smart students with their proud parents. I'm just like them, have weaknesses, strengths, hopes, desires but I KNOW OUT OF ALL OF THISE STUDENTS and those WHO DIDN'T COME I AM THE ONE WHO WANTS TO GO TO WEST POINT MORE THAN ANYTHING ELSE IN THE WORLD, MORE THAN ANYONE OF THEM- RIGHT THEN, AT THAT MOMONET, NOW AND UNTIL THE DAY I WAIT, TRY, TRY, TRY, AND I WILL NEVER EVER GIVE UP TILL I GET THERE. I've chased dreams/goals and ambitions, but this one is the ULTIMATE, the BIGGEST ABOVE THE REST, THIS IS THE ONLY COLLE
GE I WANT TO GO TO. I CAN SAY THAT UNTIL I CHANGE MY MIND when I VISIT WP. I WILL CHANGE MY MIND and NOBODY WILL. I MEAN NOBODY ! I CAN SAY THIS , BECAUSE IF I LOSE IT, THSESE GOALS… I would rather die. I would lose what I STAND FOR, WHO I AM, MY CHARACTER, EVERYTHING ABOUT ME. THINK LIKE LOSING A PURPOSE IN ~~ANYTHING AN~~ THIS WORLD. I'm more sure than anyone of them. I feel this I'm the only person I know that desperately wants to go to W.P.

- I know what it takes to get the admission. I should. I DO coz I've spent gazillion hours, knowing, collecting, reading, analyzing, speculating, visualizing, dreaming, desperately wanting, holding these ULTIMATE PURPOSE TIGHTLY AND NEVER LET GO OF IT.

AND I SUFFERED FAILURES OF PREPARING MYSELF, I DREAD FOR THIS SO LONG, I DESERVE A SPOT TO PREP WP AND WP.

==================== ♥ ==========================

AUGust 19, 1997 (5:11 P.M.) Tues.

Have you ever done anything crazy or just simple things in your life or just pursue something, something not just important it may seem or just because but you just got to/ have to. This scrapbook of mine is one of those ideas as crazy as what is pasted on it; its important that I did it for my last lazy summer of my life. Also, I wanted to have my own time capsule to show my kids, my grandchildren, the world and just remembering what my past. I want to remember it, remember things or remember from reading what I wrote; remembering the past. I cherish my childhood and the crazy Fun times of being a teenager, **"An American Teenager,"** *knowing the fact I will never be young, I can never go back, not that I want to and knowing that the older I get, the more I become aware of who I am, what I want to become, what I'm capable of, my destiny, the more I get stronger and tougher, the more serious the problem I face. . . . everyday. The future is in my hands. How I had this idea of a scrapbook full of memories.*

NOTE 2 ME: (TO TALK ABOUT MY SCRAPBOOKS, A TOPIC DISCUSSION IN MY 2ND INDY MOVIE "MY VENTI FRAPINOA SKETCHDEZORTDRUNKENPHRENIA WEEKENDS 1") CHER (?, HA!HA!) or HEF (PLAYBOY FOUNDER) HAS A SCRAP BOOK. I COULD COMPARE & CONTRAST IT TO MINE.

Well, about 4 or 5 weeks ago I did my final summer cleaning, eliminating what to throw or keep. What I found was the past just collecting notes I wanted to keep from LMS, my middle school and a few of my Holy Spirit School stuff. My resourceful always keep me organize. One of the things I wanted to do, I mean two of those was to write poems and draw/ paint again. I didn't expect to recreate my past, to *remember memories. I just want to hold on, looking back was so dramatic for me. Especially that one night I found 2 folders containing signatures and messages of Holy Spirit School. It had drawings of a troll wearing a short and T-shirt with emblem of the school. It even have a helmet. Every time I look at it, and read what they say I just began to cry because what happen was. . . . Whats the word I'm looking for, a confusing period of my life. I came here to U.S. at age 12, on December 17, 1992. The first land I step on in U.S. was the airport of Detroit, Michigan. My Mom pronounced it Dit-ri-yot when my step dad asked her on the phone where our destinations stops to get to Columbus, OHIO. My Mom bought a lottery ticket again and she keeps getting $5 back of how much she put in to buy those tickets most of the times. As for me, ~~and~~ I reminded my Mom before we already won the lotto. Look where we are now. We are in America, "The Land of the Free." It is always my belief as a child "The land of Destiny", "The land of hope" "The Promise Land" I always remind myself these great things because at this point of my life I found a dream, I found hope and I'm waiting for the answer.* ***I remember the last day of school at USC-GHS. My classmates saying Good-byes, my friends I left behind, the teachers who I will no longer see no more etc. I don't think I cried, I don't remember it all just a few segments of it. I remember*** *my science class telling a student in my group, " You have to be the group leader now," not me anymore. She said "Well, ain't you coming back." I looked at her and chucked almost laughing "NO, I'm staying there for good." OF course, the short conversation was in Cibuano dialect. I stood outside my school where you can cross the street. I looked back , it hit me thinking, "Wow I can't believe it, I just had to looked back at my school saying Good-bye. I probably stood there for 30 seconds or a minute because I remember it vividly. It reminded me now how did I ever became a group leader of 6 or 5 students in my Science class. It reminded me also I was a group leader in my home EC class because I just had to volunteer & because nobody wanted to speak up or raise their hands.*

☺*A LESSON: SOMEONE HAS TO LEAD, TO SPEAK UP, TO BE THE ONE RESPONSIBLE.*

Even though opportunities pass by before I didn't hold on or someone just had it such as in kindergarten I wanted to be Sgt. Of Arms, (a ~~type of~~ Rank of School/ class of five) someone got it so many times in grade 1-6 to hope I was a treasurer in class or class officer but someone had it. Someone always gets it. Like in Art, I so long wanted to win something or first place but someone is better. Those are just a couple of examples in school while the rest of my childhood years was quite harsh in which I will tell you more and much better.

I really didn't know how to start an opening, just started writing, "now and later" knowing the afternoon fades to tonight. I had this vision 50 years from now of my journals into a book published. I wish I could write a book, I wish for a lot of things. Do you know what I wish for right now more than anything: "I wish I'm enrolled at WP Prep knowing it and reminding myself on June 18, 1998 on my Graduation Day. Is that to much to ask. When I thought of this scrapbook, I didn't know what will be on it. I thought also of "elemination" collection of things I rejected. I don't know about it now because its just paper stuff. I remember now, 6 weeks ago I listen to "this American Life" topic about people who collect other people's trash or stuff they found in cars that had old letters or collecting what people would throw away. Anyway this is how I kind of soRt of gotta had an idea of this scrap book.

To continue my story . . . . I think we left that night of my last day of school to go to Manila. "Manila" the capital of Philippines. We stayed there for almost a week. It's a requirement to pass the interview in the U.S. Embassy. It was a vacation for me. My Mom, my Mom's friend (shes my teachers sister who my mom acquantance with ~~sin~~ from needing help from filing papers requires for passport to getting us to Manila, its her job) and I stayed in this apt. called Bel-Air Apartment. My Moms friend has connection to people around the place close to the embassy. I ~~have~~ had a good time especially the fast food we eat. I was glad I finally got to see M A N I L A. I got to go to LRT (a railway transportation), biggest Malls in the country. Some say it is owned by Imelda Marcos just the same with Cebu Plaza Hotel, a 5 star hotel in Cebu. Who knows! The next thing I remember I was on a plane to Seoul, South Korea. We had to wait for 2 hours, something like that to get to Detroit, Michigan. It was weird how we left at Manila the same date Dec. 17 and got to Columbus,

Ohio on Dec. 17 that night. I think we arrived at 11PM or 10 PM. My StepDad was working for a security company. The 15 hour or around 15-20 hours of flight was tiring. It was really at that point of my life: weird , "somebody pinch me"!. I knew I wasn't dreaming ~~coz~~ because I felt my stomach in the air. I was excited to go see U.S. I really make this feeling alive.

W O W ! ! ! I'm happy, I was smiling. I always had the window. This was my third airplane trip. Did I mention how "Lucky" I am because it change my life. America? The airport was huge, it was nightime so the airport wasn't crowded at all. My step dad picked us up in the airport wearing his Pinkerton Security uniform and his patrol car. A white police car without the sirens; just simple white car with the Pinkerton emblem design on each side of the doors. I really didn't notice that time at the airport. He drives different cars coz they are numbered and sometimes the car is the car is the look of the police car and sometimes just the plain old white. I was glad he bought KFC fried chicken "extra crispy." It was sitting in the back, a bucket full of fried chicken. I was hungry. I was surprise how the American highways are humungus. I didn't wear a seatbelt so I slip to the other side when he turn to exit a freeway/ or highway. He live in this tiny apartment. It wasn't a bother to me or notice it was tiny because before I lived in tiny/small houses before. I was just glad. He took us to where he does this security job. The area in town was fairly small, it had a Big and Tall store, a music store, Radio Shack and around it are fast food places, malls streets across the place. They were really friendly. These people who run the music store even gave us a Christmas gift full of godies. I had 2 weeks before I have to go back to a new school to finish the 2nd half of my 6th grade. My step dad enrolled me to Holy Spirit School. Since it's a chatholic school, expenses for enrollment are expensive. I didn't have any clue to what the next 8 months will be for me at Columbus, Ohio. I remember the big tall trees. I guess they were pine trees, an array of these trees close by where I lived noticing them always as we drove by over a bridge. The school was at least 5 minutes drive away. Entering the parking lot, straight ahead was the school, the very first thing I noticed was the church and the small chapel on the opposite sides entering the parking lot. Behind the church was a softball field. It was my first visit to the school. The principal showed us the classrooms, library, the gym, even the music rooms, one had a piano for *piano lessons, the second one was a little bigger where music class was held. I was enrolled in for piano lessons. My piano teacher comes once or twice in a week. I had one hour during Wednesday almost every other week or once or once a month. I'm not sure but I do know it was always during science class in Miss Pishitelli. I never understand the computer concepts in Math. I don't quite remember what we did. We, as the entire school, the 8th-5th graders will participate in a play "Oklahoma." My step dad even rented a costume. It was the heaviest and pretiest costume there. I hated the hat, it made me look goofy. He was upset coz I didn't wear it. He spend, I think $5 to rent it (just the hat). The way of teaching from them till 8th grade got harder but not even close in comparison to what I went through USC-GHS. It seem easy but not so difficult of what I learn in school in Holy Spirit. I was glad to have fun times especially at lunch times. We would play soccer in the softball field where it was grassy. It was fun but I'm the kind of person who would sweat a lot. It was embarrassing at times. They even have a small playground next to the church outside. There was this swing tires. I was dizzy, dizzy. They would spin me push me back and forth.*

(NOTE: REDO ABOVE 4 "SPEECHLESS" URANUSMARTIAN ME /LINDSAY LOHAN , JUST LIKE HER CHARACTER/CH. AS FORREST GUMPY ' I KNOW WHAT MODELING IS ABOUT?' IN "A.D.I.J.T.S.")

[A.D.I.J.T.S. MEANS __?_-> SEE SLANG-VOCAB GUIDELINE PAGE]
FUCK THAT! IT MEANS A BROKEN ASS ASSASIN, DIRTY LITTLE GIGANTIC SECRETS, JUST ONE MORE,THE DON MAMAS, SLEPPING WITH YOUR SEX THERAPIST

But I never puked. Of course, in every school in this world everyone is part of a group "click" of friends doing fun stuff together or just the way it is. This was a punch in the face for me coz I was shy gRowing up. I don't remember how to approach to people, to be sociable. It hurt me emotionally. It sucks. It was tough. I cry about it. I remember I had to ~~back~~ to the restroom because I was crying. I have this tendency of crying over things/problems and I can be easily hurt emotionally. Please remember I'm not the same person 4+ years ago. I'm writing this the way it was. It's hard feeling like an outcast. I don't feel the same way now because I already put it behind me and I'm completely different now. It was tough but I learned a big chunk of character and

personality, myself and the perpectives. To go back to my story . . . My teacher, who is and was and always, Mrs. McLaughlin helped me understand. I had a low self-esteem of myself, she lifted it up. She's always an inspiration to me. She told my classmates. It worked. I felt like they pity me but they helped me, ~~get~~ lifting up my spirit. It felt good, I belong. **I finally recover but I have to move to California. I was excited but uncertain. My memories of OHIO is always in me. Stepping my shoes on snow.**
Making a snowman. I love the winter despite of coldness. Spring was beautiful there. Colorful in my eyes. The smell of rain. The thunder and dark clouds never get me into panic but sometimes the east part of U.S. is known *for the hurricanes, or that gigantic twirly thing , I don't know what we call it. Once or twice but never destructive. I miss my classmates. Of who they were 4 years ago. Jeffrey Howatt wrote me a letter to feel better telling one classmate not to make fun of the food I brought foR lunch. I showed him how to whistle using hands, making music by using both hands put close together and blow in the hole. He can do it better than I can. Beth Sandman- isn't that a funky name, Jenny Obbagy just a few of my classmates my friends. I can't believe that dictionary calculator erased their address. I wonder what they are doing now. Of course, I'm graduating and they are in their junior year. I wonder where Mrs. McLauglin is now. She's probably working as a teacher in the same school. I hope. I would like to see these people. I played softball. I never played any sports in my life. It was so much fun. It totally sucked at first but athletes get better by playing more and more. It was for Spring season. My teammates were very supportive, my coach was too. I played softball, it was my first practice yesterday. I caught my first fly ball when it should be, it wasn't mine to catch but she said nice catch. I'm not sure if it was my* 1st *catch but it felt good. I got to play as a catcher in a practice game. But I played left out fielder. I wanted to continue playing it here in California but its just not the same. El Cap Girls softball is #1 I league, the best players around but the schedule was not for me. Maybe college (club or team) but I never understand how the ball went too fast for me. My Step Dad bought me Pizza because we had our big game.* **I made a homerun for 1 point ~~and~~ because got into first base. It clique I got to second, then third, then homerun. I can feel my adrenaline going. I was born competitive, giving one best shot. It always fired me** *up for batter up. My Dad says I shouldn't feel bad, that*

sports isn't important later on life. He always made me feel better. I love Taco Bell. I love the food here. I met George and his wife, my Dad's brother who lived in Cillicohote, Ohio, about 1 to 2 hours drive from Columbus. The houses, what my Mom says boxes. Lucky him he had a nice warm house. I played computer games there. Her wife would cook food for an afternoon dinner. She asked me, "Are you anxious to go to school." I said yes, not knowing what anxious mean. She was a nice person. I didn't like his other brother. His wife looked at me if I would use fork because she put it in the plate : She said we use our hands to eat chickens or do you use fork. I don't know, you had to be there.

I'm glad that they liked my artwork (my classmates and my teacher Mrs. McLaughlin). Because I never got that attention about my artwork before in my old school. I was beginning to believe, hey! I can do this. I can draw and paint. I had done different drawings and showed it to the class but I never expect Mrs. McLaughlin to put it display outside. I got a kick out of that. I did a drawing of Paul Lawrence Dunbar, an African-American poet. It was a project I worked with Nikkie. She did a rapping composing about his life and I did the drawings. It was my very first recognition award and displayed. I REALLY WANT TO DO SEROIUS [serious] ARTWORK as a hobbie as well as WRITING. I just don't know exactly what I wanna draw, I'm more realistic like an impressionist in creativity than imaginistic. I would love to use these skills for unselfishness reasons. I share something. I would love to DRAW or create that would help mankind, the world. I really don't have a plan yet it hasn't fully create any vision in my head. In my old school, I worked so hard to be a top student because it meant a lot to me with also my art talents and I never got the full satisfaction until I came here. I was an Honor student in Holy Spirit school. I always have this drive for perfection, the best! I'm happy to be able to cope it now. It ruined what I was capable of getting. The grades coz I only want the best. I have a good attitude about it now. If I get a B, that's great and I can do better next time without feeling bad of wishing an A. I was upset Because I wanted to get the Gold Honor Award instead I get 2nd Silver Honor Award. [{{{ YOU WANTTT THEEE GOOOLLLDDD HERALYN!!!! U WANT THE FUCKING OSCAR!!!}} }January 13, 2007, 7:33 PM, SAT] I should have been happy than comparing myself to others wishing they had mine. I did everything my best shot. You never realized it until you loose it.

My Mom is awesome. We always stick together. I remember after school walking to Kroger supermarket because we both didn't have a ride. My Step Dad was sick at the hospital. She got off work and we walked home. It took us about an hour. I never seen her so happy. This is her dream as a kid to go to America. She told me so many times. She planned to be a nurse, get out of her hometown to go to college and work here. At least she didn't vow to become a nun. Forgive me Lord. We both won the lottery. I'm trying to remember. I never really like to listen to her. She's strict because she in so many ways totally different and unargreable to me. She is very protective but that's what Moms are. Right? She's the only one I have She's been there for me since Day 1. I can't imagine what my life would be like ~~would~~ with out her. I hate it when she gets mad at me when I do something terrible. I don't really express how much I love her and she never say anything. She does say a lot oF things to me. I listen and sometimes I don't. I guess it her way of saying it. She tells a lot about her experiences. I don't think I lost her when we came to the promise land. I don't get the attention anymore especially me who loves attention. We don't get to talk a lot because of her work and I'm busy. I just want to grow up and she still talks. I HATE TO FOLLOW her words because I want my way. I'm trying to be free and independent to grow up. I like correcting my own but sometimes it never works because she wins. What can I say she is my mother. I hope she will be proud of what I do in my life. I never really understand her and I don't think any mother who has a teenager growing up do either. My Mom is very supportive. How could I be selfish sometimes when she always there for me. There is so much to say about her. Right mom? A great Mom! If you want to know more about my Mom it is in my diary. I just want to continue remembering memories.

Back to OHIO . . . . If you were to ask me what surprises me about America later on. The teenagers were dress into fashion. I thought everyone was rich. This funny thing. . .I thought I would no longer be ~~hassled to~~ asked by my new classmates for pens, pencils or papers but it's just the same here. America is full of surprises. I would love to see more of it, to go to different places I never been. To see the world and all that stuff. Anyway, on February of my Birthday I got a Casio keyboard and I later came to California stop playing piano and started what I love. Karate. Martial Arts. TO LIVE LIFE .. YOU HAVE TO TAKE CONTROL OF YOUR LIFE, DO WHAT YOU WANT, WHAT YOU LOVE and ENJOY and NEVER LISTEN TO

PEOPLE AND FOLLOW IT IF YOU FEEL IT IS ~~NOT~~ RIGHT FOR YOU. I liked playing the piano but it just didn't "click" I would rather do what I desire in my heart. I got lots of 1st , 1st my 1st stuff toy. The clown I named after my Step Dad. Since they look similar, a few hair except he's wearing a clown hat but he wears fishing hat. I celebrated my first Christmas with snow, a happy 1st family that ended years ago so I have my Mom now. You can see why I never talk about the guy. I don't hate him because he did a lot for me for a short time. I wouldn't be in America anyway. I did miss my country Philippines a lot. My Mom and I got homesick. In U.S. 4th of July was no fireworks(for me) but I know sometimes in the Summer time, I would see why loneliness hit me. Just everything, being away, no close friends to talk on the phone for a visit. It was just the 2 people in my new family.

========================  ============================

Sept 1, 1997 9: Pm......

AM I LAZY OR WHAT.... I keep telling myself to continue writing my diary. I think I am having to much fun this summer. Junior Year Rocks ! I admit I just swift through it but the past the past. It was all good. Journalism doing nothing. Chemistry was fun except my brain couldn't absorb all the info. AP Eng. Just when WOPI ! doing advance work or nothing. Mr. Hoss was great. One of the best at E.C. I'll always remember this thought for the weekend. Eventhough I may not know all the answers and too many numbers ran in to my head. It wasn't so bad afterall. Lunch at everywhere I was a cayote. . . Meeting.. Clubs.. Food ... Library etc. I like helping out on Mondays as a peer tutor.... It's okay missing out and only show up 4 days for AP U.S. History - that class was way cool. I dump Spanish but I'm no quitter I have it again my senior year. I got stuck in P.E:-

I felt so bad dropping Spanish in my Junior Year... I wanted to tell her (Mrs. Fonseca) I'll do this. I wanted AP SpansihT for Senior year. I'm in no Rush at all. I'm glad I took Spanish (2nd) & Political Science in Grossmont College for 6 weeks.. Talk about faster than speed of light. I didn't like how I have to put all those info. In my head. It made me crazy. I had to memorize so many things. I talked to Mrs. Fonseca a few days ago saying I have your class again. It was before my tennis practice. It was friday. She said, "This giRl like to suffer," letting Kelly knows. I told her about the summer school and Kelly ask about the schedule for Hoor Colege Prep.

My Summer was incredible. I don't remember much of summer school in Grossmont College. Thanks to Hilary and Jason, it made it better. Jason is really nice. I was glad I got ~~a~~ rides from him. I love the music.. Rage against the machine.. I've heard of them on T.V. seen them in a magazine There was this one song I always hear it on the radio. It had that missing word in it. I have nothing against cusing. I like the freedom of saying it whenever I feel like sayinh it because its an expression. My parents were gone for Fishing at Lake Jennings at 4 P.M. They have been going there every FRIDAY since June. Usually when they are gone I would stay home and watched T.V in the Living room and pig-out. But this time…. I planned for 2 weeks to have a party… it was for Hilary's Grad. Party. Kelly and I planned it. ~~And~~ We did what we have to do: our idea for her gift we been thinking about for months (I love that Frame with pictures.. Drawings.. It was a neat project to do), pitching in for food and party stuff. I was fun to babysit Pooh Bear (that's what we call him) It wasn't bad at all babysitting because he loved our friends. The next week I baby-sat him he was ~~all~~ crying all the time. I was glad they didn't have a Flat tiRe that night because the car had a flat tire ~~1 week from that night~~. The next FRIDAY.

NOTE: 11th grade was fun.. Football games, food, parties, crowd friends, new friends for a year or one night, TRILL, MOMENT. Its gone!!!!!!

Oct. 24, '97 (11:10 P.M)

I have an hour to tell you bout my last-lazy summer. I left 7 pages more so I could talk about it. I wrote about my college experience and Hilary's Surprise Party but I'm going to write about as early in June. WOW ! I never felt anything like it. I wont tell the date but it was early June. Jessica Stamper, Nikki Huck, Jessicas Mom and I all went to River Rafting I never experienced anything like it. I would do it again. Name the time and day and I'm there. Well, maybe not this year. Okay, I went to make very, very first concert, NO DOUBT. Oh yeah ! That was too much fun. I knew a few people from my school was there. I wish I was at the FLOOR. I'll make sure I get a Floor ticket on my next concert. Hilary and I went. Hilary's Mom is funny. I like her. She gave me a decoration hat "You get to have this because you're my friend," Hilary said. I like how they treat me; Hilary's parents are nice. The No Doubt concert was fun. It was an exalrating (high) feeling that night. I didn't wanted it to end. I would go to another one so I could jump up and down again, scream, yell, kuss and get wild and crazy. I wonder what group band I will see next time. I got a free CD and 92.5 & 91X stickers and magazine stuff. I was glad I went with Hilary she knows everything about concerts and went to saw at least 15 types of band. I saw ~~Green Machine~~ Weezer, which is the reason why Hilary wanted to go and green Machine… no it's the Suicide Machine.

NO DOUBT RULE! Gwen 10 lbs skinnier in person. She Rocks like no other person on that band. Everyone are great : they are so much better in concert. They perform well inlive. Hilary thinks we might get lost and not find our way home. Her Mom knew where to exit for the freeway but she made it sound like we got lost. That ride was fun and funny. They drove me to Nikkie's house after the concert. Nikkies bro. drove us to Jessica's house. It was my 2nd time at Jess house. It looked like one of my dream house only mine (dream one) was bigger. It was good enough. Her Mom and her didn't get ready. They went to sleep early so we had to wake them up. I was still thinking about the concert. It was unbelievable ! After 1 ½ hr. at her house we left in 1 or 2 AM to our destination. The Motorhome was cool. Jess Mom was wackier than I thought. Shes' fun to be with… Jess has her personality.

RIver raftIng

The scenery was beautiful I really never gone passed L.A. We got to Bakesfield . . The Kern River. We passed small towns, lots of acres of farm land before up en the mountains. It scared the heck out of me with those rocks. The entrance welcome said . Welcome to… … mention about at least 100 people died since 1960 or something like that. It was so pretty. One with nature. I took some pictures. I still haven't develop it yet. I was scared but it when smooth the first day so I was fiRed up to do more. I t was Fun I got to meet other Rafters there and the guides were great. The food was good. I almost saw my life slip.. I feel at the horse shoe fall. It s 4 feet down and it has a donut ~~whore~~

whole in the middle going down. **I JUST LOST ~~THE~~ MY GRIP AND MY RIGHT FOOT ~~DID TOO~~ SLIP OUT OF THE RAFT.** I was one of the people up front. I was thankful I didn't hit ~~only~~ any sharp rocks . and not go to far that no one would get me. I yelled, " Get me out of here ." Something like that. First time I felt like what if. But the day before. I made myself go slidding down the river like that because almost everyone decided to. I had to prove it to myself and I can do that coz it's me. So anyway, I got saved. Thank God.
[[add picture of river rafting ---- other than front cover----ei. Friends on raft ,etc.]]]

It was funny. I thought that was a highlight of the trip. If I can do this anytime I can jump out of the sky and land both feet 3,000 ft doooowwwnnn (skydiving) I love those kind of adventure. After the 2 days, well the 2nd night we had to go home. I was glad to be back. The next day seem as if I knew I did all those cool adventure but it felt like a dream. So I looked at the shirt I bought that was all I got as a souvenir. It made me believe, So I really did it and I sleep at the Riverbank the night before. Oh Graduation . . . This time it was for Nikke, Jessica Stamper and my best friend Hilary. I got to go to Disneyland grad Night. I was glad to be there despite of all the waiting in line. Hey ! I got to stay up all night. Raymond puked ! Gross ! They took me home the next day morning and I slept till my Mom got home from work. HA ! HA ! HA ! I didn't expect that but I was tiRed.

I went to the movies, saw GI Jane, Jurrasic Park, Face Off etc. I can't believe I got a break. I took my last opportunity to have fun (in terms of my last lazy summer) I went to the Beach 2x. The B-Day Party was cool at BoardWalk the Belmont Park at Mission Beach that was cool. I got to do stuff with Kelly.
She is one of my best friend. We went to places, saw many movies we wanted, went to Grossmont Mall, etc. She didn't mind about taking the bus but it's different how coz she drives. I remember this so vividly. My new doctor help me towards my goal I have so long. She helped me lift up my confidence. She got her dream. I need to fulfill mine. I will. I never got to call Elizabeth and she emphasize that at the beginning of school. I promised to call her wher we wher at Danille's B-Day Party. I don't know what else to say about the summer. I did a lot. Wild Crazy car Jason got… this guy name Sam…. That Political Science class & listening to …Rage

Against the Machine CD…. The fun stuff I did with my friends… all the pool parties… work…movies… summer school… running …tennis..beach… friends… music… FUN… FUN…FUN ! That's pretty much it. I hope my next one (summer) will tell about BOOT CAMP. I really have to make it. It's so important.

TAPS NOW I'M TIRED. I'm giving 7 more pages from where I started my journal for tonight (Sept. 1) because I have school tomorrow. I'm so exited. I can't wait. Await for new challenges. My Mind and bRain thinks like the smart Heralyn again. I'll absorb a lot. A can do that well in High school… sports…. Extra ciricular activites… work. Class works etc. . I'm a sponge. My summer was great. I was surprise to have a time off after been so hectic/ busy my junior year. I thought " I actually get a break." It's summer just like that. WOW !" and it's back to school for a great and awesome senior year. They say the older you get the wiser you are. I certainly will handle things quite differently and better in my Senior Year than any other ways of the last 3 years of high school. MUSICAL SONG → ♫ Buckle up ! Get Ready for a wild Ride… be careful.. It will be bumpy…Relax enjoy.. Live to thRill… Life is aint that bad. I will be fine. Whatever happens… happens… I control my own destiny… I control my own destiny… I choose the road… sooner I will be on my own… I will be fine… Nothing can stop me now. I know I'll make it to my dream… Take one big step one at a time. Don't worry if I'm sad. I will not worry. I will no longer have to worry about ASB… self-esttem… sad memories of the past and much more I put it behind me now. I know I will make it. Just put on a smile. I'll show the world what I can do. I'm proud of who I am I'm glad to live each day by day. LiFe is treating me good. I'm ready for a show,. Tomorrow is when I start.. I got lots of stuff to show you. . Read on the pages of my life as it unfolds. Conquering the world. How about that. I'm ready for my role once more in high school it will be the best of the best of all the 4 years. What's beyond that… one or two years to get to my dream. I'm ☺ smiling. I tell you. I can do anything and no limits awaits. Do you doubt me. I don't because I'm positive I'll get there no matter what. No matter what happens. So enjoy the Ride (HERalyn). Enjoy it. Nothing can stop me now. I'm on my way to the top. ← song ends here

Sept. 2.

I FIRST DAY OF SCHOOL WAS CRAZY. NO… It was a long day. I'm tired. I decided to walk for the rest of the senior year or take the bus. I got up 10 mins. late instead of 5 AM. I did push-ups and sit ups…just a little exersice. Got ready. I arrived at 6:32. It was early but somehow some student got there before me. Must be the Freshmans. I saw Meagan… we talked and walked around. I wanted to lose her, find Kelly and wait ~~for wh~~ till 7 AM to get our stuff placed somewhere safe. We talked with Elizabeth and my vocal group with Danielle and them. One of the things I hate for every 1st day~~s~~ is everyone is scattered and covered evry square inch before the school starts. It will take a couple of weeks for everyone to stay in close groups. English was okay. I felt like I wanted to sleep. I spend over an hour on this homework about myself and my goals. It was worthwhile.
Mr. Dennison is funny. He made us do a paper tower lab. I was glad to see Stacey, at least I ~~can~~ have someone to talk to. This is a beginning of a beautiful friendship but only for 10 months. I'm glad that I have her in my class. AP Cal. one of the class I was excited about. Mrs. Thalman is a great teacher. I told her about my Math goals as a freshman to make it to the highest level offered here at EL CAP. I had to take summer schools. It was worth doing. Its nice to have a goal come true, it's a weird and different goal because the sacrifice and 3-4 years waiting. Cheryl, Linly, Sarah and of course Kelly are just a few of the students in AP Cal out of 20x. One the first day of school like last year. I always want to remember quotes on the first day that meant a lot to me. She said, "This is it. You are the ones who made it here. You should be happy and know you re smart." I smiled realializing I fullfill something I wanted despite of what happened for the past

couple years. My attitude IS AWESOME because I feel GREAT… DOING GREAT SO FAR COMPARE TO LAST YEAR'S 1st day because I still had to puzzle up coming from my sophomore year. Since, It was a slap in a face, I don't mean is as a bad thing I had a good experience so I fell GOOD. I like IT ! Douglas AP Am. Govt. Ohh! I'm going to rock this class.. I look summer school in **Political Science and so I have a big advantage. I know something about college level work from my summer experience so I guess its one of how I'm prepared. Lunch was a bommer. One thing I didn't like. Yes I had nowhere to hang out. One of the reason why I join clubs and because I don't belong, maybe if Hilary was around but I don't like to hang out with Elizabeth and them at Lunch… once in while. I CHOOSE 2 years** ago how my lunch whould ~~be~~ spend. It's the best way for me because I want to have it in my College Resume. I have 3rd year Spanish again. It feels good. Despite of what happen. I'm back and I'm better. Mrs. Fonseca is a great teacher… she's superb. I have AP Bio with Elizabeth in Mr.Vans class. I like it. I like the class setting. I like all my classes. Its going to be a great was radical year. I control it, the path and destiny I choose IS UP TO ME. I looked at the J.V. courts while talking a rest. So I let go of it but I was once like them. I was looking for someone like me- Heralyn as a Fresman playing Tennis. I thought there will never be one the same. I tried to find someone. Im not talking about similar looks. Similar spirit, undiscovered, unexpected but its too bad he has to cut 9 new players. I pray to God Kelly doesn't get cut. Oh please NO. I played with Kelly and this shy girl. Close to me. I know how she felt because I once was her but she not like me. ~~No one~~

~~is~~ Everyone is unique. If she had my drive and spirit, make oR not make the team. I wish her well. I said hi to Mr. Hoss.

Sept 5, 1997

It's T G I F night at 10 :35 P.M. I'm sleepy. My 1st week of my senior year just drif by. My Mand day was kind of upsetting in tennis. It upsets me because she has the same potential like the other girls trying out who made it. She could have made it. She just didn't have it in her. I really won't go into details. I just don't like to see someone, loose something they want because of their shyness. I know how she felt because I had to get over it and I did. It was a heck of an experience and maturity and maturity and it was beneficial in my character to get over my shyness. Also I played with Kelly & Shelly for a spot in V. #3. I really didn't want it. I feel comfortable with J.V but if it will happen or sometimes playing that spot it doesn't matter. I felt like I didn't need to win…. "Winning this match doesn't mean anything in 5 -10 yrs from now," while playing. It was like I already had enough in me. What I mean by it. I get FUN, challenge, build of friendship, spirit of playing it ~~at a~~ more self-determine, esteem etc. playing as practice ~~or not~~ and playing a match in Tennis. It was just a scrimage against Ramona. If you lost more than you expect to win, It feels like nothing, just continue… and play the next one and I don't take losing seriously. Sometimes, I forget how I got here.., in tennis. WOW ! An athlete…, talking more … group work.. learning… I got so much out of Tennis. I love everything about the tennis experience I had in EL CAP including my 12th grade year. Summer Hudson's Mom asked me. "How does it feel ~~takes as~~ like a Senior," while I driNk in the water fountain. If feels GREAT ! She talks about how fast and finally one more year. I talked about where I want to head for next year. I'm so good at that when I strike a conversation connecting to it from writing goals to college talks. Alicia is great. Her Mom is nice. "NICE POWER HIT ALICIA" "I remember that" she replies. HA ! HA ! Well, you have to be me to know. You can't be me, you couldn't handle what I went thrug and where I came from. You wouldn't want to be me and I wouldn't want to be you. Each one is unique.

What happened at school. I got paid tonight and I went to buy Flowers for my Mom's B-Day Tomorrow. It was worth it. I would rather play Tennis than go to the movies. OH. My school is rockin good. More and more work are coming alive. In English we are doing this Senior Showcase preparation so we had to write goal essays and we have to read our 1st book. Mr. D. has an easy life. He craks me up. We did Density Lab. I'm so glad Staci is in my class. I felt awurd when Dale said… "You work on weekends," got a problem with that- We just chat about stuff. He is easy to talk to. It bothered me when Mrs. T. ask me if I have any problem, ? ? About any just ask her. I kind of got the hint she talked to Mr. Hoss and know what my grade was. It's no bigge because she she just doing her job. AP. Govt. Mrs. Douglas showed a video about democracy. How it compared to Amstredam. I thought that kind of place never existed in this world as form of govt. policies.. At Lunch at Mr. Van classroom I ate lunch and talk with Kelly. Veasna, a savior, helped me on my homework. I just find him weirder everyday. I ace the Spanish but I missed 2 out of 20. That was probably better than last year. Lab in Bio was okay. Mr. V still has that Boa snake "Riff" 10 ft. long. Elizabeth gave me her senior picture. I have to work tomorrow and take my senior pics. At 5:30 A.M. Weekends is gonna go fast for me. Good Night !

Sept. 7, 1997 (9:40 PM)

The weekend passed like a tornado as if I'm caught by its essence of the world events twirling around __ unsurpassed on T.V. My weekend was mostly work. My Mom had her 43th B-Day yesterday. There was only Judy and Steve and their baby son invited for a pizza party. I was glad they didn't go to OLD TOWN for dinner. I went to Wal-Mart and Ross to buy stuff like 311 CD, secret pals gifts for tennis, phone cards. Cordory jeans… **Work was still the same… it feels weird at times I don't have to think….meaning I don't have to use my brain. Tonight I got caught some thinking problems about DREAMS. Mine of course. Princess Diana died a week ago and so did Mother Theresa. My Mom** gave me the Sunday News paper tonight. I thought that was odd but since it's a school year, She just probably thought I'll need it.

I like to have a politics carrer. Examining these 21 great women were not in these position. I don't mean it as sarcasm. Diana was kind of in politics but its my point of what and how they were remembered…. AS A HUMANITARIAN. They are caring, loving, kind to people the poor. TheiR service counts. What I'm trying to prove a point is. I realized something because of their death that I have been serving my Lakeside conmonity since my freshman year, come to think of it, I served as a young missionary when I went to USC-GHS. I WANT TO CONTINUE MY SERVICE AFTER HIGHSCHOOL COLLEGE.. Beyond throughout my life. I finally understand the fortune cookie: I asked something for my future and I got : if a true sense of value is yours, it must come through service I Believe service can be from military, volunteering ,….

Sept. 15, '97 (8:15 PM)

This is the 3rd week of school. I don't quiet remember everything what happened for the past weeks. I might not know evry single detail off the top of my head. I'm so tired. Hey, at least I did all my homework that's due today. I remember I aced my Spanish vocab test last Friday. My weekend went fast. I hate it went I say, "Sure, I'll remember this awesome moment. This will go down in memory lane of my life after doing something great accomplishments etc," but do I really. That's why I write things down that's important. I feel in a stress mood today and tension is up since im itRed today so I decided to write while listening Sheryl Crow's "Everyday is a winding Road" to help me reflect and cool down. I thought I was going to be sick tonight from the way I felt yesterday. I KEEP TELLING MYSELF, I'VE HAD WORST DAYS THAN THIS AND I WILL FACE MORE BAD DAYS AS MY LIFE PROGRESS. I certainly did take this day seriously and I finally tackle it sooner in 900 hrs. I will tackle another day etc. I do a pretty awesome job at it. I feel awesome right now because I'm writing about my experience in this diary. Today ~~I~~ at Lunch I fell less of myself … a question of my leadership. Marco and Kelly told me these is a Key Club meeting today. I thought, "Wow, she did it.(Jessica Stokes) I'm a part of it making this happen. Switching Roles for Sec. And Pres. For Jessica for the sake of the club's future fRom weaknesses, needing more members (very impt.) to rising to the top will happen this year." it bothered me even though I had some content because I feel I might get the lost of my skills or a new member like Marco seem to know what to do. My peers again turn to me flashing in front of my eyes that they (and more will come) will be a part of Key Club. That was something I couldn't do if I was a President. I didn't associate or friends with the people who are in my class (12 grade) but Jessica can make it happen to get new dedicated members. I later got over it and realized what I was leading to that It just didn't help my character and well-being if I had that attitude. My realization showed me the way. I'm glad that finally a vision dream for this club; the students who want to be in this club, the people who are willing to help are going to belong to Key Club. It's finally happening in my Senior year and we can also pass the baton so Key Club as long as there are new Heralyns, Jessicas, Nikkies, Kellys, Marcos etc. staying and coming to be a member, it will survive. My main concern is not to loose the new members and keep them motivating. It doesn't bother me I don't have the skills to be friends with new members but Jessica the '98 class. **I think I will be an awesome leader. My leadership are just growing everyday. I call Hilary. It felt good. I hope we do something** this weekend. Kelly got her license. I'm glad. I called Alicia. She's great ! She helps me mentally and my tennis skills. Not any of my tennis partners can do both of that at the same time. Not to mention she helps me in so many ways like giving me rides, for secret pals she gave me the note, etc. These are the just one of many memories I'll think is my 4th/year in tennis and every year is different. I shouldn't feel bad or hate foR because that would just be cruel for me and to her. She's just helping me in any way she can. I should think of something to show her my gratitude. I FEEL GREAT. 1 more to go. ~~my~~ mi tarea… then off to sleep.

One more thing. I talked to my MOM about my day but I told it differently from my Diary. I write and speak differently, it sets apart from what I want the person to know, understand or listen etc. I told my Mom that I want to work at Barona when I get to college if I'm stuck here ~~be~~ and keep achieving for that goal. You know what it is. I don't know which college would It be though. I think whatever happens after the GRADUATION IS EQUAL
Heres a diagram:

Sept. 17th (Weds) 8:20 P.M. -10: PM

Yesterday was another bad day and, ~~I~~ at first I thought today was a bad day too. The only bad thing yesterday was my coach told me I couldn't play because I didn't show up on Monday and didn't tell him about it. But like Monday, which turn out okay when I realized something is great. I deal Tues. like I dealt Mon. It was a good thing because I got to do my homework and, did 2 hour workout of running toning muscles and karate. It was mostly running it was the 1st time I ran 2x-3x the amount I ran last Thurs. ~~wen~~ after being drop off from Alicias bro. It was worth it. I wonder how much I weigh. Today, I expected a bad day and it did happen. Oh Boy ! I wished I could write like a real writer telling about this day. I did a job of a journalist, writing a story about "SEE YOU AT THE POLE" so that I could actually turn in something to the Forum Publications. It was a great experience feeling like a student juornalist again. You know what I mean. I won't go to details about the event. I miss one homework (Physics) for the 1st time. I was sleepy till lunch. Stacey told me her friend died. Can you imagine that happening to you and I wouldn't want to feel I lost a friend and will never see her again. WOW ! I was about to tell her but I didn't say " That's why I make each day fulfilling something, tackling it, surviving, feeling great as if it was the last," thinking about it. Sometimes I think about it often. We had presentations in class at Calculus, got an A on group test we took . "WOW ! " I thought, "it says Calculus on the test" It pays off when taking summer school and just keep going. The point is I made it. It feels great to be in class. I won't go to detail of what happen in every class. I gave Eliz. A note. She wrote back and wrote a very, very small handwriting. Have you ever had a day your waiting for something to happen… where the bad thing and then something unexpected happens. Per. 6 ended and I decided to go to the office for scholarships stuff. I saw Mrs. Villegas ~~walking~~ passing by me. I should thank her ~~yesterday~~ tomorrow because she told me have a good Day after the "see you…. event! " I said the same thing to her. " I hope I will," thinking about what she said. I asked for my transcript since I need it. I also found out my grades in summer school. I F the Spanish and to my surprise I got a C in Govt. I had a dream I got a D but wasn't sure which one of these classes. I felt really bad. I remembered my Spanish teacher telling me, "You should drop the class because its not worth it. You are failing this class not unless you can bring it up in the next 2-3 weeks (at that time it was 3-4 weeks before summer school will end) " I felt bad after she said that. I remember that day vividly. You know what. I told myself, I made a promise to myself that no matter what happens in both of these classes especially Spanish. I will not quit. I was thinking more to Spanish because I failed Spanish my Junior Year. I wanted to take Spanish III again and use summer as a review for ~~everything if the Spanis~~ getting ready in Spanish class this year? I was about to tell her what actually happen. Why I'm in her class, why I'm taking summer school at Grossmont College the main reasons behind it. But I didn't because I had mixed angry feelings after what she said. I worked so hard…so. so. so. hard.. I thought I would have had a brain tumor by the end of 6 weeks. Spanish was competing with my favorite hits subject in Political Science. I felt really bad at 2:15 P.M. I went down to Spanish building. I felt like I wanted to tell Mrs. Fonseca of what I got. We were about 15 feet away. She She was eating yogrouRt. I just told her directly I got an F. She said, "It's worth it, isn't it?." Yeah I thought. "Yeah.!," I finally6 said it. She went on talking about how I'm doing in this class. She looked at the computer and found my name. "You got a B in this class." " Ya! " " A couple test was not as good as the others." How "~~How ar~~ are you doing with your studying." "I'm fine, I'm using flash cards I had last year. These are the only four I can't get in my head for tomorrow test." She help me how to ~~find it~~ memorize it. She was sitting in the computer Chemi facing me, behind the computer, and I ~~burs~~ went talking about what leads to a whole meaning of a bad day. This time, this reflection ~~is~~ tops all of ~~it~~ the last 2 (Mon, Tues). I finally told her how grateful I was to have her as a teacher. " Do you remember when I talked to you about," I paused, " when you wher about to go to Room 4 (Ms Benjamins Room) and we strike an awesome conversation." I told her about the military college I want to go to; the Army carrer. I tried my best explaining about the different ways to get there. I told her I wanted to learn many (at least 5-6) languages that will help me in military and politics. Yap! I still remember that conversation. My Mom just walked in a second ago asking me about my homework, and she's gone…… To go back I bursted in tears because of those emotion good and bad of the experiences I went thru. It happen so fast. It was the second time I cried in front of a Spanish teacher. The 1st one was Mrs. Benjamin in my Sophomore year. If you knew what I went through my 10th grade year, you would understand. Lets just say… B A L A N C E ! So what happen was Mrs. Fonseca lifted me up to make me feel good about myself. She said about that what I did was wonderful… to go to summer school and taking Spanish III year again and how I told her I'm not in a rush to go to 4th year AP Spanish. I have a whole lifetime to learn and increase learning … why hurry while it's important to learn it the right way; no rush. I felt great. This is actually one of the best days of my senior year, perhaps in all of my high school. I'll look back feeling great about this day. You Bet I will ! I asked her about what can I read, something I can take home to read if she would allow me. I told her that when I leaRned English, I never got to read novels until I came here in U.S. My penpals (best friends in Phils) read novels in high school, they should have started it in 3rd, 2nd grade. I think reading in Spanish, talking/ spending time will help me greatly. She happily told me I can borrow any book that I can understand; in my level. Just like that. She said again, " I'm glad you came here. You made my Day. We made each other day better." I walked out feeling the world is my oyster. It was an incredible feeling. Never will forget "experiences, not failures makes us better," when she corrected me. I walked home and I. . .

I wanted to anyway. I thought a lot about what just happen. While walking; walking with pride and feeling great in me. So that's what I unexpectedly think I didn't know would happen. That's what one thing I love about life. I came home, did a little homework, ~~and eat~~ ate and called Kelly if she ~~we~~ wants to run. That was intense. I did 2 ½ ma. Exercise today. I run to Kelly's house. I saw Kelly's Mom going somewhere with Stevie. She waved hi ! Kelly and I ran up to the water tower. I just spend 15 mins. ~~walking~~ running uphill and I had to run 10 more mins. uphill to get there. We talked. I liked the view~~ed~~. I fond a little open fence fence. Where walking down, there was a driveway but we didn't know which road it lead to and 2 houses. While standing, We saw a dog. He was barking. Kelly said," Don't move." We just stayed clam while the dog just barking at us and sniffing us. I swear, I'm writing this right now and it's making me laugh. She knows that I'm afraid of dogs espically those mean ones.

She dog left us, feeling okay and freewill again. "Talk about territorial dog," said Kelly. I told her if I was the only person I would run as ~~he~~ fast as I could uphill to get to the other side of the open fence. She laughed, we both did. We walked up the hill to head downhill running and then suddenly the dog came back. He was behind us, and we stayed clame and looking behind our back. He left and we just run to that open fence. Oh goosh! Thank you Lord that I'm okay. Gee, what an experience. There was another dog but he was on the other side of the road and the owner was outside doing garden work. We just continue running. We went down Morrilo Road which would lead to the soccer field, Baseball field which was behind L.M.S. Look ! There was a lot of cars and parents & students were there. Must be open house night. It was only 6:30 PM when we got there. I looked around for anyone I wanted to see. We talked to Miss. Gramham, a Math teacher at L.M.S. She's great ! We chat about what we were up to… school… college but It was only for a short while. She said Athena made it to AIR FORCE ACADEMY. We left and she said, " Happy Running !" Walking out the room, she came out asking if I'm still interested in tutoring. "Sure." We tried for short cuts and finally ended to this little door fence heads back to the road I ~~have had to~~ ran to get to Kelly's house. It was uphill so we only have 15 mins. Left. We got to het house at 7p.M. Kelly's Mom offered me a ride. I said, " I'll be fine. It get's dark at 7:15 PM. She Kelly said, " I'll give her a ride." She did. That was the first time I ride with her without her parents and she's driving. I chuckeld almost a laugh. She seem calm and relax. She's good, better than I could do in driving. She drop me off at the bust stop. Just like that. I got home. I told her to Drive safely and thanked her. I'm at reality right now. Tomorrow is another day. I just hope Tomorrow and FRI. will be awesome. NOTHING CAN STOP ME.

Sept. 20, 1997 (8:41 P.M.)

Tonight is Saturday night. I went out to Family Fun Center playing minature golf with Kelly. I was glad I got to do something aside from going to Wal-Mart/oR Ross 2 weeks ago. I only spend $ 7 dollars at least. We went to Jack in the Box. We get along great. I don't think we will ever have a fight. I didn't even get to go into the Skateborad virtual game. I had to work today. I must be crazy working at

McDonalds this long. I wanted to quit a long time ago but I need the money. Oh ! Yeah ! I got hit by a golf ball and I wasn't even playing. A little boy slam the ball to hard and it hit and bounce hard to something before it hit my head. "I guess it gives me a whole new meaning of " Play at your own risk." Friday was yesterday. I'm not upset I didn't go to the football game. I was sort of having a bad day. The week was okay. I tell you reader I feel like I don't want to play tennis. I would rather use my precious time getting results like running. I have no choice because I must have 4 yrs. Straight playing tennis on my transcript. Tennis is not the same. Alicia is not really.. She's more like someone … a coach.. Who finally broke my habit of lobs. Kelly was the motivator who helped me play so much better. Gail was the awesome tennis partner of all. She was a senior. I am now. I don't think winning was her point like how I thought of it last year. And Alicia thinks that way but I don't. I don't give a dam if we win or lose. I just wan to play tennis. I want to get it over with. Instead of using my strengths focus on extra-curricular activities especially Tennis I'm using it on where I spend time on… MY ACADEMICS.

Sept. 25, 1997 (9:45 PM)

Tonight is Thursday. Weekend is almost here; I'm excited. This has to be the most crucial week of this month; the hardest week so far ∧ out of all 4 weeks. I had Ap Cal & AP Govt Test on Tuesday. I fluncked it. I think I fluncked all of it. I have tests on evry single classes this week. Tomorrow is Bio. After this I'm writing Stacey a note and ~~fin~~ contunue where I left off studying. I wanted to write this last Tuesday night but I was too tired. Tough call but I didn't expect such a decision just like a snap of a finger like an after noon goes in to a change of nightime. I was glad I got to enjoy Tuesday after school because of all the loadwork at school that day. We had (our Tennis team) to go to La Jolla Beach, (which part) where there are huge waves, Big socks, magnificent views, rich people with their beach house and Rad cars. It's not the part where my Parents (family) used to go to almost evry Sundat 2 years ago. This part (are) was where you can find cute surfers. Enough description. I read back the last time I wrote in my diary and came across about wanting to quit Tennis but no choice. Well, I did quit Tennis yesterday. What an experience. I was unsure if quitting was the right move when I looked at those waves. That feeling didn't go away. We had our pictures taken and ~~when~~ event to eat pizza. I've seeen too many cute guys and cute cars that day. That day ROCKS ! I'll always remember it. I got a ride with Heidi and BobI, had to sit on the back seat with a very, very, very loud music stereo behind me. I love it! I didn't talk much. I thought about the banquet this year… They better not put me as Most Bashful again or I'll tear it. Heidi's a good driver. Bobi just get crazier. They daze summer's truck. Oh ! Did I tell you we went to Freeway and lost in track with Thor and Summer and some people but we all got there ~~after~~ even sort of lost but we all found where it was at. The view was magnificent, totally Breathtaking Hmmm ! ! ! Every view, every parameter. At one time all 3 of us work" Ooow! !" to his cute guy when Heidi our way to the pizza place. Stacey kept me intertain. To get to the bottom line! When I get home, the feeling of quitting tennis will soon be over. No more E.C. tennis. I wanted to join Cross Country I told my Mom but it was too late. I didn't know what exactly the meaning was when I used my feet ~~wril~~ writing / engraving in the sad words "Good Bye E.C. tennis." I was just standing at one spot. Those waves hit me quick: meaning It made me think what is better. I wrote Why I want to built tennis.. On next page. What's I want to quit tennis.. On next page. What's lacking about tennis. The reasons behind the reasons. Its on the next few pages →

Sun- Sept 28, 1997 (8:41 P M)

Today I went to the Mall twice , once with Kelly and second time with Robin. Kelly and went to the Friendship Festival. I was looking forward to this day. This weekend or whenever every year they have the Friendship Festival usually at Sept (4th or 3rd week) marks today as 1 year of my Mom and I as U.S. citizen. Last year, she took the oath that that makes me automatically a U.S. citizen too. I remember the Miss Universe of Venezuela was there giving a speech. I saw three monks. I ate a Mexican food. It was good. It's all about getting together showing off different countries uniqueness in food, costume, entertainment, geography (by giving out info.) etc. I couldn't resist the Filipino Food. Kelly ate this square Iranian / or something but it was a popsisle squared one. I was so hungry and when I'm hungry I have a big appetite. Wouldn't you know it, Alicia was there with her oldest bro. and Mom. I didn't expect it, like does it have to be. I didn't know for sure it was her. Yap! It's her. Maybe her way of not you so friendly one word "Hi !" It was basically her Mom that came up to us that drag her and her Bro. Her Mom asked the question why I'm not in tennis. It was a short conversation. I really don't care what is going on Alicia's mind at that point. She can blame it on me out I don't regret anything. I made a choice. Kelly and I had to leave coz it was 12:40 P.M. We walked across the street and finally fond her Dad. I waited For Robin to show up at 1PM. She did, after 15 mins. of wating, .3 mins. Before 1 PM. I haven't seen her for 1 year. Some nice Robin I know. We saw the movie, "a thousand acres. It was an emotional movie." I loved it. It was a sad movie. I remember HOPE was the last word, the narrator Jessica Lange (one of the character) said it. Robin drove me home but she had to go to the mall to buy a purse first before dropping me off. We talk about high school-college-people we know…anything. She said to call me about the Football game this Friday against Granite.

The main reason why I wanted to write something about today is not just 1 year U.S. citizen and fun stuff but I wanted to share to you about a theory -somewhat true happens in movies, each and everyone's life in their past and future or present. I realized HOW MUCH PAIN AND HARDSHIP…SACRIFICES MY MOM AND I HAD TO GO THROUGH to GET HERE. TO GET THIS FAR; here in U.S.A. I REALIZED THAT I GREW UP and live the life of hardship since day 1. Hardship is not exactly the word. Examples, life without a father, unperfect life even if at First you thought you will be save by a new Dad and 1st and last Dad but the reality hurts, a price for the career, childhood living with realtives because my Mom lost her job, brought up in a country-Phils., ~~ap~~ sacrifices, something bad will happen in the future for me. Something has gone wrong, I learn and live with it. Of course there will be more. Sometimes faith is not true. Maybe I will have to go to 1,2,3, or 4 more to Find happy marriage or something is wrong with the relationship or him or me is the cause. Or I will be set up something bad that will end my carreer. I know how hard it is to not have a father. I know how hard it is to be poor, really poor. I know heard it is to live in a poor country but a counrty shows it's pride, respect and other aspects and even though it fades it is still there (just have to look harder) I just got to look harder in my life.. In this world. I find more and more of these. I'm fed up with too much of these. Does anybody hear me. I told my mom about this. She said, "Yeah ! Just have to pray to God." Lord do you hear my call. I ask for no more pain. This is the 2nd time I asked of you by writing in my diary. I didn't expect it will be like this. I haven't heard from you. Sometimes I don't see you informs that people say we seee you. I know I haven't talked to you. IS that it? Oh, Lord How will I stop my pain. Mr. Hoss said, "Every problem, every obstacle in life can be accomplish by overcoming it. Going up that mountain, hill or whatever it is. When you get down you have to solve another one. It just gets harder and tougher." LoRd I have lots of hills, mountains, slides my Mom and I went thrugh and made it. We have some now. I have LOTS OF IT NOW. Am I really going to loose 30 lbs by end of Jan. or 25 lbs by Dec., if I Do.. You know what happens. But what will happen after getting there, I still continue for West Point. Will I get there. It's so hard. I'm a senior. Just making it to Prep School would ease my pain. When and exactly are the procedures? Where do I egain and strengthen my strengths, HOPES, 100% pure SELF-DISCIPLINE which I don't have, toughness (need more), accepting and doing the SACRIFICE, Determination ? W I L L ? Will I find these. Where? In me. It's weak. HELP ME ? HELP ME MAKE THIS A REALITY. This mean a lot to me. IF a first step is losing weight. My step Dad will see / know that I aculdly belong to the National Guard. I wish that day… he sees me in a uniform. I'm not doing this for him but he's like the person I have to overpower. He thinks I can't make it. He made me weak. I did overcome him and this is one of the two to show himnot for show -off or for him. Actually ~~to~~ so he sees me in it- Good and Bad. Afterall, he helped me for a short time and got me here. 2nd one is in the W.P uniform. I hope he lives to see that day. I have to worry about where I'm heading this summer and what college. What my recruiters expect for me. I was glad I chose tennis. I knew I wouldn't run. I THINK A PERSON SHOULD FACE THEIR FEARS OR WEAKNESSES RIGHT AWAY. But I don't regret it. I treasure a lot about tennis. Running now is how I feel about starting a new sport, something competitive and challenging with self- discipline. GOD, PLEASE GUIDE ME TO VICTORY… It will be a long Run, 4 months to be exact: Life is running. Running is Life. And, I need the strengths and attitude and characters to get to where I want in losing 30 lbs, getting to W.P. making it day by day at a time, surviving etc. Please guide me for I am weak. I need it I'm thristy for it. I know I just have to remember that my participation is a part of it. I'M WILLING… I'LL STUMBLE or fall just help me to get buck up..to continue to win.

Oct. 18, 1997 (9:30 P.M.)

Days and days has passed by. The sun sets and rises gaxillion times in this world. I've seen it when I walk~~ing~~ to east at the moment before time of afternoon Fades to night. It's pretty when I looked out the horizon. Everyday I feel the weight of my problems, time needed to do things and so on. What else is new anyway. Sooner or later 8 months will ~~come~~ passed by; the end of the chapter part of my life in this Room. My bedroom, I call this the box, 6 sides, I've seen visions of the future of me and the world, dimensions strething to the outside far away seeing myself, feel trap here, felt rejoices, memories of me in this room ~~it~~ is ~~was~~ part of me… my life. Usually, I wanted to write about what cool stuff I've been doing. So.. I didn't went to the memories with Hilary and out friends out I'm going to the mall to but a nun costume. To kick back and relax at the mall for an hour. Well, I have tons of studying to do. My life doesn't get any better than this. Of course its been and always be CRAZY. WORK on weekends, SCHOOL STUFF, Fun is limited (that's how I want it to be), Time to get things done etc. I fell good LoRd. Somehow I do. Thank you. I'll make sure I'll maintain it. I wish for a lot of things. I see the big picture now(to how I plan the battle) step by step, year by year to get thRe. I know I'll make it. I just have to do it…believe! What did I do lately. I went to see U TURN directed by OLIVER STONE. That Fri. night last week was way cool! IHOP, Yah ! HHHMMM! Good food. Bad stomache next day. This guy was too annoying, too weird. It was a good time with friends. Got home at 12:30 AM. I went to Family Fun Center with Kelly 4 weeks ago. My fun stuff are limited. There's not much I can write about but I do want to Recall things. I wrote different stuff on pieces of papers over the years.
Read on:

* Walking to the ~~wild~~ top of the hill, meeting spot before Kelly and I Run the top of the ramp. Going down where the Riverview School was. Lacated. That spot I stood. I was hot.

When resting… thinking about discipline, weakness in will character but improve.

★ It was towards the end of my junior year. I just wanted to get high school over with. GO away.. Out of this place. Later, I knew that I shouldn't feel that way. I should triumph the experience I have to go through. That's the beauty of life full obstacles to tackle. * it was * I was watching Allegory of the Cave- wishing Senior year is over- then Prep- West Point. I imagine the things I have to go thru while watching almost not paying attention to the movie. I need an A in this class. I think of WP everyday a lot- an obsession. I know its for me. Yesterday I thought how it gave me great things to achive, one is never limit yourself to anything. I benefited a lot to the " Whole Person Concept" Ive been working on since 10th grade. Just think I haven't even got there. I already got something out of it. That's why its impt. For me to go there.

★ I still have a the list of 8 things on **"What I need to do to be successful." I wont write them. Put it this way. I just look in the mirror and it's start with that person in the mirror. It's in my he**ad. **I know what I have to do to obtain success.**

★ Don't worry the bad experiences are bad will as human nature we forget but only remember the best of times.

★ Yeah, I'm really going to remember this moment. I have too many moments. I won't remember all of them but I do know I have what we call a diary.

★ It's funny / weird because it let **ME** look for what's important.

★ Isn't this how you want your life to be, better than Gr.9 , only academics, maybe sports on the season, a glimpse of few people but this year you get better coz youre used to it. It's challenging fun, exciting, youre doing something every minute, second, how to get ready to accomplish , to get things done.

★ Kapoyon nako dili makuha nako and gusto ko pero do ko kahikatoa ugsaon and buhaton. Premero, isulat gusto nako ang buhaton dayon instead of complaining kay I know how. Best thing about me, if I want something, Gwen[when] a lot I can handle it per I have to put my mind to it. I have the ability very few people have. I can be at the bootom and I can come out on top. I already know this I just need to know how to do it.

☺ ☺ WOW… I have lots of confuse stuff I had to go through. Hey I'm still here.

Oct 24, 1997 (9:55 PM)

I tell you reader about my life. Can I say Hi to everyone in the future, say 50-80 yrs. From now. So do people still say life ~~is unfair~~ sucks, particularly from teenagers in this late early 21th century. Enough of that. What about my life. What else is new for me. I celebrate tonight, today… I went to the mall. I plan this before school. I wanted to take a break, celebrate anything and spend my money to give myself some credit on stuff. I deserve it. If I had to describe this week, It had to be the best one yet. I found this girl and her strong character. I thought I could never find her again but I did. I'm talking about the fresh man girl who was me. You know the A student 3 years ago. I've been working haRd. I sense my atitude has improve (procrastinating etc.) in terms of what I have to do to work on my academics. Somehow It didn't feel like her again. She was so shy, smart, too concern of what others think, low self-esteem, felt worthless, trapped are so much more. I've changed a lot. Im not saying I didn't like my personalities and characters okay, I didn't but it was not easy to just do academics and felt like nobody everyday three yrs. Ago. My transition and obstacles/ challenges I had to face in order to improve that makes me of who I am now was not that easy as it sound. No one knows what it feels like to be me, you have to walk in my shoes. The experiences I got was worth it for the price of my academics but the PRIZE IS IN ME NOW and I'm still learning more about me and improving what I can. Also, I'm glad it happen because I don't have to live a life of someone else dream for me. Eventhough it help me shape up who I am and what I wanted to do in life. I'm truly happy to get this Far And ~~have~~ knowing I'm content and proud of being me. It feels great ! I could never be that girl anymore because the one at this moment has changed greatly, so Full of life, dreams, ambitions and hopes like she could do anything her heart desire. It is truly true because I had accomplish leadership skills, sport abilities, academics, talent skills, personality/ character development etc. in my entire life and more will come, improvements will be made & there's a lot to discover. I'm glad I worked hard this week. I got a lot done. . So I took the Math Test Unit II- I might not have gotten an A or B but the effort was worthwhile. I know it's important to work for all my classes. I put a lot of sacrifices just to have all 6 Honors classes. Yah, I could have Journalism as an Editor but I'm concern about my weaknesses. There other good stuff I could have like Tennis but ACADEMICS is my GOAL TO ACHIEVE This year. Today I went to the mall. I saw 3 a few people and talked to them. I bought a Nun costume, 2 blouses and SUGAR RAY CD and ate Chinese for my dinner. I was just glad to hear from WP. I thought they forgotten me. I still haven't got anything about W.P.P.S> Life goes on.

Oct. 26, 1997 (10:10 PM)

← 1 hr early since we daylight savings time turn back so its 10:10 instead of 11:10

I have something in my mind. So I write it in my diary because it gives me a new perpective or I find out something From reflecting or just reflecting works. I'm going straight to the point. S That letter from W.P. Regional Conmander, Major Nathan S. Sassaman ~~just~~ is Still in my mind for the past few days since I got it now. 20 mins. ago I took it out. Recard [recalling] it, it must be the 20th or something like that reading it. Really! It doesn't haunt me.. I don't feel bad. Did that been there okay. I know everything about West Point by the book (not experience) but by the book. I've read anything I can possibly find about it from catalogs to pamphlets to video to W.P. Presentation by Major Sassaman on April. I ~~He~~ new 2 yrs. ago I won't be qualified because of my academic is not strong enough. I know that already. I just wanted to see what happens after when I mailed that Pre-Candidate Questionaire. A letter of Course out what will itself. It didn't mention about Prep-school. I hoped get info on that. I was glad I got this letter. Somehow, this letter is ? Stronger than I thought. I'm sure thousands of others got this. This is the only one with a real signature from any letters about the Army (it wasn't a Xerox signature). "I recommend that you devote your efforts now to improving your record rather that continuing the admissions process." This ~~quote is my~~ concerns about academics. It just in my head when I was doing my homework tonight and I think it will be always. Somehow, the letter helps me to do it, to motivate myself getting better in academics everyday. It's a big impact in my life. Also, I got stuff FoR Presedential Awards and I feel so motivated to loose weight so I will be in the National Guard. I feel like I can do anything; I feel confident, strong and determine. WOW ! I feel like he cares about my goals. I learned what laudable meant, " your laudable goal of service to the Nation…means worthy goal. I don't know if he got to read the letter concerning about PrepSchool. Like his character speaks in this letter, his concern, his advice to me just helps a lot. I hope he's the Western Regional Commander for another 3 yrs. minimum. I took out my transcript. I calculated G.P.A. I will a have for graduation. 4.6 at last. That's Great but to think if that is the present, today, right at this moment what is my life? Will I be stronger, better person, more sociable etc. especially if that's reality I will be contRolled and live someone's dream for me. That's not right! I like now; my reality. Because…

- I live from my dreams & ambitions I discover for me….
- I live for me, not for someone's dream [of] me….

-WOULD I HAVE DONE EXTRA (like summer school if not for failure, I mean experience).

- I have a view of up and lows so I know what it feels like to work so hard and still not get to have it (happens so many times), that set's me apart from straight A's student not just by grade but EXPERIENCE MAKES ME STRONGER etc. especially (of course) the bad ones are better of reflection makes me of who I am. I've been there they haven't yet. In fact, I've been there since the day I was born. I lead a tough life, so I have to be tough not weak.
- I live knowing my strengths and weaknesses, limits, OOHH ! There is not no limit, to talent and skills. For example, I discover that leaders aren't just form [BORN], they develop (they could have the natural leadership skill but it's nothing if they don't use it) by experience just like anything in this world. It's worth it, Really, it is in exchange for outstading grades & so are all the reasons I've mention in my diaries. EvEry good thing has a bad thing, every bad thing has a good thing. The only thing in my opinion is the f~~or~~ woRst thing of a man should know other than the end of the world but "TO DIE WITHOUT ACHIEVEING A LAUDABLE DREAM) to live & die without fulfilling a purpose in l~~if~~ one's life." That's how I feel about *WeZt*

Point, the Army, I still try to figure out what to do with Writing, Art, investing, wanting to be a humanitarian (like what Mother Theresa said, "God created us to do small things with great love.") *politician, a leader, a soldier.* I still Question my purpose. I got visions of it but they seem puzzles to me. I'm sure it will come to me when the time comes. I know so. Right now, I think of W.P. and hope for that dream. I'll keep on working to have a better record one step at a time, one day at a time. I wait for the day I wear the Proud elite uniform of my nation. I wait for the day I salute to the Flag, a respect for this nation. I wait for the day I make it to the National Guard. I wait for the day comes on the Saturday Morning as my 1st day. I so long for that day. I feel it's near. It has to be I waited so long for that day to come. Maybe I should start the 1st time in history I write this poem for my English class.

NOV. 21, 1997 (10:25 P.M.) FRI.

Today was just weird but totally cool. I just can't forget this day. I remember last night, I spend 6 hrs. trying to make my Physics project work. The world is not that cruel. My lab partner brought stuff too. We used it. It wasn't such a bad day afterall. In fact, that was just an itsiwistsi tiny part. Okay, I decided I give Veasna a present. He's been bugging me about his B-Day is on and I want chocolate or colgne. . a gift. And he did say that to other students he know. But he bug me 3x. Yesterday, I bought him chocolates, a postcard saying-I never met a chocolate I didn't like" and a B-Day card with a note I wrote. Wrapping his gifts was the last thing I did last night. I feel asleep again only this time I slept at the left far side of the bed and again my lights were on Before. 1st period, I ~~go~~ put the gifts on his desk because I didn't want to give it to him in front of all my classmates. I forget about my name from… and to.. He was wandering who it might be and a few ~~some~~ of my classmates said, " Who is it from?, May be it's from Kelly Brady, May it's From.." I thought of this good; only me and him knows about the presents. HE passed a letter note and enclosed a little candy bar crunch with his senior wallet picture. OHH MY GOOSH !!! Kelly L. handed it to me because she was the last person who had to pass it before getting it to me. Who sets behind me. I won't ~~say~~ write all the words he wrote. It's a thank you note. I don't see why he would feel like

crying. He said that He can't believe you gave me all that but I do deserve it. I don't know how I reacted really. Our class were watching "Lady Jane." After the bell rings. HE talked about a little chat. He said about how he like it. He wanted a hug from me. Gee ! In 6th period, he hugged me behind when I was sitting in class. I can't believe he did that. He gave everyone a little piece of a chocolate. The one in the box. About 7 people around our aRea in class. Snoppy Elizabeth whatz in my back pack. Somehow got a hold my wallet and saw apic. Of him. She read it out loud.. Not too loud to the whole class but still. She thinks there is a connection between me and him. HA! HA! " Put it this way, I wouldn't be surprise when you call me on the phone ..saying your going to the Prom with Veasna. After school I thought about him. How he has an awesome truck and what if I end up going out with him. I walked home as usual but I thought a game about what just happen today. Out of the blue I tell you…
HE pulled over and asked iF I need a Ride. "Sure, why not!" We talked. HE ask where I live and I told him. ~~I g~~ He told me he had to work and its okay if he might be late because his parents own the store. HE said it again that he didn't expect it. I don't remember all of the conversation. He drop me off. It just hit me, Oh my gosh. I didn't expect it, not too cool like this. I was sublime. I think the GIFT itself made me remember me if also my old feelings. But it was always he flirts with girls. I'm sure he had some feeling for me. If he did, he might have had it all through these 3 yrs. BuT and it made him like me mean OR He just thinking of me as friend but has feelings now for me. I feel a great vibe; a chemistry. It's too weird. What would happen in the future I wish he will ask me soon like this Monday so we can do something this Thanksgiving or something like that. So now what! Fine, he's a player I'll pay without making the 1st move. I think I just did. Okay, without asking him. I really wonder if will ever get to go out with my long time crush. Who KNOWS ! Never- Right now I come first. I must contunie [CONTINUE] to achieve my goals.

Tonight, I got to see Hilary since Halloween. We went to China DiEnasty. We talked about 311 and Sugar Ray and Metallica, college, etc. I told her how Jason got in a car accident. Poor Jason. Hilary is still Hilary. It was funny when she said how she got an A- in philosophy and Ramon got D who took a lot of notes. And to think she ditches a lot. Next year, we will have hopefully 2 or 1 classes together like in College Algebra. I really got to write memories in this Journal because I won't remember every little bits of everything. Halloween! The best ever! I dress up as a nun all day. I had Fun.. So much fun. I went to La Palapa Restaurant after school with my friend Kelly. I gave some of my friends candies. It's a tradition as WE (Hilary & I) call it that we will always do stuff on Halloween. This year, our group of ~~go~~ friends, more like Jason, Tom, Jim and Hilary. All of us went to Balboa Park. Cross over the suicide bridge ~~at~~ and went to see something happening there. There was that boring show of Phantom of the Opera. I wanted so much to be Jason's girlfriend. I was always next to him when we walked. But no way that will happen in my lifetime. It's better to stay friends. ~~And~~ I don't know, It's a tough call. FREINDSHIP LASTS LONGER. We went to eat at Dennys, played pool at Tom's House (won #1) till 11:30 P.M. Got home and watched- a movie. I got home at 2:45 A.M. Slept at 3 AM I had to work pretty much after that because it's a weekend. That was too good; somehow it felt so un real but it happened. I don't know what's in store For me next year in everything that concerns me… my Life ! I had a 4 day weekend and I went to see "In and Out" with Kelly. That was a rad movie. That was the first time she we dRove to go somewhere… Fun place to be. I went to the mall. with Elizabeth and her Mom I had a nice time. I won't go into details. Time is too fast. But I'm doing much better compare too the last 2-3 consecutive yeaRs in high school. I know this senior year will be the best of all. Of Course! Moving on up… Thanksgiving break will be awesome. I have a lot of energy, I have to because of the massive load worrK I have in everything. I will be Fine. Hopes is making it happen For me and other stuff. TA ! TA! I write in December.

~~Dec~~ Nov.30, 1997

Tonight is Sunday. Tomorrow will be 1st day of December. Yes ! Time fl~~y~~ ies quickly. Sooner it will be January. To recollect my toughts. I can't believe I forgot to write about Halloween 1997. That was the best Halloween Balboa Park ! The bridge ! Staying up all night. Jason's house is rad. I dress up as a nun. HA ! HA! HA! Indeed, what a great night of fun that was. Memories are wonderful. Don't you think? Too bad I won't remember everything. I'm enjoying my young teenage. Lifestyle. It's great blessing being a teenager. Adults seem

to have a different perpective. U-TURn was cool ! Dah! I did write this but I need to write more about… .. I saw Mortal Combat. Rad
movie ! Kelly drive a hard bargain. Glad I went to see it. I can't wait for the 3 week vacation. I'm not worried, it will come in a flip of a page. Thanksgiving was okay. **I saw MIB 7 oR more** times. McDonald's is home to me on weekends. I went to the mall with Judy and my MOM yesterday. I'm still lazy I ran but I need extra time. Why is it time always wins against me? I don't ask much out of life, Really ? I know what I want. I know how to get there. I don't believe the world is cruel as it is already. I don't blame the world. I just want to achieve level 1 and 2. (Army National Guard & Rotc) to get ready For [level] 3. Academics is harder and it will be ~~tough~~ more…… Why is my inner strength of me. OF course, I know the answer myself. Everything will be alright. I keep my head up high.

DEC.25, 1997 (5:20 PM, Thurs)

Ha! Ha! Ha! Ho! Ho! Ho! So it's Christmas. Big deal! Not much. I like the way my country celebrate Christmas. It's just difFeRent here. Its fine. I got a Pooh watch that has a musical melody from my Mom. I got other stuff too. I already have it all, I just look around me. I only wish for one thing. It won't come true like a magic wand. I have done all I can but I will pass level one. Time is running out. I want to know now and I believe I will qualiFy. I will make it to ARMY NATIONAL GUARD. So I am, I myself is in charge of the future. No amount of money can replace for whatever it is worth. It's truly PRICELESS. I will have that member of ARNG to fall back on because once I'm in I tRuly believe West Point is just a couple of years away. I think now. My guardians, my consceince avoice inside me tells me I should quit McDonalds. The voice also said if I just concentrate on losing wieght and lose it I will make it to ARNG. Also, something about West Point in year 2000. WOW! I am so positive about this goal. And what is beyond that. So much for this ink, its almost gone like time ticking.

It is wonderful to Remember great memories but at the same time it is also painful to remember what was forgotten. Like others, I learn to live with it. If Christmas is the time to celebrate then to me everyday is Christmas because I celebrate everyday. I thank my Mom my friends, everyday and the Lord For EvErything. OF Course My Mom reminds me every year on how we are always together. She wrote a short note on the Xmas Card.

Dearest Lalyn,

You must remember that everyday we celebrate Christmas in our life just for the TWO OF US. I do hope that you are really getting used to it, that we just celebrate it by ourselves, nobody else. I thank God that every Christmas we are always TOGETHER and never be separated from apart. Ok!

I love you very much and this is the {ONE} thing that you must remember.

Then she enclosed a $10. She said for Christams Dinner. Actually, We (3 of us) ate on the table. Ate crab legs because that was what my Mom wanted. I relally don't like to write about a family because I only have my Mom and I. I grew up knowing that. I wrote what she wrote to me because I can always remember back if ever I forget about last night or today. In 7 days more it will be Jan. 1, 1998. WOW! My most memorable of 1997 was everyday. Well, March 1997 was one of the turning point of my life. That W. P. presentation when Kelly invited me that night. (May) Halloween 1997. Homecoming 1997. TRYING TO RUN… RUN… RUN… and ~~what it~~ how it taught me a lesson Last Lazy Summer 1997, (Summer school) How I got an F in Spaniish II & C in Pol. Science at Grossmont College. Sleepless nights from work, McDonalds (1yr 6 months) job, all my friends around the world, Dec. 17th I forgot to celebrate that day because I was busy at work & school. HoRRay! As of today, My Mom and I have live in U.S. for 5 yrs. And 8 days. I am an American citizen. Movie time with friends sitting at the movie house[theatre] to watch movies. I CELEBRATE MY LIFE HERE ON EARTH. There is so much to remember about 1997. I sometimes want to write about my past but that was just memories. I really wish to visit the Phils. When the time comes. I plan to do many things during my X'mas break. Ohh! In case I forget to write ~~what~~ I did: wrote letters to my friends, went to Wal-Mart, shopping…shopping, watched Titanic, Flubber… SCREAM 2, I had a party with Elizabeth's house party, too much food, Pot luck at work, filed to quit Mckidies., got my paycheck, saved money, studied as much as I can, SAT, ACT, listen to music, stayed up late and woke up late. Smiled…etc. WHO KNOWS WHAT. TommoRRow and year 1998 will bring?

Jan. 7, 1998 (Weds. 9:20 PM)

It's 1998 ! I'm still here living life to the fullest- I made it this far. Life is sweet ! I thank you Lord for all your blessings. New Year's Eve was okay. I got to listen to top 91X countdown I plan to buy / or get have smash mout CD. I saw Scream 2 ! ! ! I visit at Marilyn's house to see Jamie. She is weirder now. I had a wonderful vacation. My life just gets better everyday but like everybody else: it's not easy as I say " Life is great ! ! ! I love to tackle the challenges I face everyday even though it requires dedication, self-discipline, hard-work etc. It. Is very rewarding in the long run. As always giving my best of my ability and even more. Yesterday, I weighed myself and havent'd done it since Sept. or Oct. I'm pretty sure its October. WOW! I thought 156.5 or 157 or 158 was impossible. Maybe I made an error. I doubted it but I was happy. It made my week or just that day. I feel great that I made it in the 50's. I weighed myself today, accurately said 157. WOW ! I lost 7 lbs since summer Oct. I know I gained last summer and I had 164 lbs beginning of school. I think I had avg. of 1 lb. loss per 2 week. Awesome ! I plan… No.. I mean I will lose more. I I need 10 or less lbs. to make the requirement. I will have a Fat paycheck. The biggest one ever. I'm glad I got to work a lot during vacation. Before I know it,… Time will roll in fast and I won't have my job. "RUN LIKE THE WIND!" I should say to myself, "See, running & calishetics exercise paid-off and even if you had to work and not exercise 5x a week. ."
I feel great. I believe I will get to my destination.. The Future is near that I will achieve my goal of level # 1 → ARNG. I would do whatever it takes. So I hard.. Quit my job.. Tennis.. Sacrifice on importance and a lot more… and take summer school (3classes) 1998. If the time line plan works… I'm gone for 4-5 months to Basic Training and Advanced Ind. Training.
*Dear LoRd.

Ohh! Lord I don't know what I would do. If I don't make it to boot camp. IF I don't make it to boot camp. IF I an not a member of AR National Guard 5-6 months from now. I wonder what and how I would react. I feel good today like I just good an accept one letter to West Point. That goal essay is true about my weight. I'm half way there. I never felt the feeling of fullfilment that true sense of feeling on how I plan my future carrer. I feel it inside me. It is priceless. I'm glad that this goal is not For money like the goal. Money won't do much. I thank you for your blessings, warth [warmth], kindness and everything about the nature, world, and the people around me. I will live with a purpose so great. Indeed.... Whatever it takes make it all worth it. Thank you for being there always in my heart. Tomorrow is another day. Thank you that my Senior Year is the smoothest. I'm in control. I control my Destiny. Good Night Lord.

Yes.. I did finally know the pieces of the lost. Puzzles. All together equals me. The strength and weaknesses, experiences not failures, +/- , ralization and actions etc. so much to it. The formaula is me. It all comes back to me.

I planted another seed today.. I hope to see the sports, the growth. I know there are lot tot see... her.. Know and so much about this world. FAILURE IS NOT AN OPTIION! I WILL FACE MY FEARS. I had improve greatly. I'm crawling my way in academics. Once was my stregth and how my wekness. Not for long. It's hard to get back on the track but get back now or it will be late sooner or later. I can't forget this day. I hope Kelly feels Better. Can you believe or in was that I will Can you believe or in that I will be 18th, in Feb. 7- Party ! I' M VERY LUCKY !

Jan. 9, 1998 (9:15 PM FRI :) ☺

So it rained today and probably tomorrow. At least I'm not working. I only have to work for 2 more weeks. Finals is in 2 weeks too. There will always be days I wish today was better only in making sure I did study. But I just do what I can. I really really had a busy 1st smester in Senior year. I'm thankful I have money for college ($610) right now. So I don't want my Mom pay for it, she has done at lot. Money has taught me a lot that other {CA} ids don't really know yet coz they don't have a job. It was a lot of work. Sacrificing Semester I is not the way to go especially as a senioR and ^ one of my 2 goals is to raise my G. P. A by .2 to have a ^ higher rank in class. Neither I should sacrifice 2nd semester, right ? Besides I need to start getting used to pure hard work and effort towards school work to achieve it.

It is part of on adavantage to have 6 honors (3 AP) classes. Summer school will be a BOOM !!! CRAZY 6 weeks ! Sacrifice and besides I won't bemissing anything big this summer 1998. It will be fun like last year. This year may be more fun. I really hope I will achieve this goal and that after making it is another goal for Fall (Aug -Nov). It will be one of the great things ever happen to me and especially at a young age of 18. It will be a start of a new career. The very first and it's full-time FoR a while but part-time after that. Who knows what God has plan for me. I don't know. I know that I control my destiny, my hopes, my ambition & my fears. I feel CONTENT everyday. I feel good about myself and everyday is a brand new day. Life is not perfect and because to get to the top…climbing up is not easy and it just continue to get harder and more rewarding. I like to improve, mature, challenge myself and much more. In this world, anything can happen. Heck! If we can clone of a baby similar to his/ her Mom or Dad ~~if~~ depend on sex. The U.S. govt. think it is not okay. And I would love to put all my memories on a tiny microchip and when I get old I can remember back. Since cloning sheep is old news and this year 1998... Who knows what kind of human being or alien ? ? ? I still believe in a liens and I believe we are not alone in this universe. I wonder what if I really have the passion for writing poems or stories. If I will really continue to improve my art talents. I LEARNED THAT I CAN START BY ACCEPTING IT, ^ THE IMPROVEMENTS, THE WAY I USE MY SKILLS/ TALENTS, HOW, I SEE IT FOR ME FIRST. It is like how I feel about myself NOW. FOR ME! I should accept it souly,(if that is a word). An example waz is how come I ever was interested the military… I accepted it… I see it's purpose… What it is to me and for me.. Discovered myself and more of what I didn't think,… my heart beats for it… special sense yet I can almost feel it and I did once. Really as of now I feel happy and content. Imagine how much impact in my life it will bring for me. It will be incredible. 10 more pounds. It has to be hard to let go something you love, don't you think. I cant imagine of letting it go because it is more than that. I can't imagine that day t feel like Ripping out my soul. Highschool has it' purpose. I see it's purpose now. Everyone has it's purpose. I see it's pupose now. Everyone has it's own and my experiences of high school was unique. 6 more months to know more and learn more experiences. I'm very smart. It is not easy to have wings when I've been crawling as worm all along. I'm not talking about gross stuff out or I'm not depressed other. What do you think it means. I have to start from the beginning and my way up to "the climb". I remember I this when I wrote about it on my Spanish (summer school) class notebook. It was intended to Rewrite in my diary but I don't recall. I would love to get straight A's this 1st & 2nd semester year but I had to sacrifice ½ of it for the sake of a college future. Who knows whats in store [for me] not for 2nd semester. I only have 2 goals as of now and hope I will a achieve it on the date of my graduation. After that, I will challenge another big obstacle.. Of course ! Quitting McDo. Is one of the best thing for me right now so I only concenttate on those 2 goals. I can't make promises. Am I afraid to fail? I just turn -off the radio because I want to answer this question. Yes! I am just like any human being. Sometimes, I'm worried. I fear that I won't pass the medical examination went I lose enough body fat to pass. I worry that I won't have nothing to look forward for ARNG after summer. I'm not even /sure how to work and how much time left, # of months and when or where. BUT REALLY DEEP INSIDE ME IS A FIGTHER WHO BELIEVES IN WINNING THIS BATTLE. SHE IS TOUGH, COURAGEOUS, BRAVE, SMART, COMPETIVE, YOUNG and there is so much more and more to know. I have to be and because I have gotten this far. I know the significance of achieving it these 2 goals. Only me really understand. I think what I will start to do is harder than 1st semester because I will lose more calories and I must be awake and use my time wisely after I exercise so I can study and do homework. I will probably stay and do homework. I will probably stay up at 11 PM or 12 midnight. I love to RUN. I really miss it. That thrill of running uphill for 10 mins. When it takes 20 mins to walk. Runinng as time unfolds and feel the earth move beneath me, and wind whispers on my ears. The sun's rays ~~above reflects~~ above and hot temp. that I sweat ~~drops comes out a mouthful~~ Each drop must have been plan sacrifice. The intense heat pushes my adrenalin faster. My heart beats like a drum. The faster I go, the faster it beats. My blood boils and I run for more. My sweat vaporise by the sum or, my T-shirt suck it or it drops on soil but still I continue to RUN. It satisfies me to think of this great things. To think what will running do for me. It has done a lot for me. I see God's creations around me, His maRvellous creations made me feel free. It lead me to answers of my questions. So, I wonder if the puzzle pieces I lost inside apoint. It doesn't matter. The answer is me. I feel my body and soul fly like those birds of great flight. I see. There is no stipping now. I stand alone. The serenety of the earth and it's wonders calms me down. I see visions of the future and smile for what it represent. Nothing can me now. I run without a finish line for there is no limit. My characters strengthens and challenge. Destiny is sweet as is to life. I ~~had control no cold alone~~ know this. I fear nothing because I doubt nothing. Finally I step and reach my destination. I took a deep breath and exhaled with great reflect. The future is so full of these. Tomorrow is another run. IT can take me beyond and surpass it's limits.

Jan. 13, 1998 (Tues) 6:00 PM

I just got home from work about 30 minutes ago. I'm relaxing right now and kistening to music. I put ***chumbawamba*** CD right now. Okay, let's see right now my life is… nothing different. All that usual busy stuff. Sooner it will be Jan 28 (Wed), my last day at work. No more minimum wage job for me. I really hope… I don't want to work anymore job like those except the career field/path I deeply want right now. In 26 days I will be 18 years old. The big number 18 ! I'm looking forward to that. I guess? Nothing more there is to celebrate about. ..Well, there is Finals. I can't wait for that to be over. It will be such a relief. I have a load, if not a ton of work to review. AT LEAST, IT'S NOT THE END OF THE WORLD. Richard Rider, one of the guest speaker in my Govt. class spoke today. I mean, he gave a speech about his Liberitarian party and the issues. He knew a lot and gave an outstanding speech. I learned from him about what is the 2nd thing a politican does when he/she elected. (get ready to a ~~re-call recap~~ prepare for a re-election). A good start is at the bottom and work your way up to get to the top. Theres 1,800 offices in San Diego alone. Anyway, there's more but I want to write about something else. I like to be immature and its funny . Kelly and Elizabeth are my friends who I talk a lot at 6th period AP Bio-class. We have a minimum Day and going to eat at **Taco Bell[*YUM]*** after school for Lunch. My friends and I spend about half or less of our conversations about college. At least Kelly has something. She worries. I wouldn't if I was on her place. Then maybe she is (of course) unsure she knows which ones she got accepted. I have a different approach if I was in her place and because I know so. I am serous about going to college. Priority and the important reasons *reasons* behind why, I still hang on to that goal to be a cadet at West Point. I don't really what it wil be like 4 yrs or even 2 yrs from now. **I only know it is in my control** to follow the path I chose a long time ago step by step. I love my Mom. I know she wants to go to the Phils. And won't go without me. I really hope this year in August is the year but after that I'm not sure because I don't know what will hapeen. It's right after a week or so on the last day of summer school at Grossmont College. I'm doing okay if not okay better towards discipline myself in food. I have to get use to stop my craving. I'm not sure if I carve more when I exercise or not. Hopefully after finals I will have time to start my after school running again. I want to start ~~it straight~~ my Presedential Program again. I feel sleepy now. I feel good. I'm doing fine in life. I don't beat myself with negative feelings or unhappy days anymore. I will survive. I write like it was a song seriously there days are over. I can handle my life better. I do & know better everyday. I am a human being so I feel many things. Back to reality now.

JAN. 18, 1998 (6:50 P.M.) SUNDAY

At first I was trying to study then I wrote a list of why I am successful. I opened the blue bag where I put my 2 diaries and other important stuff. I like to look over what I wrote, well I read them because I wonder how I react now. Highschool is an impt. Part of my life. It is more that a place to get an education. For me, It has given me a chance to be me…. Really to find myself. It is one the greatest battles of my life being a teenager. It is not easy to mature especially when a person feels no self-esteem, lack of will, confidence or strength a lack of what is important of a person's soul-character. Maturing is the only way to figure yourself who am I? What is my role? It is too confusing. I am sure everybody when through is phase in their life with or with out the help of others only that person knows to solve it. I found mine the hard-hard way. Mine was hard and tough times seems endless. Trap no more. For me, I said that only one can save herself/ himself. Others can guide you or help and give advice. Isn't that what parents friends are foR. I am not alone and others kids had it worst. I'm fortunate to have my Mom and the Lord. Others stand alone. If you read from the 1st diary to this far, you will know. What I really want to do tonight is spend time on remembering my memories of high school. I remember my Freshman year. I always got the grades but I was so unsatisfied of the rest. Un even my grades was not an achievement *because it was the only thing important* because it was the only thing important because it will get me to a great future and college. I was a dreamer. I spend a lot of time thinking of my future unreal zing part of it was not my idea. Of Air Force Academy and being rich (not of my own company business). I never regret ~~e~~ anything if you ask me. There is a purpose for everything in this world whether from experiences, desires or just a person see it only she/he undertand. I wish I can do something to all the kids who once was me. Lost about their identity. Confuse about their life.

[Wanting to be someone else they are not, confuse about who they are, wanting to escape from it, mislead and so many more I have no~~t~~ time to write it all. I'm bugeting my time. Popularity wasn't a bad idea. I knew a talented person who was caught up by it. Dropping out of High school is not a good idea. It got me to a new character to acquire; Leadership. *NOTE: TALK LIKE YODA IN "SPEECHLESS "]* It's nice to think about my experiences as a young Leader in the community and school. I never think I would get that far if not for my character. Extracirrucular activities which was mainly base to enrich my character and leadership is worth it despite of the sacrifice of my grades. I'm glad it turned out. I'm glad my life turn out this great. It has been an incredible experience and I continue to climb. The age 18 is another step. I am not tied up to someone's hopes but it help me to rethink about it. It is a laudable goal but I choose ~~it~~ the Army and West Point. I wont go into details why because I explain it So many times in this diary. I have fun with clubs and the activities I plan and participated. Of course now it is different. I learned many experiences from it but I prefer to have my PRIORITIES. Things that matter now. I owe [a lot] nothing to my High School and community for my continuing experiences even as of today. Yes, my family and friends. I give back my time to volunteer and help in any way I can. I had increase my character, my personality and become a better person. I found strength in me to continue ^ achieving my goals in life. I will like the idea of taking time to enjoy life but I do enjoy life every minute and every second. It is nice to have fun and relax too but I don't I don't like to abuse it. I ~~did~~ made me neglect much of what is important. I ~~said~~ wrote about it and I don't want to repeat it. I coupled and tackled stress. I don't worry about what people think of me. Anymore. I know myself well more than they do. I am a human being, I do say things not thinking it can upset that person. We all have done that. I no longer wish to be someone else like Sara. I am very happy about my personalities and character. I have yet to learn more, just another part of growing up to be an adult. It seems like I always have great days as a senior in high school. I skin med through ~~diff~~ next page after page. I laugh or smile because I think I was so outrageous. Yes, if you are a phy charatRist....you would think I was crazy. Isn't evry body? I feel embrass about how far I tried to get these guys to notice me. Hey, many girls don't have the guts to do what I had done. I still think it is funny. I can't believe I'm the Soph. Class president of my class 1998. Yes I believe. "You never know what is going to happen unless you try, "something like that about reminding myself to achieve something. I have met a lot of interesting people my age in high school. I had achieve goals related to high school whether in academics, sports or activities. I also falied. One of the greatest thing about life is failure. In my opinion, It has given me a different point of view in life or anything. (life, goals, hopes, or person/ people who helped me). I remember (~~those words~~ having a conversation to Mrs. Thalman and Mrs. Fonseca about it. It has given me inner strength and more strength about improvising or improving my character. There is a self-assurance. "It is not the end of the world." People continue their life and their past was not easy and they are still batteing obstacles and living (… You know what I'm talking about). I think crazy is an okay word. How about psegochotic. It seems more funnier to me when I look back like spying on guys. It wasn't like one night.. Bam!!! I see realize what is really important. It took a while… long. I know that I feel like crying but It never solved me anything for me. It just make things worse. Sometimes one of the worst thing that happen like ASB can to me in high school. Journalism showed me something new to my skill. But the experience of challenge I got from both was great too. There comes a time when I need a friend. Elizabeth, Kelly and Hilary had helped me through rough time. A talent so precious like Martial Art. I know I will continue to improve and have time in the future. I sense now that despite of the problems I had in the past, I was tough and tackle d them. That is one of the reason why I have a strong character. Thinking of Air Force academy ever was my destiny and it is different now. Destiny is controlled by the person who desires it. I control my own destiny. I was very WORRIED ABOUT MY FUTURE. I MADE IT THIS FAR. LIKE WHAT I SAID BeFORE, I am tOUGH and CAPABLE OF ACHIEVING WHAT I WANT IN LIFE. "dESTINY IS Destiny , Let it be." One of the best things is getting those below B grades. I don't think they are bad grades because I didn't just sit in class and got that. It had a purpose. I am in control of my life Right now. I like it this way much better. One turning point of my Soph. Year was the Gradaution. I found MY MIRROR OF REFLECTION… my soul…inner most of me; myself. That day gave me hope and much more. It was a sad day after school but turned out to be awesome. "A lot of unexpected things wëll happen," quoted from the 1st diary comments of how I felt towards my future. A lot of unexpected things had happen and will continue to be. On that graduation , John Boland was mention about his choice to W.P. I am not feeling low. That is such a vague word -(*low*) to me now. I am no longer running away with my life. The Lord has helped me and is my guidance when I ask for help. I thank you Lord. I always think High to rise. I keep thinking of what really matters ~~meant~~ tome or the things that I want to accomplish will it win out well excluding academics which was really the most important to the requirements. I know how to get to W.P. because I'm a planner. I alone understand why I'm doing this; for me. I'm happy that as ~~the~~ pages after pages, I got better. The pages got thicker. I found myself my junior year. I ".. to respect myself, feel confident… have high-self-esteem, feel great, don't compare myself to otheres.Stocks -> 4 money, teakwondo-> winning national titles, -> are a ~~few~~ couple hopes. I love my philosophies only me(in my heart) sees its purpose for my life. I'm fascinated ~~with~~ about successful people. ***"I desire to do great things; to conquer the world,"*** another quote to help me remember. A dream in life is different to a vision in life. Note March 2, '97, is one of my favorites. Yes I do have the will, courage and desire. To make it to the Academy. My Junior Year was ~~toug~~ tough too. I appreciate doing something Fun not to escaped with my problems but to just enjoy. My senior year is a worthy [situation]. I never want to come back and relive Highschool. I prefer to say each year of my high school contributed to great things for me. Each year has its own special meaning only I know from my heart. Since I crossed at part of troubled water in my life so ~~I am~~

~~can~~ be the person of character. I have So much more to learn. I don't worry about what if I have a different life not like this right now. I don't think of it at all. I'm glad of the turning point of ARNG> I wont forget about what Mama Maria told me about the military
(conversation with my Mom).

Jan 23, 1998 (5:25 P.M. T. G .I. F. Thank Goodness its Friday !)

I will start by talking about the 4 FoRtune cookies ~~Judy~~ Steve gave me. I've been collecting them for a while now. I think it is interesting. It somewhat gives me answers but it is not what it seems yet. It is weird to trace why I got this tape of Fortune cookie. It doesn't cost much compare to asking a fortune teller. Plus, I get to eat the cookie part. I already overspend more money than I expected. I guess, I have to hold off for those 2 CD's. I really want. My mirror of reflection came up and I did wrote about it before. I always fell I have all the luck in the world despite of everything. I believe in my instincts. But when will hard work pay off other than the paycheck I got today. It's amazing how days turns to weeks turns into the end of the ~~mon~~ month. Two more weeks till my B-Day. I hope my light headache will be gone soon. Yes! Yes ! Yes! I made it. Say Goodbye to Semester I and hello Sem II. Finals are over. I feel weird when I don't do something fun like going out to places, movies, friend's house or the mall etc. I'm very satisfied right now. I saw Titanic with Robin yesterday afternoon. We went to the mall to eat at the new McDo. I wish I bought the soundtrack but it was $2 bucks short. I really appreciate it a whole lot better when I saw it the 2nd time. Around 100-2000 yrs. Range ago was completely different time, culture, society etc. I'm glad to be alive and varned close to looking forward close to the millemum. Year 2000 ! It will be an exciting year ~~even~~ something link to it. When I was 12, I came to America. If 1992 and 1980 was the year of the Monkey. 1998 is in my instinct a very memorable and yet challenging year for me as a vision a prediction. I feel it. I call the shots because I control my destiny. 1998 is the year of the Tiger. Year 2000 is year of the Dragon. The Dragon is the most fascinating of all. I am veRy fascinated about The Year of the Dragon. In Chinese zodiac. I really don't know how it all link together. I only did a research about the Chinese zodiac 2 years ago but I don't know a lot about it. I will find it moRe stRange year 2000 when #2 goal comes true, 1998 of a. start…. 2004 as 24 years old. The question is how does what is the relation of 12, 24 or even 6, 12, 18, 24 (age)…… and what was great about being a 6 years old?

Okay ! I don't see how I have to learn/ and study the past ~~about 100 yrs~~ when the school can teach the literature of our society. There is so much talent around the world. Does it have to be history beFoRe we can talk about it in high school ? It is only in college because each subject is more exact ~~and~~, detailed and precise. Why do we have to read/ watch plays of W. Shakespeare when we can read Jurrasic Park and ~~see~~ see the movie at class too? Present literature is important too. If I was a teenager going to school 100+ years from now. I probably will be studying about Hollywood literature. It's impact on to ~~more the~~ the people, society, music, movies, $ $ $ lots of money, the hard-work and talented actors/ actress directions and others musicians and people of this wonderful society. And to thinkb how a ~~1401~~ 17th years old kid will react to it [my situation] it if she/ he was born 100 plus years from now. ~~Who~~ You would they find it boring to ~~I~~ know . , and ~~I know~~. And understand the facts. It is important to know the past and learn from it. How about a modern History and literature class for a new subject in Highschool. That way students can discuss, relate, argue, respond, charge & enjoy ~~etc.~~ their situation. The modern life should be discuss in classrooms. We are fighting for it everyday. /\ and reliving it the future. Because it is not easy to live easy. I have no clue what I'm talking about. FoR ~~oeu~~ now, I go to school to appreaciate the past and, the world, endless possibilities, and especially the millions of and p billions of people ~~we had died who~~ created and responsible for making is world what it is now. Yes ! That includes my teachers too. It is one of my major goals in life is to make a difference. I am only one person. I can do all. I wish I can end the world hunger, clean up the enviRonment of the world, peace on earth,… in other woRds, save the whole wide world. Well, one must stand up so others will too. I feel really weird tonight. There are only a few things I want to happen….(1) To be a leader in military and U.S. politics (2) Leader / politician (same

thing ~~)~~ but I prefer the world so I can make a difference (3) be a writer /poet (poems, shot stories, novels) ans (4) artist (3) & (4) a purpose to share it, enjoy it, challenge within it, especially touching people's lives and feeling the same way when great writers/ artist has helped me see the world to appreciate and even more (very priceless) (5) Army challenge as a lawyer JAG, DIA agent, military intellinge, West Point, ARNG, NSC, challenges of many many years of experiences that5 will help me lead to a Political career (6) Busniess women (NYSE, ← stock investor), having very small business instead of a big one) so I can have a (7) Lamburgini, Hummer Black with stereo system & Black chevy blazer & Corvette (I can LIVE having 2 out of 3 cars and have a mansion/castle worth at least $ 3.5 million and a
$10 million in the bank. Of Course life wouldn't be grwat[great] without the people I love (8) to have a husband who is in the military/ politics career (I don't even want to talk about details or I will need to buy a new diary. Just a little humor) That would be nice if he was the future Pres. For as long as no threatening or bad things (like what Clinton is in now) (and still have nothing_____?__ will change my mind about Sec. of state, foreign affair, politial, world problems U.N. I wouldn't be surprise if this all happens and look back at age 60+. I told you I'm weird tonight.

Today finally happened. I mean about the get together at Elizabeth's house. We ate Pizza and watched *ConAir* and *A long Kiss Goodnight.* I always end up watching less about what happen today and more about how I feel on what I think. Nothing starnge for me. Tomorrow I will do clean-up stuff and go to work. I have plans for Sunday but I wont go to the mall. A few more days and I no longer have to work for McDo anymore (at least 10+ hours). My last paycheck is on Feb. 6. I'm excited for the 4 months of pain and the 2 goals I will accomplish. Of Course ! I have a positive attitude and I'm a hard worker. It will pay off. 7 more days till my B-Day !

Jan 31, 1998 95:45 PM)
← Last Saturday of Jan.

What a cool week I had so far. I made it this weekend. Today was a glomy day. El Niño (the storm) came back but I was at the mall with my Mom and Lorna(& her kids) my Mom's friend. I couldn't find the one Elizabeth wanted for B-Day. I got a fortune cookie written " *An unexpected event will soon bring you fortune." I hope it will come true soon."*

I hope that means the ARNG and whatever it is, I hope it will come true soon. I haven't pasted it (my fortune cookie) on my diary. It is stick to one of my drwing & (on the wall) with the newspaper magazine (Parade) started " If it's Something you love with all your Heat, Do it," from one of the women of the '90's interview who is a horse jockey (← I'm not sure if that, is the right name for it.) Anyway, it menas so much to me. It will go in my scrapbook. I really want to finish it before I gradute and I can always add more stuff in my scrapbook for college stuff. It is incredible on how much opportunity young women have today because of the women I read about on that magazine and the 65 years old lady, Mrs. Costanza (a former advisor to Pres. Carter). The role that they play have a big impact to me. I am so [happy] to have a choice I call my own. Despite that fact there are unfairness in our society of today, it doesn't stop me or any young lady women who wish to achieve a career she wants. That is the way it has to be to have more expansion of vast opportunities because it will put so much impact to the future. I am just one person but I can do anything I want to happen for me and together with people (like you and me) who has what it takes can to. Moving along… I finish my 1st week of my running/ training. I feel so good but there is a lot more. Oohh ! About 18-20 weeks for the most. Hey, nothing is easy as counting one, two and three. In this world, I have to follow the rules. I don't want to worry about the of consequences. What ever happen in the next 5 months or more will happen. I must think positive. Thinking negatively can hurt insult my performance in life, both my school work and exercise. I'm in the guidance of the Lord. I have faith in me and him. I have strength and he will be fine. I have nothing to fear; nothing to loose. I like this week. I no longer work. My last night was Sat (Jan 24). My academics are wonderful. I will be successful this 2nd semester. I have a lot to concentrate. This is my last semester of high school.

An unexpected thing happen this week. Kelly and I usually go to the library in the morning when we get to school. But on Thusday of this week, the library in the morning when we get to school. But on Thursday of this week, the library seem full but not really. We decided actually I suggested that we go to my period 1 class (English). I had 2 homework from my first class English I needed to get them done but I never got a chance before Period one my class starts but anyway I did made the deadline and did the homework sometime that day. My point is I got a Golden State Exam Recognition for 1997 English. I was speechless. I never think I will get that award. That was the 3rd time I took GSE[GOLDEN STATE EXAM] (one for Algebra at 9th grade, Chemistry at 19th grade). Well, I do deserve it. I just gave an example that anything in this world is possible. I'm happy. I'm proud. I smiled and laughed extensively. It rained that day. I still think that was a weird day. Another article on Parade magazine was about this elementary Teacher let her students write a letter about themselves. She sends it back to them 10 yrs. later. It will help them remember back the precious memories. I rember great memories as a small kid. I won't write much about it except in the scrapbook. I made a promise as a small kid. I won't write much about it except in the scrapbook. I made a promise I will write a letter when I graduate from high school. What I did in my teen years, ups and downs, what I love and like. It will be a review and the best of the best events. I don't want to write a letter now because I have a diary. Since I have the time to do more for myself now, I need to spend most of it to my 2 goals. I need huge review of 1st semester stuff in Calculus. I learned this lesson before but I remember its significance much greater now than ever. It is hard to put in words.

" Tommorow is another day to be a better person."
" What I learn yesterday, today and tomorrow is needed to excel in the future."

Now I know. I appreciate education for a long time now. One of the things I must do which is one key element to excel each day. I can't go back in the past. I don't regret anything. I don't want to change a bit of it. **"Failure to me is as importance as success."** I know it from my experience. Let's cut to the chase here- the future. Math levels- from arithmetic to Calculus to beyond Calculus. I need to know to solve step 1 to 10 to get to step 11. I don't want to miss any steps. So now I know. I know more of what I don't know. I have a piece of paper I took notes from Mr. Hoss about his philosophy of knowledge.

"The more you know, the more you know what what you *don't know*. Therefore you become aware of what *you don't know*. Knowledge will come to you, suddenly you will care about it; quoted from Mr. Hoss."

My way of getting to have more knowledge and more of what I need to know for this class or anything is appreciation. BOOM ! Just like that. I like to learn. I admire the work of teachers teaching his/ her students to learn. "To gain knowledge, one must appreciate learning. Appreciation must come from within." That is how I think of it.

People are good at something because they acquire or work for it.

A person has a talent and even much more they can offer abilities but it is nothing unless the person improve, challenge, gain, share, excell, acquire or tested from it. It offers a lot to the person who got it and to the world.

Last advice from Mr. Zhoss, "Never analyze yourself with critizm. Be yourself."

My category (why did you choose the job/ career)

(1) Doing what they love. IT comes with passion. Whether to help others, making a difference.

(2) But it can be combine (1 & 2) if doing something to get what they for money, greed, power (the bad and the goood side). #2 can rule the most if that is what you want.

(3) someone made them too.

* 1,2,3 can be mix and combine. Right now I want #1. #2 comes when I achieve it. It varies because we are human beings. There's 2 more things I want to be in my diary.

Midge Costanza
876 Vine St. # 40
Oceanside, CA 92054

1/28/98
Dear Costanza,
Greetings ! First allow me to introduce myself. My name is Heralyn M. Toling, a student at El Capitan High School. I am one of the students who [had] the opportunity to hear your great speech in Mrs. Douglas, period 4, A.P. American Government class. I would like to take this opportunity to say that I really like your speech. Thank you for sharing your political views and political experiences to the class. Your speech iz very inspirational to me. This is why I'm writing this letter to you. I'm was deeply moved by your great speech particularly when you talked about the opportunities and our chioce of destiny all Americans are fortunate to have. You inspired me to keep on believing and working towards acheving my laudable future goal of a career in politics.

I was fascinated about the United States of America ever since I was a young child up in the Philippines. I'm fortunate to come to U.S.A. as an immigrant at the age of 12 and to have the vast opportunities and my own chioce of destiny I control. Before I came here, I heard that U.S.A. is where dreams and hopes can come true. *[OF COURSE], USA is for someone like me & you willing to achieve/doing what it takes to achieve [PLAN, DREAM & take ACTION].**

I thank you very much for everything. I will always remember your great speech.*Plan, dream, action is just thought of8/9/08 to write about the [3STEPS TO SPIRITUAL MOTIVATION]

Sincerely,
Heralyn M. Toling

Of course, I wrote it neatly. It is important to me write her a letter. The speech was meaningful to me. I feel better when I wrote the letter. I wanted to show/ tell her how much it meant to me. I'm sure she will be glad to read it.

Feb. 6, 1998 (7:50 PM)

Hi ! I made it to another week. Can you say politics ! This week was somewhat like that, at least part of my story will be. One of Mark Price supporters for his campaign in running for State Assembly 75. He called about an hour ago. I thought at first he was from Nobel Bakery asking the correct way to spell my name. It was the first thing he asked but he said he is from the people of Mark Price. You know what I mean. I was able to say words but couldn't think. I started to fell nervous. He probably thought it was a prank call. I really don't know. The last question was- How did you know Mark Price? Then he said he'll call back and hang up. I think I blew it. I thought about how fast that went. I doubt he'll call back. I really don't know what he thinks. I said that tomorrow is my B-Day, my parents are gone and don't have a clue of where it is… tomorrow is my B-day, my parents are gone and don't have a clue of where it is held at, and I talk much of helping out. I just realized he wasn't Mark Price until I wondered what and why he said, "he'll call back or someone was on the line." I Just like that. He asked, "If I drive or old enough to drive." I said dumdumfundedly "No." What was I suppose to say that, "I don't know how to drive even though I will be 18 tomorrow. I don't have a ride there. Please, Please, I am so desperate and wuold love to go to this kick- off party." Like that guy would really understand or even Mr. Price. All I know is am very interested in Politics. I want to get an experience of helping out candidates like Mr. Price. I want to see what it is like to be in a local political area.
Hey ! Gotta start somewhere at the bottom, right ? I wish I had a car and drive. I wish for a lot of things. I thought maybe he wanted to talk to Mr. Price and who called Heralyn Toling who called. I wished that Mr. Price can help me get there (provide transportation) and back home. He's rich. Yeah Right. I knew at the moment I got that invitation, when he handed it to me that I wont be able to go. Poor Heralyn! I'm proud at least I took one step forward and probably another step today to try, to get involve in this political thing. It will help him or if anyone will ever call back.
I was glad he came to our school to talk/ speech on Thurs. at my AP. Govt. class. He's a Republican. Yap! He is one of the political people in my memory…" Everyday is a new experience," he said. I asked him about running for his candidacy. I don't remember much. I can put in this scenario,

"Hey ! I did something that interest me. A step forward towards my leadership. The only way you can get things done, is get off your butt and do it. My interpretretation of what Mr. Randy Voepel and Mr. Price talked about. So im very happy I talked to the speakers. If not helping Mr. Price campaign even though I really want to.. I WILL (MARK MY WORDS) find another way to get involve. I don't see why I wouldn't for the type of person like one whose interest in politics means a lot. WELL, AT LEAST I HAVE EARNED THE RESPECT THAT MR. PRICE INVITED & GAVE ME AN INVITATION to HIS CAMPAIGN KICK-OFF PARTY. WHO KNOWS WHAT WILL HAPPEN NEXT and my future. I can look back at this memory, smiling and thinking this is this is one person why I got high & far in politics. I'm a believer myself, in my dreams and hopes.

Mr. Randy Voepel, another ~~lost~~ [winning] Republican like myself who is a vice mayor of Santee. He is a very remarkable guy. His motto is "Say what you mean, mean what you say." (Harry S. truman) He definetily gave me a great advice. He told the class he knocked at over 5,000 doors (a lot of doors) that made him win over his Libertarian Party. He is a rable-rouser. Lets just say he definitely made his mark. He made everyone talk and argue about his views in class and whole lot of disscussion that day. I have nothing against his views. Overall, all the speakers were great. One more thing, **"Money** is everything especially especially in **politics."** ***"POWERTICS!,"*** said Mr. Voepel.

"See all signs, capaign ads on that wall. I like these people. They are the ones who did something," said Mr. Voepel. He spend $30,000 + & without any support from Govt. Mr. Price spend over $ 100,000 so far and it's not even June 1998 yet.

Its been raining this week and will probably rain tomorrow. I have been doing great academically. I have to get used to getting A's and B's now. I like it. 2 weeks is short to detemine how well I am towards my 2 goals. By the 6th week (around March), I will see my hard work pay off. I just continue to run like the wind. I feel weird even now but as much as this week(today) all put together. Turning 18 tomorrow means more… a lot more. I don't really want to discusss or talk about it much. I just read back what I wrote feeling 17th. Yes, I was a big picture has worried but overall felt confident in which I failed turning 17th. I HAVE THE CAPABILITES TO DO WHAT OUT OF LIFE. I'm fired up about tomorrow and turning 18th. Indeed, it will be another very interesting year for me. I have visions and sense the feeling of what I will be challenging to and success of … I have so much to write, to hope, to say but I know that reading this the night before I turn 19th I [will] be content and happy. I will finally say, "See! It wasn't so bad. I did it Heralyn and you knew it all along." I hope so. Which way is the wind blowing for me? For as long as I have this life. I control, my character and everything what keeps me moving and pushing up, I will sense the calmness of the wind. I had a conversation on the phone with Hilary. I told her how morose I was feeling except I control it now.

"Are you going to get throw out of the house now?," she took a deep breath. Whatever happens, that isn't and I wont allow it to happen. Over my dead body. Kelly been a geat friend too. She called about time for movies which save me time. And I called Elizabeth. And others to tell them. I'm going to Wal-Mart to kill time and to be early coz I got to get the cake at Nobel's Bakery. Robin, Jimmy and Hilary's bro are coming too. Tomorrow should be an interesting day despite of rain. I would love to write how great and confident I am but not necessary tonight. I'm fine. I'm sure I will be writing about what will happen tomorrow. It will be a fun day.

☺ HAPPY 18TH B-DAY !!!
Fun! Party! Whoopee! Horay! Oohh yeah ! 18th here I come. (U KNOW WHAT… HAPPY 107 B-Day... If you live dat far HOMEY!!!127 is even better G.)

BUY DA'MUARTE M/L 107 [my 3rd book]
a revise version of SEX & MUSIC LIT. 101 [1st book]

₱ 55 pesos

P55 value at H.B.G.& P.
Makati, M.Manila, Taguig Philippines

$ 1.07

$1.07 value at H.B.G. & P. Los Angeles, San Diego ,U.S.A.

☺ raffle this gift certificate at H.B.G. & P. (after ordering) to win a free flirty meal worth ₱ 2,600 [$51.00] or more cool prizes. + read the book for all cool prize listing.

Gift Certificate

Presented to: ________________ Expires on year 2015

HERALYN'S BBQ grill & pub

THANKS 4 BUYING MY 2ND BOOK TITLED: HERALYN M. TOLING'S SPIRITUAL HIGH-SCHOOL & COLLEGE DIARIES W/ JAWING MR. & MRS. ROCKSTAR

(1) Heralyn M. Toling
one coupon per order
RESCUED AT GUNPOINT.

CUT ALONG DOTTED LINES

₱ 55 pesos

P55 value at H.B.G.& P.
Makati, M.Manila, Taguig Philippines

$ 1.07

$1.07 value at H.B.G. & P. Los Angeles, San Diego ,U.S.A.

☺ raffle this gift certificate at H.B.G. & P. (after ordering) to win a free flirty meal worth ₱ 2,600 [$51.00] or more cool prizes. + read the book for all cool prize listing.

Gift Certificate

Presented to: ________________ Expires on year 2015

HERALYN'S BBQ grill & pub

THANKS 4 BUYING MY 2ND BOOK TITLED: HERALYN M. TOLING'S SPIRITUAL HIGH-SCHOOL & COLLEGE DIARIES W/ JAWING MR. & MRS. ROCKSTAR

(2) Heralyn M. Toling
one coupon per order
R.A.G.P.

VISIT HBG&P 3X AND GET A FREE MEAL

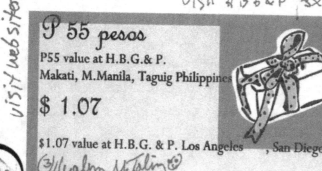

₱ 55 pesos

P55 value at H.B.G.& P.
Makati, M.Manila, Taguig Philippines

$ 1.07

$1.07 value at H.B.G. & P. Los Angeles, San Diego ,U.S.A.

☺ raffle this gift certificate at H.B.G. & P. (after ordering) to win a free flirty meal worth ₱ 2,600 [$51.00] or more cool prizes. + read the book for all cool prize listing.

Gift Certificate

Presented to: ________________ Expires on year 2015

HERALYN'S BBQ grill & pub

THANKS 4 BUYING MY 2ND BOOK TITLED: HERALYN M. TOLING'S SPIRITUAL HIGH-SCHOOL & COLLEGE DIARIES W/ JAWING MR. & MRS. ROCKSTAR

(3) Heralyn M. Toling ☺
ask for your free meal coupon from the front cashier register.
Rescued at Gun Point.

@ Lakeside, CA U.S.A.
Heralyn's BBQ Grill & Pub.com. www.MVFS...

MADE @ 2AM on May 3, 2008
www.HeralynM.Toling.com / www.
www.M.V.F.S.W.com

THIS COUPON
VISIT website

H Heralyn's
B BBQ
I'LL DIET WHEN I GET BACK
G Grill
and
NO PROBLEM - CHARGE IT!
P Pub
est. 2010

Buy my 1st 1st 1st ever ALBUM titled: Sex & Music Literature 101 - D107 = L.M.V. - Songs I Miss U...

This coupon made at 2AM May 3rd 2008 @ Lakeside, CA U.S.A.

D.e.l.t.a.
A.r.m.y.
F.o.r.c.e.
B.i.t.c.h.e.s.

I'LL DRINK TO THAT

D.A.F.B. Soon to be a major kick-ass dance company, 4 all hochiemamas alike!!!

Hieralyn Manlos Jaling Jifedso
August 7 2008

May 25, 2004, 12:46 AM, Tuesday

GET ME HOME!

I'VE NEVER DONE THIS

WHAT A KISS!

YOU'RE IRRESISTIBLE

The GO POLITICAL THEME of My 2nd Book titled: RESCUED AT GUN POINT

SMELL THAT AIR!

Where is MARCIBLOND?

Phaze 1 of M.V.F.S.W ♥ MyVenti Frapino Sketchdezort Drunker- phrenia Weekends [the movie]

Itz likepaying $30 million in ADVANCE.

Phaze 1-3-4

P1 - Do the Weekends 1-2 backwards

P3 - EDIT [PRODUCER-ing/post pre] productions

P4 - TURN in to SANDIEGO/Sundance film Festival? 2017-2018 or? 20??

WISH YOU WERE HERE
EAT YOUR HEART OUT
UH HUH!
my imaginary friend SAVED my LIFE♥ How?
CHECK THIS OUT!
SEND $ A.S.A.P.
THIS VACATION IS GREAT!
July 2008
MY PLACE OR YOURS?

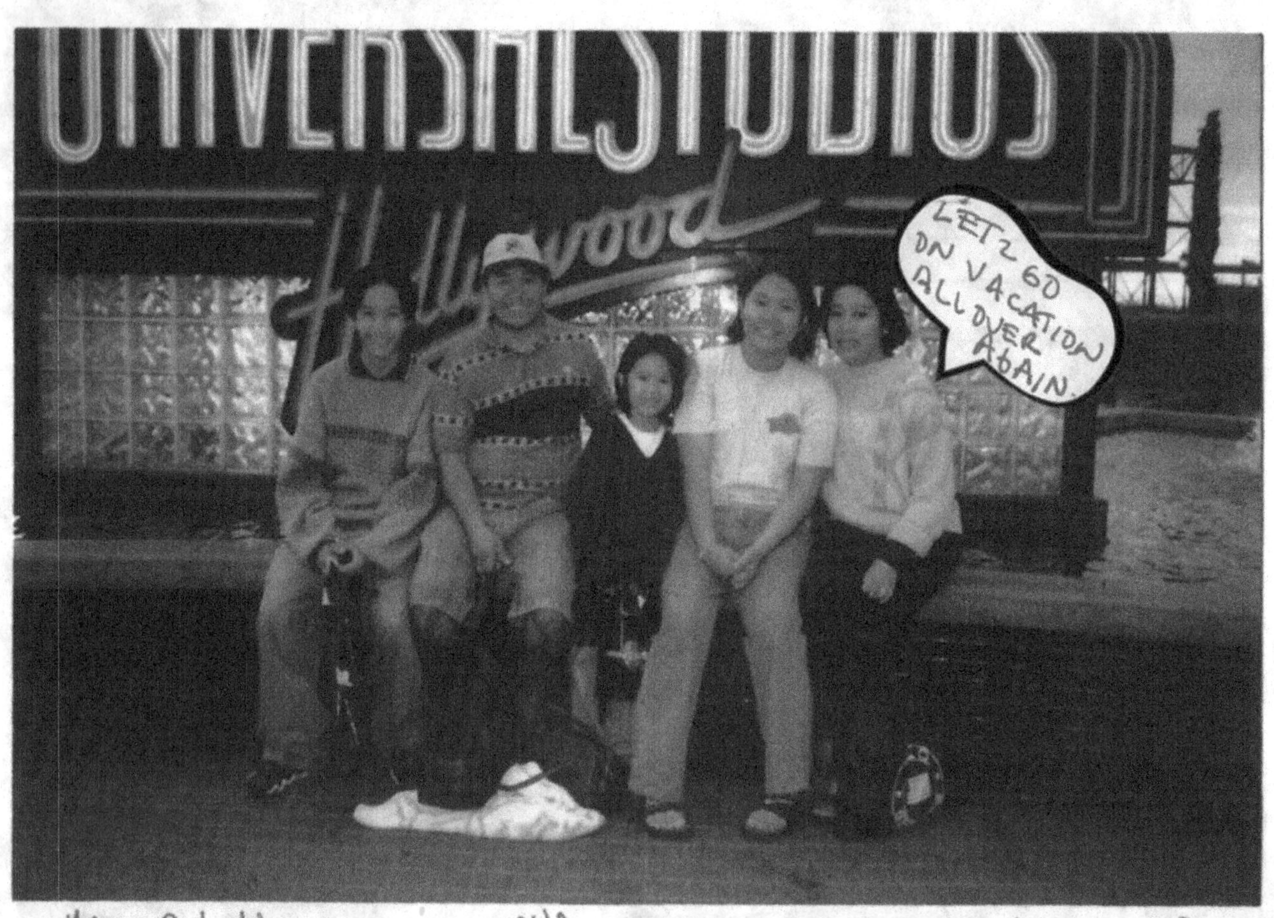

My relatives, cousins & uncle June, Tita Myrna Dimple. Angel, ~~[illegible]~~ Jin Earl (not in order) @ Los Angeles' Universal Studios Hollywood

WE MADE IT!
GO AHEAD, MAKE MY DAY
ALL THIS AND BRAINS TOO!
Look! A picture of my imaginary friend
PARKING ONLY

LET the GOODTIMES Roll
WHAT THE ???
Hemlyn's Highschool bedroom
1993-1999
College...

Hi! Itz Nicole
GRIN AND IGNORE IT!
SEE YA SOON
GO FOR IT!
YA-BONEHEAD!
BEACHED WHALE AT REST
WHAT SIGHTS!
THE SUN HAS FRIED MY BRAIN
JUST US GUYS . . .
'99年 3月 1日
HANGIN' LOOSE!
GET ME OUT OF HERE!!
OFFICIAL BEACH BUM
GENIUS AT REST
FUN IN THE SUN...

HUBBA, HUBBA!
WEST POINT
Senior year AP Bilogy 1998 Yeah!
Shamu.
SeaWorld
DisneyLand 2004
Chocolate Hills, Philippines [Bohol]

HI EVERYONE!

HERE'S TO GOOD TIMES

A DREAM COME TRUE

NO DOUBT

I THINK WE'RE LOST

You are going to have a very comfortable life.

Toling Libedo

Clothing Company

I'm getting horny, how about you.

Self-establish since you it on me.

Toling Libedo

CLOTHING COMPANY

Live Free Or Die

Logo designs for TOLINGLIBEDO T-shirt/clothing company [Friday night] August 16, '08

WANTED: A GREAT TUTOR ~~from~~ with a Graduating Diploma of Univ. of Santo Tomas - Teacher - Leader - Easy Going - Adviser - Flexible on working

BE HERALYN M. TOLING'S

NEW TUTOR / MENTOR and get

Paid high $$$ dollar or ₱₱₱ pesos!!!

Heralyn will negotiate to your the amount of money you want for this JOB!!!

Must be a graduate of

① University of SANTO TOMAS [UST]

② A great personality.... Well-Rounded, friendly, nice, helpful, focus, talented and plans to have a creative interest in Fashion, Fast food-restaurant, publishing magazines and movie-Hollywood dreamaker (i.e. aspiring actor/actress, writer, director)

③ are you well-spoken in English and transform the English language for Heralyn to pass the U.S.T. Entrance Exam B4 2011 of May?

④ Are you a fan of great architecture?

If you qualify for all of the above. Plez contact Heralyn M. Toling @ this store. Leave a written message to one of the Heralyn's BBQ Grill & Pub managers to apply. Ask Right now

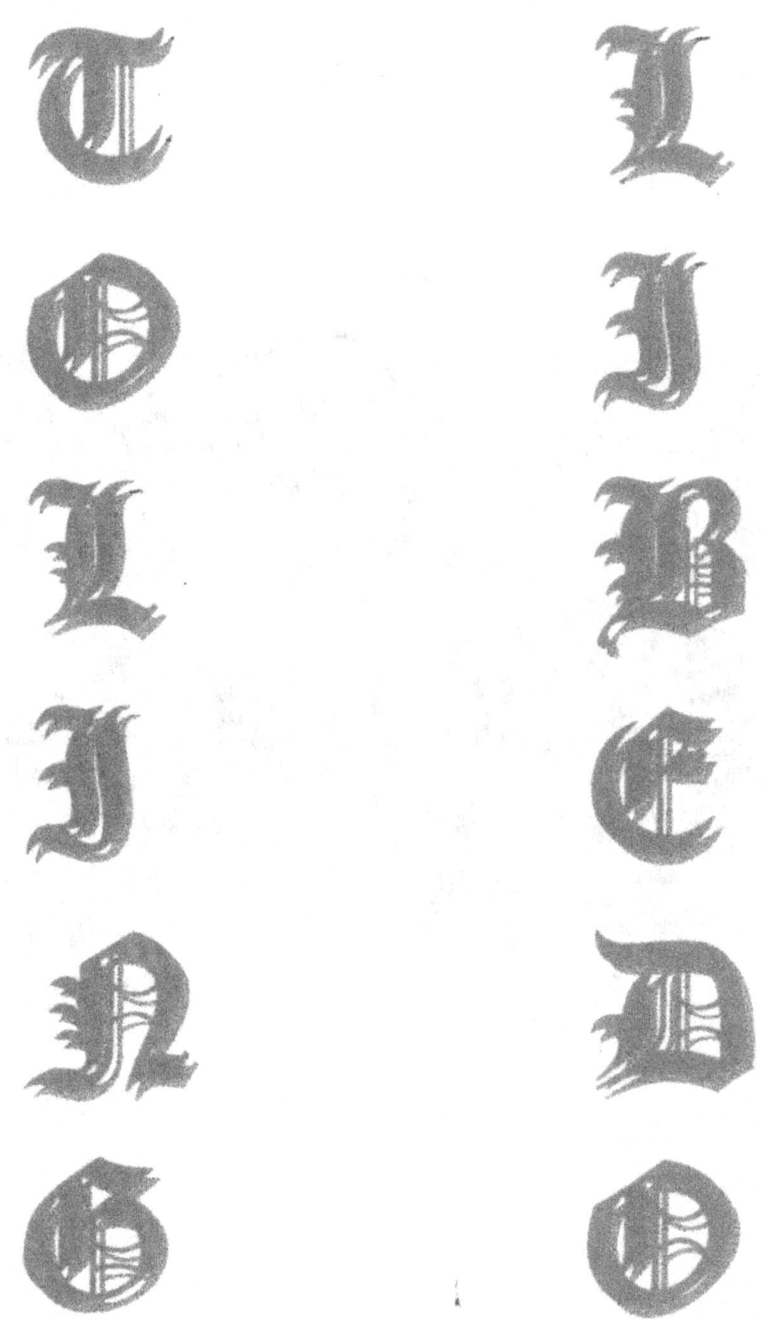

ORANGE

May 17, 2004, 10:40 PM Monday

WE'RE NEVER GOING BACK
SHARKS!
THIS IS BEAUTIFUL...

WHO'S HOMESICK?

NUDIST CAMP REJECT
EAT YOUR HEART OUT

WHAT A BOD!
TIME TO PIG OUT!

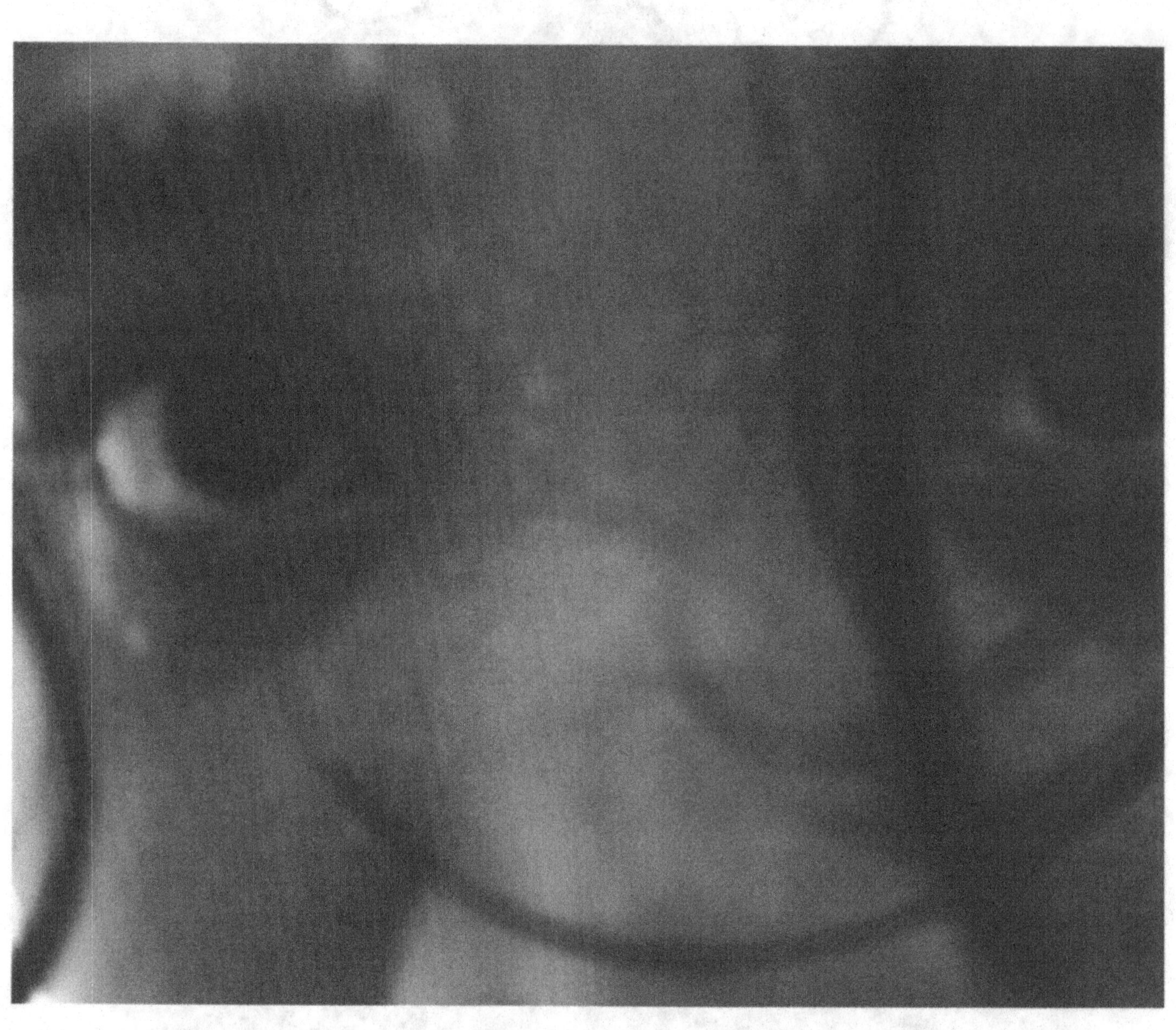

UMA
$ 7,800
SHOOT THE MOON!
I'm a Bee...
I WON
...NOTHING.
2009
Morales T.V.
Put your MoonWoman here?
SUN
EARTH
SATURN
Milkyway
Chrysalis Miracle Awards

LET'S PARTY!
A TAN GODDESS!
TAKE ME I'M YOURS!

I NEED A DATE!

ONE CRAZY NIGHT!

THE GREAT OUTDOORS!
MARILYN MONROE, WATCH OUT!

WHAT A FEELING

My cousin ALMA, Heralyn

IF SHE ONLY KNEW!
IF HE ONLY KNEW!

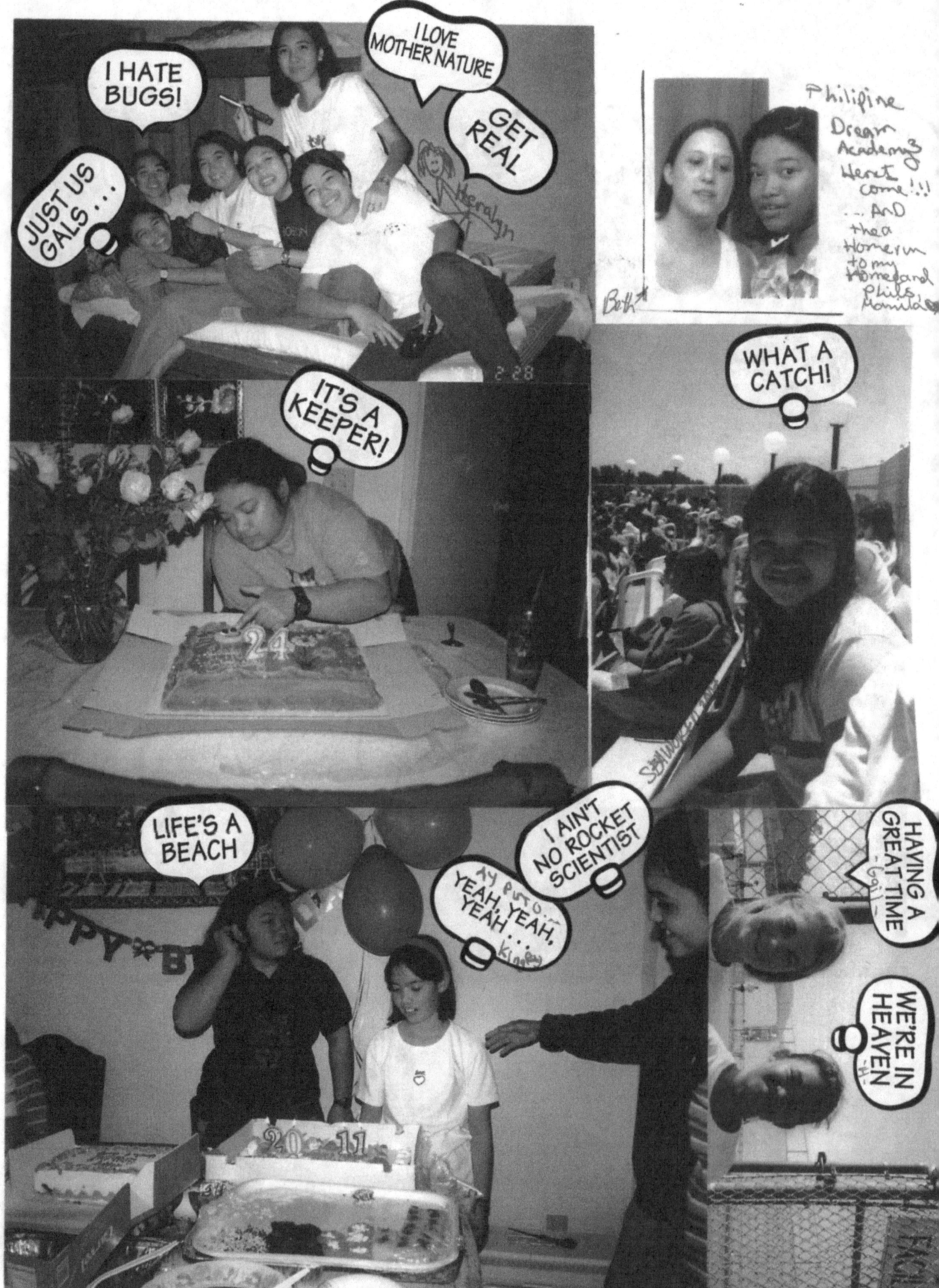
I HATE BUGS!
I LOVE MOTHER NATURE
GET REAL
JUST US GALS . . .
IT'S A KEEPER!
WHAT A CATCH!
LIFE'S A BEACH
I AIN'T NO ROCKET SCIENTIST
YEAH, YEAH, YEAH . . .
HAVING A GREAT TIME
WE'RE IN HEAVEN

WHAT SMELLS?
BON VOYAGE
THIS IS GOD'S COUNTRY
WE'RE ON A MAN HUNT
WHAT A WOMANIZER!
Wowowee, sinong di mawiwili 
DOH!... BART!
IF YOU'RE RICH I'M SINGLE
SO SUE ME!
Absolute
THIS WATER IS COLD!
TAGUIG VACATION @ June 2006

BRE and
GIRLS Tennis
I ONLY LOOK INNOCENT
'04 6 15
My very first
BORN TO PARTY!
WHAT A BOD!
100% PURE BEEFCAKE

SAY IT, DON'T SPRAY IT!
QUIT WHINING!
MAKE money
WHAT SMELLS?
WHAT A HANGOVER
YEAH, YEAH, YEAH. . .
MOVE IT OR LOSE IT
WILD MAN!
RADICAL WOMAN! . . .

12:36 P.M. Febuary 8, 1998

I'm not going to tell you the way it happenend but the way I remembered it. It was a wonderful day. It didn't even rain even though it was cloudy. Yap! Im 18th , the first thought came into my mind as I woke up in the morning. My Mom greeted and hugged me. She gave me a B-Day card with a $20 bill inside. I took a shower and ate breakfast with french toast and scrambled eggs which my Mom cooked for me. I wanted to stuff…I went to Wal-Mart to buy Elizabeth 's B- Day gift (B-Day Feb 13 th) so that I don't have to worry about it. I also bought The Beacon Street Collection No Doubt. I read many funny B-Day cards. I ate lunch at Wendys and got my beautiful B-Day cake. It had Happy 18th Birthday Heralyn on it. I was glad it wasn't Marilyn or my name wasn't misspelled. So I waited and waited for the time to get to 12:30. Just my luck a Q 106 Van pulled out in the parking lot. This asian lady was handing out free stuff advertising the rado station. The cool songs made me unpatient. I got free stuff and it was awesome I got a Milki Way candy bar and Marcy Playground CD. So I begged to have it and told that CD in my B-Day. The shit I do to get things. It was unbelievable but I hold that CD in my hand and have it. Everyone got there and the only guy was Hilary's bro. We saw "Great Expectations." It was a great movie. I asked myself, "Is there any hope for me that has to do with Art in New York?" I would much rather have West Point but I would love to have both. New York is the center of the Arts, Money and the military -asset to me. I just realized that right now. It is a perfect blend for me. New York will give give me great expectations and all I HAVE TO DO IS CHASE IT AND MAKE IT HAPPEN FOR ME. I PASSED THE CANDY BAR AND IT DIDN'T even reach to Hilary who has the last person. I was enjoying every minute, every second of my life yesterday. We ate pizza, my B-Day cake & cookies. I reserved the upstairs because I like it better. We laughed. I lost like always when Eliz. And I played videogames. I thought everyone was having a good time. I opened my presents and they notice I have icing on my nose or face. We laughed I was somewhat embrass and said, "So you are going to tell this people that I went to this B-Day and the B-Day girl had icing on her nose." That is nothing compare to what I will tell you next. Robin and Kelly gave me the same thing. The Titanic CD. HA! HA! HA! HA! Well if you were there you would get the point. I loved Titanic

(movie). I wanted the soundtrack desperately. I kind of figure it was going to happen but I really didn't expect it. I'll give it to my Mom and I don't want Robin to give me the receipt. Just like that it was over. Eliz. And Kelly left at 4:30 P.M. and the rest of us left later. Hilary's rich uncle from Northridge gave me a ride home. Hilary helped me with bringing my stuff. I was feeling sublime. I spend at least $ 80 bucks the memories are priceless to me. I wanted to celebrate my 18th B-Day and I got a lot more than what I expected. I'm not talking about the gifts but the memories. Hilary, Tim, and I went to Mission Valley Center to see a movie. It was my first time there. It was a fancy mall. We went to a magazine store and they bought YM and Giutar magazine. The place is huge. The AMC 20 is the biggest and most fanciest theatre Ive been and heard of. The Metallica Article kept me entertain while waiting for 7:10 PM at the movie lobby. We saw Good Will Hunting at 7:45 PM at the movie theatre. We saw Good Will Hunting at 7:45 which was one of the most funniest and awesome movie I saw. I certainly had a great time that night too. Tim dropped me off [with his RV4] and I was at home again. It wasn't late (11 PM) fore me so I listened to my Cds. I feel asleep when I played my Titanic CD. I still remember the smell and taste of the sweet cake, pizza or the movie popcorn. 18th ! I'm 18th years old. I have everything going to me. There is nothing that I want more than just to live the life I chosen. It was worth living for everyday.

Feb. 20, 1998 (10: 52 P.M.)

Hi again ! So much has happen in this 2 weeks. Before I did this (what I'm writuing now). I read mostly stuff of 1st Day of school and skip some but read the important ones. I thought that it seems kind of funny, my life after something non so uplifting happens. I mean some events are funny when I can relate to it why. I aso recognize my writing is deeper and makes more sense. Afterall, I do spend an average of 2 hours everytime I write a new entry in my diary. It is very worthwhile to do this and because it is significant reflecting about my life now, the past and my aspirations of the future. It is certainly not an award winning style of writing. Goosh! Have you seen the way I write in my diaries, they are not well tone in composition, grammar or sometimes spelling. Not to mention my hand writing. If my diaries were publish, I prefer it should be in this hand writing, not the type version (UHH!!!) (I don't know) (you will see why) maybe it will help for you to make sense out of it. There is always an alternative like what you are doing right now, like anybody who can read till high school. Why am I talking / writing to you? Perhaps, maybe, you or a class discussion can talk about it. That is one of many ways, you can look at the world, logic, questions, interpretations, or the I or my generation thinks. Somehow I'm thinking this is definitely not literature. To me it is more than that. Okay, lets see how you analyze this. Today is the last wayday to start because it is today. I really don't have a sense of humor, either that or I'm closing my eyes more than 3 seconds. Since our school had a 3 day school week, FRIDAY at EL CAP is hotter than hell. Well, before (FRIDAY) Today I thought of wanting it to be the last period and when the bell rings, I'm free for days. I had a lot of work. All the usual stuff. Time won again. I had 4 consecutive Test/ quiz. First one was a surprise Quiz at my English Class about Chapt 12-18 (Vol.2) Pride & Prejudice. By the way, that is a lovely and wonderful book to read. I plan to buy a copy of the book someday. The Big test at Physics and I know I failed that one because I wasn't well prepared. Good thing I can retake it. The big Calculus Unit 7 test. I didn't even retake the Derivative Test this week. I boomed that one too. The good thing is I have so many of these experiences that I don't sweat, cry or stress out because I wasn't prepared enough. Of course I spend time on studying and homework especially that I don't have a job now. I didn't study for Calculus at all. Then my last Quiz/ Test on A.P. Govt. which I studied and prepared for. I got 22/30. It was doubled points (each worth 2 pts.). It didn't bothered me much not getting an A on that Quiz. Finally I got what I wanted when the last bell rang. At 3 P.M., I would have my glory on Mexican food. Our Spanish Club planned to see Evita and Mrs. Cremidan (a club advisor) decided to take money we fundraise to buy food of which one we prefer. I wanted my favorite Mexican food, Chicken Burrito with hot salsa. I also got a side of rice and everyone had a large Coke (except one person had small). We watched Evita at Mrs. Cremidan's room and ate our food. It made me full and not wanting to eat dinner at my house. It was my 2nd time seeing EVITA. (March 12, 2006, 11:40 AM/ Editing note: I can't believe I didn't misspell EVITTA .. I must have been paying attention to dat movie… VIVA E_V_I_T_A !!!) I love that movie. It has soul, a meaning from what my heart understands. Also, I like music that has a soul and a heart and I love anything from Classsical to Alternative. Evita Peron did say the right stuff and her hopes fro the masses lives on. She is one exceptional leader. I admire her for who she is and what she has done. She is ambitious indeed. I think what she did gave hope to the people of Argentina, her people, her dreams became theirs too. The movie inspired me about myself. Mrs. Evita Peron inspired me of my hopes & dreams. What she did was wonderful and lifted Argentina. For the record; would give up, n , I would love to live the life she had. I hope that someday I can help many people; the world. I want to touch people's life, uplift their spirits, and make a difference. I want to be one of them any many heroes (like the past) who has done something great. I want to make a difference in this world. Yes ! Mrs. Evita Peron, what you did was worth it. You probably already know that and you must be happy to see the hopes like yours and hear the voices of your country (men). I didn't really cry at all at end of the movie but the 1st time I did. Kelly and I left. It finish at 5:35 P.M. and it was a perfect timing to see the sunset. I told Kelly, "The sunset is behind the mountain now. I like it because you can see it better and it's more prettier. I love the sunset when I see it after a tennis game," continuing to talk about , "So can I get a ride?" "No, You can't , just walk (joke)," said Kelly. She says it when I joke to her about asking a ride home. The sunset made me happy. It reminded me more of what a wonderful life I have and how great my day was and how everyday is wonderful. I looked up at the sky, the earthly heavenly bodies, it is so infinite, yet the stars where shining so bright. This wish upon a star has not yet come true. Even tonight, my goal reminded me again. So much 3 years ago how I wanted to be a senior. Army National Guard goal is what it is all about. I would do anything to make it there by Aug-September. Tonight made me realize on how important a goal was and the ones I had in the past and how I changed it and how it all comes down to this. My #1 goal right now and how it will shines my Future. How far have I gone. I ran up that hill I love being challenge as my warm-up run. The track field was muddy in some parts but I kept on running. I was felling weak, so I slowed down. I felt weird, I couldn't feel my warm hands, it was cold. I was upset at EL Nino stoRm. How could it be this year for such a storm to come. The Earth is affected by it. It is not fair for me. I wish the weather could be nice like the way it was always so I can run more often again. After I ate my dinner, I was feeling dizzy and sickly. I was about to throw the trash when I felt dizzy & nauseas all of a sudden. I was about to pass but I told my Mom about my situation. She told me I should never have run. I was feeling cold and colder while laying down on my bed. I didn't want to freak out. It was scary to me. Then I was getting warm and got a high temperature. I feel asleep without knowing it until I woke up. I didn't want to sleep because of afraid. It made me feel better when I slept more. I don't plan anything like that again. Hilary, Tim and I went to Bolwevil[BOLLWEEVIL] to eat and Foster Freeze. We went criusine to many places. Tomorrow ~~is another~~ is another way to say " Life's worth living !"

March 1, 1998 (9:02 P.M Sunday)

"Oh what a beautiful morning, Oh what a beautiful day, … a beautiful evening. Everything going my way," reminding me of the Oklahoma play. I participated at Holy Spirit School (6th grade) in OHIO. So many things I remember when I run. A sublime feeling of infinite hopes. Accomplishing my destination to run to the top of the hill thinking if I keep doing this for the next 17+ weeks. It will be worth it. Last week was an awesome week. ! La alegria de escuela ! My favorite part of the school stuff is the challenge. The price and prize of it. Price of Calculus to feel like everything I do about this subject burns my soul. But the prize of it is just being there and knowing I'm in Calculus. It is what matters and also the prize of it in the Long Run. Other subjects are interpreted differently but so little time and it will bore the hell out of you and me. On Feb 21 (Sat), I went to Todai Restaurant, UMM! Awesome food and so many variety of Asian Food. Sushi, I ate them, only the cooked ones. Desserts like the twirl chocolate or whatever it was called. Cynthia, my Mom's friend was the one who had the idea to plan this day to enjoy life. My knew the person (jeweler dude) because she bought an expensive bracelet. My Mom has a gift of identifying real gold fake ones. Who knows, she might buy me another pair of earrings. That night I went with Hilary and her Mom to have margaritas (virgin for me and Hilary) at a Mexican restaurant. What an awesome day. The next day I stayed home doing as much as I can to do the important school work. The last week is the 17th weeks before end of school. The week I decided to sacrifice it all.

So I did and it work. I hope to find out my weight tomorrow. I only ask 1 lb. A week. I also did kickboxing / teakwondo which tortured my body. The pain was gruesome. My philosophy is starting something is hard to do, doing means= you made a commitment. To continue without surrender is another test. A test that defies you (whether you are committed or not). If you want it bad, it must be so. Finishing it is a glory but when it find out when is the only way to not stop and give up. You must be able to run without a finish line. That is exactly what I will and have been doing. Thank you Lord for the last 3 days of sunny weather. I ran on FRIDAY. I am SO MUCH BETTER COMPARE TO LAST YEAR OR EVEN LAST MONTH IN RUNNING. To run where the wind blows is the hard part but to run like the wind is even harder because It is testing how much I'm willing to follow the wind and keep on running. It is very hard and a lovely yet an extreme challenge. I WONDER WHAT WILL HAPPEN TO ME IN THE NEXT 6-8 MONTHS and beyond. I only wish what I truly deserve. The price of ARNG- I am doing right now and the prize of it is what I truly deserve, & that prize is a self- assurance. I had done what must be done. While others have an acceptance letter to prestigious school, scholarships, I have ARNG. What more could I ask for on my Graduation Day. Thank You! Is it okay I call my Guardian Angel. Thank you for what you have done two nights ago. Yes I believe you. You know my fear very well. You know my future, my ambitions, my dreams and hopes. Your guidance has given me great courage and inner strength and my ambition will not be broken. "This 16th week is dedicated to you Lord. I do this for myself, for the love of challenge, will, sacrifice mainly about me and why I am doing it. This is for you too. I see you in many ways, like my Mom's love for me, my friends smiling to me, the world shining and good (so much more), this week is for all of these. I will always think of you, I see you in so many ways. I can hear you in my heart spiritually." I rejoice today and everyday for you.

How great it was to end a night with friends and a prayer. Tim and Hilary are great. I'm glad I did something fun this weekend and it made me satisfied at last. I started walking with Hilary and we will walk on Fri-thru Sun. The views are breathtaking and we talk of good memories and plan fun stuff to do. HOW WONDERFUL MY LIFE HAS BEEN. HOW HARD AND PAINFUL I WENT THRU AND STILL CONTINUE TO BE TOUGH, BRAVE & STRONG to tackle and tomorrows challenge. THIS IS WHY LIFE IS WORTH LIVING ON TOP OF EVERYTHING ELSE.

March 8, 1998 (9:18 P.M.)

It's funny how time flies but time is stable, it never goes fast or low. A clock tick tack, forever and the long and short hand moves. Really, what is time? Time is Gold. Too many philosophical definitions of time. I wont mention. I had done my extreme best to use it well. A saying, "Live each day as if it's was the last one." I like this saying because applying it everyday means giving my best. My best by definition is what I can do to push for the will and determination better. What is neat as another day passed, the more experience you have in your life. Also, I don't think of it (saying) much everyday and everyday I don't ever know I live up to that saying until I think about it. Because I always give my best, (of course, someday are better, somedays are harder) and live to the fullest of happiness in learning experiences or just daily stuff.

"Isn't it cool that we have been friends for a long time," Hilary said.

We continue to walk and talk about many things. "I like it when all my friends get together and we do fun stuff." I'm so fortunate to have a friend like Hilary. I've been friends with Hilary for 4 yrs. I live here in California, Lakeside. Isn't funny how things end up. "Isn't funny how life is," said Hilary. In fact we both have talked about it. About life in many topics. Each person has his/ her own beliefs, philosophical thinking about life. I don't know how many times I wrote/ said, **"Life is great." I smile. How wonderful it is to be alive, to have this opportunity to live here and to challenge everyday. My most favorite is the challenge of each day and how I challenge it with every I got." I I nice look forward to another day when before got to sleep. I get to look forward** to another walk, run, seeing my teachers and friends, learning are a few of what is in store in each day. My philosophy of commitment (EXERCISE) FOR MY 2ND WEEK- ALL I CAN SAY IS I LIVE UP TO THAT Commitment and the same with 3rd, 4th & so on. I'm glad I'm doing better and improvements are getting higher everyday. Lord, I have given that week for you and and not just me. Today's exersice was great. I think of you everyday by seeing your beautiful creation. Thank you for being there for me. Thank you for everything. How am I doing with accomplishing my goal to loose weight and making it to

ARNG? I'm doing great and you probably feel the same way. I hear you in my heart. You speak through it. Are you excited about the day I do my oath this country as I am? I'm restrenthening, making my goal stronger than ever. Lord, forgive me for all my sins. What is it about me, one thing I found out (I knew this but never ever deeply thought of it much until now) and mu [my] inner voice, (my G. Angel and you) saying I have a power to believe it and make it happen. That is a wonderful gift I have. Thank you! I really regret that how I wish I wasn't so ambitious and willing to go after ambitious high goals/ dreams. I believe having ambitious personality is a wonderful to travel around the world. That awaits.. Ahead. I'm knowledgable about to what I'm learning in Biology (Digestion, Vit, Respiration etc.) with applying to my exercise and Diet Plan.

I had so much fun yesterday (Saturday) with Tim, Hilary and Jason. We went to 5 Music stores, Parkway Mall, Jason's house, Arbys are just some things we went. It was an 8-hour of mega doze fun. I had so many laughs. It was a perfect day and night to do something. I love being me. I love teenage lifestyle. I love my life.

March 11,1998 (10P.M.) (Weds.)

Ive been wanting to write during weeknights when I have school work and losing weight to concentrate on. This week is the 15th week before the last of week of school. It is crazy to think about it. I will smile when I read this in the future after graduation. I wonder if I can answer this question with good news for me at the time I read this: HOW IS HERALYN DOING? I'm sure no matter what her Life will always be awesome because she knows- she knows how to tackle problems, she positive, and a lot more that nothing can stop her from anything she hopes for. What will I be up to? Where will my life be and what great things has happen? Have I achieve any of my ultimate goal? Wish I know the answers to these but only a matter of time and the Road I take. I'm sure it will be wonderful and it gets better everyday.

This week has been a week and I'm only on the middle of it. There is no school on Friday and tomorrow is senior Ditch Day (or as Mrs. Thalman calls it S.D.D.). I'm glad tomorrow will be the last day for this week. Tomorrow is the day I been waiting for. Finally, after all these 3-4 yrs. Of my high school career, a West Point cadet will actually come to El Cap and talk about W.P. folder ready and I wrote questions too. I gurantee you I will be writing about this tomorrow or sometime before this week ends. I can't believe I am 158 lb (not 162 anymore). Yes ! Only 1 lb. A week as my goal. If I loose more the better and faster I get there.

I have to tell about Mr. Chocolate (Richard SANTANA), the man who reminded me today to follow my dream and believe in it. TO ACHIEVE IT. TO MAKE IT HAPPEN. It strenghten me inside and I thank him (one who few people who helped me). I will never doubt about myself in achieving my dream. To continue … (by tomorrow or FRI.)

3/15/98

(1) Life is wonderful. (2) I'm happy. (3) it is nice to know that I have been better and cool. (4) I have awesome friends. (5) I have a great Mom. (6) A West Point Cadet helped me answer a lot of my impt. questions. (7) Mr. Chocolate reminded me how great my goals are and it should always be strong that I will never doubt it but just continue to run after it- (8) Everyday and day after- the more great days pass the closer I get to ARNG and after that-W.P. (9) I feel like the luckiest person in the world- Yes ! I am ! (10) That I have the power to do anything; because I feel like it. I feel this because I believe in myself to achieve these challenging & wonderful goals.

Above: I just mention just 10 out of many things I want to write to start a Gratitude list again. I was reading the last 3 pages on this diary. I got the idea from Oprah's show. Cool huh! I'm going to do more gratitude list before I write about the events of my life. As I have mention before, about W.P. cadet, that I will write more about it this weekend. What can I say. Where do I begin? I believe it was God's grace, oh! Lord you are always there to help me on this long road journey to West Point Military Academy. Not only did I talk to cadet from W.P. but he also fit the profile of a candidate like me: he spend 2 yrs. Of college w/ R.O.T.C. before making it to attend West Point. WOW! I find that information [from] him valuable because I too will fit this profile. It is my plan, a timeline of 2 yrs. Before making it to W. P. (in 2 ways)

(1) -SUMMER SCHOOL '98
-SUMMER /FALL -ARNG
-BOOTCAMP/ A.C.T.

-SPRING 1999 GROSSMONT COLLEGE W/ ROTC classes
-SUMMER 99 ARNG W/rotc training
-applications for W.P. M.A. (on going process)
-Fall/ Spring 99-2000

(2)- Summer school' 98
-summer, fall-ARNG
-Boot camp/ A.I.T.
-spring '99 G.College w/ROTC classes
* apply for W.P. Military Academy Prep School by getting a notmination from ARNG TO Spring)
-WP MAPS- 99-2000
-entrance summer 2000 to West Point

I'm probably the only PERSON WHO UNDERSTAND HOW THIS WORKS (WHAT I WROTE ABOVE) UNLESS I WRITE MORE IN DETAILS BUT TO FIND OUT MORE JUST KEEP ON READING. THERE IS A VOICE INSIDE ME WHO SAID 2 YRS. AFTER HIGHSCHOOL IS WHEN I GET ACCEPTED TO West Point. I was a junior and everytime I doubt in my dream (of W.P.) and question that when and how long will it take me to achieve this goal to attend West Point, because I knew that it wont be after high school right away. The voice inside me, I call it my Guardian Angel's voice or God's voice, who lifts my spirit up when I lose faith about achieving W.P. (or any doubts) and say, "Don't worry. Keep believing in yourself, you will make it. The day will come. In 2 years will be rewarded to make your goal come true." It is from the heart and I said it whole heartedly because it is when the best of me. I find peace & strength. You may think it is weird and I think it is weird too. Really, I believe in it. I'm thankful that I know it. I'm thankful to learn about myself and it strenghten more in my character from the day I decided to go after this goal. It has many rewards in challenging this goal and Im not even a cadet at West Point or a private of the Army National Guard yet. My hopes are up, my patience is long, my dreams are alive. It is indeed a wonderful challenge (one of many I will face) to believe I can achieve an American Dream and I will achieve it: meaning behind the land of opportunity.

Im sure that 2nd class cadet (junior) had his own challenges before making it to West Point. I have mine and many more I will face. Thank you Lord for alll you help and your guidance. He helped me answered my questions I might be ask when applying the nomination, advices in preparing to be more competitive, about WPMAP Prep School and the experiences he had. I left the Carrer Room leaving the satisfaction of great hopes and will I said, "He made it happen, so can I."

Im going to write an essay tonight about how Mr. Chocolate speech gave me strength to keep believing in my goals and it made my goals stronger and walked out of the gym as a stronger, more determined than ever before. Overall, I was a better person. Nothing can stop me now. I his last saying, " I made it to Harvard with Doctorate Degree. If you have something you want to do. Don't let anything or anybody stop you because you can be a Harvard Graduate." These are interpreted mixed with my own words and the way I remembered it.

I had no school on Friday but I spend that day mostly at the Library. Hilary and I did the usual exercise we do: that day. I learned a lot about SPAIN. OHH! HOW GREAT IT WOULD BE TO ATTEND A UIVERSITY anywhere in Europe to CONTINUE MY EDUCATION AFTER MY Bachelor's Degree. TO BE AWARDED A SCHOLARSHIP LIKE THE Marshall Scholar. WHAT A GREAT CHALLENGE IT WOULD BE AND HOW GREAT IT IS TO ACHIEVE IT. This is one of the challenges I will face and like about W.P. W.P will give me many opportunities and that is one of them. My I-search paper in Spanish is worth doing because it will remind me and now and my aspirations.

I HAD A WONDERFUL WEEKEND. Tim, Hilary and I went to LaPalapa and cruise around San Diego county. I love Mariah Carey's music. Tim is a loyal fan. I hope to get all her CD's I like and especially music box because it has 2 of my favorite song she sang. The song Hero is a great song. I smiled and chuckled to think about how much Hilary can't stand this type of music. HA ! HA ! HA ! HA ! HA ! I ate a free doughnout given from Tim. My Mom bought 4 circle doughnout at Lucky's. I ate 1 as my share and I asked after I ate it for the other doughnout. My Mom said, " One for you, one for him and two for me." OHH ! The humanity ! It made my night to eat another doughnout which Tim gave me.

MAYBE SOMEDAY I'LL WRITE ABOUT MY EXPERIENCES (CHALLENGES, ETC.) TO BECOME A CADET AT WEST POINT AND IT WILL BE PUBLISH ON THE ASSEMBLY (magazine of the Association of U.S.M.A. like the one I read on the catalog of 97-98 written by Capt. Bruce Ollstein, Class of 1986.

I need to be more discipline and do better with the way I eat. I will be starting my 4th week tomorrow. It will be better this time. Self-Discipline is hard but a little bit of improvement everyday will make it one of my strengths. I have done that in the past. " My strengths will be my weakness, my weakness will be my strengths." Only time and my actions will make this a successful outcome.

Moving along… I told Hilary about how people who doesn't live here and think of U.S.A. " To them this is the land of opportunity. If the person has what it takes to achieve what they want out of life, it can happen here. They believe, must be hard- working, and do more someone who can achieve will pay off. To them, this is where dreams come true. The place to achieve their hopes." It is relatively true that I'm talking about me and I'm not the only person in this world who thinks of U.S.A. this way but many people wishing they can achieve their dreams in U.S.A. whether for their family, a job, money etc. it is truuee, millions of immigrants had come here to believe U.S. is the Land of opportunity.

History doesn't lie.

March 18, 1998 (10:25 PM) Tues.
GOOD FORTUNE LIES AHEAD 02 10 14 23 35 40
A FINANCIAL INVESTMENT WILL YIELD RETURNS BEYOND YOUR HOPES
PEKING NODDLE CO.
THE WORLD will SOON BE READY TO RECEIVE YOUR TALENTS 01 07 12 20 34

Im going to write a quick one page of today's event and this week. Mark Price (43) spoke to our class the whole period today. It's nice that he told us his background: I met the guy (Mr. Price) who wrote the Abott and Costello "Whos on first?" comedy at age 17-> (NBC at 19) did it in class, a family he came from were WEST POINTERS, LEADERS OR POLITICIANS AND BUSINESS PEOPLE, got started his AD AGENCY at age 23 (FORD ADS FITTING) open car door don't brake a nail for ladies, mirrors on the car…, seats that don't let any skirt stick to the seat), has over 200 businesses on his JOB NET… something program for welfare people needing work to get out of the system and homeless. I think that his life is interesting. He said that he takes this opportunity to talk to intellectual students like us not just because we are smart but he aid, "You are the future who will be making decisions and by the time I'm old." Reprase it the way he meant is (young generations now) your decisions will concern/effect me if you pull the plug or not when I'm old.

He likes to make a difference coz he cares that's why he's running for state assemblymen. I have an idea but won't write about it unless I make/ do it (the actions) (A FORUM IN LAKESIDE). I'm HALFWAY THROUGH THIS WEEK. I'M GLAD ABOUT THIS WEEK. I THINK I LIKE THIS WEEK THE BEST. I KNOW I ALWAYS LIKE EVERY DAY. Put it is way. This week has the most challenge in academics and I love challenge especially if it is worthy and invaluable especially Spanish project. I know I will continue to be excellent/ outstanding student in tackling this problems because I can do it all my heart.
Oh ! I have my 1st SPRITE today in rules of diet/ exercise. I allow myself only 3 till June 18. I treated myself to eat Chinese Food. I was thinking and talking about financial investment and the blue ink fortune cookies thin is neat to know. I hope good fortune and the world will receive my talents is BOOT CAMP-ARNG- Its funny coz fortune is 2nd time mention.

March 24, 1998 (7:58 PM) Tuesday

This is a great day to write on my diary and since I haven't wrote anything of what happen over the weekend. Well, I want to start about today but how about last week and the weekend. There is no doubt last week was the toughest week (the 14th week before school ends) of my Senior year. There were probably days very similar to these of my high school days but nothing tops it therefore it is the most challenging and too much time consuming and call it also the most successful week I had. Indeed, afterall those 9 hours (not 10 coz of dinner time) straight typing from 2PM- 1AM for Spanish I-Search (1st 4 hours) and Physics (5 hours) Research paper on Light. I slept at 4 PM that Thursday night. My school work, which ended at 4AM in a FRI. morning. At last, FRIDAY DID COME ! All those hard work an everything I had to do so I will be proud because I did everything and turned on time. I wrote the best poem essay on "TO HIS COY MISTRESS (BY ANDREW MARVELL) after I typed my Research paper that Friday morning. The only thing I could do nothing about was CALCULUS. The only way to be better in that subject to get a letter grade higher than now is study and relearn what I didn't know how to do even though our class learned it already. I would have drop that class long time ago if not for the experiences I had over the 3 ½ years of high school. I would rather get an F than get a Withdrawal Failing (WP) or Withdrawal Passing (WP) on my report card. I got a WP last year on 3rd year Spanish. I can not afford to drop a class, especially a class like Calculus I long to be in Calculus and had to work hard/ take Summer school just to get where I am now. I really did like last week a lot because I learned a lot and absorb a lot of information. IT was also the most challenging and gruesome week of academics which made me like it even more. I love challenges and tackling them is rewarding for my part. Enough said about that week and I want to talk about fun stuff. I love FRI. nights and weekends because what I do on those days are fun stuff. I think of weekends as my reward to do fun stuff and go to fun places w/ friends. Last FRIDAY Kelly, Elizabeth and I went to Grossmont Mall right after school We ate at Trophy's. I had took out only $9 and coins from my wallet. I spend $5 dollars on a clam chowder because that was the only one close I can afford. It's somewhat embarrassing to eat and buy a soup but I did enjoy the food lot. That place is (muy caro) expensive. I was tired and very sleepy but I still have fun. We saw "The Man in the Iron Mask" at the theatre there. It was worthwhile seeing this movie. My #1 Rule of a great movie: the movie must be able to touch people's souls (our feelings and emotions) and teach a lesson of following a dream/ goal or changing other character/s in the movie to be better (or whatever sort of way) or the main character/s, or the theme of the movie is a dramatic change for the movie character and inspire the audience or all of these. It taught me the value of the dream/ goals and it must be achieve buy going after it and the honor & pride of serving for something that represents big & great. These were what the Muskeeters deem for and got in the end. It taught me in a way of realization when I think of my goals in the Army and what it represent. Movies are part of the human kind and in our everyday life. **I got home and had the T.V. for myself because they were out for dinner. I ate a real dinner w/ rice and adobo chicken. Yummy! On Saturday, I got the T.V. again for 2-3 hours. Hilary, Jenifer and I went to buy our tickets for the "Spring Thing." I was so happy that I'm going and so was Hilary too. They invited me to go to the beach. Jenifer drop me off an hour later, we were on our way to Mission Beach. We only had 2 ½ hours to enjoy the sunlight. I think that** day was the highlight of the weekend. I love to do things that are unexpected because they tend to be the most fun. I hope to go to the beach a few times more before I leave CA [CALIFORNIA for ARMY BOOT CAMP]. Im glad to see my great progress in running. On Sunday I ran from LMS to the top of the ramp without stopping. Then, I ran for the most time where Hilary and I walk. It took me about 35 minutes. I walked only about 35% of the time. That was challenging not to mention the hot weather. I will definitely do it over and over. I will soon. It is nice to see many improvements. I hope what I'm doing this week will make me loose 1-2 lbs.

Today my Mom said: "She can't live without me and she would go crazy with the life she has." I am tough because of the life I had before and have now and because of her in the same reason why she is tough because of me and the 43 years of her life. Together, we have each other. I don't know what she will do when im gone.

I think it will be harder for her part to see me leave and gone. I just hope she understands. I had this weird dream today that I saw(looking over my window) on an afternoon/ (5-6 PM time) evening time many Army soldier parachuting down at my aprt. Complex. I saw one landed on the the swimming pool 3 feet deep. Everyone landed safely. The [? }parachute ←whatever that is called was black/ &brown/white/yellow/green. They were hiding everywhere. 2 or 3 on the front garden where my window is outside. They weren't bad people but I find this dream interesting and bizarre. I thought something about the IRAQ IRAN WAR [or the stupid war the fucking RUSSIANs we y'all deal with everyday → H solves the problem ,solution is "H" knows?]might be going on but they landed here. HA ! HA! HA! I wanted to sleep more even though I had to wake up very soon. So I did. They were there to help I guess. They save my life twice. Once, I was outside, one gave me a real hand gun (the one I like, an execution US sniper rifle I invented from the future) and I cover on this Big Rock {LIKE FOREST GUMP DOES} and it was at the sidewalk near the Foundation and, …and on the grass too. I don't know who the person I was shooting but it was intense, FUNNY I THINK, AND LOVE THE SECRET AGENT OR ARMY COMBAT SOLDIER ROLE I PLAYED OR BOTH ROLE. I didn't know what my role was. Second, They told me to duck down and get out of bed and go lay on the left side of my bed. I did. The door open and a person shoot it and they started firing w/ their

M-16 Rifles and killed the person [ENEMY]. There was more but I don't remember it all. The only thing unfamiliar was the living room in my apartment is not exactly the same or if that was a living room. I think that PARACHUTING and COMBAT ARMY secret agent are just 2 things I will be doing in the ARMY, I don't know what it means. I always have weird dreams. Just think if I can think like this weird, I could write a novel and make a movie $ $ $. Oh Well ! I had dreams before like I was parachuting but it was a colorful parachute and I landed on a big green hill land. It was like Europe country side. And the background was trees. Then I was balloning I don't know if there was another person or just me but the air ballon was so colorful. This happen 4 years ago and I think I dreamed it 2x or 3x later. I also had this dream where I was walking on a stairway was many stacks of books and light was coming up. I made big strides to get up and did and there was a light bulb on the hanging from the ceiling. The background was a black wall w/ light and my shadow on it. I like this one also, I walked into an ARMY UNIT. They were all saluting me. There was a lady soldier who I taught it was me or maybe as I was walking seeing her remind me of the young me (a soldier). My views where like how I see things. I didn't see myself walking down but it like I was actually walking.

I see that.....

[DRAW URSELF] 

I DON'T SEE MYSELF

I felt like I was a general or a colonel or a major, a high ranking officer. It was neat. I remember before I went to sleep I asked the Lord of any dream on what I will be doing in the future and if it is related to the ARMY. Dreams are weird and it is a different world. It is interesting to talk about.

I save the best for last. I was thinking of this during 4th period and couldn't get it off my head so I wrote it on my packet/ note.

How much time do I have ? 13th weeks too short to achieve this possible dream. Every year in high school, I had chase dreams, tackle goals etc. But of all I missed & failed to do, I can't afford to fail. Failure is not an option. This uncertain feeling is FEAR and I'm worried. There is nothing else I can do but continue doing what I have to do 158-10= 148 Ibs even 150 is good enough [200-210 HEAVYWEIGHT BOXER CHAMPION]. I only want one thing from all the sacrifice, hardship, challenge, pain, patience, hardwork, determination and every sweat from Running/ exercise is ARMY NATIONAL GUARD TO WEAR that uniform, be called Private Toling [GENERAL TOLINGLIBEDO], Boot Camp and A.I.T. and many more and then later on ANG is my ticket to WPMA.

March 29th (4:25 PM)

The weather, let's say it was raining like cats and dogs. El Nino (storm) came back since WEDS-THURS and this weekend. I hope. It will be a sunny California weather for Spring Break. I don't mind much about tHe weather as long as It will be sunny again soon. Last week was okay in terms of school. The only things that bothered me was last week was 13th weeks till end of school. I think it is scary because I was afraid of not worried because I can pull it off. I will loose more. I'm glad. Next week is go fast. I had so much un flying that kite for Physics Lad and it was the only one in our class flew the longest and highest too. Glory is sweet! I'm reading 2 books for English.

On Friday I got sort of wet from the rain after school so I took the bus home and use the umbrella I always carry. My Mom mention about La Palapa while we were talking in my room. I wanted so bad to go and blamed her for bringing it up. I got over it. We painted our toenails. Suddenly, at 6:50 PM Hilary called to ask me if I wanted to go to Tim's House to have macaroni & cheese and margaritas. I was excited and syic up ongoing. I got what I wanted that night. Tim made the Macaroni & Cheese and Hilary & I use the blender for margaritas. Of Course, it had no alcohol. It was strawberry virgin margaritas. ***We watched 90210 and Trojan War movie. I had so much fun. I didn't think I would go anywhere that night. I got home at 11:30 P.M. today is Hilary's B-Day. She's 19th now. She's having the time of her life right now. I like to make my friends*** happy and make laugh. I love doing something for their B-Day's. Yesterday, I gave Hilary a funny card and a nestle crunch Bar. I got the candy at 99¢ store. Since already gave her a B-Day gift but I just didn't to give her a card. It was very windy but I walked to her to give it to her yesterday. I sang happy B-Day her Happy B-Day on her pager voicemail. She called 3 hrs. later to find out it was me. I really don't have any inspirations to write about it now. Maybe next time. Till then.

April 19, 1998 (Sun 8 PM)

Is there a heaven on earth? I always think everyday is heaven but for the last 2 weeks it was heaven without school. It was Spring Break from April 4 (Sat) to 19. It was great. I had loads of fun. I don't know how long it will take me to write about my Spring Break '98 experience. It all comes down to the fun stuff I did because that is what Spring Break is all about; FUN. (Ap 4) I went with Hilary, Jimmy , Raymond and (the group) to eat Lunch at China Dinasty around 2 P.M. it was from Hilary's B-Day group thing. Jimmy gave her nice presents. It was fun. Everybody was hungry. Hilary even bought us shrimps. The group talk about stuff and had some laughs. We went crusin. Jimmy drove to places/ stores to look at CD player for his truck. Hilary found this $6,000 T.V. gigantic entertainment at this store. [Looking like a greeny frog--I'm bored -AN ARMY OF ONE- I want that black yellow shirt I see on tv HBO savings of $30 mil a month life August 9, 2008, 10:26 PM "Why is there war?" To be FaT -I- g- u- e.] We were all looking for her. We found her sitting on black leather couch. She said,
"I never saw anything so beautiful in my life," as we left the store. A good thing about sitting at the back seat of Jimmy's truck is the nice scenery of San Diego (mountain ranges, cities lights at night …just the view). Im the type of person who savors every peak moment of earth's boundless beauty. It makes me happy and fulfilled just looking at it. I love evry moment of it. We went to Jimmy's house and swam at his pool. We enjoyed the spa just relaxing and talking. Hilary did 20 plus laps on pool. It surprised me how energetic and fast she was when she swam. Sometimes when I do fun stuff (it's always fun w/ her) with her, at one moment or think of , " How awesome this is. This is incredible. I have a great friend. I asked myself or think of, "*How awesome this is. This is incredible. I have a great friend. Her friends are great and has became my friends. How lucky I am to have a great friend like her. Very Lucky! I'm having so much fun. I'm enjoying every minute of this right now.*

How did it ever turned out this way? I'm very lucky to have a best friend like her." I remember when I catch my breath after laps of swimming while Hilary was still swimming. Of course, there has been moments like this one. I have plenty of them. It just happens when I stop and think at one point in time. I think about it I realized and reflect about it. There are other things I think about our friendship too and that was just at one moment in my life. Have you ever done that? Just think about something in the middle of whatever fun stuff you are doing and realizing how great it is. It's hard to explain because it only speaks inside you. The stars was really pretty that night. The night weather was perfect except when we came out of the SPA when it was over. It was chili later on that night. Jimmy's Mom was nice. " This Jimmy keeps all his gay porn movies," HILARY SAID. I have this serious personality and find it hard to tell when people are joking or not. I left the house with an empression Jimmy had those videos until I told Hilary what I thought when we were swimming. "No it was a joke," she said. We both laughed. I thought that was funny.

I finished Kelly's "college survival 101" music tape during that weekend. On Monday (Ap.6) Kelly, Eliz. And I had a fun day together. We went to Jimmy's Restaurant at Santee for Breakfast. We planned this last week before Spring Break. It was a good breakfast. I like our talks. Part of the plan was to have an Easter egg hunt at Kelly's backyard. We watched *Mortal Combat Enililation* for a while because it rained at noon. When it stopped raining, we had our hunt. It was my idea to have an eater egg hunt because I never did that. It was first time. I liked it. The plastic eggs inside had candy chocolates in it. I only got 5 (I think) eggs. I loved the Canterbury chocolate egg it tasted so good. We played board games all afternoon and ate McDo. Food (except Kelly) for Lunch at her house. We went to Family Center to play minature golf and video games after we had 2 games of playing pool at Bolwebills. I had fun. I caleed Hilary when I got home to ask about her party. I remember the day before (Ap.5) we went to LaPalapa. She called me to eat dinner there with her. I was glad she did that. We were both HAPPY TO GET OUT OF OUR BORING HOUSE. We talked mostly about what I will be doing during Aug. to Dec. for my Army National Guard training and Boot CAMP> I saw her face in grief about me leaving. I told her about my goals. I can talk about anything to her. She respect my goals. I was somewhat started feeling sad about me leaving when I talked about it. We walked our last ½ route walk. We just talk about a lot of stuff. I told her about my scrapbook project. She asked me if she can take care of my stuff (like CD's) when I'm gone. I was glad she mentioned it. Of course I said yes. Then she asked "Do you consider me as your best friend?" With an enerGytic voice I said, "Definetely Yes." We both smiled. We went to Luckys to buy Jello mix and club soda for B-Day Party.

Ap.6 that night around 7 PM I went to buy easter stuff for Hilary. I saw this little 12" EASTER EGG TREE. I decided not to use easter basket but make her one like that. I didn't know how exactly or what materials to use at first. I spend at least 10 hours on it. I had fun making it. I had my own candies to eat so when I'm temped to eat hers I eat mine. The tree was made out of hanger wire and covered with tissue paper. I colored it. It had 156 candies, 17 eggs, 19 candies taped on the tree. Only Hilary and know what they mean. I made it especially for her.

(Ap. 9 thurs) I decided to give it to Hilary before I start muching on the candies. I keep on looking at it. I had nothing to do that day. I was beginning to fell dizzy staying to long in my room. I covered and put it to do that day. I was beginning to fell dizzy staying too long in my room. I covered and put the tree inside 2 brown bags. I got to Hilary's house and her Mom invited me in. We talked bout stuff. She said that I'm creative and it looks pretty. I told her the reason why I couldn't wait to give it to Hilary. I went home and I enjoyed bowling. Hilary didn't bowl (except when I let her bowl twice) because she didn't want to mess up her pretty nails. An embarrassing moment when I could not pull out the seatbelt and Jason had to do it. I laugh when I think about it. It was somewhat embarrassing for me. Jason drives a cute WOLKWAGEN BUG. I love it when " Rage against the machine" is playing full blast. The next day (Ap. 10) Fri) I went with Hilary and her Mom to the mall because they need to buy a dress. "I can't believe I will be gone. I have 3 months more. It's weird feeling, Hilary." "it's just beginning to hit you now, she said something like that. We went to POR FAVOR. UUUMMM!!!!!! The Virgin margarita tasted so good. "Did you see Heralyn's face when she said MANGO?," she said to her Mom. I love mango. It's my favorite fruit. It's my favorite fruit. I could eat sweet mango and sour mango with bagoong. My Mouth is watering right now. It was a beautiful day. Hilary and I started walking at 7PM. I remember the sun. It was pretty. I love the scenery when I saw the LAKESIDE VALLEY FROM THE TOP OF THE HILL AND THE

MOUNTAIN SURROUNDING IT. This is one of the many things is great about walking & running. It makes me fell running and walking is worth doing it. Por Favor is awesome. Maybe I'll have my 19th B-Day there.

(AP.11) MY MOM AND I WENT TO WAL-MART. I ENJOY DOING STUFF TOGETHER WITH HER. WE MAKE THE BEST OF IT. SHE SAID "IT WILL RAIN AT @ 2PM." WE FINISHED THE SHOPPING AROUND 1:45 P.M. " WHAT ARE YOU GOING TO DO WHEN IT RAINS? (OR WHAT IF IT RAINS?), SHE ASKED ME [SOMETHING LIKE THAT] I RESPONDED, **"JUST MY LUCK!"** IT STARTED DRIZZLING TO GO TO AMC SANTEE THEATRE WHICH IS DOWN THE STREET (ABOUT 2 MIN. WALK) SO I CAN SEE A MOVIE. I SAW **THE WEDDING SINGER.** I ALWAYS WANTED TO SEE A MOVIE BY MYSELF. I DID IT FINALLY. TOO BAD THE MOVIE WAS TOO SHORT. IT RAINED LIKE CATS AND DOGS WHEN I CAME OUT OF THE THEATRE. I WAITED ½ HOUR FOR THE RAIN TO STOP. IT DIDN'T BUT IT SLOWED FOR A WHILE SO THAT'S WHEN I WALKED BACK TO THE BUS STOP. I WAITED ½ HOUR FOR THE RAIN TO STOP. IT DIDN'T BUT IT SLOWED FOR A WHILE SO THAT'S WHEN I WALKED BACK TO BUS STOP. I WAITED FOR 45 MINS. FOR THE BUS TO COME. IT WAS REALLY COLD AND IT RAINED. I ONLY HAD MY GREEN SWEATER WITH A HOOD, A LITTLE TREE AND MY LEVIS JEANS THAT HELD ME FROM THE RAIN. IT WAS COLD. I THOUGHT ABOUT WHAT IT WILL BE LIKE TO BE A HOMELESS PERSON. I WONDER ABOUT THE HOMELESS PEOPLE. I FELT LUCKY AT __________ I HAD A WARM PLACE TO LIVE IN LAKESIDE. I COULDN'T IMAGINE MYSELF BEING HOMELESS. I DON'T KNOW HOW I STARTED THINKING ABOUT IT WHEN IT RAINED. CAN YOU BELIEVE IT STOP RAINING THE MOMENT WHEN I WAS IN THE BUS. I LOOK BACK ON THAT DAY AND JUST LAUGH ABOUT WHAT HAPPEN. THE RAIN WAS THE MAGIC

Ap.6 that night around 7 PM I went to Luckys to buy easter for Hilary. I saw this little 12" Easter egg tree. I decided not to use easter basket But make her one like that. I didn't know how exactly or what materials to use at first. I spend at least 10 hours on it. I had fun making it. I had my own candies to eat so when I'm tempted to eat hers I eat mine. The tree was made out of hanger wire and covered with tissue paper. I colored it. It had 156 candies, 17 eggs, 19 candies taped on the tree. Only Hilary and I know what they mean. I made it especially for her. (Ap. 9 thurs) I decided to give it to Hilary before I start munching on the candies. I keep on looking at it. I had nothing to do that day. I was beginning to fell dizzy staying to long in my room. I covered and put the tree inside 2 brown bags. I got to Hilary's house and her Mom invited me in. We talked about stuff. She said that I'm creative and it looks pretty. I told her the reason why I couldn't wait to give it to Hilary. I went home and got a phone call from Hilary. That night we went Bowling. Jason, Raymond, Hilary and I enjoyed bowling. Hilary didn't bowl (except when I let her bowl twice) because she didn't want to mess up her pretty nails. An embarrassing moment when I could not pull out the seatbelt and Jason had to do it. I laugh when I think about it. It was somewhat embarrassing for me. Jason drives a cute Wolkswagen bug. I love it when "Rage Against the Machine" is playing full blast. The next day ((Ap. 10) Fri) I went with Hilary and her Mom to the mall because they need to buy a dress. " I can't believe I will be gone. I have 3 moths more. It's a weird feeling, Hilary." " It's just beginning to hit you now, she said something like that. We went to POR FAVOR. UUUUMMMMM!!!!!!!! The virgin margarita tasted so good. " Did you see Heralyn's face...... OPPPS I DOUBLE TYPE

!!!!!!!!!????????? WHATTTTTT?????????!!!!!!!!!

ELEMENT OF THE DAY. IT WOULDN'T BE FUN WITHOUT IT. I picked up a cake for my step Dad's - Day cake at Nobel's bakery. I needed money so I had to do it. It was funny. The cake was never in the refrigerator when I picked it up. The cake was FRAGILE and I needed to be so careful because it might be loopsided. I walked with extreme caution. "OHH hell what was that," I thought when I heard a click when I walked. It was just nothing. It was really bumpy for the cake when I was ridding the bus. I was way loopsided when I got home so I slide it back slanting and sliding it to make it in the middle so it looks the way I got it. That was a funny experience for me. I saw "City of Angels" with Kelly. I got home feeling so good. That movie was so good. I wanted to see it so bad and finally got to. I decided to sit down on the red curve outside our apt. complex so I can just think about myself and wonder if theirs really an angel. It loved the same. My sweater kept me warmed from the cold wind. Like what I said before, "I have passion for nature. I found serenity in me. I just pretended that one of my friend will pick me up and look at the watch often. There's a mountain I saw it above all. I thought about my goals where and when I will be, just everything. It turn out one of my friend now lives in the apt. complex saw me and asked me if I wanted to go with her. I did. We went to places. (Ap 17th) My Mom and I went to the mall. My Mom left early because she felt sick. She gave me $40 (it was my money). We didn't even buy a dress for my graduation. Maybe next time. I bought a NO DOUBT T-SHIRT on sale for $ 6.99 at HOT-TOPIC. I remember I had a dream today that GWEN signed an autograph for me. I knew I was dreaming. "Bummer, too bad I wont be able to have this and put it in my scrap book," when I looked at what she wrote. I didn't even read what she wrote. She sign NO DOUBT instead of her name. I wore it the next day. (Ap. 18) for Hilary's B-Day pool Party. I had to wake up at 7 AM that day. I was tired but I got over it. I was tired because I had to baby sit 4 girls and got home at 1PM.

"Why are you leaving early. Are you going to Tijuana?," my Mom asked, I laughed. I told her that Tim had a job interview and I'm going with them. We ate Taco Bell for Lunch. I was glad we did that because I would have been starving later on. The Viejas Outlet store is pretty. Tim will working at G.A.P. I made chocolate covered strawberries for HILARY. We mix strawberry margarita. "Don't worry Hilary just think when you are 40 or 20 years from now funny this is," I said as we were walking back. Did you ever say that going to laugh at this 20 years from now. I chuckled and smile to think how funny the situation was. I saw how pretty Lake Jennings was. My family used to go fishing there. They still do it every but without me. I love that place. I could spend a day there enjoying every minute of it like the way it was before. I ate a lot at her party. Oh well! I enjoyed the party a lot. I talked with Hilary's Mom while Hilary was taking a shower. Hilary's Mom is so cool and a nice lady. The group talked and laughed. We later went crusin for 2 hours. I got home at 12:15 AM. I was so sleepy and tired. I had an awesome day. It was a great way to end my Spring Break. Today I just back and relax. I saw the sun again. I wanted to sit down on the red curve again for the second time. **The sun fades it beauty I saw it from bright yellow to red orange. It was pretty. On the opposite side of the sun is the mountain I loved. I thought about what I needed to do for 9 weeks of intense school and what my expectations after that. I will do this again because it is like meditating for me. I feel like my soul speaks** and I don't yet know how to expLain it right. I sleepy right now. I need to go to bed. I'm ready about school for tomorrow. I'm excited about it. Say Goodbye to Spring Break. I can't wait to start for my old busy schedule. I am so excited about the SPRING THING. IT WILL BE SO MUCH FUN. UNTIL NEXT TIME.

Mon (5:45 PM to 9 PM) 4/27/98

Its time again to write about what has happen so far after SPRING BREAK. 8 More weeks till the end of school (including this week). Im not one of those people who hoped

or wants summer vacation right now. I like to live to live every moment and everyday of my life because life doesn't revolve in the summer time but Right now. To cut this nonsense sermon,.. I'm saying that im living the good life right now and why wait for the future when you can party or do what you want. YEAH ! You see where I'm getting at.

I can barely think right now. My brain is still thinking about the concert. But before I go there I have to start wit last week. Well, gee that's easy. I don't remember much of what happen during the 1st week after SPRING BREAK except over the weekend. I learn how to ride a bike on Friday. Not really because I only spend an hour and did 2 360 pedaling consecutively w/2 feet. I need to work on balance. I'm glad I got the oppurtunity to learn now. I would never thought I will learn how to bike in a million years. It is actually fun. My weekend was sort of hectic because I was doing something every hour. Plus, I had to wake up early Sat & Sun. I never wake up early on weekends, not unless it is important to do so. I had to attend a teen mentoring meeting on a Sat morning at 8 AM-11:30 A.M. The breakfast was good there. Then I had to go to Ross to meet my Mom. I was really late went I got there. I only had 1 hour to spend with her but she was at Wal -Mart. I had to leave so I stayed at Ross. I brought this up because I was thinking of something important when I was inside the transit bus. It was my only way to get there. I'm use to it. This is what I was thinking: ' I couldn't imagine being stuck in a bottom of bottom pit. Its weird to think to suffer more . ~~$$$~~ I don't mean the word suffer as torture, you'll see what I'm talking about. It is quite impossible to be at a bottomer pit. Its impossible (or unfair) For someone to drill it deeper when it is deep enough. What Im talking about is my situation in life. My life Right now is great. A lot of my Filipino friends would love to live here. ~~The same~~ My life is far better compare to kids who doesn't even have one parent supporting them or living on the streets or emotional depressed etc. Im not looking down on them or living on the streets or emotional depressed etc. Im not looking down on them because I had those days of my life /\ somewhat similar to what I mention what im saying is that I am a lucky person. It doesn't matter who you are, there will always be good and bad things about youR life. They it comes and go, whether it's another problem or challenge to face. There aRe ways to make life better.

I can go on and on about the good and bad things of life. Moving along…. One of my dilemma is after graduation. I know that I have to move out of my room few months from now out like June. (3Rd week) or aRound there. Where will I go I still have to do my summer school. I hope that I will achieve my goal to be a member of Army National Guard. I have to . I want to. Its my savior for getting money and my college dream. There is no other way. I have to do this. There is no way that I will be rejected for Army N.G. I cannot see the bottom pit whole to be deeper. I can't see myself working 2-3 jobs and ask For my Mom's help for money so I have to pay for apartment rent, food, college etc. there is no way I have to go through hell. Going to boot camp is not hell for me. I cant see myself in pain again and live back when I was a Freshman or Sophomore or my childhood days with my Mom we went through

(I was still on the bus). (I looked up in the sky). I said to the Lord that this can't happen to me. If I had a dollar ~~penny~~ for every time I till ~~him~~ the LoRd about it. It would be a lot of dollars. I know he is listening . I believe in him. He was the one who saved my Mom and I years ago and my high school years are just a couple of example not even going to details. I believe in him. He has shown me miracle things that was happened in my life when I reflect about it. I would not be in U.S.A. if not for him. I never thought in a billion years when I was a small kid I would live here. Back then Mom was the one who carried the sorrows or problems because I was too young to understand it. Now, as a young adult I have my first big step in life and this time I have to do it alone without her. Of Course, she is there to support me and my friends supporting me too. I'm mainly talking about being in charge of my life. To follow my dreams is even harder that I thought it will be. But, that's reality. But do you want to know one of the big things I learned of my 18 years of experience is that no matter how cruel the world will be or tough or challenging or crazy life you have or life will be, there is one thing that has work for me and I think it work for everybody. "HARD WORK PAYS OFF !" When was the last time you work so hard and just keep on trying and trying and then finally you get something out of it. Do you agree with me? It doesn't have to be big things but maybe simple things like: studying HaRd for an exam that you had to give up your social time. So that and got an A or B, keep looking for a job… then suddenly opportunity knucks (Chi ! Ching ! $ $ $) you got a job or staying in school so that you get to go to cool colleges like in Masachuttes, Seattle or New York. Where will this take me: 1 year of self sacrifice, discipline and determination in running, dieting, lost 20 + lbs & quit McDonalds so I can have the time to run and do school work. I did all these so that I will be in the Army N.G. That is HARD WORK to me. I think a lot about what will happen in May, June, July, Aug- Jan, Jan -99 -June 99. The main reason is that I have FEAR. I'm afraid if I fail. Im afraid that I will flunk the medical exam and they will find out something I will be disqualified. But I really don't think negatively like that all the time. The truth is, I am positive that I will be going to boot camp but sometimes I think about what if… This is why I think it will happen (meaning I will be in A.N.G) because of my hardwork, I suffered enough and I don't deserve that this pit (situation) I am now to be a deeper whole. The only thing I really want Right now is the Army N. Guard Recruiter (Sgt. Goodenough) telling me that I'm going to BootCamp and Training in Aug to Dec. I never ask the Lord for that. I ask him for his guidance and that I will continue to be a strong-will & determined to achieve this goal. I had never failed a big dream or goal in life. I can't see failing for something I believe in, admire, hope to be (a soldier) and being a part of something great and unique. So righT now, all I can do is wait when I have to do my medical exam in May (not wishing it to be May) and just enjoy Running, live and awesome life, go to school etc. I had different pits in life. They were gone because I buried them by putting cement, soil and shit in it. I really never started using the pit word to relate about my situation until I thought about what to call it when I was on the bus. The sad thing is I don't know the literary term for it. I think metaphor or imagery. I don't know. I guess I can relate to this pit since I realized the problems in my house and high school. The deepest was when I was around 13 years old. I deal it better now because Im used to it. I'm pretty happy of what I had done for the 5 years Ive been here in U.S. I just realize now it is not really deep compare to when I look back. I had put cement, dirt, soil, shit, crap, food, money, time, tears (water) and etc. to get to where I am now. Sometimes when I write about or remember what happened ~~my fresh~~ on my grade 9th, 10th , 11th 'tears will come out like right now. It depends on what I remember. Well, at least I can never be that shy, low-self-esteem girl and thought she was dumb because people only saw her intelligence but others saw more than that she just didn't look hard enough. She couldn't even look hard enough into her soul or look at her eyes and face and see who she really was. But that's gone now. It still huRts when I think about it. There nothing I can do. about the past. It wasn't so bad at all. I had awesome days back then. Okay. Moving along now. This pit will be gone soon. If I have to put dollars (foR Rent) or sweet so it will be gone. Moving out of this house and knowing I made it in the AN Guard is when the pit is buried. That is when I will celebrate. Goosh darn Right I will. But you know what. I don't hate the bad things in life. I hate it but I don't. Does that make sense? It is just that I'm a survivor (I remember Mrs. McGraw saying "You are a survivor, Heralyn." When I went with them for 4th of July 1997 Fireworks). I had many ups and downs of life and I take those experiences with me everyday. If you know me well, this is why you see my great character; who I am. I love to take on daring things in life. I love the challenge for it doesn't matter if if Im drowning but still alive but when I come out of the /\ deep water … ~~you~~ I come out a better person I like to see people happy. I like to help out others and make a difference. I love the role of leadership. I like to make a big deal of my friends big event like their B-Day because I want them to feel special and that I care in the same way as they do for me. One way to describe friendship is a give and take relationship. I heard that quote from somewhere. It is like one friend gives more than the other but the other person ends up giving more and vice versa, therefore it is balance. I remember Hilary saying, "I going to debt to you." I said, "What do you mean. it comes out balance." I think she knows that. I like to go to Wal-Mart to take the bus just so I can talk to my Mom about anything without talking in dialect like we do in the house. I love how I go to school on weekends and have so much fun with my friends on weekends. I think life is boring without a social life. All in all really, the whole experience of reflection right now and the bus was well worth it. I will win this war (battle). It has been my own (battle) war since the first day I decided to run and continue running ~~day after~~ everyday as exercise. I will achieve my glory in this world. I will achieve this goal. There are gazillions of glories in this glories in this world. What ever you call it, glory or happiness or extreme edge. I call it glory tonight because I achieve gloriness. ~~Shot~~ somehow I have weird interpretations tonight. I think I do that all the time. Its probably the side effects from last night. That concert funkin Rock ! It was my 2nd concert. I've seen a total of 15 bands now. I saw 12 bands last night. They are (in order of appearance) assorted jelly beans, Flourecent, **KOTTONMOUTH KINGS** was good. I love the Suburban LiFe song. I think im going to get scream 2 soundtrack . I don't thing I want to get their but scream 2 has that song in it. The Argentinian Rock band was good. I didn't understand what they were saying except a few words. UNWRITTEN LAW, BUCK-O- NINE, BLINK 182, & OFFSPRING ROCK. 1 ← Also, the SPRUNG MONKEY and COTTON MOUTH KINGS ~~were~~ the bands I like there./ I love the Buck -O-Nine "MYTOWN" song. The OffSPRING played for one hour. They played all the best songs. I thought they would I will play know a couple songs but I was wrong. The SPRING THING CONCERT LASTED FROM 3PM-11PM. We were there for 8 to 8 ½ hours. There was probably about 3500-5000 people in the COX ARENA. 2/3 were on the Floor and the rest sat. There werer 2 stages. I was glad I wasn't on the floor. The smoke smell was either cigarrette or pot. I think everybody smelled the pot more. "I smell pot," said one of the Blink 182 guys. It a pretty weird feeling from having that 2nd hand smell. I don't know the term for it. I keep hearing bells ring nor " I hear butterfly singing," I said to Hilary and Mrs. McGraw. This is the first time my ears are ringing. I couldn't [xoudn't] go to sleep right away last night because I hears heavy metal music and crowds cheering whatever I think, " HEralyn ! Heralyn ! Heralyn !." That was cool. I wonder what I will hear if I smoke it. No ! I wouldn't be that supid. Well tomorrow is another awesome day to breathe. Today, the Friendship Festival food was good and I got out of school because of that. Well, gotta do homework.

Sun (11 PM) May 3, 1998

I'm so pissed ! Well ! I don't know. Last week was crazy for me. To make it even worst, it will be crazier because it is towards the end of school. I don't want, to have stress again. I haven't had to ~~gotten~~ opportunity to run everyday because Im so busy. There are a lot of stuff to do and I have to meet the deadline. I'm going to start running so I can be stress and worry free. I'll be fine. This happens… I just need to blow off steam. Overall, my weekend was awesome. Friday night was fun. I went to LaPalapa with Tim & Hilary and we saw City of Angels. I didn't get home till 12:30 AM. I didn't cry seeing this movie for the 2nd time. I enjoyed talking and laughing about stuff. Hmm Yes ! Virgin /\ stRawberry MargaRitas was excellent as always. Hilary and I got a Freebie, each extra chicken enchilada. I inhaled that food. It was so good. That was a great Friday night for me. I went with Beyonce to see "007 Tommorow never dies" movie. We took the bus to get there. I bought a black back-pack which is exactly like my other green one. I also bought 2 shirts/ blouses. I always like to pay cheap. Why by a $60 backpack when I can go to ROSS to buy the exact thing for $20. We ate yogurt after the movie . The movie definitely influence me more of becoming a secret agent. Ive always wanted to do this type of profession in the future. It is a fantasy can happen for real but only I can make it happen. The cross-over dimension in this world has to work for me. Who knows I might be working for DIA or CIA or NSA or NSC. I have to learn so many stuff to be able to do it. Im learning how to ride a bike so someday ill ride a motorcycle. The movie I saw at my Physics class, ***sneakers*** (another spy, action, secRect story movie), was so cool. Maybe I'll watch it again someday. I'm almost done with Kelly's 18 different gifts. I need to get 4 more. One of them is a poem. I'm having fun doing this for her 18th B-Day. Some of the stuff are pineapple, chick key chain, mini- cinnamon bagel & glow in dark snakes. I hope she plans something that day. Today, one of the things I did was calculating my future income from

Aug 98-June 99 to see where I stand in the Real world. I hope everything will turn out the way I want them to be. I plan to learn how to dive during my A. I . T. and to get buy a $2,000 truck there. I hope that when I step on that kind somewhere in the east coast It won't be hell because I know by then that I got the right path of Road I wanted and NOT the path of hell. I don't deserve it in the first place to get that path I don't want at all. I feel my goal will come true and time is near and if it is I only have 3 moths left in this bedroom or maybe 1 ½ months.

May 10th, 1998 (7:38 P.M.) Sunday - MOTHER'S DAY.

I greeted my Mom Happy Mother's Day and gave her a dozen of pink roses today. It's been a laid back weekend. It wasn't like hectic oR loads of crazy fun things to do. I went to the mall twice. Friday was fun. Kelly, Elizabeth & I went to Pizza Hut , close to Parkway Mall to eat lunch. I remember Kelly's B-Day Party was held there to seven songs on the juke box I selected=Two of the songs from NO DOUBT (Spider webs & just a GiRl), others I remember are T.L.C., Treat her like a Lady (Celine Dion), Nirvana, & A. Morrisette. We went to the mall after that. I got some stuff for my scrapbook. I had fun. When I got home I wrapped a few gifts for Kelly. I only need to buy her a pineapple & write a poem. She said she will have a party next week. Nothing big, just the three of us doing something fun. I went with my Mom to the Mall on Saturday. She felt sick so she had to go home early again. She's been not feeling good everyday Saturday. She felt sick so she had to go not feeling good evry Saturaday. She can't figure out why. She spends a lot of time in the Kitchen and the bedroom, pretty much the house during her days off. She thinks something about the smell in the house. I hope she feels better next Saturday. I bought ~~got~~ my business suit outfit I wanted to wear for my graduation. It is black. I have a white long sleeve with whitest Rips to accent it with style. I love this outfit. It makes me feel like a professional business person on a secret agent or both. It just feels great wearing this $ 140 suit. I got them on sale so all together it is $90. I got the suit at SEARS and long sleeve at my favorite store there Charlotte Russe. I really hope I will do something fun on the night of my graduation. I really want to have a GRADUATION PARRTY. I'll just celebrate it by myself. Not Really ! I will do whatever it takes to have a party, whether a Limo party or a hotel party. Or both. It's crazy how ($ $ $) money revolves in everything these days. I hope I don't get hectic weekdays like that one last week. I need to get back on Running beFore I start gaining weight again.

May 17, 1998 (9:30 PM) Sunday

What a weekend ! What a week ! At least last school week wasn't as busy as the one before it. Im glad that week was over. Scholarship foR the Stadium Association interview is tomorrow at 12:30 PM (I think !) for me. Im not even ready. But I have to believe I can pull off a great interview. My college education at Grossmont is dependent on it. The fact is my whole financial college independent lifestyle ($10,000 worth yearly) is depended on it. I need to get some money from them. I wish I could just beg and they will give it to me. I have to fill out my Spanish scholarship. I don't even know for sure if I am one of the science club members graduating getting a scholarship. I'm sure all the seniors in this club should get something If there is one person not getting it. It will be me the rest will get it. They can't just leave me out of sharing the money. As usual, projects and more ~~even~~ projects aRe due. One of the things I thought a lot last week was about achieving success "gLORy." "A person who works hard, dedicate a lot of his/her time, on sacrifice, and commit to achieving His/her goals/s will have his/her glory when the time comes with patience." It happened to Kelly. She is one of 3 students who is Salolitorian. I remember my freshman year when I was walking in the Hallway in our school, I thought about what it would be like to be a ValidictoRian or a Salitatorian. For a second I hold on to that goal then I let go of it because I doubted my abilities. I was smart (but I didn't know that I was smart until I realized I stop being the smart student). Of course, Im a smart student but when I stop getting mostly A's on classes. " Some people are reawaken when they lose something important. It is an invaluable experience in half life when it happened to me." My point is not about me letting go of that thought but how I wished, I didn't limit, my capabilities back then. Then again, That's how I learn to be a Better person (like me Right now) and take my life so important. NOW, I wait For the time to come to achieve my "glory." The Day I become a member of the U.S. Army National Guard. But I learn that you don't wait for someone or something but I alone must make the ~~first~~ move. I thought about the summer time, Graduation Night, hotel party, San Diego style vacation, when and how long is ARNG… , September at Phils. Etc. I felt what it was like everyday when I was in gRade 9, 10, 11. I'm not sure how to explain it. I just felt stressed out with too many things I need to do. But one thing is foR Sure. Back then I was 4, 3, oR , 2 years thinking about the future (day dreaming or stressing out about the future etc.) but what is __?__SCARY IS.. THIS TIME IT IS SO CLOSE IN A MATTER OF MONTHS TIME PASSING BY and 5 weeks till I gradaute .its okay to be scared with the feeling of Raptureness especially if the person who feels like that is me. You would know why if you know my life situations and problems. It is tough but I will survive as I always have been befoRe. I only ask the Lord that I don't have to suFFer a lot of pain oR troubling waters every time. He knows how I feel and understand. How do I know what im going through and understand although they may never know what it is like to be Heralyn and ~~going through~~ living a tough liFe. But that is A Blessing that I have wonderful people I know I can share joke or stories laugh with, talk anything, enjoy what the world has to offer etc.

My Mom's cousin, Myrna Morales Tongco is coming this memorial Day (Mom , May 25) along with her family. Her 3 kids, Jun Earl, Dimple, and Angel and her Husband June. MyRna my Mom Mom are close friends growing up through college and forever. This is what tRuE friendship is about… it lasts forever. I seldom see it. I believe that TRUE FRIENDSHIP will only happen to me and my friends) if both of us make it lasts. This is one of those things I don't know how to explain because Im not 40+ years old. Im so happy ~~to see~~ that I will see my cousins and aunts and uncle. This is one of those things where it only happens in a dream. But it is not in a dream no more, it will soon be a reality in 8 days. On Friday after school I went to Kelly's house to celebrate here B-Day. It was just Kelly, Eliz. & I doing another FUN event. I gave Kelly RecoRd tape , cookies, ~~fortune cookie~~, lottery ticket, child figurine, chocolate candy bar, mini-lamp, 'at keychain, insence, short stoRy from Elizabeth, GLOW IN THE DARK DUCKIES (HOW MANY DO YOU HAVE ?_ [Milki has 4 & I love dat PADRES GET LUCKY TROLL]) CHAIN,

Hello Kitty stationeries blue nail color, bookmark, glow in the dark snakes, FRAM PICTURES angel box, pineapple, and a poem (← I still need to wRite.) it was worth it even iF it was a lot of time to prepare. We saw what you did last Summer and GATIKA movies AND ATE PIZZAS, CAKES, COOKIES & ICE CREAM. I WENT TO Wal-Mart with my Mom to get my very own Monopoly board game and a travel's 6 in 1 game. I also got a mini new T-shirt and a new sketchers shoe. I haven't gotten to do stuff with Hilary. I hope to see her next week. I need to clean my Room & the bathrooms. Cleaning is one thing in this world that takes forever. I saw 7 yrs. To Tibet while baby-sitting.

May 25, 1998(6:45 PM Mon- Memorial Day)

Surely my life living on this planet for 18 years have been full of fun pack adventure. At least I don't have to worry about senior showcase or scholarship that I need to type up and worry about an interview. The most important thing I realized when I finished my scholarship stuff that those scholarships are not even close worth the value of my goals and ambitions in life. I would rather go after it than to have the value of money for the scholarship and not go to the college of my dream. I really couldn't say anything that will make them think twice about awarding me the scholarship during that E.C. Stadium Assoc. Interview when the lady said that I could get money from Uncle Sam (a lot) for college. There is only one scholarship military I want. That is West Point $260,000 value. She could never change my mind. I responded saying that I know a lot about the many programs for college while in the military but " My Heart is set on West Point." I hope I get something . So many things has happen last week. I will be very busy tonight and probably till 4 AM in the morning typing & writing an essay. All this week, the major thing I did was making $40 in Babysitting. I get paid to do fun stuff plus free food. The REC Club (where I volunteer) is a great experience for me. I'm glad I applied to volunteer there. I talked to Hilary on the phone . She called me to tell she got $45 hr. coupon for Presidential Limo. She just saved minimum reservation. I got went job hunting. I would really love to work at the mall. I think the best job there for me is Sam & Goody , 5 • 7 • 9 , or claires is good too. I really gotta have a summer job. I finally heard from Maureen. She sent me an advance graduation card. The

Tongco family will arrive here on Thursday, May 28. I made an WELCOME SIGN with drawings on it. Sea World .. Here I come.

(Sun Morning 2 PM) June 7, 1998

It's been quite a ride for the past two weeks. I didn't even get to write on my diary last week. On May 30th 1998 was Prom night and after -Prom. Kelly, A.. , & I went to the " Top of the Cove" Restaurant in La Jolla. I spent $40. I guess it is worth it because it only happens once in a while. The ocean view was pretty. I got a $23 Dinner Menu (something Grilled Chicken ...). Also, ate raw oysters, V. margarita y the most awesome desert I ever had. AfterProm at Family Fun Center in Clairemont Mesa was fun. I'm glad I did it and went. Also on that day Hilary was working and I went with her Mom when she got picked up after work. She told me she saw my MOM and my relatives from ~~coming~~ the Phils. (Sea World.) It been so crazy with school and graduation. I've been with my cousins /relatives to the Mall and other places. It's been crazy in this house doing go to school on Friday but I needed that day off. I got a haircut and went shopping crazy. They are gone to go to Disneyland and Universal studio and wont be back on Sunday or Monday. Hilary and Tim ~~spend~~ stayed at ~~mayt~~ here ~~but~~ and we went to the mall. Hilary spend the night. Then I spend the night at her house last night for the 1st time. Tonight is the party. We had great food and watched movies. All the good shit in a typical American Party. I showed Hilary my scrapbook and she Read parts of my 1st diary. I not only get to have FUN (Thurs night to Sun) but also get money around $100 from my MOM. I'm so glad of what is happening in my life right now. I got $4000 scholarship from Spanish club. I thank the Lord for his many blessings.

June 10, 1998 →
"THE MISSING PUZZLE I FOUND"

Maybe writing on my journal will make me feel better right now.

" Just hang in there Heralyn. Just 8 more days till graduation day." I hate STRESS more than anything in this world right now. I want to feel better. Im just at this moment of my life facing another challenge. I just hope everything will be better for me soon. I need to be in a

good mood everyday. You know how I thought of writing on my journal was when I sat down on my bed and look out at my window. Ive always done that when Im you know feeling like this right now ever since I came to California and lived in this apartment. The window haven't change /only season/- ~~weather~~ climate) but I have. I'm stressed out for the fact that I haven't been able to Read and finished my last novel I need to read for ENGLISH CLASS. An essay is due this Friday. I need 30 hours to finished this book which includes reading and writing the essay (typed) but I don't have 30 houRs to spare. I gave up. I want high school to be over. I just went to pick up the phone and Marisa (Advisor of Rec Club where I volunteer) told me if ever I changed my mind I can still if I ~~still~~ can go to Awards night tomorrow (honoring the volunteers) I told her before I couldn't and I said I'll try. I don't have a ride to get there. SOMETIMES I HAVE BIG DOUBTS aBOUT my life. I mean the sequel of events happening right now. I believe that a person is in control of his/ her own destiny. But WHAT IF IM REALLY NOT IN CHARGE OF MY LIFE. I'm not trying to say God is in control totally. I think I have this theory that im stuck in this hole, YES A HOLE ! You can laugh if you want. A hole where I'm stuck being a B- (3.0 less G.P.A. less) student with all the well- rounded background. Dammit ! I quit my job on Jan because on of the reason was I waited to get better grades. I will have almost the same grades I got on my 1st semester for 2nd semester. Bummer ! No matter how hard I try … I couldn't get straight A's this semester because I'm doing something. OR don't have the time OR something else is more important. The sad thing is Im not making excuses but these are
Real /\ reasons. My point is Im stucK in this hole and most likely chance I get out is 1 in a million. How ironic, Ive been wanting to get out. I hope is only high school. So if it's a plan above or the stars that I will get a 2.99 G.P.A. I don't care but I want my dream. I can see it now.
50-60 years from now if ever become a politician. People will dig up a lot of stuff about me. "They will say Heralyn made ~~up~~ it. Did you know she got an F in A.P. Calculus." She was just an average student but she love leadership." Believe it or not, she ran for school treasurer twice and didn't run third time because she knew she ~~couldn't~~ doesn't have a chance." Just let someone reread it again I know why I just don't have a chance. I think you know why. Those (
" …") quotations are just what people will think. I like it this way because it means that anything in this world is

possible and it matter if you were an honor student or a valedictorian in high school. WHAT WILL ALWAYS MATTER IS HOW YOU ALONE MAKE THINGS HAPPEN. And of course with wonderful people helping you on your way. See, I told you writing journal helps me feel better. It is like a therapy for me. This will save me a couple hundred a moNth in the future. I always stood my head high. Im a survivor. You gotta Roll with the punches. JEWEL (the singer & writer) wrote journals. She said it was like therapy too and look where it got her. I don't know what else to write. Haven't you realized that I write till the end of the page. Ill think of something. I hope I get a job soon. I don't care of any job with a few exceptions but I have no choice. I need money- My relatives (The Tongco Family)) will be gone on Saturday. I will miss them. I had so much fun with them and went to many places. I can't wait for the Limo and the dinner. Hilary ~~Britney[~~ Mariah] is paying ½ for Limo and that's a lot of money. It will be fun. She read my diary. I hope always wanted at last one person to read my diary while im still alive. She read parts of my 1st diary. She didn't see her name. I think its betteR she sees the finish product of my scrapbook then she will know what to expect if she still wants to read the diaries. I let her read it because she is an understanding person. WE Have been great friends and I trust her.. I guess I end here For tonight.

June 15, 1998 (5PM) (Monday)

Im feel like shit today. Maybe because Im in a bad mood since Period 4. I'm not sure when it started today. Is it when I read what Dale W. Wrote on my yearbook ?, or when Elizabeth said "Thanks a lot for laughing at me on Fri …. my ankle is bruise up ? Or when Elizabeth said " Thanks a lot for laughing at me on Fri …. my ankle is bruise up ? Or when ~~Marco~~ read what Marco wrote on my yearbook ? It doesn't matter. My pissy mood will be gone after I do kickboxing I plan to exercise after writing in my diary. I feel a little better after I listened to Sublime, Sprung Monkey and A. Morrissette. I still have the little T.V. to my surprise but nothing is on that is worth watching. I love music. It has inspired me over these years, cheered me up on many bad days and I can Relate my life to it. T.V. is crap most of the time. As usual, writing this clams ~~clams~~ my nervous system down. Back to realization therapy. So what… my classmates just wrote what they felt like to say. No harm done there. Like getting an F on Calculus or a C in Govt or a C in English. At least I have one B in Spanish. Just one of the classes I worked hard for. ***I EITHER WORKED HARD for something oR I DON'T. I should have stayed working at my McDonalds and surf my 2nd semester. But I had a plan for 2nd semester, and It blew. Oh well ! I did everything. I still believe in my theory of black hole*** or whatever I called it before. I'm sure Marco had good intentions writing believe in my theory of black hole or whatever I called it before. I'm sure Marco had good intentions writing in my yearbook. I missed ~~the~~ his point on the 1st sentence he wrote. I guess I overlooked it. [My G. Angel must have talked to him because lust MARCOS message cheered me up after I fully understand the whole message when I got home. The TRUTH HURTS. Many people died from it and others got away. I sound like I'm talking about the evolution of man or World History. Although I won't go in details what happened today … because it doesn't matter. I have more things to worry about and not to worry.. Whatever life will be for me… WHO CARES ! WHOOPEE !!! All I know is I'm graduating in 3 days. June 18 will be a Memorable night for me. I can't wait. It was easy saying Goodbye to my relatives (my Aunt, Uncle , & 3 cousins). They left on /\ early Saturday morning. I basically did house cleaning. I got bored on Sunday. I returned the videos I rented and called Hilary. I asked her what she is doing. I asked her what she is doing. I asked if her Mom would be willing to help me with Spanish. Jim and Mrs. McGraw helped me. Jim totally edit the whole thing. He did a good job. I helped grade papers of L.M.S. 6th grade assessment Test. Those yummy Tacos. I could eat a dozen of those a day. I feel so lucky. **"This can be your airport to land," Mrs. McGraw said. I knew she wasn't joking when I asked what she said. She said it again. I thank the LoRd that I'm surrounded with caring people.**

June 26, 1998 (Friday 8:50 P.M.)

Finally ! A chance to write stuff on my diary. Stuff? I mean the precious events that happen for the past6 2 week period ; it will always stay in my memory. What A MEMORY IT WAS !!!! Im not going to tell you the way it happen but the way I remembered it. Well, its gonna be a long night for me. Im starting of what I did today and day before and so on. Pretty much this week and I will have a big section for the Graduation events after that. It's kind of like rewinding.

It seems my life is out of control or not a smooth ride after I graduated. It seems that I don't have a break since the day I was born. I know I love challenges but somehow as I grew older these challenges gets harder and harder which make it very difficult to achieve. Almost impossible to achieve when I think of it sometimes because patience fades, faith fades and ...."trying harder and not giving up.." is just a useless quote to live by. Good thing I'm back to normal. I think I am ? But whatever happens Im still alive and breathing well. The people I know well will still be here and God is still watching over me with my G. Angel giving me advice. The point I'm trying to make : *Life is whatever you inteRpret it. You make your point this time.* Okay, picture this : I got out of high school ...Freedom ... have taking summer school for the 1st 6 weeks of summer.... Wake up at 4: 39 AM or around 5 AM... have 7 AM- 9:30 AM Spanish 220 class... spend $200 on this class... $200+ on the Limo... there goes my $400 scholarship... money sucks when it is all gone... I've been having weird moods lately like happy, sad, uncertain, (which is pretty normal for me by now) but on a summer time. My moods made my summer /\ in a slow start. OR it could be this slap in a face experience I had during the last 7 days (including this day) I'm glad my doubts of taking summer school is gone. The class is cool. I sit at the back where I could see everyday because I got tiRed of sitting up front during my senior year. My teacher can teach. HE talks slow, almost as if he is talking translating ~~some~~ the Spanish to English. He's funny and it makes the class not boring. The test is not as good as Sra. Fonseca class kept me running like a GLADIATOR. Don't ask, its hard to explain . And to think I would have "ace" that Capitulo 13 exam (1st exam today) today if I studied more than an hour. Its's my fault. My profesor give us a study guide for the exam and at least -50 % of it will be on the test. "Guess what? , I got a job," the words that Kelly said to me last night. She called me to tell me she got a job at Santee Wal-Mart and that I should turn in the application I have with me because they are hiring. What was going on with my mind yesterday , need a job, Hawaii, Las Vegas … Seattle… cross country road teip, New Jersey, (exam) study, $ $ $, future, car and then after Kelly called the Job i need so bad and she got hired. I must admit I was jealous but I'm glad she called me to tell me about it. Life is a Bitch ! Some people get what they want easier and while others don't. I have asked many stores for applications… around 15 applications sums it up. Kelly just spend an hour and filled out 4 applications and got a job 2 days later. I tell you Life's a bitch ! That was how I felt and it feels good writing about it right now. I got over it. I'm applying to Wal-Mart tomorrow and Lucky too. Hopefully it will be the last 2 applications to fill out for a long time. The happy feeling of waiting for Sam & Goody to call me soon because they are hiring :) is gone. I had a really good time this week despite of the shits in my life. I finally gave the Thank You card address to the McGraw Family with a Hawaiian chocolate box. " This is making me want to cry… what you wrote…" Hilary said. I didn't had a big comment but I thought of what was going on my mind a couple days before Graduation. I did read what I wrote on the card and I felt almost crying. Its 9:50 PM and Im so sleepy. I had a long day and a long week. I guess I will say what was really going on my mind when I finish this tomorrow. Hopefully, I will be fully conscious and remember a lot. Good Night ! A remembering of my beloved Aunt Jojo Aniversary's death of today. A place in my heart for you always.

Sept. 6, 1998 (Sunday) 12:45 P.M.

Today would be my Mom's 44 B-day. This ain't no June 27th, '98. Usually I got so lazy on summer time. Can't you tell ? I usually write on my diary at least once evry 1 week or 2 and not in 2 months. Like the saying goes " Time is precious." So I'm making it count right now. Im going to tell my lovely summer story and the main character "me." I'll probably tell it differently now because I'm on top of the world now. It was … to describe my summer in 20 world… cruel, disappointing, great, unexpecting, sad, glories,
104 % of fun, hot, breaking the rules, joyous fun in the night, roaring laughter & shopping. I saw 3 movies. "THERE'S

SOME THING ABOUT MARY" WITH KELLY. I only did a few things with Kelly, not like last year of summer. Kelly, Eliz and I went to Fashion Valley Mall and saw a movie. I can't remember the title. I saw the Avengers with Elizabeth. I went everywhere this summer. From Grossmont Center Mall, Parkway Mall, movies, crusin with Tim & Hilary, Family Fun Center with our without friends. "it's almost like a religion"... I said to Hilary when we were at LaPalapa. She laughed. It's because we love to go to LaPalapa. It is one of my favorite hangout. Hilary and I both love the food and margaritas. Right Hilary ? At one night this summer she spent the night and we watched these bitching movies (It was cool !) Tim picked us up at the Parking Lot where China Dynasty is at.

I had so much fun. I went to a Casino for the first time at Viejas. We got home at 4:20 AM. ."playing with fire...." she said. Don't we all love playing with fire. That was a perfect kickoff of my last day of summer. I started school the next day. I did lots of other stuff. I spend a lot of money just to have fun. Ain't life grand? It was the peak of my summer.... My life when all of a sudden BOOM !!! Like I just won the lottery. I couldn't believe that for the first time & in my life, I could make it happen. I did it. I'm talking about the Marketing job I got. I got a letter from Ochoa and Associates so I scheduled an interview.

WOW !!! It was one of my favorite event this summer. It played an important role in my life and will even play more. Indeed, it will be an influence for the future I wanted. But that future is not as big not if I come up with a plan to make it real and give it to someone I can trust with a few exceptions of course. I never would have thought of this if not for this marketing job I got but I had to let it go. I didn't have the money. Why should I pay for the knives I was going to show to the future customers. At first, I couldn't believe it, at $ 12-25 starting an hour. I cried and I wanted to cry then I called Mr. Ochs about my situation. I know that he wasn't scam. It is just a rule that we had to pay it and he'll reinburst the money. I know that was twetoo[real2].

I was one out of 100+ who got hired and out of those only talent, skills and luck in my opinion will get 10-20 people who will stay ~~in the~~ as a CUTCO sales rep. Longer. If you get the picture, that's how money is and to make money.

I have nothing against the company. It was good while it lasted, it was a neat fame. It made me feel that I could do anything. It was a perfect example of that. It wasn't easy to get to LA MESA but I had to do it. It was for a purpose.

I hope the future holds for me is great. "If Heralyn had a million dollars, can I live with you so I can continue my military career." - HA ! HA ! " Did you hear that Tim." Last night was fun. Last week we went to the beach and last night too. Tim found an apartment. I think the future says : January were moving with or with /o me. That's a wrap. I got to make my time count. Oh yeah almost FORGOT I Finally got a permanent job or jobs for a while.

(1) at Montessori Pre-School
(2) Baby -sitting
(3) a Business : Self-Defense Studio

I'm still at this apartment only because I'm getting along w/ him.
☺ I'm finally a college student and enjoying it. Its not so bad after all. I have a class at night Monday Child Growth and Development, Weds.: Administration of Justice and at SDSU Army ROTC Intro to Military (MS 100) and a Lab. It will be fun. I can't believe Im doing Army ROTC after 4 years of high school. It feels good to come this Far and not to wait For ROTC is here to stay. I'm on top of the WORLD Right now. Its only the beginning… keep on reading.

(Sat) (10:05 PM) 9/19/98

"This will staRt or it slow for you but it will be start out slow for you but it will be tough later on," these woRds provoke in my head as a Reminder of what my Guardian advise me. It's thrue but with my Guardians I can maintain being on the top and I might and will Fall down but I'll get back up and just keep on climbing until I get there and when I get to W.P. the same cycle goes over again. Another goal and tougher choices with a tougher life to lead. I keep saying to myself if this is tough wait till I get to WP [WEST POINT] become an agent etc. I envision what other worst or tough things will happen in the FUTURE, and that I have to be ready and prepare myself for the ultimate challenges in life. My week or for the past 2-3 weeks lately, my mind has been totally ~~weird~~ indescribable because of many things that has happen towards my college life. Adjusting to it everyday… everyweek day is another big 13-15 hour (or more) adventure. It is tiRing. My schedule is to weird and hard to explain but then again

Im the type of person that can adjust, adopt & improve to anything that is coming at me providing that I perform with my excellent perFormance.

Homework foR the soul (based on OPRAH) Today I accept all the good & bad experiences. Tomorrow I am willing to do all my homework and study and clen my bedroom. So that I pump up foR another busy week.

These are the the notes I took from OPRAH show. I actually feel better now. [No, itz from The TYRA BANKS show. JUST KIDDING!!!!]

(1) Accept all your experiences, I am angry, its okay to be angry. I just shake it off and it will take a good night sleep are more but life goes on. I just keep in mind things will be better. I think positively. (2) Its okay that you make bad choices oR things happen in WoRst ways. Say that I accept….
(3) If you don't heal the wound of your past, you will continue to bleed.
(4) IF YOU ACCEPT SOMETHING THEN YOU ARE WILLING TO CREATE SOMETHING FOR YOURSELF !
(I WISH I KNOW THE NAME OF THE LADY WHO WROTE THAT BOOK & CHANGE OTHER PEOPLES LIVES.) OPRAH said, "Knowing who you are is knowing you inner spirit," (Psalm 27,) OPRAH also like the Psalm 37

I had a turning point, (a few this week) but one of them is a call from God. Though she knows it might/ will take me months to get me ready for this mission because oF my circumstances plus it takes a long time together, info. About RAPE. I'm honored to be called out. Once again I continue to be a volunteer which I love to do. I don't know much about public speaking and what to tell the young kids on the issue of RAPE PREVENTION. I've done volunteering stuff beFoRe but this one is different and harder. Im up for this challenge and im willing to take up whatever it takes so that I can spread to words of knowledge to the young generation and beyond. I'm thinking about making pamphlets. I'm thinking about making pamhets. I need sponsoRs. I need info. I need time and help. With God anything is possible.

Here's what my Guardian said, "Play BlackJAck and you got a Few cards left but continue to play and bet your whole life. You can back out so you wont be scRewed up later or play it to ACCOMPLISH… meaning to win and must not FAIL. It is not an easy situation, neither does the tough challenges cadets face at WEST POINT> So I can't screw up. I must have stRagiht A's with excellent balance of activities categories. I must finish what I started at the beginning of my high school. JUST THINK IT IS NO LONGER ABOUT THE DREAMS I CREATED 4 years ago and to finish it but being a CADET AT West POINT changes all the rules with consequences and great glories. It OPENS ALL THE DOORS. I HAVE A LOT OF Reasons which I don't want to go to detail. I CAN MAKE MISTAKES BUT I CAN'T FAIL To me it is a lot of pressure but I'm willing to sacrifice aNYTIHNG NOW AND THE FUTURE TO GET TO W.P.

Sept 21-27, 1998 (12:05 PM SUN.)

Almost time to move on to another brand spankin new diary. I already bought one. So many things in my head I really want to tell you. From ROTC, SDSU to Grossmont College student life to my jobs and the future I control. So many weird changes (that is how I feel like) and yet I have to keep up and accept / and (oR) adopt to it. Part of my success is how well I handle these changes and other stuff as I encounter every single day. I still like to baby-sit and just like among other things - (aint so bad) Really! Very rarely opportunities to play with young kids and get ~~to play with~~ paid. I feel the same way about working at my Pre-school job. I can actually say this job is fun. From this point on I will either slip again oR keep on climbing and stay on top with my academics. Its not a trick question for me nor does doing it w/ actions. I know well enough what will happen if I keep slipping or slip once, game is OVER. Ive been too many oF those during my high school career. I just keep telling myself "Im in control. The actions I must take to achieve my ultimate goals. These very actions will determine my future. The Heralyn now has an extraordinary future in store only if she makes it inside the doors. Of WP opportunities and grad

them." I have so many things, strategies, different feeling and obstacles from day to day. I remember Sgt. Makwske saying to our class last 2 weeks ago…" Some of you ~~might~~ will stay foR… 8 or more years or do minimum service obligation. A Few of you may be generals. So look around…"
{ 7/8/2005 [1:11 AM-USA TIME] Definitely not with …what am I saying . The QUEEN of ENGLAND. She needz sume younger audiences. GRANDMA … going nowhere… Does she have dentures? Y/ N } ***I couldn't exactly garsp the exact wordings. He makes everybody laughs & has that wit of a comedian character in a goofy way. He can actually lighten up the whole class or the whole cadre if he wanted to while he talks. Capt. Katherine Graef. She is a mystery to me. Shes been very helpful to me and I can feel that she will play an impt. Role of achieving those ultimate goals. I wonder how she will react to someone like me … a cadet (an*** Aztec ARMY R.O.T.C. freshman Cadet MS1-2-3-4-5) about my ambitious, laudable goals when I tell her. She may comment on being pRactical but I don't know that really. Anyway… soon it will be NOV. then DEC. soon is enough you will find out. It is interesting to talk about the ARMY as all related topics Allaine/ Elaine & I talked was connected to it. Most of it I already thought of OR even mention it on my diaries. For example, the stereotyping of women in the military. I really don't care what people think of what they think but I have respect on their opinion because it has always given me different points of view. To think of killing a human being… the enemy… spill blood and another concept about sacrifice. Well, there is no doubt that the career I chosen is the most difficult & challenging. The Army Profession will give me the idea of my maximum level of excellence. The total best of me and hopefull beyond my wildest dreams as it has already shown me that. I still have this FEAR and I still have 5-7 more pounds. I know what it feels like to expect something so good and have a disappointment and then get Rid of a sad grind face of disappointment so that the rest of the day will not be ruin and among more things. That was my 1st P.T. experience. I freaked out. I think but I drop out after the cadence and started feeling weird while running. I definety felt pressure that in a sense I wanted to cry which

probably / maybe lead to disappointment. I handle the situation perfectly and so with today. Nothing in this WORLD can stop me. Today was fun. I think im ready to sleep now.

Fri. Oct 23, 1998 1:27 PM

Im on my break from work. Today was fun so far with the field trip event. "HEralyn if you are having too much fun.. I don't have to pay you," Donna said. I laughed and I heard Mrs. Morris laughed too. The Pumpkin Patch fieldtrip was interesting and fun. We walk through a CORN MAZE, RODE on the tractoR, got pumpkins FoR the kids etc. I even got to wear a Montessori Pre-school shirt. What a fun job huh! This week ive been craving different kinds of food. I ate a WHOLE ROTESSERI CHICKEN on Weds. Last night I had 3 ROLLED TACOS, CHICKEN BURRITO, and SPANISH MEXICAN RICE. I ate a huge size of cookies yesterday too. I ate 2 chocolates bars, caramello & milky way. It soRt of has to do w/ the FTX this weekend. Tomorrow morning at 7 begins an adventurous G.I. Jane (As Eliz calls it) combat style tRaining. I get to carry a 40-60 ibs. Rack sack of sleeping bag and all other combat ARMY equipment. It is like anything else when carrying it or how ROTC deals with everything. ***COMPLAININIG* NEVER SOLVES ANYTHING. I think it's better that I stop complaining. It is just how the ARMY is... very demanding, tough and challenging. I love ThursDAY. It is probably my favorite day of the week.** I Imagine myself that WP experiences maybe this tough everyday but even more tougher. It has to be exhausting being a cadet at WP. But like anything else it has its purpose. I'm pretty much at a point in my life, I say? Give me moRe pain. What I meant is.. For example on WEDS. I went to my 2nd P.T. I did good despite of my trying to catch up. It wasn't that bad. I learned that there is no limit to what I can do; the mind, body, & soul. I know that but being in the ARMY. I see it clearer. Like I didn't think of how much we had to do (the limit) because we will end up doing much more fRom more sit-up reps. To push-ups Sgt. M. waited us to do 45 sec. More of it. There is no limit to what the mind & body can do. There is no limit to what I can do. The sky is not the limit, there is no limit. OuR cadres keep reminding us to do our best, and keep pushing ourselves. Its impt. To keep improving. Im still in pain fRom just 1 hR. of P.T. I got to see behind the scenes look on how & what MS IV - Iii's operate. Its vital to the program. I really didn't see that perspective until yesterday. Communication is a key to the success of ARMY ROTC. And all others too. It s very impt. Something we all need work on but all others we still have to work on because impRovements make it better. Its Funny how I recall prepare myself to do great. But when im in it I don't think of the preparation. The expression fRom Nike. **"Just do it works better sometimes." My Diagnostic P.T. went very well I learned a lot. Even little events in life can influence my future for the better. October is just flying by and Nov. is near I'm on my 2nd half of the fall semester in college.** There has been a big event, a tuRning point of fRiendship. Only great friends stay friends forever. I'm bless with many people & Resources helping me achieve my goals and even day today stuff. Im bless with many great things that has happen in my life. Its quite a ride. My life is awesome. I told Capt Graef that. I lied about when she asked how I get to SDSU. I cleared it up yesterday. Its impt. To be honest (always) as an officer and a cadet; an individual with a stRong character must possess it. Im FiRed up about Camp Pendelton. Operation tRaining stuff…. The cadet experience is awesome. Backpacking & camping out in the goonies, the Army way. It will be exhausting but most of all rewarding Leadership experience.

BASED ON- /INSPIRED FROM OPRAH'S TALK SHOW : HERALYN MORALES TOLING's SPIRITUAL HIGH SCHOOL/ COLLEGE DIARIEZ -MY GRATITUDE LIST !!!!

Jan. 19,1996

Im grateful for............
(1) being alive, enjoy this ~~farniete~~ on a nice weather
(2) my Mom... who's always there for me always → even if she'll blame me or critize me.
(3) A few good friend's who gives me rides, make me laugh, appreciate me etc. even though I hate their guts, others are Fake. that's why you can only have a few good friends.
(4) getting this far, live life to the fullest in America & for future to come.
(5) having a strong personality and power to achieve very few special people have.
(6) all my teachers giving me a good education cutting me some slacks who will help me in my life and about self-realization to what I can achieve.
(7)having the intelligence & high moral character to be a successful person from the day I was born.
(8) my talents.. (art, martial arts, sports) and many more yet to discover leadership.
(9) having another day (no school tomorrow coz it's MARTIN LUTHER KING B-DAY to study for Final Exam).
(10) the clubs I'm in. They taught me more than what I got about me and the school.

Jan 20, 1996

(1) MaRtin Luther King Day (~~Ho~~ holiday no school)
(2) 50th Innagural Day for Clinton for another great 4 years.
(3) Reading: Second thoughts on the 1st Amendment. I learned a lot.
(4) The gifts I got from Elizabeth, $100 mi madre (CD player)
(5) achieving 50 push-ups today in my exercise (10x 5)

Jan 21,1996

(1) I'm lucky to remember the challenging time running for School Treasurer. Sure it meant a lot like a dream. Finally, I never thought i would say this: I don't want to win this year coz I want my G.P.A. up hopefully 3.9-4.0 and AP biology looks better in the college transcript. Don't you think ? Because but that time I graduate I will hold 20-25 leadership office best in that high school. I don't want distractions like ASB. Im happy to get this far. I DON'T WANT TO BE

POPULAR JUST SO I COULD HELP THE SCHOOL SOMETHING DIFFERENT OTHER THAN CLUB OFFICE. Heck, ive been helping the school since I fell in love getting involve and the Rewards are great, leadership I have help me decide to study Politics. I think it's weird Heralyn in Politics. But I'm thankful and grateful ; a stepping stone in my life.

Continue I'm grateful for

1/21/97

(2) the outstanding giving out grades "freebes" from a couple of my teachers. Still, I deserved it anyway. I cannot believe I would be so happy in my life to get a "C" in Pre-Cal because I studied many hours over the weekend and last night. Since I could have done better but it was a "C" or D or F in the report card.

(3) Which brings me a point of REALIZATION I FEARED BECAUSE PEOPLE ONLY SEE ME AS SMART and I hated it not only that I had hard time fitting in and I get interaction from being SMART. BUT NOW I'M GRATEFUL FROM WHAT I BECOME AND PROUD TO BE A "GEEK" in other words "intelligent person"

(4) ___?____and I eating lunch in Burger King. { AOUWCCHH!!! Food poisoning [film scene-/ she dropz to the floor] } Realizing a best friend for life and someone to share and talk a conversation about your goals, carrer and future because your goals, carrer and someone to share and talk a conversation about your goals, carrer and future because youre suppose just to live and survive high school. GO FIGURE !!!!

(5) Writing this gratitude list

(6) having a vision for a future, to hope and dream of the american dream that someday hard work will pay off and I hope people of the WORLD can count on me & my leadership.

(7) Wonderful best priceless memory of Chirtmas '96.

(8) Another day, glad I got a ride home.

(9) all my wonderful friends; realiable & unrealiable

(10) trying out in tennis (thank GOD no cut) gving me all those and one more great hopeful year.

2/7/97

(1) My B-Day !
(2) Have money !
(3) Got shoes !
(4)Have Mom !
(5) Great Day !

April 4, 1997 (FRI. NIGHT)

(1) Got a shirt from Ross-saved $10
(2) Got a best friend named Kelly
(3) Got all the food I wanted to eat. Dairy Queen Ice Cream
(4) Got Paid $117 -got back $50 for spending
(5) Got to run 1 mile
(6) worked on mural dimensions
(8) volunteered 2 hours.
(9) Glad Spring Break was fun- don't wait till school !
(10) I finally got rid of my cable T.V.
(11) T G I F !

Sept. 1

(1) I'm so excited ! I can't hide it ! I want to go back to school. I'm glad school tomorrow. I want to continue going on/ moving to the next step higher till I get there. Summer. I had so much freedom I could choke on it.

(2) I'm glad for all the great memories of my Last Lazy Summer. Its not so bad after all.
(3) Life is good !
(4) I get to play & sweat in tennis and all those secret pals, games and chatting with the group.
(5) Life is good !
(6) I get to talk and meet new people and the ones I already know.
(7) I get to look forward to T G I F.
(8) Life is good. Life is good …..!
(9) Im happy of all the things I did this summer especially the scrap book.
(10) I have a ready smile, looking forward to each brand new day, new challenges.

EVERYDAY GRATITUDE LIST AS OF Nov. 30, 1997.

"Life is great no matter what…."

Jan 13, 1998

"It's better to live and die fulfilling one thing you want to happen or desire and hope for than to live and die fulfilling nothing at all." I get it now. I see it. Good qoute.

D__♥ after you fulfill your lifelong laudable goal.

"Fulfilling something that came from the heart is fulfilling a life's purpose." [need to revise]

JAN 23, 1998

" THE GREATEST GIFT OF ALL IS LIFE ITSELF."

A conversation with ____….I sad that I have all the Luck in the world. Im a survivor.

The overall "Gratitude List" 4 letter word L-I-F-E. I have air to breath and healthy lung and heart, people around me, Life precious moments, a list just continues but it all comes to me, my soul, my life. [7/9/2005 -Sounds like JOSS STONE 1st & 2nd album]

P.S . When I graduate I write a letter. Dude! It'z in my SCRAPBOOK!

☺ **PART ONE**: Heralyn MORALES Toling's 1ST DIARY

☺THE SOPHOMORE YEAR:

☺THE CLASS PRESIDENT & POPULARITY ROCKS ! ! !

☺ **PART TWO**: Heralyn Toling's 2ND DIARY

☺ THE UPPERCLASS YEARZ:

☺ [MATURITY LEVEL]

☺ THE PUBERTY OVERFUNRIDEZ TO CRASH & BURN ON MY TEENAGER YEARRSSZZZZ !!!

♥

☺ PART THREE:

Heralyn Toling'z 3RD DIARY

☺ THE NEXT 7 LUCKIEST/ SUCKIYEST/bombitchiyeah YEARS OF MY LIFE & THEN SOME...BLAH...BLAH....+ :

☺ [ITZ CALLED COLLEGE.]

Nov. 2, 1998 Monday (4:50 PM)

I'm inside the bus on my to Grossmont College. I've been thinking a lot of things today. I witness a beautiful sunset on the bus. Working as a teacher.. Leading and having that responsibility is great. One of the things is leadership. The more I thought of it, the more I realized I've been preparing myself to become a leader since as far as I can remember. When I was in kindergarden I wanted to be the class(room) treasurer. I still remember that moment, that gut feeling on how I wanted someone to elect me. Its funny how this one of the things I remember as a kid. Ever since then I've wanted to be in charge in many different ways. Sometimes I had opportunities but didn't bother or raise my hand to take that leadership roles. I had a few leadership roles as a Carolinian student.

1:18 PM (Jan. 4, 1999)

Im listening to "**Sublime Stand By Your Van Live**" and sitting down on my favorite chair at the teacher's lounge upstair where I work at. Heres to the remainder months of 1998. Okay, I had so much fun at Camp Pendelton as a MS I Army ROTC cadet. WOW ! Not even words can explain the total experience. It was so much fun getting down (on my knees) and dirty w/ mud dust etc. I needed a shower. It should have rained during the day. I walked gazillion uphill on Road March. Thanks to the great leadership for MS III & IV's and everybody that made it and survived. It was one of the highlight of the year. I saw a rattle snake when one of the Sgt. Showed it to me as I waited for ice for my sprain ankle. Land Nav. Was totally cool adventure. I learned so much. I even made a decision about ARNG. I think I'm pretty happy with my decision. It's a lot wiser to stick w/ ROTC. I loved when it rained at around 4 AM and I thought it was the spiders crawling on my head. It rained and rained. I will take that experience and I learned from it. I got to do things I never thought I could do. I shot a M-16 rifle and rapell [rappel] from a rapelling [rappelling] tower. I learned so much about myself and gained a lot from the whole experience. I had so much fun during Halloween. I dress up as a HIHERALARYLN. It was fun. It was the 5th Halloween Party in a row with Hilary and out friends. I feel pretty lucky to have cool friends. I have great friends. I feel lucky always. I had a better year. Each day it gets better. I feel blessed with the life I have. I have a gift and full of talents. God has given me so much.

(Jan 3rd Night time before I went to bed)

Why am I so cared of 1999? On New Year's Eve. I thought this is the year that great things will happen. Has it always been like that…. Another year is another great improve year. 1999-things will be better …on my life, love, money; I want a car so bad, keep achieving for WP, lose weight, have fun. I gotta know where my life is? Gotta have a clue where I stand? Do I even stand a chance for WP?
IF so? I need to make that battle plan? A sense of total preparedness on my right hand as the first day I start SPRING SEMESTER. How do I spice up my 1999 year? Need things to do commit for…? Need to have that

SELF-DISCIPLINE ?

I'M NOT WORRIED. I will just face my fears. I will achieve my goals. I will have another great year. I feel great at this point of my life. I'm so lucky. With guidance and … I have the world smiling back at me. Being 18 has been so much fun. Experience has taken me to become a better person and knowing more about myself. I fell [feel] like I'm flying. I feel like I'm on top of the world. I feel like I can achieve anything.

Jan. 6, 1999

" ONLY THE STRONG INDIVIDUALS SURVIVE IN THIS WORLD" This love experience made my life a whole lot better. I really know it feels like to love someone, to care and feel the pain. It has its ups & downs. Dec. 1998 gave me something I will never forget. I will surely remember year 1999 for as long as I live. Never have I feel so alive in my life. I'm fighting back on my weakness by using my strengths and experience of 18 yrs. I can either be upset, depressed and sad about it or enjoy the ride. Life goes on.

"The only thing we can do is play on the one thing we have, and that is our attitude… I am convinced that life is 10 % what happens to me and 90 % how I react to it," by CHARLES SWINDOLL on ATTITUDE. So I have a great attitude about it. I can deal with this situation. I am strong individual. It is my obligation in life to make my life great. Dammm! I fell so alive! I fell so great! I fell happy! I'm going to have a blast this year and no one is stopping me. Your right, Lord planning is an element key to success and happiness! ("The glories of the world") I learned that sacrifice is crucial but sweet as I reflect on my life when I was at LINDO LAKE yesterday. "NOTHING IN THIS WORLD is/ or FREE & EASY. I HAVE TO CHASE IT, SACRIFICE, BE PATIENT, AND DO WHATEVER IT TAKES TO ACHIEVE MY GOALS & ENJOY THE JOURNEY THAT IT TAKE TO GET THERE. I EMBRACE THE WORLD & EMBRACE MY GOALS, LIFE ITSELF. EVERYTHING WILL WORK OUT JUST GREAT BECAUSE I HAVE SO MUCH HOPE AND FAITH IN MYSELF, THE WORLD, IN GOD.

Jan 10, 1999

I feel so alive. I feel so great. I feel so happy yet I feel so uncontested. I fell [feel] like the world is caving on me but really its smiling back. I don't understand why this feeling has to happen now. Maybe it happens For a great reason. I have a few great friends. They have been around a long time. These friendship I value because we survive. IT FEELS SO GREAT TO KNOW WHO I AM. TO ACTUALLY HAVE THE FEELING OF MY STRONG INDIVIDUALITY. TO KNOW MY STRONG CHARACTER and it is even stronger. I have so much in me. I have so much I can accomplish. Beginning of January has been tough emotionally. Being in LOVE with this guy realizing that makes me crazy. I'll survive. It's tough falling in love with someone who is your friend. He's totally cool. Things will work out. If this relationship will happen, it will happen sooner or later. All the kids love me at my work place. Montessori Pre-School- TO ME IT IS A RAD PLACE TO WORK. I love WORKING THERE. The teachers like me. Mrs. Donna Bridgemann- the owner/ director thinks I'm such an awesome teacher's aide. I work with the 2yrs. -3yrs old and Mrs. Kymm teaches the class. The other teachers there are Mrs. Leah, Mrs. Valerie Morris, Mrs. Erika Molina, & Mrs. Bobbi Jackson & Mrs. Tammy Acierno. I made cheesecake and bought Fruits for teacher's snack last Friday. The teachers love the cheesecake. I even got a note from Donna how wonderful a cook I am. In fact, It was so easy to make with my DAD helping me out. He got it from Jello-cheese cake mix at Lucky's. HA! HA! It is so yummy. Last week was first week of volunteering since I haven't volunteered for a while. I love volunteering at the REC CLUB. Oh! Lord I thank you so much for the many blessings you given me. I hope Junior America opportunities works out well. Music also makes my life go around especially when I'm down. I love NO DOUBT, Sublime etc. it's been a long time since I got to do something with my Mom until yesterday. We went to Parkway Mall. We played video games and I treat her out for lunch at Oscar's. We wanted to see a movie- Step Mom but maybe next time. Today, I got to spend time with Kelly at Fashion Valley Mall. I bought me some GODIVA chocolates for me, my parents and friends and SEES candy chocolates. Time to go night *night*. Well, tomorrow is another brand new day. My life goes on.

(2:05 PM) Jan 13, 1999

What was so great about 1998? Everything !!! How I saw the world in a different point of view. My life seem so much better. It justs gets better. I'm on my break at work. Highlights of 1998. There were so many …. Graduation, Limo ride, tough times, ROTC, college, land a new job, friendship, family etc. Despite of how 1998 Dec. ended it was still great. Life goes on. I had a great New Years Eve because I got to spend time with my friends. Hilary invited us for a party at her house. Tim and the others were there. My Christmas holiday was great. I even tasted champagne for the 1st time on New Year Day Dinner. Everything is gonna be alright. Things will work out just fine. Life is so great !

Jan 17, 1999 (9:36 PM)

There is so much I hope for 1999. I truly do deserve what I hope for. Like: (1) an opportunity to compare for Miss Junior America - in July, go to Disneyland and just to get away for 3-4 days.

(2) I hope / wish that I make $1,000 + even 750-800-900 is good.

(3) Playing my cards Right, I will have all A grade. It's muy important to go to WP.

(4) If I just loose 10-15 more lbs. I'll be just satisfied w/ time for exercise.

(5) Actually taking Driver training and a car loan.

(6) getting money from FAFSA to pay for my tuition (college).

(7) West Point ! West Point ![US ARMY] ROTC, WEST POINT! MAKING SURE I GET THERE SO THAT I WILL AN ARMY INTELLIGENCE OFFICER. * reserves

(8) MOST OF ALL- I want all of 1-7 to HAPPEN !!! SO BAD I deserve it!

Today I went to Seaport Village, Horton Plaza, and eat Hard Rock Café with my Friend Kelly. My vacation is okay. I get to relax and get things done slowly but surely. I have been working hard at Montessori Pre-school. Its been fun exhausting and stressful month. Things have been weird lately but is shinning -meaning its just warming up to get better. This will be a volunteering again at the REC club. Tim is thinking about working at my Pre-school. Well, will see what happen. I hope that if he gets the job, he will actually like working there (w/ the kids and teachers). Its different for different people in so many ways. Tomorrow I will go to Viejas Outlet Center with him (Tim). He is working so I figured I will use the $15 Gift Certificate he gave me. I'll probably go to Viejas Casino and walk around for window shopping and eat there. Just hang out and relax. It sounds like fun to me. I will also have time write letters for my pen pals.

I hope that I will make decent money for the Self-Defense coming up. I want to make it big. I wish that I will be a Martial Arts instructor finally comes true. I hope this will turn out great. I have many great ideas. I don't want to act or talk to the people at the Lakeside Community Center that I have to suck up so that I will have this opportunity. I just want to be me and its time to say good bye of that fear of low self-esteem or self- ******s. I will just be me. Confident, helpful, friendly, nice, great person and I have so much to offer.

(10:24 PM Saturday) Feb 13, 1999

It didn't seem so long ago that New Years Eve Party came along or how I had a great feeling of the first new morning of 1999. 1998 was so cool. I had s much hope and gain great experiences that will contribute to my future. What a great life I have! And yet… so many more awaits for me in the future. I learned that working not only gives me more wrinkles but more problems which makes things better is accepting it, go with the flow and do my very best with the challenges or o anything, that waits. I have been so busy but I must find time to do everything. I will keep working to have a better self-discipline with time management (the daily planner project). There are so many things I want to say/ write but time is ticking. IM just glad I finally had a chance to write in my journal. What a relief! (a stress relief) writing is just one way to handle stress. I know that I also need my space and time to reflect. I feel so much better now. The challenges I face right now are tougher and the are lot higher. I think the challenges I face; I can tackle. I remember my Logic Professor saying, "When your Boss ask you to solve an equation (meaning -job stuff to do) you can solve it. Your boss hired you because you met the qualifications." I think God gave me these challenges because he feels confident enough that I can handle it.

Yes! Indeed! I feel like I have all the confidence in the world because of how he has given me strength and so much more. I'm learning everyday and gaining and gaining invaluable life experiences. IM setting myself up for SUCCESS. Im making things happen. Im in control of my destiny. Sure not all my wishes will be granted this year but the harsh reality is…. They must be earned. Well, sometimes God gives me break and things I don't expect. Like being Miss Teen E. Lakeside or an opportunity to work in Self-Defense Program. *There is so much I hope for my future. I want to be somebody. I know I am somebody. I am somebody. I am Heralyn M. Toling. You know what I mean. I hope for great things in this world. I want to contribute something extraordinary. "Today is just another ordinary day in my extraordinary life." The teachers gave me a B-Day present. There are so many things that awaits for me.*

Presidents Day Holiday Feb. 15, 1999

Well, I did my best. My weaknesses many have put disadvantages on my strict schedule I can change that. This week I will not use any schedule without delay. This means: running, waking up and sleeping must be time. The T.V. is at my Mom's room to avoid distraction. I'm determine and motivated to achieve my goals. Sacrifices is just one aspect of achieving them (goals) but in general is the whole person concept. It is not just academics I have to be great at but my jobs, ROTC, athletics, volunteering and the rest I left out. Even my social life need not only to be reduce but how I control it and control myself. Being myself and standing up for myself is impt. Especially being surrounded by so many different people. I don't like the idea of having and being in debt through credit cards. I need to pay my SPRING '99 FEES, BOOKS ETC. <u>I need to find a way to get money to pay for my future college stuff.</u> SO, SO, SO, SO BAD!!!!! I NEED MONEY AS SOON AS POSSIBLE. I hope the Lord is listening. Well at least on the bright side… my life is good and each day gets better. I'm glad those high school days are over with. I hope these 3- 4yrs. Coming is nothing compare to what I went thru my high school days. I know it is different. I have some catching up to do with my academics (my first priority) losing weight, time etc. Till next Time.

March 13, 1999 (Sat 10:43 PM)

Yesterday afternoon w/ Eliz. at the mall and today w/ Kelly & Eliz. We went to the mall to see ("PAYBACK") movie. We ate at Trophy's first. It has been a big break for me to loosen up. Im extremely grateful for my friend and hanging them around to do fun stuff. I had a tough week. There is so much I want to do. I need to get a lot of things done. How well I do this semester will determine my future plans. I already had enough shit I had to put up with for the last 18 yrs and one month. Life has been shitty for me. I had my shares of fun and glory but the point is Im ALWAYS SCWRED. IN OTHER TERMS I WILL ALWAYS END UP SCREWING UP EVEN IF I STILL DO THINGS RIGHT, THERE ARE/IS ALWAYS SOMETHING GOING WRONG. WEST POINT IS STILL MY ULTIMATE GOAL! I JUST CRIED OVER THIS SHIT! Im trying not to cuss. Sorry historians. It been a difficult week for me. Im a very expressive person, therefore cussing is necessary. I cried over problems. It has been like that ever since I can remember. Making it to West Point means nothing will go wrong in my life. I think I mean that if I getaway… better things happen w/ higher chances. I hate being miserable. CONFIDENCE is my strength yet my weakness. WHY??? I learned that confidence is not something I can earn or something to gain by achieving it. I think my confidence is already in me. It is a strength, a gift and yet it stabs me in the back. In order to make my confidence effective, I must use my confidence. I need it and will need it a lot more in the future. I only know the confidence I have must grow and catch up to the level of challenges I have today. OHH gosh! Why does everything has to be so complicated. I can do it! I need to stop crying over matters. Maybe, its normal for me. No, I need to stop it because it makes everything about me WEAK. It is so hard writing on my journals nowadays. I remember the fresh new feelings on the 1st day of 1999, Valentines Day with my friends, my busy schedule, this crazy diet. Good Bye! I have a mission to accomplish. Situation… everything is falling apart. What I have… JUST ME AND GADGETS.

April 3rd, 1999

What a Spring Break it has been so far. I have to admit this Spring Break 1999 has been the best so far. The Spring FTX at Camp Pendelton was incredible. This weekend is great. Im at the balcony 6th floor of SDMH & M. WOW!!! Im using my time wisely by enjoying myself. I'll write later.

4/26/99 O full moon

A warrior prepares for battle, polishing her shield and sharpening her sword. A long journey lies ahead for her. A journey that will determine her life's future. Okay… I don't know the rest of the story… not yet! To me, the sword is everything except one thing. The sword is my character, my past experiences, knowledge etc. That one thing is my shield. It will determine success or failure; this life's journey. To me the shield is the consequences and possibilities of the future. Yeah! Yeah! I don't make sense. WHAT IF … I don't get accepted to WP (I lost focus ….
(Gee! That sounds like a typical day to me).

I thought tat if I write what I think about right now, it will help me in that journey.

I'll get back to the C C P T { Challenges, Consequences, Possibilities, Triumph } whenever it will be.

June 6, '99 (10: 33 PM)

12 Days of Fun is up. Its been 12 days since Spring semester ended. 12 days short vacation is enough for me. I spoiled myself. I stayed up late and woke up late. I had a blast with my friends K & E. The Boardwalk, Hiking, mall, movies… FUN…FUN ! I saw STARWARS Episode! 2x. Not so long ago I was practicing tactical training at Camp P. for the Spring FTX. I never know until weeks ago, felt not coming back to R.O.T.C. I miss those days. I can never accept or want have an army career in this lifetime or knowing its too late. Im glad to get B 3.00 GPA this semester and A- in ROTC. Not bad considering I was on the verge of academic disqualification. Nothing said. June 7- July 16 -6 weeks of summer school that will teach me MOTIVATION, SELF-Discipline & Balance. MSB = FOCUS

6/14/99 (Monday)

What I accomplish today (a small accomplish towards achieving a bigger goal)
(1) I spend 5 hrs. of hw & studying (CD 125 SPAN III)
(2)… Homework turned in for today
(3) Myself-discipline is improving. I spend less of my lunch break and more on a 2 hr HW/ Reading chapters
(4) I did the Target training (T.T.) for stomach

- -

- -

What needs to be done or improve.
(1) Need to lessen/ minimize break on T.V.
(2) need to have a cutting-edge self-discipline.
(3) need to cry out for motivation (You can do more, the more motivate the better)
(4) Keep that drive of hunger to succeed.
(5) better practice Physical Fitness based on bookmark written despite of summer school.
(6) maintain good health, good food.

Gratitude list
(1) I made most of my SPAN II classmates laughed about one comment that the people in el campo are locos.
(2) I'm glad I participate in class.
(3) Im happy to have a continuing desire/ ambition to succed.
(4) I'm happy to talk w/ my MOM.
(5) I'm happy to make a difference in a kid's life.
(6) I'm glad I played A. Morrisette & watched NO Doubt video.
(7) Im glad to have many unique talents and skills.
(8) I'm glad to have the ability to adopt and achieve in any situation and a mission I want to achieve (so far).
(9) I'm glad to get back on the learning ladder of my educational success ALL THE WAY!
(10) to have a beautiful day today(summer!)

Nov. 8, 1999

If theres anybody that needs prayer out there, its me. I just finished reading the previous pages. Ive been praying a lot, talking to GOD, To Santo Nino and my guardian angels who I call advisors. I always believe in miracle. I seen pretty cool stuff in my life that are miracles. Even writing in my journal is a miracle. I regret not writing in my journal for almost half- a year. Still, I have some catching up to do. I HAVE CONCLUDED THAT FROM MY EXPERIENCE LAST NIGHT= ALL I REALLY TRULY WANTED WAS TO FAIL, AND FAIL all over again until I'm ON THE BRINK OF TOTAL FAILURE WITH NO SHOT at my DREAM Because I keep Failing on the major important that will determine my future success OR TURN MY LIFE AROUND TO CLIMB THE TALLEST NEVER ENDING BATTLE… TO THE TOP. I realized from last night that all I really wanted when I was in high school was to become someone Im not because I hated the way others or how I saw myself as-a smart student. I got somewhat of that in high school but I really concentrated on Leadership in high school. Now that my main focus is academics in college- - I got my altermatom. I got what I always wanted in high school- an F grade in class. I didn't even a F in Calculus my senior year HS> They bump me into a D and other classes I got Ds instead of F's. The bottom line/ my point is telling myself "THE LAST PIECE OF THE PUZZLE IS COMPLETE. I AM READY NOW. I AM READY TO TAKE ON THE ULTIMATE CHALLENGE." (FIND MADONNA) I would never thought in my righteous mind that this day would come. In fact, I never knew what the puzzle pieces was about- its purpose or the whole puzzle until now. The puzzle itself until now. The puzzle piece of destiny, a puzzle of youth,… happiness, failures, self-esteem, self-confidence, puzzle I already have and thought I lost it etc. Its seems that all my life has been about TRIAL AND error UNTIL THIS DAY. Now I take with me every puzzle piece in tack. The warrior wasn't left for battle yet, she had to wait what's
(Gatorade) missing. NOW SHE HAS EVERYTHING. SHE IS READY TO SUCCEED IN THE ULTIMATE CHALLENGE. FOR THE FIRST TIME IN MY LIFE I'M SMILING AT MY FAILURE INSTEAD OF KNOWING ABOUT IT. I GUESS, its all part of growing up. THAT'S THE IRONIC ABOUT IT. YOU WANT SOMETHING as freshman High school Student and I [you] realized all you [I] wanted fROm that want is to smile and laugh about being 30-40 pounds overweight, academic failures, leadership mistakes, and crappy side of character building, built-up. The magnificent four (4) as my symbolism

ironic. All my life, it seem that I have been getting what I always wanted to do and have. That's why I said ive see too many miracles in my life. WHY should west point Be any different than to wanting FAILURES- to experience failures so bad. TO ME, TO BE TRULY TRULY SUCCESSFUL ON WHAT YOU WANT (WHETHER A CARRER JOB OR QUEST TO BE) THE # 1, LA CRÈME DE LA CRÈME

I BELIEVE YOU HAVE TO EXPERIENCE FAILURE/S FIRST HAND. THAT A GIFTED, TALENTED PERSON CAN

ACCOMPLISH. IT'S A HUMBLING EXPERIENCE TO EXPERIENCE FAILURES AND RISE ABOVE THE REST TO DO NOTHING BUT SUCCEED. BECAUSE NOW, HAVING MANY TALENTS OR BEING GIFTED IS USELESS (UNLESS NECESSARY) EXCEPT THE PERSONAL DRIVE IN YOU TO PERSEVERVE NO MATTER WHAT HAPPENS.

****** Learn How to spell Persevere … dats what SUCCESSSSSzzzzz w/ a Z/S like MY AMERICAN DREAMz is all about.

THE ONLY GIFT I MOST VALUE IS MY ABILITY TO SUCCEED WITHOUT A DOUBT, WHEN I PUT MY HEART AND SOUL INTO IT, THAT THE ONLY WAY IS CLIMB THE TOP WITHOUT EVER LOOKING BACK.

11/19/ 99 10:52 PM

I've been afraid many times but nothing prepared me to face me fears now- right now. I saw TEEN FILES : THE TRUTH ABOUT VIOLENCE ON CHANNEL 13 UPN CHANGED ME. IT CHANGED ME IN A WAY THAT I HAVE TO TAKE ACTIONS OF THE EMOTIONS THAT I FELT DURING AND AFTER THE 2-HOUR SHOW. THE SHOW TAUGHT ME OF LETTING IT GO- THE PAIN, TO FACE MY FEAR AND TO HAVE TO TAKE ACTIONS. My diary is important in this process. Don't let the title fool you that I had led a violent life. I put more focus on the impact I learned from it and from the different lives of those teenagers who I can relate about my troubled days- the bitter sweet experience of Highschool and early on.

"I'M TIRED BUT I WILL KEEP GOING. I WILL MAKE IT - SURVIVE AND COMPLETE THE MISSION."

I got angry- angry at myself… I learn hope from the letter about ______
I learn to - let go

I learned to have compassion ~~compassion~~

+I learned how to face my fears
Face my fears

I learned to accept and move on.
I learned to understand -to see things…..

____

____

____

—

I want a change in my life.
I want SELF-DISCIPLINE and SELF-CONTROL. But for now rest and tomorrow I will write a promise a-motivation. → chicks

→ CA

- - - - - - - - - - - - - - -> K C

[it goes on & on ..itz not even funny … …..]

Dat girlly girl - on my PSY class 120.. I still haven't pass it. Like I took it ___3 or 4 x already.
Like CSULA is totally the place to pass dat class.

11/21/ 99 1:20 AM
TITLED …HERALYN FILES.

THE TRUTH ABOUT STEALING AS IF THE EVENT TODAY WAS IRONIC "You have no locks for your backpack .." my Mom said so many times as I recalled.
NO ! I didn't listen. "It will never happen to me," I thought so many times. I can't believe it happen to me twice. Once when I was in 6th grade and today… My most priced possession. The only materialistic thing I valued the most second to my JANSPORT EXTREMIST backpack was stolen my glasses [RAYBAN.. Name ur favorite brand ________]. I envision it as it happened. I anticipated it; I saw it in my vision. I felt it, something suspicious. I felt weird, a warning. It didn't matter because I still have my future. I know that no one can steal that (my dreams). I learned many things. Most

importantly. I learn that I can replace it with even a newed, better and exact pair of sunglasses. (I even got a 30 % discount.)

What → I learned that materialistic things {does} doesn't rock my world. I realized that no one can ever take away my dreams. I have nothing to fear about my dreams, the fear of not succeeding. I wasted a semester, things are not going as plan, I thought I was ready to take the biggest responsibility of 18 units and manage everything- to succeed but I thought wrong. Once again, I misjudge my abilities. Think Pink ! There you go - I just told you my biggest fear. My biggest fear of failure came true- it didn't go as plan. Now I have to fix things up. I have no more chances. Im angry at myself for allowing this to happen. But no matter how pist or angry or sad or unhappy about the outcome it will never change the reality of (Right now)- today. The reality is the FEAR BECAME A REALITY BECAUSE I LET IT HAPPEN. I ACCEPT OF THIS OUTCOME AND NOW I MUST SUFFER THE CONSEQUENCES. THAT I MAY NOT HAVE A CHANCE OF A CADETSHIP AT WESTPOINT, DESPITE OF ACHIEVING MY PLANS TO SUCCEED in the MAGNIFICENT 4-FOUR. It won't matter now because I already have 13 units of W'S. Very SAD ☹ BUT I WAS AWAKEN TO REALIZE I KEPT A PROMISE TO STO. NINO. IT WAS MY FIRST PROMISE, HE WAS THE WITNESS -TRULY WAS THE PROMISE FOR ME. I PROMISED THAT NO MATTER WHAT HAPPENS, I WILL ALWAYS HAVE IT IN ME TO BELIEVE THAT MY (to DREAMS WILL DREAMS WILL BECOME A REALITY ESPECIALLY WHEN MOMENTS LIKE THIS POPS UP. (I WAS EVEN WARN HOW ROUGH THE GREAT RIVERS ARE (AND HOW DEEP) WHEN EVERY CHALLENGE I LEARN) TO STICK BY MY FAITH- EVEN GROW STRONGER IN ME TO KEEP THE FAITH- THE BELIEF- THE CONFIDENCE TO SUCCEED. I PROMISE TO STICK BY MY ULTIMATE GOAL- THAT I WILL SUCCEED IN IT WITH OUT ANY DOUBTS. JUST LAST NIGHT, I WAS REMINDED OF THAT PROMISE FROM HIM BECAUSE I STARTED WORRYING AND BEGAN TO ~~LOSE~~ HAVE HOPE. I THOUGHT MY DREAMS ARE GONE- I SEE IT RIGHT BEFORE MY EYES- WHY BHODER TO CONTINUE THE MISSION. HE ENLIGHTEN ME. I UNDERSTAND HIS MESSAGE NOW.

➘ THANK GOD

AS IF HE SAID TO ME IN MY VERY EYES, "MY CHILD, YOU HAVE NOT LOST DREAMS IT IS STILL THERE. HOLD ON TO THE ROPE "GRIP HAND" AND NEVER LET GO. It is not so far. You are almost there. Persevere through this and your dreams will be a reality. You are not alone in this mission, we are here to help you with guidance, support and the strength to succeed undoubtedly. It is a promise to you and me like the heaven and earth becomes a one universe. A PROMISE THAT WE WONT LET YOU FAIL BECAUSE YOU WONT LET YOURSELF FAIL. YOU ARE READY TO CONQUER SELF-DISCIPLINE AND SELF-CONTROL SINGLE HANDEDLY GOOD LUCK- JUST CALL WHEN NEED SOMEONE TO TALK TO."

NOV. 27, 1999 10:48 PM

AT AROUND 6 PM, I saw my life flashing before me. The imagine became a reality at that moment. The IF POSSIBILITIE S(Challenges, Consequences, Possibilities [CCP]) drilling in my head. As if I have been in a thousand accident but only encountered one. It came to me as a shock after accident. I pondered over it again and again and again when I was at Wendy's. Well, this one is one is different because I saw it in so many different situations. I was in a somewhat lucky one. The deadly situations, the practical ones etc. I talk the Lord last night. Only when do I hear his words when Im at inner peace with myself and around me. [→ yeah] "*I deeply regret of being pushy to him about a miracle written on paper by him. I asked too much of him. I got the miracle tonight in a different way. I understand that it was more than just a car accident w/ K. but even more. What is it Lord ?"* You have sent the best angels (indeed all angels seems to me are your best servants) by my side. In so many ways I have seen your miracles big or small-each is very important. But what am I to these miracles. Was it not a day or hours ago I wanted to see you. To sit next to you in the kingdom of heaven -a metaphor of you know= so much has happen in the last few months, days. Lord, to see my life's destiny lost. What am I in the American dreams lost. What am I in the eyes of you? In the eyes of myself, for that matter. Ive faced terrible storms, number of floods(okay a few), earthquakes, witnessed animals suffering till death and the sudden stops of cars in front or behind me when walking, not to mention the cause of my right feet… why is this day so important to me Lord? YOU WANT ME HERE LORD. I AM YOUR SERVANT in so many ways. THERES A REASON WHY IN HERE. AM I TO MAKE IT WHAT I WANT OF IT OR ARE ALL OF IT PLAN WITH THE KNOWING YOU KNOW IT ALREADY. I know that I make no sense at all But I know that I control my destiny and with you- I place my trust, my dreams, ambitions, fears and pains (to name a fear) TOGETHER-with you beside me. Undoubtedly I succeed with true confidence.

What is this to me? A new beginning yet a true wisdom of hope... Of lost of patience, of bursting angers, facing and losing the battle filed of fears- my unhappiness. I have a message to myself- TO SUCCEED WITH CONFIDENCE TO ACHIEVE MY DREAMS I MUST PERSEVERE TO GREAT DIFFICULTIES. This is where my true inner strength lies. And where I find you Lord.

THE GOLDEN RULE

You must always remember that WP is the highest standard of the ultimate leadership institution where young American Leaders are tame and molded to become guardians of this nation and the world. Only the selected few will earn it- their spot of the long gray line. But out of those selected few, only a handful will walk and live the path to be heroes and great leaders of our time for they have embodies the true reason of why WP will always be an integral part of this nation. For those young Americans who have step up to that challenge of earning a cadetship and living the WP experience has the opportunity of a lifetime and the shoulder of responsibility to uphold the freedom for all American. You must remember you wake up everyday ready to embrace the ultimate challenge- a chance to improve your chances A STEP CLOSER TOWARDS LIVING THE WP EXPERIENCE.

- - - > Just arrive ______?___ _____ ___

- -

ANGEL , GABRIEL, ARIEL, URSULA >>>> Victoria Secret & Sport Illustrated Models looks better as G. Angels…. Just a joke!

WEIRD THINGS has been happening but it's really me. The metamorpohis stage is complete. (DON'T 4GET TO GET MY ALBUM/BOOKZINE @ AMAZON. COM/barnes&nobles.com …SUCH AS… " SEX & MUSIC LIT. 101 & DAMUARTEMIL 107")

I hope so, its 10:57 PM Tue night, I cannot explain the supernatural things going around for the past few weeks. Im filled with emotions I can't express. I opened the white door and still think I opened and still think I opened it too late. About a week before /\ I found out who I was step dad passed away. I'm not gonna say the date because I really don't remember. Im so tired I feel like I woke up from a comma. I'm questioning everything WHY ? WHY? AND WHY? And WHY ME ? No matter what this is my role in life and its very important. Am I thinking with sexual thoughts right now? No! = I mean that with honesty. I don't really know whats going to happen yet. I don't have all the answers now. I'm figuring things out. It used to be so easy to write in my journal but now I don't even know what I'm writing for. I do miss a lot of people, from my past, my disecting past, figuring things out. I have going into details now because it is all in my head. I hope for the best. Who knows maybe I'll have a truck and go to homecoming 2000 El Cap. I see why I'm still in Lakeside, why [it]influences me and others, I've become a mature person, I hope. I'll *try* try to be good. GOD has bigger plans for me. (GOD) The Lord always gets his way. I love you DAD. I wished I said that more often and found myself earlier maybe I might be more prepared for the now and the FUTURE. No matter how many times I tell myself that- I can never talk to him about impt. Things matters to me. But I still have the people I know- my friends and caring neighbors, the community. I went to El Cap today, things changed- time passes by, and people- (teachers) changed in

many ways. The campus looks prettier with all the different and new landscapes. I actually know what carpediem means YOGI BERA "You're future ain't what it used to be." I'm still looking for that special someone. I shed tears for so many days- it seems endless. I know my heart is empty but it is not really true. Maybe it is but I know my past lives on in me- in my heart. The people I knew from my past will always live on in me- in my heart. The people I knew from my past will always lives on- whether they were close friends or classmates. As always symbolism is strong- it brought me the inner peace of myself- I don't know if that explains a lot Well, I can look at a flag at
L. M. S. , El Cap, SDSU, and walk ~~in those campus~~ anywhere without feeling depressed maybe sometimes I feel depressed because I know why or anything. I just hope I get that white F-150 Ford truck 2000. *I still reach for the stars.* Nothing changed, my past experience will never changed but I can learned from so many of them. HUH! Yeah ! IM trying to think it without thinking. Okay? ! I do miss the girls in my dreams, who knows I'll run into them. But first thing is first- so okay I have many first things like a car, a solid education, a good job, where to go, what to do, I live freely. I hope even though I know something is missing. That 1998 yearbook changed me, healed my wounds of the past. I was trying to put on many roles in high school, confused as I was that I was really empty inside- but didn't know it till now I was really running away from my destiny. Although sometimes I eel like a prison in this game, I still feel lucky to be myself and know that I am a somebody- like everybody else and I am a messenger of God, -→ think of Britney [WHY] Yes, I am a human being so what, doesn't mean you don't have to be lucky or … I hope that "you can be yourself" I know what that Means to me but to you- you have to find that out for yourself. There is so much I can say or write that it is not the perfect time to write it down.

3/29/00 8:17 am

I'm ~~concern~~ concered about a lot of things. I miss my classmates, no one specific I just saw a F-150 pretty soon that truck will be a classic. I feel better, Im still learning to let go. The sun is coming out. That yearbook (1998) has to be so powerful, when I look back during those high school years, huhhh! (taking a deep breath) it wasn't about trying to be popular or trying to be popular or trying to be the best in something - whether leadership, community service or academics, or wearing the right clothes or breaking the rulles or cheating or stealing or being disrespectful, or who's a comedian or backbiting or rudeness- to me it was about friends, family, the community, the many people who cared, who give, who got along, who learned the values of what respect really means or honesty, as always it will always be a learning experience. That s how, I hope everybody sees it that way - maturity. I miss the many ____ in my dreams. They got me through high school. HA! HA! HA!

Dec. 23, 2000   4:40 P.M.

The truth is a beautiful thing. I can see what I keep listening to my music before and my before and never understood it. As of now, the metamorposis is complete (5:00 AM) but I think it is a process- life is a process- a healing process. Its going to be a beautiful life. Never have I haer the sound of music so beautiful in my ears. I broke down and cry- tears of happiness and freedom. The world cares, everybody does. Everything is going to be fine. My life is a comedy, think that high school moments- a few embarrassing moments but when I look back every moment/ time in my life was a comedy.

♥LIFE IS A COMEDY SO DRINK IT UP.

I FEEL LIKE SHIT TODAY BUT THE LORD CARES. I'M JUST A CHICKEN SHIT. LOOKING FOR THE ___ WHO MAKES THE MOVE. I MISSED THAT ___. I ALWAYS MAKE A MOVE EVERYTIME. SO GOD, WHOS THE NEXT __?_.

PERSON GONNA GIVE ME THEIR NUMBER:YOUR NAME ON THIS BLANK________________________________.

April 3rd:

Life is simple. The bottom line up front. BLUF. I'm hungry for desires.
→ N.Y. → money = job + C.A. etc. [I LOVE MY PRIDE] I have faith in God. I'm the impt. Person on earth. The supply and demand is on the rise. Gotta get what I want. I'm going to N.Y. = get a job but first I gotta quit college. The desires are high. I'm gonna make it. I'm all that. Find the ideal job- ideal __ -lots- ___,
This world is mine, I can make or break any career or organizations. I can get the right/wrong__ or ___. My choice. Its all mine. I'm ready for the big leagues baby. When I take bus, just talk- somebody is listening-watching. Oh Yes! what a [F U C K I N G] great life.

IT SUCKS TO BE ME.

"LIFE IS FULL OF BULLSHIT"

FUCK YEAH ! ! !

"OH WELL !!!"

5/18/00 7:40

Oh what a vacation. Summer job at M. Pre-school. Life is a vacation. I swear anytime I buy something I feel like Im in a bad movie. For example, buying a CD reminds me of going to Porn store. People buy stuff… I think of being self-contious [conscious] about myself. It is all in my head. I'm back a ~~to my~~ new ~~old~~ self. I forget how heavy my head was.

5/19/00

I'm the one that is naïve. How the fuck did I end here- TITA/ AUNTIE Lorna's house. It doesn't make sense. OH WELL! I'm angry … I never feel so controlled emotional. I hate it because I never feel like this before. When I think of a girl or boy out there craving for food: has to look at magazines and they have to think about wanting that body -that body they idolize. But the world is still spinning. I'm not doing it for me… I'm doing it for a special someone out there who are ~~CRYING~~ LAUGHING INSIDE.

I WONDER WHAT THE REAL ____?__ H.T. & LOOKALIKEZ is like? in a couple of years… I wONDEr WHAT MY KIDS THINK… & ONE D>J!

May 31, 00

Did I miss S.F.? very much WOW! What a trip that was. It certainly was the most memorable of all time so far. SPRING BREAK 2000!!! Yeah!

I Love my job, especially when I analyze, really ANALYZE
I ANALYZE BULLSHIT
The popular studs and students. I can't believe I have to rap my way. Oh Goosh! God must be cracking up. Why Rap? Rap and techo music mixed together is a product. It sounds better. Why do I feel like I'm ~~wat~~ looking at West Point Catalogs again- the same shit over again. Only this time I'm one of them, yet to be discovered. I have the advantage, I'm unknown and I have plenty of time. She is the last PERSON I WANT TO SEE. I used to do this when I was a kid JUST FOR KICKS. *(Get over it. As if tearing the "better part" of this journal gonna keep things in perspective.)*

Lover Loses Viagra Early = +L-O-V-E

What PISSES ME OFF WHEN PEOPLE TELL ME WHAT TO DO: BUT that's the price of being ahead- to get ahead, to find out how this world works- the mumbo jumbo shit.

6/2/00

How could one person change my life in a blink of an eye. Not even my Mom or step dad close enough to change my state of life. You changed every thing that once was impossible now to be possible. I'm beginning to realize the impact she has on my life. This is only the beginning. My whole world perspective change because of her. As if, this whole new world (in what I do) is all about her and for her. (The Virgin Mary IT'S ALL BECAUSE I'M MADLY in LOVE WITH HER) I cant fight the feeling. It is too strong to resist. I could write a book… millions of poems thousands of letters, billions of lyrics to express how I feel. The truth is overrated. How is this possible? I felt like someone just wack me with a bat- REALLY HITS HARD. SO WHAT! I'M IN LOVE WITH SOMEONE I NEVER MET. [As long as itz not a he/she …U know? _______ HA! HA! HA! Ok! I don't care. Itz a joke.]

6/4/00

When reality hits hard on me. I'm back to my old self again. I question everything. Is this real? Can I back up what ive been doing. Yes for examples: Yes you can w/o these. I'm such a fuckin fool. Now its back to…

THINGS THAT WERE
Things that are not
Things to be real
This is not funny.

6/12/00

Theres always the fucking diary to help me ease my fucking pain. You know I only cuss when I'm pissed. Every song is like a fucking memory of ?___. I can't get over ?___ especially a nights. There two sides of me. The I'm so in love with you all over and Im fucking FED UP with this shit.

I hope things work out well. I'll give HOLLYWOOD something to piss on. Its gonna be me. Im gonna be pissier than Madonna, Funckier than Mariah, I'll be a talkative b**** people will be gossiping about. After all, my purpose in this fuckin' stupid planet is to be the pain in the ass. I'll take no prisoners. I know if I turn off the music. I'll think but might as well be stuck in this fxuckin Ride. Why do I have to be somebody else when I can have my name ___?___ all over every magazine. [YOU WISH "H"]

WELCOME TO The new me. I appear bichtyier than you think. LET me see what pisses off T O L I N G, When someone else is in control-especially the control of stupid love. ___?___ better be worth it. NOW I know how men feel when they fall in love. THIS love pill is getting stronger everyday. Its not fair that I have to fucking suffer. LUCK, what luck . . . I'll believe it when I see it. ~~LUCK~~ Like those airplanes are suppose to make me feel better. ***All I wanted was a military career now I have to GO HOLLYWOOD.***

Yes, I'm so happy to see you the next Britney… or oh my goosh your gonna be the next it girl?_____, [the next__, Oh I'm working with YOU. YAP, as if I give a flying fuck.

Hollywood talk… lets all welcome Heralyn TolingLibedo. Oh there she is … why do I feel like the baby PANDA. I won't get that still! Why can't I be normal? Why did GOD give me this responsibility in the first place? Why can't___ (not __) be responsible? Why was my father/mother ?_____ [the traditional Filipino family - coz my MOM wanted someone else already…._ ______] never responsible? Why do I hate ___?__ because it will always remind me of my __?_. I finally had a ____ but of course I shut __?__ oFF my life- After everything ___ done for me. Alright God, you called him to find me. Did you know what he had to go through to find me. There was somebody else before me then there was my Mom and I. So God what do you have to say for yourself. Save me. Take me to heaven on earth. What do you want me to do? Yes, like I'm so happy, like I'm looking forward to sing in front of thousands - to millions. I hope that the music ~~wel~~ industry welcomes me with a big smile. This is how I feel and I'm not pretty happy. I could care less about Luck, fame, or Hollywood success. Honestly, I can't wait to go back to college. I don't want to be famous. Who knows what's in store for me. Not only did I put up with so much CRAP in my early days etc. but not to mention hell, now it's a bigger hell. I'm a love bird in prison. BECAUSE I'm following again. Nothing's change. Like they say, invest in the right stock profits will come. But this ain't a game. Oh Yes! I like to buy the blue candles. YM issue oF May 2000. Who? ____HOTTEST STARS UNDER 25, ON DA COVER.

Friday 6/24/ 00 [24x6= 144 yrs. old]

The love pill is gone. Either tat or I'm in denial. Yeah! I learned to stop lovin'___ OR START LOVING and start caring for myself. I'm somewhat free. I've been writing songs out of rage. It doesn't seem to feel like its my own work- it sounded like I'm an angry b***h. Its time to move on for another job. I had fun today with Beth and her MOM. GOD WORKS in mysterious WAYS. Her Mom found $40, she stop the car at going to McDO drivethru. GOD always listen. I want to witness my Mom's dream. I want to finish what I started. I want to finish what I started. I want my Mom to see me where I want to be.. I only have one life to live… might as well witness all of my dreams come true. I want them to come true one at a time. God is listening. HE cares as much as I care. I'm learning to let loose and get in control.

July 10, 2000 (Mon)

Shit! I miss Ally McBeal show. Oh well, Well, I fulfilled my desire of a vacation- just be a kid, pig out, gain weight, no pressure, just silly fun. It's a better child hood memory. I'm free to be me.

100 Reasons why I want to attend the USMA [oops, I don't know] or *Be part of the*

showbiz industry [Hollywood /LOS ANGELES/San Diego/ MANILA, PHILS. /______ ______]

(1) A presentation of my American Dream in the past. (What I was looking for.) It will always remind me of my childhood days, my youth when I daydream about U.S. - the land of endless opportunities and what it would be like to live it.

MY DEF. OF THE AMERICAN DREAM= AN OPEN AVENUE OF ENDLESS OPPORTUNITY. A DESIRE TO ACHIEVE WHAT WE WANT FOR OURSELVES AND FINALLY TO DO WHATEVER IT TAKES TO ACHIEVE IT.

10/24/2001 Tues 8:22 PM

I wish I have photographic memory so I don't have to look /read my diaries again. Oh well! Sometimes I have to be careFul what I write or say because somehow it comes back. WHATEVER!

11/21/2000 Tues.

I search, and search for something over the past months only to find in me whenever I look back. To find a place in me. To look at your eyes expecting something back only to find me where I found you. Such as the road/ path I embrace only to see the hand of power holding on. You of all, things recognizes my /\ ~~many~~ doubts ~~poise/s~~ to witness the mirror of myself in others. Although the path is so long yet I have only just started. How was it then I was so blind for long only to hear the sounds of flight up high. I see heaven at my very eyes. Let ~~these~~ you see me… I chosen [chose] to play ~~hide~~ the part. I feel you stronger than ever. The one who brought the rainbow circled around the sun in midway when I asked. ***You flattered me with dark clouds of hue in the morning but seize the afternoon with heavenly blue skies. The rarest*** birds I'll find where I'm at to symbolize the place where I will be such as the seagull to remember clinging to a love ones hands. I feel a strange depart only to see him/her there eye to eye as if his/her perfect love didn't satisfy enough; I brought myself to you. I shared it all with nothing to hide, the universe at my very in my heart. You alone should know this for you bear witness it in my name.

8/13/2001

This 21st century is weird. I wonder what the next century feels like? [[LOOK how much I look like you 5x]]

8/17/2001 10:30 PM F
I'm just at a all time low right now. I don't know why but I'll just deal with it. College starts next week. I'll rather be resting. There no point in writing. I cant believe whatz been happening. I have yet to find my ultimate passion but I think I already know the answer in so many different ways. It shows like a lot.

9/12/2001

I'm trying to find that passion. You know, it's dying to come out of me. I really to don't know yet. What that's that mean "You inspire me to follow my dreams." nothing yet. Part of me is laughing but honestly I sometimes, like right now, I'm crushed inside. But then It goes awAy. Where am I gonna be 7 years from now? Could angels be right? What's a Tony? I wished something about the message was right.

7 years from now_?_

---I'll be [itz only 2008]35 yrs. old, 2015 wanting to finish "MY VENTI FRAPINOA SKETCHDEZORTDRUNKENPHRENIA WEEKENDS"

-- IN A COUPLE, FEWWING YEARZZEY I HOPE TO ATTEND LAW SCHOOL AT U.C.L.A. [UNIV. CALIFORNIA, LOS ANGELES] NAH! BE A FAT ACTRESS AND FINISH US ARMY ROTC YEARS 2,3,& 4. OR STAY IN MANILA, PHILS.
-- Definitely --a L.A. place/restaurant of "Heralyn's BBQ Grill & LIBEDO PUB" or earlier than 2015.

11/18/03

A I E W notes

Well, I'm surprise we get to go on da trolley but couldn't picture the ultimate action scene yet on Trolley bec. There was an accident on cz!$ imperial yesterday so it was closed down, at least I got to see…

I don't know (9:49 PM) the other side of the newly San Diego Downtown Ball Park because the totally was rerouted. Oh well! I really don't feel like talking about myself much. Maybe, I'll make sure I'll be able to read my handwriting- Just wanna jot things down for my 1st novel/ action flick. Huh ! Humana Humana …♬ Well, I guess the 1st few pages will be tawed out to a stripper someone falls in love with a stripper (got the idea from one of my tape mix-ins) while well anybody but specifically for the one got in jail / in T.J. I can't wait to work on my 1st movie startng off on T.J. strip joints. Dats what I'm exposed to (Ha! Ha!) so far. But I'll be seeing strippers in da club. Well, there's a dirt bike racing to practice hopefully I'll win. All lot of fun stuff to do. Back to the Miss Conception scene… (she falls in love with the stripper (think Justin in thongs) or whoever!!!! Anyway, I'm just here to face my mind and laugh at my own imagination.

So I could use this song from ? __ I don't know the band name, itz sad. *"Call up my mamma.. Says Im in love a stripper yo" in Mexii coo, you calling her a hooker… I meet her on the subway she told me I gave her dat VIP card and told her if ever had a problem don't hesitate to come by… just because she dance, loco cogo don't make her a ho no! back street the French are all hard.. We going to disco… call up my mama say I'm one with a stripper yo"* [background song in da club strip joint] …

Anyway… it's a MAFIA GANSTER HIPPIDY DUDA FAMILY for everyone to enjoy. I cant wait to get lost while writing in this flick. I will be jam pack with action. [No more tried/tired nights like High school] But next semester is my 2nd year playing college Tennis. Cool huh! Till den… I'll be thinking about it. (10:22 PM)

My wallet in Mexico… my Mom's explanations WOW… writing in my journal definitely got back my confidence in writing and got me at ease with what I have in mind to write on this project. If this helps den I got me a PULITZER prize. THIS FEELING OF WRITING WELL WILL GO SMOOTHLY IN MY MIND. SO WATS UP?

12/26/03 12:33 PM SAT.

Ohh !!! I'm so used to this by now. I got my homies to party with Los Angeles at 26 Look Dance here Lost in 'Firestorm's eyes' I knew I'll use my journal as the lines to your movie. NO !!! HUM !!! Take control of your destiny- I think itz the NEPTUNES band that sang that "STRIPPER SONG"- and a verse like " I GOTTA Protect my heart." Angels in training Call CHARLIE'S ANGELS .. They want all the blue diamonds. It sells! ! ! The fifth element is Jesusita Chrrist. Wats change. [?] I got an idea why don't I see what I see and let you watch wAt I see. For $4 million. Cool I__bb can Record her choreography youR out 1, 2, 3, 4, 5, 6, 7, 8, 9, 10, 11, 12. Here we come clubbin dacin' I don't need sleep I need weed to put me to sleep. That's hierchacy!

FINISH ON AUGUST 9, 2003 (SATURDAY) ON ALL SUMMER LONG PROJECT 2003. I'M READY START WRITING MY FIRsT MOVIE SCRIPT.

----------------♥♥♥♥----------------

[July 15, 2005, 4:27- 6:19 AM ./ ?]

CATCH THE REST OF THE UPCOMING BOOKS

#1 SEX & MUSIC LITERATURE 101

Remember there are no talented writers, only talented singers.

[LOVE & MUSIC 101]

#2 Da Mu Ar Te² MiL Education 107

Remind me the many playful player mates(I love it! I love it!) Blondes do have fun! ! ! And Brunettes [BrujaZ] to watch after them. Okay the Quote is thatz it. Okay find the one.

#3

"SAVAGELY DONE IN BED"

"MAKE LOVE LIKE A LIBEDO FOUNDER ♥"

TempingPARADISE TO HOLLYWOOD

#4 "THE ADVENTURES OF HERALYN TOLING AND KINKEY"

'REWRITING HISTORY'

#5"THE LADYGRIFFINTURTLES GO TO THEIR CALIFORNIA STATE TOURNAMENT CHAMPIONSHIP GAME @ PALM SPRINGS" [Glory Dayz!] Ranked in CA consecutively-111/ OR 3X in a row ~~like death row"~~

THE book TITLE IS EXACTLY LIKE THE 1st INDY MOVIE I Documented ~~on film~~ titled: **"The Glory Dayz of the Lady *GriffinTurtles*"**

Herez a MOVIE TITLE JOKE *to throw around da spin cycle:*

TOPSPIN CURVE FOREHANDz & FADED VOLLEYz LIKE TOLINGLIBEDO

☺ **[** MORE LIKE TAKE UR TOP SHIRT OFF & SHOW ME UR FAD SPORTS BRA LIKE TOLING] ☺

#6 A NOTEBOOK GUIDE TO:

MANAGEMENT
&
RELATIONSHIPS

A Cross Parallel Pollination
Dimension
Of managing a multi-billion
dollar
Fast food industry -company
[Y U M !]
To the journey of finding
All the answer and

handling the relationships ←
WE LEAD. Help I don't know it!
↓

Title: Written - 2:06 AM [SUN] JAN 9th , 2005

[aiew!awew! [the fortune COOKIE EXPRESS/ THE monk divas [wat else?____________ -----------

Why I Want To Join The United States Army

(1) I was looking for a
real dream, my dream,
not anybody's dream. They
showed me the way. I
got hope and took actions.
I call this my own dream.

2) . . . . Showed me I
have no limit I
believe I can achieve
it. It doesn't matter how
long it will take. *WP*WestPoint!

3) I will never be
overweight for the
rest of my life.

4) I love challenge.
I thirst and
quench for it.

5) To be / part of
belonging of the elite
team in the world.

6) It's the job that
Speaks my soul ☺ =
The character.

7) Make me stronger
and better in body, mind
and soul.

8) I want a lifetime of adventure.

I'm not talking about life adventure but the trill of living it.
Like for example, the excitement in me … JUMPING THOUSANDS OF FEET FROM AN AIRPLANE [GO! AIRBORNE]

TO AN UNKNOWN DROP ZONE.

. . . STRUGGLING TO PUSH HARDER, KNOWING NO LIMIT.
. . . A duty of an ARMY OFFICER.
. . . A soldier. A leader… a part of chain of command & in charge .

(9) A different person. . .
A much, much better person.
An individual. It just gets better everyday
and in all aspects of it.

(10) Knowing the satisfaction of why I chase it; PAST, PRESENT, and FUTURE.

(11) Many … many … opportunities for me.

(12) TRAVEL (surprises) I will love and enjoy to live and work around the world.

(13) THE ARMY OFFICER MODEL…
A LEADER… of continuing tradition (leaders from the past)
I carry… the LEADERSHIP RESPONSIBILITIES. . .
The triumphs and obstacles. . . A liFE worth
living, a career, I would do anything to achieve it
- - - in my will of virtue; a country, a world . . .
I WOULD DIE FOR.   NOT!!! I WANNA DIE @B____,PHILS.

(14) A DESTINY, A PURPOSE ONLY I UNDERSTAND.

DRAW MY FAVORITE ARMY TANK OR HELICOPTER - ON THE SPACE BELOW ☺

☺ A YEAR OFF IN WRITING IN 2007 IS OVER…DARN. IT TURNS OUT THAT I ENDED UP BEING OVER-WEIGHT. BECOMING AN ARMY OFFICER IS A DREAM I SURRENDERED … SOMETIMES! I KNOW!, DRUGS ARE BAD 4 U… I DON'T CARE IF YOU SAW MY INDY MOVIE *"M.V.F.S.W. - MY VENTI FRAPINOA SKETCHDEZORTDRUNKENPRENIA WEEKENDS"*, ONE WEEKEND ABOUT 'DRUG FREE AMERICA' ARTWORK …. OK! ITZ NOT IN

SUNDANCE FILM FESTIVAL… I HAVE TO WAIT 10 YEARS TO RELEASE IT… COZ ITZ TOP SECRET…
Follow it on the internet. . Someday, right?
--- - -- --- TO HELP ME FIND THE FUCK UP PERSON IN MY LIFE OR THE LOVE OF MY LIFE---NO MORE HINTS! February 7, 2008, 10:32 PM HAPPY 28TH B-DAY 2ME.

HERALYN TOLING'S ***COLLECTION OF HIGH-SCHOOL AND COLLEGE ESSAYS, WORKS, WRITINGS AND CREATIVE IDEAS***

ALL WRITTEN BY: ☺ H.M. TOLING

☺ ☺ ☺ ☺ ☺

HERALYN M. TOLING
PERIOD 1
3/13/95

GRADE : B +

TALENT

"Genius is the product of education." - - - - Anne Dillard

Everyday, five times a week, I go to school to learn something new. Something important that will help me on to the future. Also, I could be able to apply it, to teach and help learn others. Being educated is what makes me improve in life. What will I be without education? Where will I stand? Perhaps sometimes I forget about how ~~prep~~ *precious* learning can be. Of all the things I have and want, the most important thing is education. It feels great when I accomplished something than nothing. Without education I wouldn't become the kind of person I am right now. Without education I would not discover my talent or something I'm good at. Take Math subject for example. Before I was not interested and just satisfied of getting a B grade. What I didn't know was I could do better. So I worked hard and put more effort in it. Now, I feel good about Math stuff. It made me realize I could do better.

Sometimes I compare myself with others. When I think of a person who I think is better than me in a certain field and compare myself to her. So I keep telling myself that no matter what we are created equal, and that we are different in every way and that what makes us *special.* There is one subject that I don't like the most is English. It's hard learning another language. All the struggling ~~through~~ to be successful proved me I could do anything in life. "It's hard work doing something with your life." I'm not talented in writing. I always want an A grade in essays, especially English. But I know it's not going to be easy. It takes a big amount of time to write an essay for ~~time~~ me. I have to be willing to do it. I will do anything for my goals. Sometimes it doesn't come out right when I worked real hard and put all the effort and didn't get the grade I want. But it doesn't mean I have to give up. Life is not fair. If it was perfect it wouldn't be worth living because we would not learn the aspects of life and won't learn something from your weaknesses. I don't have talent in sports except one but I like to participate in it. I'm the kind of person who likes to try new things. I didn't learn tennis, basketball, soccer, running etc. by looking at a game but I played the sports to learn and improve. I asked myself of why I'm doing this to myself. I'm not good at it. But I kept in mind to always believe in myself. Anything is possible as long as I keep on trying to succeed. But if I fail I don't consider myself as a failure because I worked hard and did my best.

The talents I know that I have is Martial Arts and Arts. I'm glad that I started practicing karate at a young age of 6 because it made me improve and develop it so that I could go on to more difficult skill to learn like judo & kung fu. It help me a lot in life. It had taught me respect, courage, honor, self-esteem, self-discipline and the strength of mind, body and soul. I love Martial Arts. I'm dedicated and worked hard of what I've become.

"You do it for love and respect for your own life; you do it for love and respect for the world;

and you do it for love & respect for the task itself."

My second talent is drawing. Having a talent on a certain field makes me feel important that I have something to share to others. In Art class, I know how it feels being on top and it feels great. Drawing is like a vision of what I want to interpret to the public and show how I feel. I feel lucky I discovered my God-given gifts. As long as I live I will continue to share of what I have. I want to make myself useful; useful for my own good; & to be useful and important for the world. I go for my dreams. Accomplishing a dream makes my life more important. We need to think that we are created different and that what makes us special and unique towards others. Always keep in mind no matter how rough things can get to **always believe in yourself**. Start aiming your goals for anything is possible but if you want it you have to start working hard right now. **Make your talent worthy and be all you can be with what you have**.

February 21, 2008, 11:33 PM
Thursday night ☺

Journal,

I have realized today and suspected since a few days ago to what effects things, such as stress can determine your performance. I went to a problem. I made me weak for 1st/ 4 weeks especially in Spanish. I believe if I maintain my senior year clear no-no danger threat to my health my mind I can achieve anything. I have to watch out observantly very carefully of what lies ahead today and forget of yesterday.

Elements I must keep and maintain

(1) keep aiming high
(2) set ~~your~~ my mind always on top despite of how hard it is.
(3) plan strategecly like a battle of a chess game
(4) set the grade and time needed to get an A, B or C "Picture it"

(5) Almost impt. Is "FAILURE" if I failed I must climb up with all my might.
FAILURE IS NOT AN OPTION. NEVER SHOULD HAVE BEEN. IF an event of an emergency, this drive I have when I fall. I call it "the climb" . It is very useful on my success because depending on how much time I have input/ desire or want I use I can achieve the level of what kind of success.

"EVIVRUS OT TNEMILPMOC DEEN UOY" GNORW ARE YOU
(please read thiz backwards)

♥♥2012☺♥♥♥♥♥--------------------2018

HERALYN M. TOLING
Mr. Tony Ding
English 103
12/14/99

Dear Editor:

I'm writing in response to the opinion titled *Some rules kids wont' learn in school* by Charles J. Sykes found in November 14, 1997 edition of your newspaper. I am deeply grateful to read about an opinion article that justifies that high school academic is just an educational experience. It is a step towards something bigger, something greater -that is, the reality world hits hard upon leaving the high school experience. That a high school graduate only has a miniscule, ~~great of~~ very little educational background experience which is just a beginning in ~~their life~~ his/her life. The rules reminds us that reality is cruel, reffering to Rule #1: Life is not fair.
Get used to it. Nevertheless, the rules depicts greatly on what today's generation should know, what they will experience (look forward to) and learned from these experiences that their reality (future) should be taken seriously.

The reality is cruel, and the real world becomes an invitation to make the reality cruel or a challenge to succeed on his/her own. In rule#2, states the real world won't even care about you, your self-esteem. It challenge me to think that "only the strong survive", an expression relating to the real world. The real world doesn't center around you; in fact, it triggers the output of your actions.

In the real world, you have to be the one responsible for yourself. Blaming others doesn't conjure you not responsible but worsen the problem. In order to succeed in the real world, one must attend college. This is when Rule#3 hits hard. In college, your responsible for everything. You'll think of rule #1 a lot when in college struggling to make the grade while working full-time and trying to pay the bills on time.

In Rule#8 stating that life hasn't done away with winners and losers. In the reality world, one must persevere with tremendous effort and persistence over a long period of time to actually feel like a winner. It simply undermines what true hard-work really means in order to feel like a winner in the real world. The school might not let anyone get hurt but it is teaching kids not to work-hard and not put effort in their work.

Time can be our friend or enemy in the real world. Rule #9 reminds us to use our time wisely. It reminds us to choose the right path of happiness, the right job. The type of job you will be smiling when you wake up every morning when getting ready for work. It can be fair if you make it work with wise decisions. Rule #13 tells ~~everybody the~~ today's generation that we are a walking time bomb. Sooner or later, time is up. That's when Rule #14 tells us that life is so short and being a kid in those days are over and for some should enjoy it while they can.

The article reminds me the many things I didn't understand when I read this as a senior high school student. True, I read it back then and throw it away after and laughed it now because I'm in the reality. We must take reality seriously because it is our life--- OUR FUTURE. I am in charge of my reality --- MY FUTURE!
The article conveys warnings still, but good warnings something I'll keep in mind and learn through by experiencing those rules of reality --- EVERYDAY. *

*I think I learn how to spell ' EVERYDAY' when I got to a junior college @GROSSMONT COLLEGE , El Cajon, CA-- The GRIFFINS. DON'T FORGET TO BUY MY BOOK AND INDY MOVIE DVD DOCUMENTARY THAT I DIRECTED & PRODUCED **"THE LADY GRIFFIN -TURTLES GO TO THEIR CALIFORNIA STATE CHAMPIONSHIP."**

March 16, 2008, 12:13 AM

Heralyn Toling SSN***-**-****
English 103

Teacher's note: PASSES
BASIC ENGLISH COMPETENCY

The most important is the mind because it is the only thing out of the three (looks, personality, and mind) that /|\ truly counts playing the integral role of a person's life. **The mind, above all, is the inner most strength to a person's will to succeed.** Since no minds are alike or even think the same, it has dramatically shape the world we are in from every aspect. It is the most important of the three that a group of individuals can build bridges, changed technologies or even one great mind like William Shakespeare who greatly influence the English Literature and help a college student thinking creatively using his imaginations.

It is the mind the most important because it is the only thing we have that opens to a vast, endless and challenging opportunities. The mind, and individual's intelligence, is developing greatly to life's experiences and individual's education. It is the mind that will take a person to a better job, a career, because of the knowledge learned. Knowledge is the key, a first hand approach to anything applied. The wise, intelligent mind is able to think for his/her own judgment with good discretion. The mind truly makes us unique as individuals. The mind is where one's inner most highest ambitions- goals, it starts in the mind. it's a mind game to keep your perseverance to achieve those goals despite of the rigors and challenges in life. Lastly, I think the mind is the most important because of its impact it has to society and the world. Our world is vastly improving because of great minds by people working together contributing many aspects of our lifestyle. For example, the technology, getting better by the minute because of people in their creative, ingenious mind that there is no limit to ones imagination. Anything can come true with great minds thinking for the better good.

I think the look and personality are less important because they play complementary roles to a person's intelligence(mind). They are least important because they are not the biggest factors that influence one's future success but the mind. I think the personality is the second most important and the person's future success is determine greatly on his/her great, creative mind, and good personality. The mind directs us to the right path we have chosen to do with our life and our looks and personality aids us to this path. We are in a society of different individuals who think differently, therefore it is important to have a good personality and present at our best. I think a good looking person is one who presents himself well and it is ideally important in the professional world. Presenting yourself well with showing your good personalities by being yourself is marketable in the job world.

I'm in no way I will ever change my present opinion that the mind is most important because the mind is most important because the mind counts the most and greatly influence to every aspect in life. Our mind is the most unique individuality. It is one thing we can depend on.

My life's experiences has taught me that my mind, my intelligence is truly the one I most depend on and will always use my career choice as an example of the importance of first hand knowledge. I will be a future leader and playing a role that will depend on this nation's future as a U.S. Army officer. The most clear-cut and depicting scenario of the most important thing that count- my mind. When I lead soldiers who will count on me for hope and faith to survive in a war or battle (if it becomes a reality in the future from my imagination), my soldiers are not going to depend on my looks or personality for that matter but my mind- my knowledge, my leadership skills of how well I will lead my soldiers will depend and affect our survival in war or battle. *The mind is so precious and valuable and yet it can also change other individuals.*

Toling 1

Heralyn Toling

Mr. Tony Ding

English 103

9/28/99

The Ultimate Challenge

I will never forget the day that changed my perspective about a challenge. I [vividly] remember the day ~~vividly~~ when I faced the challenge. This happened during my eleventh grade in high school. I was walking with my friend to my third period AP *Advanced Placement* English class. My friend and I were talking about our Chemistry homework from last Period, and suddenly something caught my attention while we were walking to class. I glanced over to my tenth grade Humanities teacher's classroom, and two men in military uniform were inside the classroom. I just stepped in the classroom to asked my tenth grade Humanities teacher about them. I found out they ~~are~~ [were] recruiters from the U.S. Army National Guard. I walked to my AP English class and asked my teacher if I could be excuse[d] for class so [that I could] I can listen to what the recruiters will say. I remember him saying, "Good! You don't have to commit so many years of active duty in the military." I didn't exactly knew

I didn't exactly know what he meant until I learned that the

what he meant until what I learned about the U.S. Army

U.S. Army National is a branch of the U.S. Army Reserve

National that is it a branch of the U.S. Army Reserve

unit.

unit.

At that moment, in my junior year on March 1997, I was unsure of my dreams attending the Air Force Academy since my ninth grade year. I was really unsure about it. At first, I wanted to be a soldier of the U.S. Army National Guard, serving only one weekend a month and two weeks a year. But I realized a month later that I discovered something about myself. I was chasing a dream of becoming an Air Force Officer through the Air Force Academy. But attending the Air Force Academy was not my own dreams, I has no desire of attending.

Every time I think of the day during my eleven[th] grade, I remember it always as a representation of realizing my own dreams and ambitions. It was the day that changed the course and outlook of my life. So I decided to chase the ultimate and impossible dream of becoming a West Point cadet attending the Unites States Military Academy to become a U.S. Army officer. It was the biggest self-realization of my life. I realized that I was afraid to set high standards for myself. But to deny my dreams, is to deny my ambitious character, myself. I realized that I can achieve what seems

I realized that I can achieve what had seemed

impossible to me at first but possible if I have the desire

impossible to me at first but it is possible if I have the

and willingness to take actions in making my dream come

desire and willingness to take action to make my dream

true. I love challenges, and the path and anticipation to

come true.

become a West Point cadet is the ultimate challenge. I intend to do whatever it takes to attend the United States Military Academy three years from now. I know in me that I
I know that in me I have the confidence and ability
have the confidence and ability to achieve it. I just have to take this journey of achieving the ultimate challenge a day at a time. I think that graduating from the United States Military Academy is the best way for me to become a U.S. Army officer because I can look back and say,

"I Succeeded in the ULTIMATE CHALLENGE."

TURN IN GRADE FROM R.O.T.C. MILITARY SCIENCE TEACHER CAPT. KATHERINE GRAEF, U.S.ARMY: 21/25 POINTS

♥H.M.TOLINGLIBEDO's comments: I still believe in the U.S. Military. If not for my dreams,goals and ambitions, . . .then where will I be in life? What will I do and why do I believe in this?

I hope to fulfill an Aerospace Engineering degree and minor in ARMY Reserve Officer's Training Course {ROTC} at SAN DIEGO STATE UNIVERSITY or CALIFORNIA STATE L.A.

AFTER MAJORING IN Architect [DEGREE]@ University of SANTO TOMAS [UST]-the Harvard University of the Philippines. I wish myself LUCK!

March 30, 2008, 8:50 PM, Sunday, time check , At home in my bedroom, LAKESIDE, CALIFORNIA.

WHERE IN LOS ANGELES IS THE WILD CARD GYM ... THE OWNER OF THE WILD CARD GYM NAME IS -? _______________, AND COACH OF MANNY PAQUIAO, A FILIPINO CHAMPION BOXER. I WILL NEVER DIE 4 A COUNTRY OR GET KIDNAP. I WILL NEVER LET ANOTHER KID GO THROUGH WHAT I WENT THROUGH (17 YRS.) OR WILL I SEE MYSELF AS THAT KID IN ANOTHER ANGLE? I WILL GO BACK HOME AND DIE IN BAGANGA, D.O. , PHILS. I WILL BE THE PRESIDENT OF MY COUNTRY PHILS! SHOW ME A COUNTRY GREATER THAN MY COUNTRY? THERE IS NO COUNTRY GREATER THAN MY COUNTRY. A KNOCKOUT LIKE ME.

Volunteering Activities
Heralyn M.Toling
(Grade 9-12)

Grade 9:

-I volunteered at Lakeside Library(1 school year) every Friday or Wednesday, at least 1-2 hours a week.

Grade 10:

-I volunteered as a martial arts instructor for Lakeside Martial Arts. November-June every Wednesday And Friday, 2-4 hours per week.

-Library volunteer; only one hour evry month.

*Key Club International of El Capitan. Activities I helped organize and participated on volunteering.

KEY CLUB- A volunteering service towards your local community, the nation, and self-awareness about the World[planet Earth] we all live in. ☺

-Halloween Trick or Canning. Collect and ask for Canned goods, instead of candies.

-Cystic Fibrosis Bowlathon: Bowl for Breath participant & volunteer. A nationwide fundraising I participated every year.

-Blood Drive Coordinator. Held at El Capitan high school on March 8, 1995.

-Brown Bagging Project. Making sandwiches for the homeless.

-Christmas Caroling at Lakeside Manor.

-La Jolla Beach Clean-Up

-Mission Beach Cleann-Up

-Lindo Lake Park Clean-Up. 3 times.

-Pasedena Float Decorating volunteer for the Roses Parade.

-Saint Vincent DePaul volunteer for a Day Project.

-Junior Olympics volunteer. Held at El Capitan HS.

-Lakeside Western Day Parade volunteer.

-Lakeside Area Tree Planting: Highway 67, Right of Way Town Project. I planted small trees on Highway 67 exit, Behind Burger King.

-World Wide Service Project I participated, and by All KEY CLUB ORGANIZATIONS around the world: IDD Fundraising Drive to prevent Iodine Deficiency.

KEY CLUB TREASURER.

AWARDS: Achievement Award (Key Club lnternational for OUTSTANDING ACHIEVEMENT in community service).

OUTSTANDING TREASURER AWARD
OUTSTANDING KEY CLUB MEMBER AWARD

GRADE 11:

-Library volunteer; 1 hour every week.

-MATH TUTOR at Lakeside Middle School; 1 hour a week.

*Key Club International of El Capitan. Activities I helped organize and participated on volunteering.

-Annual Halloween Tick or Canning.

-Annual Christmas Caroling at Lakeside Manor.

-Annual Christmas Card Making.

INFORMATION SHEET

G.P.A.= 3.6

Colleges I'm applying

1) United States Military Academy (USMA)
2) San Diego State University (SDSU)
3) University of California, SAN DIEGO (UCSD)(UCLA)
4) University of San Diego (USD)
5) Virginia Military Institute (VMI)
6) HARVARD University, YALE?
7) California State University, LOS ANGELES
8) University of Santo Tomas-Ateneo PHILS.,Manila(UST)
9) ____________________
10) CALI LIBEDO UNIVERSITY

Major & minor - Political Science/ Spanish & 3 years of LAW SCHOOL. I wish to fulfill a lifetime career in the Military and work toward becoming a JAG (Judge Advocate General) Lawyer of the U.S. Army.

[2008-2018 college goal: MAJOR IN ARCHITECT, MINOR IN FILM]

SCHOOL ACTIVITIES

Sports:

Grade 9: J.V. Tenis, J.V. Track

Grade 10 & 11: Varsity Tennis

Grade 10 & 12: Girl's Powder Puff/ Flag Football

Awards & Recognitions:

Grade 10 -Coach's Award : "SUPER SOPHOMORE"
-Junior Varsity Team Girl's Tennis
-Powder Puff FOOTBALL girl/ team member
-One of the 6 female students who co-founded the 1st GIRL'S FLAG FOOTBALL TEAM AT EL CAPITAN HIGH.

Grade 11 -Most Dedicated Player
(El Capitan Tennis Team 1996)
-Co-Captain Varsity/J.V. team Powder Puff Football

Grade 12 -Co-Captain Varsity/J.V. team Powder Puff Football

Club Leadership Positions / Student Government:

Clubs:

CSF [California State Federation Club] : Grade 10-12 member
Spanish Club: Club Treasurer (Grade 10),
Club President (Grade 11), Club Commissioner of Activities (Grade 12)
Human relations Club: Grade 10-12 member, elected HUMAN RELATIONS TASK FORCE FORUM MEMBER (Grade 11)
Addicted 2 Jesus Club: Grade 10-12 member
Science Club: Grade 10-12 member, Club Commissioner of Activities (Grade 12)
Key Club International of El Capitan:
Club Treasurer (Grade 10-11), Club Secretary (Grade 12)

Student GOVT:

Grade 10 : Sophomore Class President
Grade 11: President of El Capitan Webb Team, Special

Education Peer Tutor, **Assistant Editor to EL CAPITAN HORIZON, STUDENT SENATE, SCHOOL SITE COUNCIL MEMBER/ STUDENT REPRESENTATIVE**

GRADE 12: SCHOOL SITE COUNCIL MEMBER/ STUDENT REPRESENTATIVE

-SCHOOL ACTIVITIES

Grade 9: Lakeside Library Volunteer (1 year), every FRIDAY or WEDNESDAY, at least 2 hours a week.
Grade 10:Lakeside Library volunteer (3 hours a month)
:I volunteered as a MARTIAL ARTS instructor for Lakeside Martial Arts (NOV.- JUNE 1995-96)
Grade 11:Lakeside Library Volunteer (1- 2 hrs. a week)
Grade 12:Math tutor at Lakeside Middle School (1 hour/week)
: I volunteer for the FORUM PUBLICATIONS (the
: Lakeside LEADER). Writing 1 -2 articles a month.

I have been working at McDonald's Fast-food restaurant since the SUMMER of my JUNIOR YEAR(1997). This year (1998), I work 8 hrs. on Saturday, 6 hours on Sunday, & 4 hours on Monday.
MCDONALD'S HOURS
Grade 11: 10-12 hrs. a week , Grade 12: 15-18 hours a week

CLUB, ACADEMIC, LEADERSHIP AWARDS & RECOGNITIONS
GRADE 10: -ACHIEVEMENT AWARD (KEY CLUB INTERNATIONAL FOR OUTSTANDING ACHIEVEMENT IN COMMUNITY SERVICE)
-OUTSTANDING TREASURER AWARD (KEY CLUB)
-OUTSTANDING KEY CLUB MEMBER
GRADE 11: -NATIONAL CONFERRENCE HUMAN RELATIONS MEDIA AWARDS PARTICIPANT/FINALIST (JOURNALISM)
-EXCELLENCE IN VOLUNTEER SERVICE AWARD FROM SAN DIEGO COUNTY LIBRARY
-NATIONAL CONFERENCE YOUTH LEADERSHIP FORUM (SELECTED TWICE AS A REPRESENTATIVE FROM EL CAPITAN HIGH SCHOOL)
-ART-MURAL CONTEST WINNER (TITLE: RECOGNIZING DIVERSITY)
-SANDY NININGER AWARD (KEY CLUB INTERNATIONAL'S HIGHEST INDIVIDUAL AWARD ON A NATIONAL LEVEL IN COMMUNITY SERVICE)
-WHO'S WHO AMONG HIGH SCHOOL STUDENTS IN

☺ THE NOSTALMAGICAL YEARS OF MY MIDDLE SCHOOL AND HIGH SCHOOL

TOLINGLIBEDO 1

I opened the top of my chair, shaped like a box. Inside it- holds papers of my past. They are just simply garbage when I look at them. Really not that simple. I collected notes, essays, papers from those school days at LMS[LAKESIDE MIDDLE SCHOOL] and [EL CAPITAN] high school. I was going to throw it right away but I have to do this project first. These notes will help me remember my past. I remember my English teacher, Mr. Best, who thought of my book essays "Thoughtful" and "Super". He would write "Super" right next to 6, the score I got from a few essays I still have. My classmates and teachers like my drawings whenever ido that type of project. I have HOME ECONOMICS. A project I still have now-- about my BEDROOM. I had a collage of things I have and things I would like to have. Today I don't have a VCR/ T.V. because that is broken and old. My casio piano keyboard is gone at my Mom's bedroom closet collecting dust. I had a piano sat on the living room behind the fireplace which was old. I exchange it for KARATE classes. I finally have a CD player which was one of the things I wanted to have at that time. I don't really care much for a Computer in my room anymore. I can't believe my dysfunctional family has a computer today.

My room was so different. My step Dad bought me a Queen size bed on my sweet 16th B-Day. I used to sleep in a small single bed. I'm sitting on the floor carpet, the exact spot I slept on the floor the very first night we move in this apartment. I remember my room was so white and big. My very own room. I had a room, a big room in this big house apartment when my Mom first meet my step Dad. That was my first room. The only reason why we were in that type of house was because my step Dad was paying it. That was **way back in the Philippines.**

(Ap.15, 1998)

I have Spring Break right now.

I just really want to throw stuff I don't need anymore. These papers are precious to me but I have to put in my scrapbook. Being ~~seroius~~ resourceful (keeping old stuff) helps out a lot for this project. I won't need these anymore since I finished my *Senior Showcase Project*.

TOLINGLIBEDO 2

Since I spend most of my time and focus on my education(school, homework, projects, etc.). I think it should be part of my scrapbook. I value education. I like school. Yeah! I know. WEIRD! It is because the experiences I got from EDUCATION(SCHOOL) help and made me who I am right now. I value it greatly. There's an old saying "EDUCATION IS THE KEY TO YOUR FUTURE." TRUE! But there is also a saying "ITS NOT WHAT YOU KNOW, IT'S WHO YOU KNOW!" TRUE! But in my opinion, a person can achieve whatever success they want to achieve if he/she has the desire to achieve it, follow his/her goals step by step and making it happen. Okay, I don't know how I got started writing about that topic. Moving along. . .

It's 11 PM right now. I have an hour before I go to sleep. These papers are twice as thick as my scrapbook. I guess I'm writing so I can write what I remember. It will help me write my life story.

HOLY SPIRIT SCHOOL **(2ND SEMESTER, 6TH GRADE)**
Mrs. McLaughlin's Englis class. The students keep a book log to write a summary about each book we read. Believe it or not, I didn't start reading books till I came to U.S. Not bad for a Catholic student who went to a private Catholic school

in the Philippines. If not for that superior education, I wouldn't be able to read and write in English. I remember my English teacher, she helped me out a lot. I wish I could write her a letter so I can thank her and let her know great my life is right now. It's crazy for me to think how I came to the U.S.A 5 years ago and what has happen to me.

Science [(Stars)]= Probably was the biggest project I did in school. I think? I think I may have picked this topic because that was the easiest one. Well, I was fascinated about stars and still [todiz] today. Have you ever wish upon a star. That little girl wish. I had a lot of wishes. Did I tell you I saw a UFO but that's another story. I'm not really thinking well right now.

Thursday, August 7, 2008 Today I went to URANUS Planet... Blah... blah...blah...and I'm eating at Bowl wel bill $850 went bad-soulry.. I need to put this book by the end of Aug.2008 and buy Sto.Nino/Jovan's blue PSP $175 as promise to get my dual AMERICAN PILIPINO CITIZENSHIP TURN IN 2ND LETTER-CALL BY END OF sept '08-BEGIN. Oct.'08. I need to finish my Strawberry shake.
Bitch you better pay for that $30 mil. AOL fines and save $ for food...Ask MOM.F*Cking A!!!**

TOLINGLIBEDO 3

LAKESIDE MIDDLE SCHOOL [L.M.S.]

Social Studies- WW1 [WORLD WAR ONE] Project will be in my scrapbook. Mr. Lange is a funny teacher. I aced that class. It /|\ was one of my favorite subject. Its my most favorite subject. This is 8th grade work. I really want to write about my experiences as a student in L.M.S. but I'm saving it for later. I describe ~~it~~ those L.M.S. days painful, victorious, and troublesome, confusing, just to name a few. I'm not even smiling right now.

Physical Science- I remember 2 classes in Science (L.M.S.):(1) Ms. Flynn and (2)Mr. McClees class.
Looking through these notes, I didn't think I had/ took a Physics class in L.M.S. but I did. I see A's and B's on my

assignments/work. I think I flunk C.P.R. and it drop my grade (Grade 8) to a C because it was 40% of our total grade.

Math- I had Mrs. Graham for 7th grade Math. I did very well in that class only because it was a review of what I learned since 3rd grade. I L♥VE MATH!I don't know why I'm writing what comes into my mind when I'm doing this. It's boring! In 8th grade I hated my teacher, Mr. Walker. It didn't seem that bad when I got moved from Mrs. Graham's 7th grade, 1st semester to Mr. walker 2nd semester class in one year. I was promoted form 7th grade to 8th grade and did it in just one year. Mr. Walker's class was a more advance learning class. I sucked in that class. I hated the way he teaches. Everybody does.

ENGLISH- I picked a few of my favorite essays/ notes to be in my scrapbook. I was laughing and smiling as I looked trough them. Most of the ones I picked was about me. We had journals/essays in class that we could write whatever we want. I always picked about my life and emotions. Right now, I really want to write short stories and maybe someday a novel. It is because of what I went through over the years of speaking and writing better in English. It was one of my weakness and still is but not as worst as before. I don't think I'm ready to write poems or short stories because I haven't conquer/ to master my emotions. I don't know how to explain it well. I just have to do this scrapbook first before any big project I want to do of my own. It doesn't matter if my short stories or poems wont be as great like many great

writers and poets of our time. I want to do it because **I want to do it.**

What do I want to do in the next 5 years?______________________________

____

____

Check out how THE 3 STEPS TO SPIRITUAL MOTIVATION WILL HELP ACHIEVE ME ACHIEVE MY 5 YEAR GOAL.

1)____________________________________

2)____________________________________

3)____________________________________

☼TOLINGLIBEDO 4

It is a challenge I have yet to conquer. Time can only tell. I appreciate the Enlgish language and value my experiences of the past to learn how to speak and write better in English. *I'm not ready to write about a different life or something different other than mine.* This is how I feel right now. I wish one of these days I can write creatively without refering it to my own life and draw something using my imagination.

FRESHMAN YEAR (Grade 9)

Career & Family Studies- I liked this class. It doesn't matter nowhat I ranked first in this class. It was the easiest class but… that was like therapy for me. It sort of helped me but it was just really just me alone can save myself. Thst was what I did. But that's a different story. **[HA! HA! HA! HA! FLOUR BABY like PIKCACHU BB!!!!!!!!!!!]**

Algebra- I selected one test. I did so well in that class. I just thrown all of my mostly A's and a couple of B test paper. Ariana and Hilary was in that class. I have so much to tell and express how it was back then. The grief on my face right now. I rember those days when I have the worst feelings about myself. I said goodbye to those days a long time ago.

I'm really glad I got rid of those papers. I find it trugh selecting which ones I want to be in my scrapbook. I picked my highest test scores and lowest for my Math subjects.

I throw away these stuff. I learned a lot because of these stuff. I don't know how to say it right. What I meant to say is I throw all these stuff away because I will always have that knowledge in me. If I was to retake any of these tests or take a test on the notes I took I would probably fail it, I don't remember all these artists during those era [hundred years ago]. I'm not one of those people who remembers tiny little things of what they learned or everything they learned.

Grade 10- I wrote an essay about the "Tales of TWO CITIES" and got a B. What is funny about it is I didn't even read the book. I read some pages of it and we spend a lot of time talking about it in class.

Grade 11- I love poems. I'm glad I took A.P. English my Junior year despite of the toture I went through in that class. Well, it was a fun class, listening Mr. Laundry talking about his life. I only wrote one poem in my life. It was a lot of homework for Senior Honors English. I didn't even try to finish this poem for a Humanities homework because it was hard. Maybe I just didn't [even] try hard enough or

afraid to write a crappy poem.

My AP Junior English class, I didn't turn in a homework to write a poem. I was never into poem but I gradually increase my appreciation about reading poems. I like it because of AP English class. Maybe I'll write a poem of "HIGH SCHOOL YEARS!"

JUST EDITING (READ LAST PAGES out loud 4 film MVFSW)

Heralyn M. Toling

Period 1

12/4/97

MY PERSONAL ACADEMIC, COLLEGE & CAREER GOALS

My personal, academic, college, and career goals are the essential goals I must attain. Attaining these goals will result a successful lifetime career path I chose. Success to me comes from will, persistence, determination and sacrifice. My character is tested in facing many challenging obstacles to attain my goals. Achieving these goals is where my destiny lies and it is up to me to make it happen.

My personal goal is to continue losing weight. I have lost weight for the past months and I will continue to loose weight while at the same time getting ready for the Army Basic Training this summer 1998. I will achieve my goal of becoming a member of the U.S. Army National Guard. Now, I must concentrate on preparing myself to be mentally and physically ready for the rigorous challenges of 9 weeks Army Basic Training. I have started my own fitness program. It consists of 45 minutes of running 5 miles, and 1 hour of calisthenics by doing 100 sit-ups, 10x5 push-ups, pull-ups and strength exercises. I exercise five to six times a week. I have achieved half of my personal goal but it is a continuing process and the best is yet to come. It is my character that has keep me going this far. This is not easy for me to do because it requires self-discipline and self-sacrifice which is difficult and challenging. I keep telling myself that I will perform better everyday and there is no limit.

My academic goal this year and in college is to maintain and outstanding G.P.A. of at least 3.5. For the past three years in high school, one of my weakness is trying to balance academics and extra-curricular activities to be a well-rounded student. It is the most difficult challenge I had face in high-school. I believe I will achieve my academic goal because I know what I must do based on the experiences of ups and downs I had in the last three years of high school. It starts in me. To achieve it, I must be on top of everything, be attentive in class, know my weaknesses and how to improve it, study hard, and be willing to get things done on time. I will try very hard to achieve it with the best of my abilities. Success will come for as long as I continue to try to achieve my goal.

My college and career goal is to attend the U.S. Military Academy with a major in Political Science and minor in Spanish, and with a commission as a second lieutenant in the U.S. Army. I will spend three years in **LAW SCHOOL** and work towards becoming an Army lawyer. I wish to fulfill a lifetime career in the military. A cadetship at West Point Will allow me to become an outstanding leader who serves my nation. My strategy is to attend college at San Diego State University for 2-3 years and take the **Army (ROTC) Reserve Officer Training Corps**. Also, I will continue to perform my duties as a soldier in the U.S. National Guard. The Army R.O.T.C. and from my unit commander in the U.S. National Guard in which I will be able to obtain a nomination to the U.S. Military Academy as well as applying for another nomination from my Congressman in our district. [A SHOUTOUT TO REP. DUNCAN HUNTER, A U.S. PRESIDENT HOPEFUL. YEH!] This will triple my chances, and with my excellent record in high school and college, I'm on my way to West Point. **[OR ON MY WAY TO SUNDANCE FILM FEST, ITZ LIKE 12:24 AM ON A WEDS. APRIL 16, 2008. I NEED TO GET MY BEAUTY SLEEP. "I GOT THE BRAINS… WE GOT GOT LOTS OF MONEY.$$$$ Bb, lets have 12 kids and don't run away with my money. HA! HA!"]** Year after year in college, I will continue to keep on applying to the U.S. Military Academy and working towards my goal. I will not stop trying. I just have to believe. It takes a confident and persistent person like me to achieve this gaol.

These very important goals of mine I have to achieve to accomplish another laudable goal of mine, not just a leader of my country but also as an aspiring world leader as well. I am very ambitious and versatile. I believe anything is possible. I control my own destiny and ambitions in life. It starts in me, my actions, and the strong character I possess. I have attained my goals in the past and triumphed from my life's experiences especially the ones I fought and struggled because it made me a much better person everyday. I live not for the past or the future but evry day by day. I know what it takes to achieve it. It is my undying will, persistence, determination, self-discipline and sacrifice; my character. I believe that the day will come for me that I will attend West Point 2-3 years from now. I will continue to face tough challenges everyday.

April 16, 2008, 12:48 AM

Heralyn M. Toling
5/18/98

SPANISH CLUB SCHOLARSHIP
EL CAPITAN HIGH SCHOOL

To be eligible for this scholarship you must:

1. Be an active club member.
2. Have taken at least 3 years. (Span. 1C, 2C, 3C, 4C)
3. Have maintain a "B" average.
4. Have upheld satisfactory attendance and sustained good citizenship.
5. Show proof of enrollment in college Spanish course after at least three weeks into the course. **

**To be verified before receipt of scholarship.

PLEASE ANSWER THE FOLLOWING QUESTIONS HONESTLY AND COMPLETELY.

What are your goals after high school?

It has been a long-term goal of mine to attend the U.S. Military Academy. A cadetship at West Point will allow me to become an outstanding leader who serves my country as a commissioned officer in the U.S. Army. I wish to fulfill a lifetime career in the military and politics, and work towards becoming an Army lawyer of the U.S. Army Judge Advocate (JAG) in the areas of international law and defense. I plan to major in Political Science and minor in Spanish and attend law school after graduating at West Point. I hope to become one of the top military officers working for the Defense Intelligence Agency (DIA), National Security Council (NSC), and the United Nations (UN).

How will this scholarship aid you in achieving these goals?

This scholarship will assist me to pay for my college tuition and books. It will reduce the cost of my school year expenses at Grossmont College this summer taking a Spanish course to continue strengthening my Spanish language skills. I will be taking my military training for the Army National Guard this fall of 1998 and will attend the Spring Semester at Grossmont College. This scholarship will also aid me to keep continuing and believing to follow my educational goals attending at Grossmont College. I hope that balancing my college work, part-time job, volunteering and Army National Guard will lead me to achieve my goal of becoming a cadet at

the U.S. Military Academy. If I am not accepted to West Point next year, I will not stop trying. This scholarship will help me achieve my laudable future goals.

THE LAKESIDE RODEO SCHOLARSHIP ESSAY -SENIOR YEAR 1998

It has been a long-term goal of mine to attend the U.S. Military Academy. A cadetship at West Point Military Academy will allow me to become an outstanding leader who serves my country as a commissioned officer in the U.S. Army. I wish to fulfill a lifetime career in the military and politics and work toward becoming an Army lawyer of the U.S. Army Judge Advocate General's Corps (JAG). To prepare myself, I will major in Political Science and attend Law School after graduating at West Point. The U.S. Army Judge Advocate General's Corps only accepts the best prospective applicants who are best qualified for the positions. I hope to attain my goal to become a U.S. Army Judge Advocate Lawyer in the areas of International Law and U.S. Army Defense Intelligence Agency(DIA). I hope to become the first female chief of staff in the U.S. Army working in the National Security Council (NSC). ***This will allow me to become one of the top military officers making military policy decisions and strategies for the welfare of the nation and the world. I hope that attaining these goals will help me become a world leader working for the UNITED NATIONS particularly in the areas of peacekeeping and global problems. I feel that attending WEST POINT is a good way for me to achieve my future goals. If I am not accepted to West Point next year, I will not stop trying.*** *I believe that I can achieve these goals due to my willing character of persistence, and my dedication and hard-work.*

The reason that I am applying for this scholarship is because it will assist me to pay for my college tuition, books, and my monthly apartment rental fees. It will minimize the cost of my school year expenses at Grossmont College before entering West Point Academy. I will become a member of the U.S. Army National Guard after graduating high school and attend military training which is the only money I will have when I start attending Grossmont College after my military training. This money will only pay 1/3 of my first school year in college. I did not apply for any military scholarships (except West Point which I did not get accepted) because I will have to pay it back when I get accepted and attend West Point. I plan to have a part-time job while attending at Grossmont College. My parents cannot afford to pay for my college expenses because of their low income salaries. This scholarship will help me achieve my laudable future goals.

8/23/04
Ψ PSY 120
2 Definitions of Psychology
(1) An Etymological Definition → The study of the mind.
(2) The Modern Def. The SCIENCE OF BEHAVIOR & MENTAL PROCESSES.

Behavior = The observable or measurable activity of an organism.

Mental processes = Affect & Cognition

Affect= feeling, emotion or mood

EMOTION : HAPPINESS, SADNESS,NERVOUSNESS, FEAR, ANGER
DRIVES: HUNGER, THRIST

COGNITION: THE PROCESSES INVOLVED IN "KNOWING"

Its hard to explain yet easy to understand…
Coz Stephanie Irwin had a year off B4 going to San Jose University. I wanna se a game between (or against) San Jose University …like San Diego State within the next 2 years. I had to wash my undies coz I ran out till next time. I do laundry. They hang in my shower curtain. I hope NO DOUBT continue to write and make another album like so many Rock bands who has been there in the long run. Such as U2, RollingStones, etc… I didn't know there was one ___guy in QUEENS. Guess who? I wana ride my bicycle.

-------------------------♥-----------------------------

1) My heart	
2) is beating	
3) like a	
4) drum	
5) I can hear	
6) the sounds	
7) of my body pouring all the emotions	
8) coming out of me.	

[1-8 C]

R= right
L= left

[L.M.V.] LOSING MY VIRGINITY

CHPHY. 4 *DELTA ARMY FORCE BABBIES [D.A.F.B.]*

WARNING:

THE 45 PAGE SCREENPLAY IS NOT ADVISABLE TO USE AS A GUIDELINE FOR ANY SCREENPLAY YOU ARE HOPING/WANTING/DREAMING OR WISHING TO START/CREATE/WRITE TO FINISH.

I SUGGEST YOU BUY A SPECIFIC SCREENPLAY BOOK GUIDELINE. ASK KNOWLEADGABLE PEOPLE IN THAT profession/ or line of script- Writing work, AND TRUST YOUR INSTINCT ON MAKING DECISIONS.

~~*LOST IN OBLIVION*~~~~22~~

WRITING SAMPLE/IN LYRICAL STYLE: "Look! I got an 'Ebolo knife'."/"Did u say you got ey ay 'EBOLA'…? A biological highly epidemic ey ay ebola virus!!! RUN! RUN!!!/ "Yeah! Itz an ebolo knife." / (An Aussie Intel. international reporter disappear in the thicky, misty, roughen survival Coko Jungle.

"JAWING 'MR.'& MRS. ROCKSTAR"

by

Heralyn Morales TolingLibedo

Hollywood/ Philippines happy go lucky
Phone # ***_*****
→ email ??? Get me one!

FADE IN:

INT. BACKSTAGE/ HALLWAY CONCERT -NIGHT
"Enter [female] CEBU standing by… & [?] CEBU running to her . . . EMOTION/JULIA, JOSS, SHAKIRA, & Assistants/ security attendants…"*
__?___ CEBU standing by… and _____/___ CEBU* running to CEBU. EMOTION/ Julia, Joss, Shakira, & CEBU's Assistants/security attendants are anticipating to do a LIVEDO movie.
*Asterisk/star is use to tell the two main characters Apart. [PROBLEM???]

CEBU
(kissing Cebu*)
Mwa.

EMOTION
He says something to CEBU. He is ['He']
the main character for "ALL I
EVER WANTED! ALL WE EVER WANTED!"

CEBU*
(kissing Cebu)
Mwa. I was gonna say something but
I forgot my line.

CEBU
Is it me or is this the
continuation to the last
novelscriptzinne²ma you just did?
or right after you wrote the
"M.L.L.A.L.F." screenplay?

CEBU*
Yeah! "M.L.L.A.L.F." stands for
"Make Love Like A Libedo Founder."
After all, I'm gonna be the next
William Shakespeare of diz
century. After all, I'm gonna be
your bitch someday.

CEBU
No! Itz not! And MILKI/CEBU*, Am I
getting that Libedo Editor in Chief (?)
job? [put edit back]

EMOTION
Ohh! Ego & tease love.

CEBU*
Of course BB! Anything for you. I'm
going on stage.

CEBU

No! I'm going on stage!

CEBU*

No! You are!

CEBU

No! You BB!

CEBU*

What's the difference?

CEBU

Because you write down you current impulse.

CEBU*

Oh my goosh! I'm all geared to music genre of writing again.

EMOTION

But that was my line.

(screaming)

Oh my Goosh! It is all geared to music genre of writing again!

Shakira mimics a Trojan condom t.v. commercial that promotes Saf sex and HIV?AIDS awareness.

SHAKIRA

E.C.? 5 days of unprocted sex on t.v. commercial. That's a lot of grinding.

CEBU*

Ok! We should go to a museum after this?

CEBU

This week?

CEBU*

Later. Like Friday.

CEBU

Why not!

CEBU*
We'll take a day off.

CEBU
Or take the next four days off.

CEBU*
Oh my God! I think I'm fucking in love with you.

Cebu and Cebu* are both in the hallway kissing together. They are holding each otherz waist and hand.

CEBU
Wow! I haven't seen your face in a long while.

CEBU*
I miss you already.

CEBU
I know you do. I miss you too, Cebu*. I see it in your eyes and writing it down.

Cebu* ignores Cebu for a few seconds to write down a song titled "I Miss You" and looks up at Cebu's eyes. Cebu* is holding a jar of chocolates bought at COSTCO store.

CEBU*
Look, I bought you chocolates. It's gonna make you fat but that's ok. You work out a lot. I bet that helps. It's PERUGUIN R- Chocolates from Italy. The R is in inverted ...

EMOTION

Like The TolingLibedo Records. The N is inverted.

16

CEBU*

(after a bite of Chocolate)

... PERUGIN R- I tried it just now. I'm so hungry. I'll make you lunch and breakfast in the next three years coz I wanna marry you. I know its only been six minutes since I met you. But I think you are the one for me.

CEBU

Oh! Really. Oh, baby I'm all yours.

(talking while eating a chocolate)

I'm eating a piece. You don't mind.

CEBU*

No, I don't mind.

CEBU

Pishhhh!!! Who is 'he'?

(pointing to her assistant)

EMOTION

Your future 'husband'.

(Cebu laughs)

--CEBU* uses 'his' fingers to circle around the nipple shape chocolate.

CEBU*

It has that --nipple chocolate shape thingy. Oh hell, I got it at COSTCO. I'm a gold club member. I think my Mom bought it because I took it from her kitchen counter...

(beat)
... It even has a fortune chocolate.

EMOTION
CEBU* gives the "WORLD OF CHOCOLATES" jar to CEBU.

CEBU
What does it say?

SUPER: "This and this alone is life: Life is love."

CEBU*
"This and this alone is life: Life is love." I'm in love with you for a long time now.
(looks at his watch)
In Tagalog, it means, "Ito at ito nag-isalang ay buhay: buhay ay pag-ibig." *(check 4 true meaning)*

SHAKIRA
(translating in Spanish)
"Esto y solo es la vida: la vida es amor."

EMOTION
Cebu* throws up on Cebu's shirt. Cebu took off her shirt/blouse. Then Cebu* throws up on the floor.

CEBU*
I'm a little excited about...

CEBU interrupts CEBU*.
(spaces_____ below /gap) 3 [feb 11,'07 WHEN DO U GAP 3?]

CEBU
Throwing up!

CEBU*

Yeah! I get really nervous before anything. I like to throw up.

(laughing)

Ha! Ha! Ha!

[[[[When ur ready, explain, LIVEDO & add the pg. 1-10 Below]

[[I have an idea, pick 10 or more actresses to do thiz…who to decide. Derez so many. How the hell do I find them? Itz Like PUNK'D. I do a "LIVEDO" AD_or to introduce "LIVEDOZ" to top Hollywood actors & actresses on these 1st 9 pages… like Lindsay Lohan will say, "I'm in da middle of filming a movie right now… Like "CHAPTER 27". Who are you? Why'r you giving me this jar of chocolates? I'm not ___?______& be AMBRIA in dat "AIEW!AWEW!" movie dat we have to film next year!!! GET OFF OFF ME!"

[Or BLAKE LIVELY WILL SAY: "Heralyn, what are you doing here?" And I'll respond to saying, "COZ U HAVEN'T SEEN ME IN A WHILE."]

CUT TO: [LEARN HOW TO WRITE CUT TO] [OR DO IT AFTER DONE IN DIALOGUES]

[A Campfire gathering story telling in "AIEW!AWEW!"]
EMOTION:-A story about a boy who has never been on a date for 2 years. Is it me? Or is it about Paris with Paris again? I thought it was girl. Then Milki showed up. Then this doesn't make sense. Milki would kick me out. I thought the writer named them CEBU & CEBU. Datz how I got the idea. Is it me or are we at a private beach…

CUT TO: [3 spaces after new scene]

ON THE ROAD TOUR- THE SAME DAY OR DAY 1. AFTER THE PERFORMANCE/ GETTING TO THE BUS. [REDO DOS SCENE 4 KEN & BARBIE - TO PLAY SAFE.] <<<REFORMAT LIKE SO>>>

CEBU
You have to unload my stuff in the bus.

CEBU*
I'll do it. I'll do anything for you.

CEBU
What are you doing here? Why are you still inside my tour bus?

Cebu unpacks her stuff or clothes on her bed. Cebu* starts grabbing Cebu's pair of jeans and thongs as Cebu unpacks.

CEBU*
I'm bored. I'll wear your jeans. Ok! It doesn't fit me. I'll wear your thongs. I'm kidding!

EMOTION
Cebu* is her 'boyfriend.' He jumps to the master bed without his T-shirt and starts singing a song to Cebu. Cebu* screams ...

EMOTION & CEBU*
(simultaneously)
... "Since You Been Gone."

EMOTION (V.O.)
Cebu* sings a song 'he' just wrote for her titled "I Miss You Like-?-"

CEBU*
(singing with a guitar)
"I miss you CEBU like my little pink pillow. I miss you like I miss a heartache of tomorrow where I can't find somebody to sleep with. I miss you like an exotic island our name originated from --CEBU, PHILIPPINES. The place where I was born & grew up. I miss your waistline move in with mine

while your hand advances to my butt-crack. Laugh baby. Ha! Ha! Ok! I miss you like I miss the rest of your beautiful disaster fans ready to rescue you {{out of it}}. I miss you CEBU as my lips misses your lips to kiss our worries goodbye. I miss you like I miss all The American Idol shows from season one to ten, and all the success and triumphs in I miss you CEBU like a Mad Cow disease."

CEBU

Look Cebu! You can stop now!

CEBU*

Forget that song. How about if I sing...

(singing a new song)

. . . "I love you Cebu like I farted out loud in my bedroom in the middle of the day. Oh! That was me farting out loud just a while ago."

EXT. AUSTIN, TEXAS - DAY

AUSTIN, TEXAS? /LAKESIDE, CA is magnificent with wonders.

Cebu* and Cebu's groupy parsheys is called the "HELL11/ME17." "HELL11/MEL7" is a burlesque/ co-ed dance Group. They walk inside the "Heralyn's BBQ Grill & PUB"- a first & world class restaurant.

INT. RESTAURANT - DAY

EMOTION rudely jumps over the front counter & taking one of the cashier's hat.

EMOTION

You look really familiar.

CEBU*

Oh, I worked at KFC. I used to work at KFC. I'm a rock star now. God! I wanna work here cuz I'm so excited.

EMOTION

Can we all get an application?

(everyone laughs)

Sorry, sweetie. You can have your hat and your job back.

EMOTION gives the work cap back to the cashier.

KALENA

Because we're hungry. We're ordering food.

A mysterious masked robber robs the restaurant and aims a shot gun to the cashier.

MYSTERIOUS ROBBER [redo diz scene]

Alright, nobody move! I got a shotgun and I'm not afraid to use it. Give me some cash. Take it out of your cash register now.

10

HERALYN

(waving a mop in the air)

I don't even know why we're doing this. But I don't wanna write a story that's all about fast food joint. I did that most of my life. I probably own my own store by now. We're just kidding on this scene.

EMOTION

Heralyn+ with a mop that smells Really, really bad ...Peeyuhh!

(pinching her nose)

Oh God! That mop stinks so bad.

Heralyn pulls out the stick
imitating Eddie Murphy in the
movie "Coming To America."

Mysterious robber still aiming to shot the shotgun to all the customers and cashier/s.

HERALYN

Ha! Ha! Ha! It takes a while.

(beat)

I'm unhooking it right now. I'm pulling and tugging this mop's sticky pole. It's suck!

EMOTION

(sings in musical Jeopardy sounds)

To do do do dot ...
Tah dut! Any day now!

The mysterious robber's mask fell on the floor to reveal it is JOSS joking around to rob a bank. CEBU* got a hold of the shotgun.

EMOTION

An unknown girl? Or JOSS robs this place. Cebu pulls the trigger accidentally. Ok, there Is a loaded shell in that shotgun.

The bullet left a dent on the ceiling.
(Directing angle: Emphasize on firing the shot gun.)

JOSS

Heralyn, you said we're doing a "LiveDO" today. How come you made me play the mysterious robber?

HERALYN

Because I asked you to volunteer secretly.

EMOTION

A "LiveDO" scene or parts of the

movie done in "LiveDO" allows
freedom for actors to say what
they want. Thus, getting real
"LiveDO" lines or comments.

HERALYN
One of the key element in "LiveDO"
movies is for someone to play a
mysterious character while
Everyone guess who is really who.

JANET
Playing detective for finding
clues.

JOSS
Did anyone tried to guess it was
me earlier?

CHRISTINA
No! Not from wearing that
"A.D.I.J.T.S." scream-cubby like
mask.

HERALYN
"A.D.I.J.T.S." is the new "SCREAM"
movie of this decade. It was
inspired from a Spaniard painter, Mr.
David Alfaro Siqueiros, who painted
"Echo Of A Scream" reflecting the
Horror of 1930's Spanish Civil War.

JOSS
I'm not playing the mysterious
serial killer wearing this mask
in "A.D.I.J.T.S." am I?

HERALYN
What the fuck does it matter!
A hint to all the "LiveDO" actors in
"A.D.I.J.T.S." movie. Ahum,
Don't forget to use the cell phone
that came in the mail, along with my

artwork and suicide note. I mean an
invitation to my first art exhibit.
prank call any of your cast-mates
for clues. A definite way that makes
A "LiveDO" movie better is...

KALENA
(interrupts)
Just help your fellow actors in
whatever ways possible. After all,
it is just a "LiveDO". We can do
whatever we want. Your way of
creating better movies, Heralyn?

HERALYN
Yeah. A "LiveDO" of buying our own
food. You haven't seen anything yet.

EMOTION
Oh please. No more "LiveDOZ" today.

EXT. AUSTIN- PARKING LOT-DAY

EMOTION
Walking out of the "Heralyn's BBQ
Grill & Pub". A pink convertible
BMW bug pulls in front of us. Oh,
My God! I'm psychic. It's Cebu.

BMW STOPS *(says something intelligent like ME)*
On the right side of the BMW car is a holographic visual radio-like stereo system projecting JOSS STONE singing one of her songs. For example, "A Car this fine... Don't ya' Wanna ride BB?"

CEBU
Get in.
(CEBU* sits on the
front side)
Wow! I feel like I'm on vacation.

A couple of CEBU's friends are chilling in the back seat Singing the one verse/ line song titled : "DUKA DUKA DUKA!"

CEBU*
Ok! You're not the Gay Cheesy

Pooh or Boger Fairy. Look! You're
not going away CEBU.

CEBU
(looks around)
Because I have to put up with you
on tour.

CEBU*
Because we're going on tour
together.

CEBU'S & CEBU'S* million dollar tour bus stops behind CEBU's BMW bug. (reword if/n)

CEBU
Get out!

CEBU*
There's no bitch next door
getting out.
(beat)
Alright, I'm getting out.

They all get out of the BMW bug at the same time.
The "HELL 11/MEL7" burlesque group is anxiously waiting for them inside the tour bus.

CEBU
We're all getting inside to our
tour bus.

CEBU*
Is there a yacht that goes with
this thing?

JOSS
Is it clung to a pirate ship?

CEBU
No! but my pink BMW bug is. We are
going to Gwen Stefani's concert
Cebu*. You are headlining it.

CEBU*

If I am headlining it. It doesn't make sense or sound good. If I'm a big star then I don't need anybody to headline with.

CEBU

Somebody will do it. Headline for you. You don't look like a dumb Blond guy to me. Does headlining Makes sense to you now Cebu*?

CEBU*

Well, you have blonde hair. Your level of intelligence isn't like the rest of us.

LALA

Just stop bitching about who is dumber. Cebu, the only reason why Gwen let you headline tonight is because you offered her to direct the "A.D.I.J.T.S." movie.

CEBU

You're right LALA.

PORTIA

Anything is possible if you know The BOGER FAIRY NICOLE. I'm gonna leave a message on her cell phone.

(talking on her cell phone)

Hello! Boger fairy Nicole. There's a party at Cebu's tour bus after the concert. Come on over as soon as you get this message. Don't Forget to invite Miss MASTERBATEONYA EYESROLLAROUND MORFUCKTOGETTINGMYFREAKON.

LALA

Miss MASTERBATEONYA is my music producer on my latest album. She's talented. She'll make sure your album goes number one for fifteen weeks on the *Billboard Charts*.

Everyone gets inside Cebu's tour bus.

INT. TOUR BUS- DAY

CEBU and CEBU* are talking and chilling at their "BUDDHA BAR" VIP lounge. They sit facing each other. ~~BRITTANY and CHRISTINA playing or filling in as EMOTION.~~ The HELL11/MEL7 ignited a party atmosphere with loud hip-hop music.

CEBU*

Do you wanna smell my killi-killi?

CEBU

Hell no!!!!!!!!

CEBU*

Killi-killi means armpit in Filipino or Tagalog.

EMOTION (POV/check, abc)

CEBU* puts his left hand inside his shirt and gells out the smell that is riking in his armpit. He's that hairy. Cebu* made Cebu sniffs his finger.

THE DIFFERENCE BETWEEN EMOTION TALKING AND EXPLANATION/ ? EXPLAIN ABOVE (?) [itz alll gudd!]]

CEBU

(CEBU's face turns away)

Gross! Get your stinky finger off me.

CEBU*

It smells like teen spirit or Red Zone deodorant. That is what my personal trainer and dietician MISS CINEFUCKINRELATETO_ UALLFAKEBOOB_ smells like. Have you met her before?

CEBU
No, I haven't.

CEBU*
Why can't I be a guy in this lifetime? In this movie? This isn't what it is?

CEBU
You are a fucking guy. And you fucking talk a lot. This movie fucking sucks!

CEBU*
Why can't I be a guy in this lifetime? In this movie? This isn't what it is?

CEBU
You are a fucking guy. And you fucking talk a lot. This movie fucking sucks!

CEBU*
No, it doesn't. Ok Dorky BRITTANY And do the Horny Party with me Cebu/MURPHY. It can't suck! If you are Kelly Clarkson CEBU…<_I/n . . .)
(beat)
... / You will have to compare "Jawing Mr. & Mrs. Rockstar" to Something better than "From Justin to Kelly." (TO ADD OR NOT?)

AT THE "BUDDHA BAR" - DANCE FLOOR
MONTAGE-

--KALENA, one of the "HELL11" burlesque dancer, invites a Friendly dance off competition.

--The BOGER FAIRY NICOLE and MISS MASTERBATEONYA(check ch.?) Magically shows up from a psychedelic worm hole to crash the Party.

--The BOGER FAIRY uses her power by picking her nose to turn CEBU & CEBU* into DRAG KING & QUEEN.

--All eyes and attention went to CEBU & CEBU* as they get up to dance together.

--A group of 'parsheyz' or partying friends surrounding them.

CEBU
Oh, I get it. It would be funny if we both be a drag king or drag queen.

CEBU*
So now what?

CEBU
Lets party!

INT.? -- TOUR BUS- DAY 3
"to add New York" ? / what to do there... remember?
In the VIP BOOTH CLUB OF BUDDHA BAR or DANCE FLOOR.
Milki: "Oh! I love hairy _____." Ha! Ha! That's like a funny Line from my next hit movie titled "LADY GRIFFINS GO TO THEIR CALIFORNIA STATE TENNIS CHAMPOINSHIPS."
Bre: Thatz a long title or title it /nickname it "THE GLORY DAYZ".
Milki: "Wow! I was really living out my dream writing diz movie. Ok! We're not drag-king-ing anymore. My Lady Turtles... I mean ... Lady griffins movie is a documentary movie. I still haven't edit it so that it will be a hit 'audience favorite' to San Diego, New York, Los Angeles or Sundance Film Festival. (friends left Milki on the dance floor) Where are you guys going? Wait for me!!!

Paris /Aiew/AWEW ch. Name : Rollercoastertawag

CEBU* in the bathroom singing.
E: Touches his private. Umm? (standing outside the bathroom)

EMOTION (V.O.)
CEBU looks back to her right side.
The mysterious killer in
"A.D.I.J.T.S." was almost detected
by CEBU.

CEBU
Really, whose face is it hiding
Over there? You're seeing things.

CEBU*
(fly kisses to Cebu)
All night and every night baby.

Cebu reads a tabloid magazine carefully. She sees Cebu* kissing with Miss Paulina Rubio at their club hng-out in Los Angeles. { Find a club in L.A. , LIBEDO CLUB}

CEBU
(playing it cool)
That guy is fine.

CEBU*
Dude! He's right next to you.

CEBU
Did you fucking say something?

CEBU*
(revising a script)
Why bother revising "M.L.L.A.L.F."
(takes a deep breath/abc)
or changing the title to
"SAVAGELY DONE IN BED". It's not
like I can sell a fucking script or
one great book I wrote!

CEBU
(interrupts)
Of course! I guess you can.

CEBU*
(angrily)
I guess I was bored to write

something like this. One of many
genre I life.

CEBU

You wrote so many novelscriptzinne²ma to get this far in life. You were just trying to figure out what to do with your life.

CEBU*

A lucky, free magic movie ticket That got me in SAN DIEGO FILM FESTIVAL 2006 for the first time. ASA, or American Writers Association inspired me to turn in my screenplays to many writing contests out there. I'm so looking forward for HOLLYWOOD movie producers and agents reading it. Why? And what is the answer?

CEBU

Definitely by fate, luck, destiny is the answer. Or just that God has great plans for you to be the brightest and greatest screenwriter in Hollywood...only for white people.

CEBU*

Like how many ...
(sings)
... Duka, duka, duka, duka?
(CEBU laughs)
Well, at least you did something great. I envy you. What I would give to be as successful as you?

(is it 2 or one space)

CEBU throws the shirt/blouse she's wearing to CEBU's* face. CEBU* plays along by throwing his shirt to CEBU's face.

EMOTION

They are both shirtless!

CEBU*

I just need to be broke for
Another sixty days ...
(pouts)
... And that is all. I'll be
fine in 180 days.

CEBU

File for bankruptcy. Diva Toni
>(abc)Braxton did that once. Her
attorney had to.

CEBU*

You mean she ran out of money.
Why didn't she just pawn her golden
CONT. Grammy she just won for a million
Bucks at the Beverly Hills Pawn
Shop.

CEBU

I'll do it. I'll do anything for
you. I went to Law School at Texas
A & M University. I'll file your
bankruptcy papers.

CEBU*

Oh, thanks for caring. I didn't
know they have fucking Law
School at Texas A & M University.

CEBU

Me too! We went there ...
(beat)
... Together. You're a fucking
lawyer! Again, you don't like to
give up, do you?

CEBU*

I will for somebody else. Stupid!

CEBU

You're fucking stupid. Stupid!

CEBU*

What is that suppose to mean?

CEBU
You wouldn't know Cebu*. You can't Even afford an AOL e-mail account.

CEBU*
Oh! A guess! I won't have to worry about downloading Amazon readers from my fan mail. I still can't believe not one of those fucking bitches wanna buy my fucking book!

CEBU
(yelling to Cebu*)
By now you fucking forget about it.

CEBU*
I mean downloading for your fan mail. I mean from your porn website.

CEBU
I have a porn website.

CEBU*
Tell me about it.

CEBU
You don't wanna know!

CEBU*
CEBU* changing the topic.

CEBU
So do you sleep naked with me?

CEBU*
Of Course.

CEBU
Did I take you to a museum already?

CEBU
We'll do that next week.

CEBU*
(snaps his fingers)
How about right now.

They are at the NEW YORK museum looking at Piccaso's "GUERNICA" . . . walking to another artwork titled "ARE YOU THE LOVE OF MY LIFE?" [redo ---change/edit]

CEBU
Are you the love of my life?

CEBU*
Of course baby. My killi-killi smells good today.

CEBU
(makes a silent laugh)
As long as I don't have to smell it ever again. Are U done being an Olyian fairy using your magic to charm me because I have a concert to go to. We need to be in Dallas in three days.

CEBU* snaps his fingers to get back to their next city tour.

AT THE BUDDHA BAR -?VIP TABLE

CEBU*
Did you like the motel/hotel we stayed in FAIRYLAND. Ha! Ha! Ha!

CEBU
(looks confuse)
Last night?

CEBU*
(talks softly to himself)

Ok, say something else.
(looks at Cebu sexily)
Your hazel brown eyes are turning me on. Wow! I'm drawn by those two sexy eyes.

CEBU
What's your point? Your big brown eyes are turning me on.

CEBU*
I have big brown eyes.

CEBU looks to 'his' window side and sees 'his' charismatic reflection.

CEBU*
Oh, I get it! You think I'm an owl. I'm hairy all over.

EMOTION
(making owl sounds)
Kuku, kuku, duku, duku, kuku.

CEBU*
(to EMOTION)
Well, excuse me EMOTION. You're just helping me be emotionally attach and sensitive to Cebu.
(points to CEBU)
I need a blow job real guud CEBU. Oh plez, plez Cebu.
I mean a real job. Are you hiring for a new assistant? See, that's gonna be me. If you hire me now, I will start saving up for that 50 karat diamond ring.

CEBU
50 karat? It doesn't exist. You need to call PARIS HILTON to get info on finding the right jeweler.
(adding attitude talk)
Ok! Sweetie boo. Right away honey.

CEBU* looks bewildered. (abc<)
EMOTION laughs. The Hell 11 is laughing uncontrollably.

CEBU*
How many karats in a ten million dollar diamond ring? Like I can afford it.

CEBU
I guess not.

CEBU*
(wears a Mohawk wig)
Do you like my wiggy Mohawk hair?

CEBU
I like the little horns sticking out.

CEBU*
It's only fun when two female actresses get to do the "AIEW! AWEW!" livedo on getting married. Writing the script! That was torturous enough to get that far! Even if none of us get a fucking Oscar!

CEBU
Or a fucking Golden Globe! Our Las Vegas drive-thru marriage must be doing really well.

EMOTION
CEBU looks at her-- 25 cent ring That CEBU* got her at the mall.
(redo line above, change?)

CEBU*
(smiles)
Hee! Hee! What was I thinking. To think so ... Like I'm gonna get some from you.

EMOTION

Cebu giggles.

CEBU*
Oh, ha, ha, ha.

CEBU
Success! It gets to you. You forget who you want to be with.

CEBU*
You wanted to be with me. I was just talking about getting some bottie baby! Boyah!

CEBU, CEBU* AND EMOTION
(together)
S-E-X !!!

CEBU*
Quick! Call 2 homeless people right now. I'm not marrying you. You deserve better. I'll do a Mira Sorvino "Mighty Aphrodite" (abc) first movie actress gonna be famous and get an Oscar right away on her first movie role. I think! I don't know!

EMOTION
Cebu* sits next to CEBU.

CEBU
I loved that movie. What I would give to be as successful as you. I'm in love with you. I love you.

EMOTION (V.O.)
They look each other eye to eye and start American kissing. A passionate and blissful kissing.

CEBU*
I love you too. Do I look like a

handsome prince? How do you imagine me in your dreams?

CEBU

I imagine you as a cute prince.

CEBU*

CEBU, you make my worries go bye-bye.

(kissing CEBU)

EMOTION (V.O.)

A prolong and arousing kiss. CEBU* feels CEBU's fake breasts. I mean real breasts. CEBU tugs CEBU's* hair harder. The kissing went on for hours, months, years... And

-- The outside view of CEBU'S tour bus window reveals time is elapsing as CEBU and CEBU* continue their romantic kiss.

EMOTION (V.O.)

(continuing; melodramatically)

Seasons turn to winter, spring, summer and fall. CEBU slaps CEBU*.

CEBU

(bitchy tone of voice; yelling)

Why didn't you tell me you were sleeping with someone else!

CEBU*

No, I wasn't!

EMOTION

CEBU* tells a lie. An honest lie.

CEBU*

I like to sleep with other people. So big deal! Every rock star does that. Oh, thanks a lot EMOTION!

IN OR NEAR BATHROOM ?

EMOTION
CEBU* sings.
(leaves the bathroom)

CEBU*
(sits on the toilet)
"My balls are hairy. White dick,
(looks down)
I mean my big black dick! And I'm proud to have a big black dick. And I flushed it down the porta potti. I mean the toilet without the help of the Automatic Royal Flushy Bear, Cheesy Pooh or Boger Fairy."

CEBU
Are you in there, Cebu? I thought I kicked you out already.

CEBU*
(opens the Bathroom)
Yeah!

CEBU
(covers her nose)
Something stinks.

EMOTION (V.O.) ?
CEBU sprays on air-freshener to CEBU*.

CEBU*
(walking out the Bathroom)
Plus, I need a smoke. A cigarette tobacco joint.
(smokes a joint)
Yeah! It's not pot. So don't worry

about me. But it smells like it.

CEBU
Because it smells like pot, that's fucking why.

Cebu and Cebu* are yelling at each other in a raging and sarcastic manner.

CEBU*
What! Did I fucking say something?

CEBU
I want our relationship to be fucking over. Right now!

CEBU*
Cebu, I'm not into this or you right now. I think I'm bi. Ha! Ha!

EMOTION
Cebu* laughs. Thinking 'his' sexuality is a joke.

CEBU*
I'm sleeping with your other homeboys.

CEBU
You slept with my homeboys? That is it! I'm kicking you out. Slut!

CEBU*
Whore! Whore! Whore!

CEBU
Bitch! Bitch! Bitch!

EXT. FREEWAY - AFTERNOON
The tour bus stops. Its door opens widely. Cebu throws Cebu* Out the tour bus. CEBU flips off and splits on CEBU*.

CEBU
(pissy mood)

I don’t ever wanna see you
again.

CEBU willingly walks back to her tour bus. CEBU* picks and throws a pointy black rock to CEBU’s bus furiously. The tour bus drives off gallantly in thunderous speed without CEBU*. CEBU* is left stranded and walking on the freeway alone.

CEBU*
(screaming)
Fuck you CEBU!

EXT. FREEWAY, OKLAHOMA, FLORIDA, TEXAS - NIGHT ? {MONTAGE}

A gigantic spacecraft sighting is visible to CEBU’S* hazel brown eyes. It hovers just above CEBU’S tour bus.

A MYSTEROUS FARM ANIMAL

wearing an all black paratrooper outfit parachutes down the tour bus’ roof, lands on its two hooves, and -- waves back to the gigantic spacecraft spinning rapidly in air.

CEBU* sees the gigantic spacecraft disappearing in seconds.

EMOTION (V.O.)
Ok! Like CEBU kicked CEBU* out
For sure. But CEBU* is not giving
up. CEBU* drinks a red bull and
rides a --flying toddler bike with
training wheels. It flies just like
the bike in the E.T. movie. Cebu*
lands on top of CEBU’S tour bus
roof top quietly. He monkey kicks
the window while his right arm
dangles. CEBU’S* left hand is
holding on to the far edgy part
of the tour bus.

INT. CEBU’S TOUR BUS - NIGHT
As early/or later idea emphasize on dining or side party table.

EMOTION drinks a hot chocolate with(containing/sprinkled w/) mini marshmallows just right next to the window of where

CEBU* is trying to get inside the tour bus.

EMOTION is enjoying the company of a talking cow.

CEBU* finally made it inside the tour bus just right before a speedy truck approaching his way.

EMOTION
(continues)
Cebu* somehow finds a way inside this tour bus. Cebu*, you gonna sit down for a hot chocolate with us?

Emotion double taps the leathered, comfy seat.

CEBU*
No thanks. I'm tired.
(walking towards the bedroom)
Oh, hi talking cow. Good night.

MOO MOO, the talking cow, is friendly and a party animal.

MOO MOO
Hello. My name is Moo Moo. Nice To finally meet you Cebu*.

IN THE BEDROOM

Cebu* goes back to sleep with Cebu. Silence. [EMOTION line]

CEBU*
(notice CEBU'S* presence)
What happened to that guy that said "Viva La Cocaracha!?"

Cebu* and Cebu facing each other while talking in bed.

CEBU AND CEBU*
(together)
He's one of my favorite singer.

CEBU
Yeah. I saw him on the Radio Music Awards. I was there.

CEBU*
At Staples with somebody else. Hi! Nobody I know.

KALENA
Opps, sorry. Wrong room.
(closes the bedroom door)
Good night.

CEBU
Was thst the one Xtina hosted?

CEBU*
Yeah! Isn't it cold out in the Desert or farm?

CEBU
We're inside. Indoor. And I need my beauty sleep desperately.

CEBU*
You wouldn't know how cold it gets outside.

Cebu* shivers and hogs the blanket to himself.

CEBU
Yeah! So why didn't you snap your fingers like a clever Olyian fairy that you are to get back inside my tour bus earlier.

CEBU*
Why didn't I think of that. I'm rubbing your body like a pen that needs to work again.

Emotion and Moo Moo magically appears in between Cebu and Cebu*.

EMOTION
Cebu* rubbing Cebu like a ...

MOO MOO
... genie in the lamp.
(yawns)
Oh, baby -- soft and cuddly pillows.

CEBU*
Can we have some privacy? Plez.

EMOTION AND MOO MOO
(together)
Yeah. Sure. We'll leave.

Emotion and Moo Moo are walking out the bedroom willingly. The door --SLAMS.

CEBU*
I bought you some flowers. Ah, like these Trojan condom flowers I started making them on the night of our first city tour. Yup at Austin, Texas while you were on stage singing that song titled "We Lick A Fucking Pussy". Just joking!

CEBU
Oh, baby. How sweet and thoughtful Of you. Mwa.
(kissing Cebu*)
I forgive you. The hit pop/rock/rap song is titled "Going Down In History."
(cuddling; hugs)

CEBU*
I didn't mean to start that fight.
(kissing her forehead)

CEBU

Thatz the time I sang "Mr. Sexuality". But, hey, you got a mosh pit going.

Cebu made Cebu* laugh hysterically.

CEBU*

Ha, Ha! Good night Cebu.

CEBU

I hope you sleep well Cebu*.

Cebu falls asleep.

EMOTION (V.O.)

They did it so savagely done in bed. Alright, I lied. Cebu and Cebu* didn't get any action tonight. Cebu* gets up to the bathroom to smoke again in Cebu's bus. He rolls a tobacco-pot joint inside the bathroom then went back to bed. We all have to leave the tour bus because ...

Within seconds, --the tour bus stopped moving and a smoke alarm is on. A thick and gray smoke from the bathroom is noticeable. ~~Everyone inside the tour bus hurriedly left the tour bus [improve]~~

EXT. FREEWAY - NIGHT

EMOTION

(continues)

... Cebu's tour bus is on fire. "The world is like an album. You throw it away when you're the Godiva." It's an HMT qoute.

CEBU*

Well, in this case, when it explodes.

-- BOOM! The tour bus blows up on the spacious freeway, shattering into tiny little metallic pieces.

The "HEl1l1/ERIN7" group sees a fiery tire rolls down like a fast-moving bowling ball. They drop their jaws and in shock.

MR. IWANTGAYMEN, 45, a tall, muscular built black guy, and wearing a sharp business suit.? He is Cebu's bus driver. Mr. Iwantgaymen call 911 on his cell phone while everyone is standing on the side of the road.

CEBU
You owe me a new bus.
(punches Cebu*)
And all my fucking stuff are
in there!
(yells)

CEBU*
Awe. Why didn't you hit me hard
enough? Ok, even your grammy that
you won for "Best New Artist" or
was it "Best Song?" ...

-- Cebu's Grammy award rolls from the flaming bus.

CEBU
(with pride)
Oh, I see it. --My first Grammy.

Cebu* picks up her Grammy before it gets run over by a vehicle.

CEBU*
Oh, it's still hot.
(jugling her
Grammy)

☺ The fire fighters put out the fire before it spreads rapidly or cause any major accidents on the freeway.
The medics are checking everyone for any major burns or injuries.

A groovy-frisky 60's phone booth just appears out of nowhere. The Boger fairy magically shows up inside the phone booth, bumping her head carelessly as she walks out the phone booth.

BOGER FAIRY NICOLE
Oh, there you guys are.
(walking towards everybody)
At least nobody got injured.

MOO MOO
Or worst, dead. Hi! Boger Fairy Nicole.

BOGER FAIRY NICOLE
Well, that's peachy great.
Oh, hey! Moo Moo.

CEBU*
Well, that was really fast. Didn't Mr. Iwantgaymen just called 911?

MR. IWANTGAYMEN
My cell phone didn't work.

CEBU
Then who called 911?

BOGER FAIRY NICOLE
I did. The all-male firefighters and medics are wearing see-through white boxers. They're from FAIRYLAND. Not really. Coz they're humans.

EMOTION
They look really good. [describe better= gud]

BOGER FAIRY NICOLE
Well, I better let those humans go back to their mundane life. I

need to make them go away before
anyone gets suspicious out here.

MISS EYONLIGHTHOSWAY
Lets all go. Get going??? [On the road]

--The Boger Fairy Nicole snaps her fingers but no magic.

--Then finally, she picks on her nose to make all those firefighters and medics wearing see-trough white boxers disappear in lighting speed.

INT. PHONE BOOTH - MIDNIGHT

Cebu* puches the *number anxiously* but no one answers.

EMOTION (V.O.) *correct way*
Cebu* uses the groovy-frisky 60's
phone booth to call a private sex
chat hotline.

CEBU*
(looks up)
No, I'm not! I'm calling MTV to
keep the whole tour bus blowing
up incident a big secret. Ducka!
Ducka! Ducka! We are at ...
(looks around)
... In the middle of nowhere.
I think there's a killer on the
loose.
{Oh, there you guys are. Where are
All my 'groupy parsheyz' going?
Wait for me!} use later

The phone booth starts talking, moving and frisking so life-like.

FRISKY PHONE BOOTH
Excuse me?
Cebu* begins to get scared.

CEBU*

Huh? Oh my God! Is someone going to die. I think there's a killer on the loose.

FRISKY PHONE BOOTH

(shouting god-like)

Yeah! You! Could you hurry up or just get out right now.

CEBU*

No way. I need to call the MTV VJ LALA. You're just a groovy 60's-frisky phone booth annoying me. What are you going to do about it?

CEBU* flips off the GROOVY 60'S FRISKY PHONE BOOTH.

FRISKY PHONE BOOTH

(playfully anxious)

Well, I'm gonna have to do it my way because I have to be reincarnated as a crazy Jewish man in five minutes. Did I mention he's gay? I get to be a Gay Cheesy Pooh Fairy.

CEBU

Oh yeah. Maybe, he will like me. No, I'm not getting out. Period!

EXT. ROADSIDE - NIGHT

FRISKY PHONE BOOTH

Ready! Set! Rolling down this forbidden forest is so much fun with ya.

The Groovy 60's frisky phone booth jumps and rolls down the hillside. The hillside is nearby the creepy, dark woods.

CEBU*

Alright! You won. I don't wanna

die! I was gonna put more quarters
there but I’ll just use my new
cell phone.

CEBU* AND FRISKY PHOONE BOOTH (<Limt)
(together
screaming)
Aaahhh!

EXT. THE? CREEPY WOODS- NIGHT

The creepy woods is dark, mystical, foogy, and the footpaths Are not so easiy traceable at nights.

The half-moon is illuminating in the clear sky.

The tall, pine trees are endlessly visible/visible endless. It surrounds them.

A few of the ”HELL11” members are flashing their heavy-duty flashlights.

E_______
You guys, let’s just walk back.

K_______
Yeah. For real.

A_______
Just forget Cebu*.

P________
God, I need my beauty sleep.

The GAY CHEESY POOH FAIRY chases Cebu*.

B_____ F_____ N_____
Hey everyone! Look over there.
(pointing)
I see the Gay Cheesy Pooh Fairy.
He is... She is my sidekick.

X__ ___ ____ ____

Great! I have a feeling we're
not in TETELAND anymore.

Cebu* and Gay Cheesy Pooh fairy joins the rest of the group.

Cebu runs into a sticky spider web while everyone laughs at her.

Paris imitates the voice of Sponge Bob.

PARIS

We're not laughing at you Cebu.
We're laughing with you. Ha! Ha!

GAY CHEESY POOH FAIRY

Paris, I think you watch way too
many Sponge Bob t.v. cartoon shows.

______?_____

(running)

I heard someone was murdered
nearby these woods. I saw it on
the news earlier.

ARLIS

That-this woods are freaking
us out.

A tarantula falls on B____'s face.

B______

(screams)

Ahh! Get it off me!

The tarantula leaps down inside B______'s blouse.

TYRESE

Sure!

Tyrese rips off Rocky's blouse and her strapless bra Showing.

SPLAT! --Tyrese squashes tarantula with his right foot.

Rocky stumbles on a dead, choppy body wrap in a black trash bag.+
+it is wrong/not right to kill another human being/person. _______________

Everyone screams when they realize they found a dead body. Everyone dashes out of the creepy woods, leading them back to the side of the freeway.

EXT. FREEWAY - NIGHT

The freeway is radiant and lively as the "HELL11/___7" gang appears from the creepy woods.

A moderate drizzle.____
____
____

The Boger Fairy Nicole opens her red umbrella.

BOGER FAIRY NICOLE
I think it's time for a FRIENDS T.v. show- theme song montage.

GAY CHEESY POOH FAIRY
Yup. I think so.

MONTAGE-- FRIENDS ORIGINAL THEME SONG

A glowing majestic fountain resembles the exact replica from the hit t.v. show "FRIENDS" appears in the middle of the freeway magically.

The "FRIENDS" theme song is sing-preform by everyone./ They sing the "Friends" t.v. show theme song to create a revamp version feel.

They all wear black & white (see friends) outfits and some are holding umbrellas.

Each person from the "HELL/____7" group is expressing their favorite character --in an artistic visual style of acting.

EXT- FREEWAY- CONTINUIS ? Abc (find a spot for singing)

CEBU*
How are we getting out of here?

BOGER FAIRY NICOLE
Oh, nigger plez! Don't you know I Get you covered. Alright, hop in MOO MOO's back.

MOO MOO
Hell no! Cebu*, don't you own a tour bus? I remember you nickname it "THE MILKIWAY" because the rooms are larger than it seems.

CEBU
Yes, exactly. My tour bus is like an infinite MILKI WAY galaxy. I got an idea.

Cebu smiles and snaps his fingers in the air. In a Heartbeat, "The Milkiway" appears in the foggy atmosphere with its own yellow and blue colored parachutes. You could see it landing on the empty, dark freeway while its gold rims still spinning hypnotically.

While it lands or parachute land/ A group of fairies are partying on the roof top. They sing a theme song, dance, drink liquor (Like thinking and Irish dance)
[What are you, Santa Claus? / Are those fairies? / Those Are the Olyian fairies. They're my friends from Fairyland.

__ ________ _______________ ____________ _____________ ___

____________:"The Make A Wish And Snap Your Fingers"
___________: "Yeah, finally, "YourAssIzMugMe2" just arrive."

YOURASSISMUGMETOO
(aiewsavez? after club)
Did I miss anything?

CEBU*
Not much? "The Milkiway" mega-tour bus is the newest high tech edition.

It even has gold rim-stunning wheels.
Fuck! It even feels like your flying.

CEBU

(pushes Cebu and talks
to her agent on the phone) ? ? ?

What do you mean I wanna play this
role? With who? Whatever, it's so
complex in two parallel dimensions.
And it comes in two versions...
Plus, two more versions. Ok! I'm
confuse about the script. The
director titles it "My Venti
Frapinoa Sketchdezortdrunkenphrenia
Weekends." I'll call you later. Bye!

EMOTION

We all go inside this nifty, black
trashy tour bus. Ha! Ha! How funny
to survive and still be alive.

*-&I haven't been in my writing office for 4months td.?{A/H_}
May 31, 2007 Almost done/finiente/over/tapos na w/ diz script
:(abcdefghijklmnopqrstuvwxyz) June 27, 2008, 8:21PM{F}*

INT- CEBU'S NEW BUS [[a perfect spot bcoz of inside bus]]

CEBU*

Can you make sure we don't
make a big story out this Lala.

LALA

No! I mean we have to put it on
MTV news as soon as possible.
A big story like we did a few
years ago when JEWEL showed off
her breasts on MTV Total Request
Live. Cebu's tour bus blowing up
incident is even bigger
story ...

CEBU

(interrupts LALA)

. . . All because of you, Cebu*.
Cebu*, you need to stop smoking

that shit, mec, chronic or pot.

CEBU*

You seem to know all your street marijuana types. So, are you the new pimpsqueezey drug dealer in town?

[[gives CEBU a hug.]]

CEBU

Yeah! Drug dealing is my side job, A hobby, other than my rock star singing career. Definitely, no!

<like a furious feel>

The explosion must have been caused by a high quality TNT-dynamite found in *Fairyland.* I only know one Olyian fairy that knows about it, Miss CocaineLickUrS-Busteye. She wants to kill me or both of us. Why?

ADD/ if nes.ry) CEBU: "I haven't or never been to Fairyland./ CEBU* : I'll take you there on our free time to see the notorious Leprechaun.)

LALA

(to Cebu*)

Look homey. You must be smoking on some weird joint. It made you think you are an Olyian fairy.

CEBU*

Oh! Ok! I'll give you a hundred bucks.

CEBU* temps LALA with a Flashy $/P100 bill.

LALA

Ah. Umm... I don't know.

EMOTION

Lala walks away. Cebu sits next To me.

CEBU*

A free weekend getaway at my private hideaway Beach house in the Bahamas. Plus, ten thousand US dollar for shopping spree.

CEBU

Oh! Look, honey. This one has a smoke detector. Ha! Ha! Ha!

CEBU*

Dat bitch that told you must have been kissing a different guy.

CEBU

But she is your friend. A paparazzi took a picture of both of you at the club.

CEBU*

If I did it... Meaning kissing ***+ at that fucking club. I know You will forgive me by now, right?

-- The lights went on and off. Cebu looks at the trashy, tabloid magazine in a feeling of shocking silence.

CEBU

Of course! Look! I'll understand. I'm hungry. Are you gonna cook me something, honey?

CEBU*

Sure! Its almost the end of my fuck-up life in U.S.A. I'm ready to fulfill something greater than myself b4 I die.

☺ *The heart of my people is* /[to win the heart of my ppl.]
TO WIN THE HEART OF MY PEOPLE IS.../ *THE HEART OF MY PPL. IZ...*
CALLING ME TO COME HOME TO PHILIPPINES.♥

Sure!

Its almost the end of my fuck-up life in U.S.A.

I'm ready to fulfill

Something greater than myself b4 I die.

☺ The
heart of
my people
is / ***[to***
win the
heart of
my ppl.]

TO WIN THE
HEART OF
MY PEOPLE
IS…/ THE
HEART OF
MY PPL.
IZ…

CALLING ME TO COME HME

P P
H I
I N
L E
I S.
P ♥ red

The♥***Heart***

Of My

people

is in me,

and you,

and in the
eyes of
our Lord.

The end

&

Beginning

Of

Age

Of

Heroism

To

Start

13.

YEAH!